MORALS
AND
ETHICS

Second Edition

CARL WELLMAN

Washington University

PRENTICE HALL
Englewood Cliffs, New Jersey 07632

Library of Congress Cataloging-in-Publication Data

Wellman, Carl.
  Morals and ethics.

  Rev. ed. of: Morals & ethics. 1975.
  Includes bibliographies and index.
  1. Ethics. I. Wellman, Carl. Morals & ethics.
II. Title.
BJ1025.W39   1988   170   87-7202
ISBN 0-13-600719-8

Cover design: Lundgren Graphics, Ltd.
Manufacturing buyer: Margaret Rizzi

 © 1988, 1975 by Prentice-Hall, Inc.
A Division of Simon & Schuster
Englewood Cliffs, New Jersey 07632

Printed in the United States of America

10 9 8 7 6 5 4 3 2 1

ISBN 0-13-600719-8   01

Prentice-Hall International (UK) Limited, *London*
Prentice-Hall of Australia Pty. Limited, *Sydney*
Prentice-Hall Canada Inc., *Toronto*
Prentice-Hall Hispanoamericana, S.A., *Mexico*
Prentice-Hall of India Private Limited, *New Delhi*
Prentice-Hall of Japan, Inc., *Tokyo*
Simon & Schuster Asia Pte. Ltd., *Singapore*
Editora Prentice-Hall do Brasil, Ltda., *Rio de Janeiro*

SH

CONTENTS

PREFACE

The purpose of this book is to introduce college and university students to ethics through a study of six pairs of problems. In each pair the first is a specific moral problem like "Is civil disobedience ever right in a democracy?" or "Is genetic engineering desirable?" These are practical questions in that they arise in practice, in the ordinary course of deciding what to do. They may not face everyone every day, but they confront many people on many occasions and are familiar to most observers of human conduct. The second in each pair is a related theoretical ethical problem like "What makes an act right or wrong?" or "What is intrinsically good?" These problems are abstract and general in that they are somewhat removed from immediate practice and concern a very wide range of instances. They are theoretical in that any fully developed answer to such a problem constitutes an ethical theory. Specific moral problems are the subject of odd-numbered chapters, while theoretical ethical problems are presented in even-numbered chapters.

There are very real advantages to this organization. First, each pair of problems begins with an issue that is a live one for students today: civil disobedience, genetic engineering, rape, abortion, preferential admissions, and capital punishment. Since student interests and concerns change, three of these are new to this second edition of a tested textbook. These problems were selected after several student polls and then revised on the basis of classroom experience. By leading students to think through some of the moral problems that concern them personally, there is a much greater chance for genuine learning that brings real understanding and carries over to life outside the classroom.

Another advantage is that this organization virtually guarantees that the study of ethics will be practical. Traditionally, individuals have looked to ethics for practical guidance, and I am old-fashioned enough to believe that one measure of the worth of the discipline is its ability to enlighten human action. It is not the purpose of a course in ethics to solve students' problems for them, but it is surely a virtue in such a course to help students think through their moral problems more effectively. By studying six specific moral problems at some length, students can learn how to formulate their own practical problems more precisely, seek out the relevant considerations, and evaluate critically the various pro and con arguments. Ultimately, the study of ethics can give guidance toward making intelligent moral choices.

Third, a course structured around pairs of moral and ethical problems can help students to understand the theoretical questions that ethics is concerned to answer. It is easy enough to pose an ethical problem, such as "What is intrinsically good?" It is not so easy to convey the point of the question. The student may not see where the question comes from or where it is leading. His predicament is like that of someone walking into a movie that is half over; it takes some time to understand what is going on and what the dialogue is all about. This text is organized to show that the beginning of ethics is the practical moral problems out of which ethical problems grow.

The fourth advantage of the distinctive structure of this text is that it remains true to the nature of philosophy by presenting ethical theories as answers to ethical problems. No introduction to ethics would be complete in which the student did not meet some representative ethical theories. Ethical theories can be studied as the personal opinions of great thinkers or as portions of intellectual history. Each of these modes of presentation is legitimate in its own way, but each misses the essence of philosophy. The purpose of philosophy is to think through philosophical perplexities, and one grasps the philosophical point of a theory only as it is seen as an answer to one or more philosophical problems.

Within this basic organization of pairs of problems, moral issues and ethical questions are treated rather differently. In chapters dealing with moral problems, the first step is to define the problem as clearly and precisely as is possible in a few words. An important aim in these chapters is to teach students to distinguish between closely related problems by isolating a single central question and defining the question in unambiguous language. In Chapter 5, for example, the question "Is the rapist morally evil?" is quite distinct from, although related to, the question "Should the rapist be legally punished?" It is essential to differentiate between such intimately related issues because an argument that may be crucial to one may be entirely irrelevant to the other.

Once the central moral question is brought into focus, the most common and compelling arguments on both sides of the issue are summarized. Specific moral problems are formulated in such a way that the issue posed is two-sided. Instead of asking "Is civil disobedience always right or never right or sometimes right?" the question is put "Is civil disobedience ever right?" The discussion that follows then places emphasis on the reasons usually given for taking a stand one way or the other. Every effort has been made to state both pro and con arguments fairly and convincingly in order to show that on live moral issues, sensitive and intelligent individuals may disagree without either party being uninformed or irrational.

Certain arguments are selected for closer examination and debate, with an eye to seeing what objections might be made to each argument and how each might be modified or defended. The purpose here is to encourage students to think critically about the arguments presented—to think through each argument, to perceive its strengths and weaknesses, and to assess the relative weight of one argument against another.

Finally, I examine some of the arguments again when I explain to the student why I take the stand I do on each moral issue. By developing and defending my own position, I hope to illustrate one possible way of evolving an informed conclusion by critical and rational analysis of the arguments. It is very important, I believe, that my balanced and objective treatment of moral issues should not suggest to the student that intellectual rigor and responsibility require complete neutrality. There is a considerable advantage in projecting the persona of an author who is not merely an observer of and commentator on philosophy and morality, but someone engaged in philosophical thinking and committed on moral issues.

In the chapters dealing with theoretical ethical problems, the first task is again to carefully define the central question. Emphasis in these chapters is on the theories most commonly proposed as answers to such questions. Each theory is explained briefly, with occasional comparisons or contrasts between theories. One important goal in discussing the various theories has been to show how ethical problems arise from specific moral issues. To fully understand a theoretical question debated by philosophers, one must see how the question arises from human choices and how it bears on practice. The easiest way to demonstrate this connection is to show how many of the pro and con arguments bearing on a specific moral issue presuppose some answer to a more general ethical issue. A second goal has been to give the student some sense of the range of answers philosophers have given to each ethical question. This is not to say that every possible, or even every important, ethical theory is discussed in the text; but the most important ones are here, and some of the ones commonly neglected in introductory textbooks have been included. It should then be clear that philosophical thinking of ethical problems involves choosing between alternative theories.

An advantage and a disadvantage of each theory are cited to indicate that the choice between ethical theories is not an arbitrary one. By mentioning a strength and weakness of each theory, I hope to suggest that any philosophical theory is to be accepted or rejected on the basis of rational argument.

Finally, a summary of my own position attempts to show how I weighed alternative theories to reach a conclusion, if only a tentative one. I also suggest how my answer is linked to my position on a related moral issue, outlined in the preceding chapter, to underscore the relationship between ethical theories and specific moral problems and to stress the importance of adopting a consistent position.

Study questions and a bibliography conclude each chapter. Questions are provided to guide students in continuing their own critical thinking about moral issues and ethical theories. Bibliographies at the end of odd-numbered chapters record the sources I have found most helpful in writing. Bibliographies at the end of even-numbered chapters include, wherever possible, a reference to at least one philosophically respectable statement of each of the theories summarized in the text. Some reading in original sources is important, because the full meaning and force of any position can best be communicated by a writer who sincerely believes it.

The experienced teacher will find many ways of using this text in an introductory course in ethics. It contains enough material to be the only textbook assigned to a class. Classroom time could then be used for expanding upon issues and theories summarized in the text and for discussing additional arguments and analogous questions. Probably it would be advisable to ask each student to write one or more papers, either on some moral issue parallel to one treated in the text or on some ethical theory presented briefly in it. For more ambitious students, this text might be used in conjunction with readings in classical and contemporary ethical theories.

I want to thank those who have given me the greatest aid and comfort in writing this book. William Frankena's sound advice on the overall conception of the text and the treatment of some individual problems, Joyce Trebilcot's perceptive comments on drafts of the entire work, and Gray Dorsey's trenchant criticisms of those chapters relating to jurisprudence have all helped to shape the manuscript. Continuing philosophical discussions with Stanley Paulson, Joseph Raz, and Joyce Trebilcot have improved this second edition. I am happy to acknowledge my gratitude to the many students whose responses to my lectures have influenced my treatment of these problems in striving to make this book philosophically sound and pedagogically effective. Above all, I am deeply grateful to Farnell Parsons, whose sure eye and keen mind found more errors and infelicities in the proofs than I could remedy.

CARL WELLMAN

INTRODUCTION

Philosophy is best characterized as the activity of thinking through philosophical problems. If one does not understand the nature of philosophy, one may be disappointed in any course in ethics because he is looking for the wrong things in it. Philosophy is not a body of knowledge, not a set of established truths on which all competent philosophers agree. It is therefore unrealistic to approach a course in ethics expecting to be told what one's duties and obligations are or what goal is most worthwhile. Students who want only to learn the solutions to their problems will be constantly frustrated because philosophy is not a set of answers to be accepted unconditionally, but a set of questions to be thought through carefully. Anyone who is uncomfortable with persistent questions and nagging doubts should steer clear of philosophy.

The nature of philosophy as thinking through philosophical problems implies certain things about what it is to learn philosophy and, therefore, about what goals one should work toward in studying this discipline. The student of philosophy may acquire a good deal of information along the way, but this is only incidental to a genuine philosophical education. Since philosophy is not a body of knowledge, it cannot be learned by memorizing a lot of philosophical truths. One learns philosophy by developing certain rational skills used in thinking philosophically. The skills required for philosophy include the ability to define a question narrowly, to state an answer precisely, to explain a position clearly, to find the relevant arguments, and to examine every argument critically. Students should aim primarily at acquiring these skills so necessary for wrestling with philosophical questions.

Not all questions are philosophical. "Where did I leave my cigarettes?" is, I suppose, an ordinary factual question. "Does smoking cause cancer?" is a purely scientific question. "What is the square root of 42?" is a straightforward mathematical question. (Some questions are *both* scientific or mathematical *and* philosophical; many of the questions that puzzled Einstein were of this ambivalent kind.) It is not easy to say just what it is that distinguishes philosophical questions like "What is the Good?" and "Do human beings have an immortal soul?" from other sorts of questions. Typically, however, philosophical problems are more basic than nonphilosophical ones, and they are inseparable from other philosophical problems.

Philosophical problems are more basic in at least two ways. They normally arise only after reflection on nonphilosophical problems. If I happen to notice a wallet lying on the sidewalk ahead of me, several very ordinary questions are likely to spring to mind. Whose is it? Is it empty? Shall I pick it up? Is anyone looking? Should I keep it? Would keeping it be stealing? Only after reflecting on questions like these am I likely to ask myself the philosophical question "Is stealing really wrong?" In this way, then, philosophical questions arise from prephilosophical questions. What is more, the answers we give to prephilosophical questions are dependent on our answers to more basic philosophical questions. Thus, my reply to "Should I keep it?" will depend on my conclusion about "Is stealing really wrong?"

A second characteristic of philosophical problems is that they are inseparable from one another. This does not mean that they are indistinguishable. Philosophical questions do differ in meaning, and it is important not to confuse one philosophical question with another. Nevertheless, solutions to distinct philosophical problems are intricately related: the way a person answers one question will affect the answers he may then give to other questions. Correspondingly, changing one's mind on a particular philosophical issue may require, for the sake of consistency, modifying one's views on other issues. For example, the question "Is stealing really wrong?" is closely connected with other philosophical questions like "What is it to steal?"; "Is the institution of private property morally justified?"; "Is the prohibition against stealing merely a convention of our society?"; and "What makes any act right or wrong?" Such related philosophical questions cannot be answered satisfactorily in isolation from one another.

Philosophy is the activity of thinking through these basic and inseparable problems. *Ethics* is one branch of this discipline. The other main branches are *metaphysics,* or theory of reality, and *epistemology,* or theory of knowledge. Metaphysics concerns itself with philosophical questions about whatever is real. What are the fundamentally different kinds of things in our world? What is human nature? What is the ultimate nature of reality? What, if anything, is the source of our world? Epistemology considers questions about the nature, grounds, and limits of our knowledge. What distinguishes knowledge from mere belief? Is all knowledge based on experience? Can mortal beings know God? Ethics deals with those philosophical problems that arise out of practice or human conduct.

In the end, every ethical question is tied to the problem of choice, the practical problem of deciding what to do in a given situation. Choice is essentially a matter of deciding which of several alternative acts, each of which the agent could do under the circumstances, is to be performed. Judgments regarding such decisions are naturally expressed by words like "right," "wrong," "should," "ought," "obligation," and "duty." The part of ethics that deals with philosophical problems of right or wrong action is called *deontology,* or theory of obligation. In a derivative way, choice involves objects; in deciding which act to do, the agent is deciding which objects, entities, or states of affairs he will produce or destroy, gain or lose, modify or preserve by his action. Judgments about the things, persons, or other acts related to any chosen action are usually expressed by words like "good," "bad," "desirable," "harmful," "beautiful," "wicked," and "admirable." The part of ethics that treats philosophical problems of goodness or badness is called *axiology,* or theory of value. Theory of obligation and theory of value together constitute the core of ethics. This core is often called *normative ethics* because it affirms and applies norms or standards by which actions and objects are judged right or wrong, good or bad.

It is helpful to distinguish between ethical theory and moral philosophy, even though the difference is probably one of degree rather than kind. Since the distinction is not clearly marked in ordinary language, the words "moral" and "ethical" and their cognates are used in a special technical sense throughout this book. A moral problem is relatively specific and practical; for example, "Is civil disobedience ever right?" An ethical problem is more general and theoretical: "What makes an act right or wrong?" Civil disobedience, the act of nonviolent illegal protest, is one limited species of act. The issue of whether civil disobedience is ever right is consequently limited to a fairly narrow range of actions. In contrast, the question of what makes an act right or wrong applies generally to all acts of all kinds. Again, the issue of civil disobedience is very closely tied to practice. It arises for the black person restricted by discriminatory legislation, for the white citizen asked to join a civil rights demonstration against which an injunction has been granted, and for the judge who must pass sentence upon the person who has violated the law because his conscience so dictated. The problem of identifying and defining some universal right- or wrong-making characteristic is less likely to confront a person at the moment of choice. It is more closely connected with the typically philosophical activities of constructing, testing, or criticizing theories of obligation.

One further qualification is required, however, to define the sphere of moral deliberation. Not all specific practical problems are properly called "moral." The question "Is it ever right to brake on a curve?" is not a moral issue in the strict sense that the problem of civil disobedience is. One of the rules of good driving is to brake, if necessary, on approaching a curve in the road and then accelerate slightly on coming out of the curve. This technique holds the car on the road for reasons best known to students of mechanics. But what if the driver fails to brake before reaching the curve and has to fight to keep the car from flying off the road? Some drivers advocate braking slightly on a curve; others suggest letting the car progress at its own speed or even accelerating a little. Their disagreement is practical enough and applies to a specific sort of act, but we would not normally regard their disagreement as a moral one. Similarly, the question "Is sunbathing good or bad?" is not a moral issue in the way that "Is genetic engineering desirable?" is. Devotees believe that lying in the sun is a pleasant way to spend leisure time, an effective way to acquire an attractive brown color, and an aid to good health. Critics contend that it is no fun to feel hot and sticky, that the sun causes unsightly blemishes on the skin, and that excessive sunbathing leads to skin cancer. Why is this issue not really a moral one? There are a number of loosely connected characteristics, one or more of which might make a specific practical issue into a moral problem. The moral sphere encompasses acts that are momentous rather than trivial, that affect others as much as or more than the agent, that subject the agent to blame or punishment if he chooses incorrectly, and that are a matter of conscience. Narrowly defined, ethical questions are general and theoretical; moral questions are specific, practical, and something else—for example, momentous or personal—that varies from case to case.

Normative ethics includes both theory of value and theory of obligation. Its judgments may be general, specific, or even particular, but they are all normative in that they affirm or apply norms. Normative ethics takes some stand on what is or is not worth pursuing or what is or is not to be done. Contrasted with normative ethics is metaethics. Metaethics does not make judgments of value or obligation; it analyzes such judgments epistemologically. It is called *meta*ethics because it is on a higher level of language than ethics. While the language of ethics is about values and obligations, the language of metaethics refers to the language of ethics which in turn refers to values and obligations. Its purpose is to explain the meaning of ethical words and to determine what sorts of reasons, if any, can be given for or against the conclusions of normative ethics. The question "Is civil disobedience ever right?" is a normative question because it asks us to accept some norm of right conduct and apply this norm to acts of civil disobedience. Questions like "What does the word 'right' mean?" and "What evidence determines whether some judgment of rightness is correct?" are metaethical because they are questions *about,* not *in,* the language of normative ethics; that is, the answers to these questions would be statements that refer to the statements and arguments of normative ethics. In philosophy, clear metaethical thinking is essential for effective normative thinking.

The problems presented in this text provide a sampling of moral issues, normative ethical theory, and metaethics. The odd-numbered chapters discuss specific moral problems: Is civil disobedience ever right in a democracy? Is the genetic engineering of humans desirable? Is the rapist always morally evil? Should abortion on demand be legally permitted? Do black Americans have a moral right to preferential admissions? And is capital punishment ever morally right?

This range of moral problems leads very naturally into the most important theoretical ethical problems, both normative and metaethical. Any reflective attempt to decide whether civil disobedience is ever right in a democracy must presuppose some answer to the ethical question "What makes any act morally right or wrong?" As we consider the alleged benefits and harms from genetic engineering, we seek out ultimate judgments of value from which all other evaluations are derived. This raises the question "What is it that is intrinsically good, good for its own sake?" In this way, thinking through any specific moral problem raises more general theoretical normative questions. Each of these questions is theoretical because any fully developed answer to it would constitute an ethical theory. Each is normative because any answer would necessarily affirm some norm or standard by which the rightness of action or the goodness of something might be judged.

Debates about whether black people in our society have a moral right to preferential admissions seem to presuppose very different conceptions of moral, natural, or human rights. Some people argue that there cannot be any natural rights because by definition every right is social. Others allege that desert is the only possible ground of any right because by definition only something that a person can claim as an entitlement is a right. Accordingly, a consideration of the moral issue of rights raises the theoretical problem "What do we mean by 'a right?' " Again, discussion of almost any live moral issue, such as whether capital punishment is ever right, ends in disagreement as often as agreement. Moreover, we are often hard-pressed to explain, even to ourselves, just *why* we take a certain stand on the issue. Meditating the doubt and disagreement so common and persistent in morality and ethics, we may well ask, "How, if at all, can one know which act is right?" This, too, is a metaethical problem because it concerns the rational justification, or lack of it, for the statements that make up normative ethics. Metaethics is not added on to moral problems and normative ethical problems as a gratuitous bonus. It grows inevitably out of any thorough thinking through of moral and ethical issues.

The moral and ethical problems presented in this text are important and representative ones that have occupied the attention of many moral philosophers and people of practical affairs. Careful study of these selected problems that arise out of situations involving choice, out of deciding what is to be done, can stimulate and help students to go on and think philosophically about their own practical problems.

1
CIVIL DISOBEDIENCE

I do not think any man ever has the right to break the law, but I do think that upon occasion every man has the duty to do so.

William Sloan Coffin in *Law, Order and Disobedience*

Martin Luther King, Jr., holds an important place in recent American history. He earned this place by his own courageous acts of civil disobedience and by inspiring and organizing others to engage in similar acts. The impetus and direction of the civil rights movement in the 1960s reflected the acts of sitting-in at lunch counters in Greensboro, North Carolina, and demonstrating in Birmingham, Alabama—both acts of disobedience to legally constituted authorities. Although King's own activities were largely dedicated to the civil rights movement, it is fitting that he received the Nobel Prize for Peace because the techniques of civil disobedience he developed were widely used by those who protested our involvement in the Vietnam War. From the mass sit-in at the Selective Service office in Ann Arbor to the quiet refusal of various individuals to report for induction as ordered, the antiwar movement used civil disobedience as one of its main political weapons.

More recently there have been several occasions where public servants, like teachers or firemen, have violated the law by going out on strike to protest what they regarded as unjustly low wages or morally unjustified working conditions. Even today we read newspaper accounts of groups of citizens who protest and seek to obstruct the construction of nuclear power plants by sitting-in upon private property or illegally blocking access to it.

Understandably, political authorities discourage and resist civil disobedience and, where they can, punish those who engage in it. Many private citizens are morally outraged at such acts, and some even brand them as disloyal. The civil disobedient not only claims that such acts of protest are morally justified, but usually asserts that they contribute to the public welfare. Other citizens applaud the motives of the civil disobedient at the same time that they feel there is something wrong in any violation of the law. Obviously, civil disobedience is a matter of great moral concern in our society.

DISTINGUISHING BETWEEN PROBLEMS

For us as members of society, civil disobedience poses a number of distinct moral problems:

1. *Are acts of civil disobedience right or wrong?* This is the central moral issue confronting any person trying to decide whether to engage in a contemplated act of civil disobedience, but it also faces the person trying to decide how to respond to an act of civil disobedience performed by another.

2. *Are acts of civil disobedience virtuous or morally reprehensible?* This is not the same question as the previous one because the moral goodness of an act is not the same as its rightness. Consider a courageous and conscientious act of civil disobedience that unpredictably triggers a riot in which many innocent people are injured and some killed. It certainly makes sense to say that that act is wrong because of its dreadful consequences. Yet it may be virtuous because the harm is unintended and the agent's motives are noble.

3. *Are acts of civil disobedience beneficial or harmful?* Like the second question, this question has to do with the value of civil disobedience. But the previous question concerns the specifically moral value of the act, while this question concerns its value in the broader nonmoral sense of desirability or usefulness. If a responsible and conscientious act of civil disobedience were to have unforeseen disastrous consequences, we might judge it both morally good and highly undesirable. Conversely, an irresponsible and unscrupulous act of civil disobedience might turn out to be very useful in promoting social improvement.

4. *Is the civil disobedient, the person who engages in acts of civil disobedience, morally good or evil?* The moral value of an agent is clearly intimately connected with the moral value of his acts. I can hardly claim to be a morally fine person if I am continually, or even frequently, engaged in morally reprehensible acts. Still, I may occasionally make a mistake or error in judgment without giving up all claim to a good character. Thus, the issue of whether the civil disobedient is morally good or evil is not quite the same as whether acts of civil disobedience are morally good or evil.

5. *Should society punish the civil disobedient?* Like the first question, this question bears on the rightness or wrongness of some act. Unlike the first question, it concerns the act of punishing by society, not the act of disobedience by an individual member of that society. The rightness or wrongness of the act of civil disobedience does not necessarily settle the question of punishment.

There are probably some wrong acts, like acts of intentional rudeness, that society ought not to punish simply because such punishment would be either ineffective or harmful.

Civil disobedience, then, raises at least five distinct moral problems in our society. Yet these problems are closely related to one another. Precisely how they are related is a more difficult, and more controversial, matter. Consider, for example, the relation between the third question and the first. It might seem that *if* acts of civil disobedience are beneficial, then it follows that they are right; while *if* they are harmful, then they must be wrong. Accordingly, it might seem that the answer to question 3—are acts of civil disobedience beneficial or harmful?—would determine the answer to question 1—is civil disobedience right or wrong? This would be true if *act-utilitarianism* were true, for this theory asserts that what makes an act right or wrong is its utility or disutility, the amount of benefit or harm it does. We will examine this theory in the next chapter. At the same time we will see that it is only one of many plausible theories about what makes an act right or wrong. If act-utilitarianism is false, then discovering whether civil disobedience is beneficial or harmful does not answer the question of its rightness or wrongness. How these two questions are related, therefore, depends on which ethical theory of the grounds of obligation is true.

Again, consider the question of whether society should punish the civil disobedient. *If* the civil disobedient is morally evil, then punishment would seem appropriate; and *if* he is morally good, then punishment would seem most unjust. At first glance, it appears that the answer to question 4 automatically enables one to answer question 5. But to argue that society ought to impose punishment *because* it judges the civil disobedient morally evil is to presuppose that the proper function of social punishment is to reward virtue and penalize vice. Plausible as this assumption may be, it is far from self-evident. It is notoriously difficult to provide conclusive, or even very strong, evidence to establish reliable conclusions about the motives or character of a person. This suggests that courts of law or other social institutions would be highly inefficient if they aimed at punishing vice and rewarding virtue. They would seldom know how much reward or punishment to apply, because they would seldom know how virtuous or wicked the person before them really was. And what would be the point of aiming at this apparently lofty goal, for virtue must express the inner spirit of the moral agent—it cannot be imposed by external coercion.

Finally, it is commonly held that society ought to punish the virtuous lawbreaker in order to discourage similar acts by less virtuous persons who would do great social harm. This suggests that the primary purpose of social punishment ought to be, not penalizing vice, but preventing harm to the members of society. If so, the question of punishment by society does not hinge on whether the civil disobedient is morally good or evil, but on whether acts of civil disobedience are beneficial or harmful. It cannot be taken for granted, however, that society ought to punish all harmful acts. It has been argued that punishing individuals for doing evil simply compounds the amount of evil by adding the badness of the penalty to the harm of the act itself. What is the justification for making a bad situation worse in this way? Once more we see that the relation between distinct moral problems depends on which ethical theory is true.

The question of precisely how any pair of moral or ethical questions is related is itself an ethical question about which philosophers may and do disagree. One of the objectives of any moral philosophy is to show how moral and ethical questions are logically related within an *ethical system*. An ethical system is a coherent set of ethical theories, or of answers to ethical questions, that provides a framework for solving all moral problems and perhaps even all practical problems. Different ethical systems relate to distinct moral problems in different ways. But within any given ethical system, the logical connections between moral and ethical questions are clearly defined. Deciding what the logical connections really are boils down to deciding which ethical system is really true. This is the final question each moral philosopher must pose.

DEFINING THE PROBLEM

If the end of ethics is a complete and adequate ethical system, its beginnings are in specific moral problems. Moral problems are practical because they pose the question of what is to be chosen or done; they are specific because they concern some limited kind of conduct, such as keeping one's promises or disobeying the law, rather than any and every kind of action. In order to avoid confusion, it is best to take such practical issues one at a time. Let us begin with the question "Are acts of civil disobedience ever right?" I do not claim that this question is more interesting or important than the other moral questions that can be asked about civil disobedience. I do suggest that it will take us to the heart of ethics faster than any of the others, for the central problem of ethics is the problem of decision, the problem of choosing between right and wrong alternatives in a given situation. Moreover, in a society where political organizations and legal procedures for change seem incapable of solving our grave social problems or preventing gross social injustice, the problem of whether to engage in civil disobedience is a very practical one for every morally responsible citizen.

The urgency of this problem does nothing, alas, to guarantee its clarity or precision. The first difficulty is to define the nature of civil disobedience. Popular and philosophical usage varies so widely that it is impossible to find any single definition that captures the meanings of all writers and speakers. Most of them, however, would not be outraged by my stipulation that an act of civil disobedience is a nonviolent illegal act of moral protest. Thus, we shall use the expression "civil disobedience" to refer to a distinguishable class of acts, each of which is (a) *illegal*. It is this feature, violation of the law, that makes such acts a species of disobedience. Sometimes this also involves disobeying an explicit order of some civil authority, as when students sitting-in at the Selective Service office in Ann Arbor refused to leave when ordered to do so by Selective Service officials and later by the police. In every instance, however, the act is one that breaks one of the laws of the governing political unit—city, state, or country.

Every act of civil disobedience is also (b) *nonviolent*. Not every moral philosopher uses the expression in this restricted sense, but it seems useful to distinguish between nonviolent acts of breaking the law and violent infractions of the law, because somewhat different arguments can be used to justify or condemn these two classes of action. Just how violence and nonviolence are to be defined is itself a difficult philosophical question. Is an act of throwing a brick through a store window a violent act? Some hold that it is because it is forceful and destructive. Others claim that only force injurious to people, not property, is "true" violence. Some even suggest that what is definitive of violence is the violation of rights and not the use of force at all. Without denying the moral significance of these attempts to redefine "violence," we will retain the ordinary dictionary definition for our purposes: an act is violent when it is characterized by uncontrolled, rough, or destructive force. Acts of civil disobedience are just the opposite. They are gentle and nondestructive; or if they are forceful, the force is carefully controlled to achieve its purpose with the minimum of injury to persons or property.

Finally, an act of civil disobedience is (c) *an act of protest.* The purpose or intent of the act is to protest against some law, policy, or action of the body politic. Not every objection or rejection is a protest; it is understood that the civil disobedient is objecting on moral grounds. The grounds for protest may be that the law is unjust, the policy bad, or the action wrong— but it is not enough that the agent dislike the policy or be unwilling to abide by the law. It is this purpose of limited moral protest that distinguishes civil disobedience from ordinary crime and from revolution. The criminal is not protesting the law; he is simply trying to evade it. The revolutionary is not repudiating or denouncing some particular statute, policy, or act of the civil authorities; she is trying to change the entire political system either by a radical transformation of the constitution by which it is governed or by a change in the person or persons who hold the power and authority in the system. The purpose of the civil disobedient is neither criminal nor revolutionary; it is moral protest against some part of an otherwise accepted political system. Whether this moral purpose serves in part or whole to justify illegal acts is one question we are to discuss in this chapter.

Specifically, our question is whether civil disobedience is right or wrong. To this question, there are three logically possible answers: civil disobedience is always right, always wrong, or sometimes right and sometimes wrong. Although logically possible, the assertion that civil disobedience is always right is obviously false. No serious moralist would defend very harmful acts of civil disobedience done to protest some very slight social evil under circumstances where the evil could easily be remedied through legal avenues of reform. The serious moral problem is whether acts of civil disobedience are *ever* right, whether there are any occasions on which it is right to disobey the law in moral protest. Granted that the citizen ought usually to obey the law of the land so that the burden of proof is upon anyone who would violate the law, the question is whether there are exceptional circumstances in which the evil protested is so grave that civil disobedience is justified.

To make this issue a live one, let us add the qualification "in a democracy." Since we are living in a democracy, the problem of whether to engage in civil disobedience for us takes on this more specific form. Whether or not civil disobedience might be morally justified in a landed aristocracy or in a totalitarian regime is only peripherally relevant to our decision as to whether civil disobedience is ever right for one of us. Also, to allow an affirmative answer to rest on the case of an externally aggressive and internally repressive government, like that of Nazi Germany, is to reduce the moral problem to near triviality because the answer seems to be beyond serious debate. But whether any person who has had a voice in making the law and who has access to legal procedures for changing the law may still violate the law is a much more debatable issue. This is the issue we shall now examine: *Is civil disobedience ever right in a democracy?*

ARGUMENTS AGAINST CIVIL DISOBEDIENCE

Many public officials, solid citizens, and moral philosophers deny that civil disobedience is ever right. However laudable the motives of the civil disobedient and however restrained and nondestructive the manner of acting, the act is always wrong. Let us see what arguments are most often given for this moral judgment.

Political Obligation

By very definition, each and every act of civil disobedience is a deliberate violation of the law of the land. This in itself is an important basis for moral condemnation. As a citizen, every person has certain political obligations, such as the duty to pay taxes and the duty to vote. Among these obligations is the duty to obey the laws of society. Just *why* the citizen is morally obligated to obey the law is a matter of considerable debate among moral philosophers who agree that one has this obligation. The moral principle that everyone ought to obey the laws of society provides the basis for a straightforward argument against civil disobedience. If everyone ought to obey the law, then it is always wrong for anyone to disobey the law. Since every act of civil disobedience is, by definition, an act of disobeying the law, every act of civil disobedience is wrong.

The Principle of Democracy and Majority Rule

Democracy is government of the people by the people. Anyone who believes that democracy is the right or morally ideal form of government is committed to the principle that the people ought to rule, that those who are governed by any society ought to do the governing as well. This is the central moral principle of democracy. If unanimity were possible, this principle could be followed with no real difficulty. For then the laws of society would reflect the wishes and choices of every citizen. In practice, however, people will disagree on any important issue; in practice, therefore, the law in a democracy is imposed on the minority by the majority. This is a deviation from the moral ideal of all the people ruling all the people. The answer is not for the minority to seize power and rule over the majority, for this would be an even greater deviation from the ideal of democracy. Thus, the central principle of democracy, that the people ought to rule, implies under practical conditions the corollary that the minority ought to abide by the will of the majority. Since the law in any democracy expresses the will of the majority, this in turn implies that anyone who dissents from or objects to the law ought, nevertheless, to obey the law. The civil disobedient is inevitably in the minority. If one were in the majority, one would have no need, in a democracy, to resort to illegal means of protest. The majority can always change the law or modify a policy or rectify an action it judges to be immoral or wrong. Accordingly, the central principle of democracy excludes civil disobedience. The argument can be summarized like this: In any society, the people ought to rule. Since the people ought to rule, the minority ought to abide by the will of the majority. In any genuine democracy, every law expresses the will of the people—at least the will of the majority of the people. Thus, the minority ought never to disobey the law in a democracy. In every act of civil disobedience, the minority is disobeying the law made by the majority. Therefore, every act of civil disobedience is wrong.

Unnecessary Evil

Everyone can plainly see, or so it is alleged, that civil disobedience is an evil. This is not to condemn civil disobedience as wicked, or morally reprehensible, but only to say that acts of civil disobedience are inevitably bad or undesirable in important ways. At the very least, they violate the law, and most likely they serve as examples to stimulate further lawlessness. They usually result in punishment, which means suffering for the offender. This does not in itself imply that civil disobedience is wrong, for not all evils are wrong. The dentist's act of drilling into a tooth or the surgeon's act of amputating a limb are obviously evil in that they cause suffering. Still, these acts are right because they are necessary evils. They are required to prevent even greater evils—the loss of a decaying tooth or the death of a patient with a gangrenous limb. By contrast, acts of civil disobedience are unnecessary in a democracy because there are other less objectionable ways to remedy social evils. Possibly such acts really are necessary in a totalitarian regime where the conscientious citizen and the moral reformer have no other way of changing an unjust law or calling attention to an immoral policy. But in a democracy legal procedures for change are open to everyone. Ultimately, the majority can rectify any social evil through the vote. And every minority, even the individual, has access to legal means of capturing the attention of the majority and converting it to its own opinion. Real democracy requires the rights of free speech, assembly, petition, and demonstration; for without these rights the people have no effective control over their government. Where these rights are protected, civil disobedience is an unnecessary evil. Since acts that do unnecessary evil are always wrong, civil disobedience is always wrong.

Lawlessness and Violence

Each act of civil disobedience is a violation of the law of the land. This fact was recognized in the first argument. The present argument is grounded on a different fact, or alleged fact—that each act of civil disobedience is a cause of additional acts of law-breaking. For one thing, each act of civil disobedience is an example for others to follow. When one person breaks the law, particularly if that person is respected for violating the law, others tend to follow suit and break the law also. For another thing, each act of civil disobedience weakens the agent's own respect for the law. Having once broken the law, the civil disobedient will find it easier to break the law on other occasions. In these two ways, each single act of illegal protest tends to foster other violations of the law. The result is an increase in lawlessness in the society. And when the rule of law breaks down, widespread crime and general insecurity follow.

A second result of civil disobedience is violence. To be sure, the civil disobedient has renounced the use of uncontrolled and destructive force, and his renunciation may inspire others to the same self-restraint. More often it does not. The end or goal of civil disobedience is to protest some law or policy by means of action in deliberate violation of the law. This end often arouses strong feelings, and the means often attract others far less responsible and restrained than the civil disobedient himself. The less disciplined participants in a mass demonstration may forsake nonviolent disobedience and engage in violent acts. Or nonviolent protest may be met with violent resistance on the part of those who oppose, often irrationally and forcefully, the cause espoused by the civil disobedient. Even the police or other legally constituted authorities may respond to acts of civil disobedience with violence of one form or another. Thus acts of civil disobedience are inevitably the cause of lawlessness and violence, two grave social evils. Any act that produces grave social evils is wrong. Therefore, civil disobedience is always wrong.

Universalizability

As Kant recognized so clearly, a necessary condition for any act to be morally right is that it must be universalizable (see pp. 42–44). An individual act is right only if every act of exactly the same kind is also right. That is to say, it cannot be right for one person to do some act in a given situation unless it would be right for every person to do the same kind of act under similar circumstances. For example, the mere fact that it would be inconvenient for me to keep an appointment with one of my students this afternoon does not justify my breaking the appointment unless it would also be right for anyone to break any appointment whenever it proved inconvenient to keep it. It would be unreasonable for me to claim that it is all right for me to break this appointment on this occasion and yet to insist that it is wrong for others to break their appointments with me when it is equally inconvenient for them to keep them. Any individual act is right only if it is universalizable, only if all acts of precisely the same kind are right. But acts of civil disobedience are not universalizable. Although some individual acts of civil disobedience appear right when taken by themselves, reflection clearly shows that if every person in similar circumstances engaged in the same kind of action, the consequences would be disastrous. Since it would be wrong to produce social disaster, it would be wrong to act on the universal principle that all acts of this kind should be done. And since no act of civil disobedience can generate a morally acceptable universal principle of action, no act of civil disobedience is right. Take the act of an individual black person who disobeys the law in order to protest some injustice to his or her race. This individual act is right only if it would be right for all black people to engage in similar civil disobedience to protest the same injustice. But if over twenty million blacks violated the law, social chaos would surely result. Since the individual act of civil disobedience does not remain right when universalized, it is not really right in the first place. Again, it would be right for an individual worker to engage in civil disobedience to protest some immoral economic policy of the government only if it would be right for every other worker to do likewise. But if all workers protested illegally in this way, our economy would break down, causing suffering to masses of people. Since it would be wrong for all workers to engage in civil disobedience, it is never right for any worker to engage in it. Complicated as the notion of universalizability may be, the argument can be stated quite simply: An act is right only if it can be universalized. Since individual acts of civil disobedience can never be universalized, they are never right. This amounts to saying that civil disobedience is always wrong.

These are the five most popular arguments against civil disobedience. Acts of civil disobedience are always wrong because they disregard the citizen's political obligation to obey the law; they are inconsistent with the central principle of democracy; they are unnecessary evils; they cause the grave social evils of lawlessness and violence; and they cannot be universalized. Each of these arguments places the burden of proof on the civil disobedient. But the civil disobedient is quite prepared to advance what he considers cogent and compelling arguments to justify his actions.

ARGUMENTS FOR CIVIL DISOBEDIENCE

Preservation of Moral Integrity

Civil disobedience is sometimes right because it disassociates an individual from moral evil. At times the law commands one to commit a great wrong, as when the Fugitive Slave Act required citizens to capture runaway slaves and return them to continued servitude and cruel punishment. Or a policy may commit a country and its citizens to an immoral course of action. Many believe that our Vietnam policy led to unjustified intervention and inhumane modes of warfare. The individual citizen may or may not have an obligation to eradicate all evil, but each person does at least have a duty to refuse personal involvement or complicity. To obey an unjust law or to allow an immoral policy to go unchallenged is to assent to and even participate in moral wrong. Under such circumstances, civil disobedience is the only way to protect the individual from being an accomplice in moral crime. Since one ought never to participate in moral wrong and since civil disobedience is sometimes the only way to refrain from being a party to moral evil, civil disobedience is sometimes right.

The Duty to Combat Immorality

It is not enough for a person simply to maintain a neutral position by refusing to participate in moral evil. The individual citizen must actively fight any great moral wrong that exists in society. Civil disobedience is justified by its central purpose: to protest some immoral law, policy, or action of the society. Although the civil disobedient may sometimes protest something that is really not morally objectionable, there will be many occasions when the object of protest is a genuine moral evil. The law may be unjust, as the ordinance requiring bus segregation in Montgomery surely discriminated unjustly against black persons. Or a policy or course of action may be evil, as many contend our policy of intervention in Vietnam was. In such cases, the conscientious citizen has a moral obligation to remedy injustice or evil. Morality does not allow one to stand idly by and observe great evils. It is the duty of each moral agent to combat immorality wherever it exists, by whatever means are available. Civil disobedience is one weapon in the fight against immorality. Therefore, civil disobedience is sometimes one's duty and, accordingly, right.

A Means of Social Progress

It is surely right to improve society, and civil disobedience is one way of accomplishing this. Other ways are writing letters to the editor or to elected representatives, working in the political campaign of some enlightened candidate, or organizing a citizen task force to study and publicize an unjust law or immoral policy. By its very nature, however, civil disobedience has certain advantages over alternative political techniques. Actions speak louder than words. Committee discussions and public speeches can do something to educate the public about some social evil, but they reach a limited audience and can be too easily ignored by those who do hear. An act of disobeying the law commands the attention of the entire society, for society cannot afford to ignore those who challenge its laws. Moreover, the media of journalism, radio, and television give extensive coverage to such a newsworthy event, and the act of civil disobedience tends to win widespread respect from the general public. No doubt some will feel annoyed, resentful, or threatened, but many more will approve the conscientiousness of the civil disobedient who acts on moral principle and the courage of the moral agent who dares to withstand the criticism and punishment of society. In this way, civil disobedience communicates the need for changes to those in society who, if only they recognize the evil and come to oppose it, can remove it from the body politic. On some occasions civil disobedience is the most effective political technique available for social progress. Since it is right to remove social evils and improve society, civil disobedience is sometimes right.

No Practicable Alternative

Democracy provides many procedures for social change. Ultimately, any unjust law or immoral policy can be revised or removed by means of the ballot box. Where the public is ignorant of or indifferent to the social evil, free speech and a free press provide the avenues for arousing public interest, and free political parties provide the instruments for organizing public response and making it politically effective. There are times, however, when such legal processes may be useless. For one thing, they might take too long. When disaster is imminent, action must be taken immediately. There may not be time to publicize the danger and organize political action to meet it. Many people believed this was true just after the Second World War, when they felt that nuclear war might break out at any moment between the great powers. Again, when resentment against racial discrimination and poverty in the ghettos becomes so intense that violence becomes an immediate prospect, something has to be done here and now. There is no time to pursue legal channels for social reform.

The legal procedures provided in a democracy may also be effectively denied to certain groups. It need not be that these groups are forbidden by law to use these procedures; it is just that they lack access to them. The mass media are available to anyone who can afford to pay for their use, but minority and disadvantaged groups may simply lack the financial means to publicize their cause. And if their cause happens to be unpopular with the establishment—big business and unionized labor, as well as the government—they will find that the establishment has informal but effective ways of censoring the media. Again, the political parties are there to be captured by any cause, but most minority groups lack the effective political power to take over or even greatly influence either of the major parties. Thus it may be that those persons most sensitive to and concerned about some unjust law or immoral policy may find themselves unable to utilize the legal procedures for social and political protest. Under such circumstances, the only practicable alternative is civil disobedience. This becomes the only means of influencing public opinion and forcing political action. Since it is right to use the only effective means to some socially desirable and morally justified end, civil disobedience is right under these circumstances.

Government May Exceed Its Authority

No doubt it is normally wrong for an individual to break the law. When the government is acting within its authority, it has the right to make and enforce the law; accordingly, it is wrong for the citizen to disobey the law. But sometimes the government exceeds its authority, either because it enacts some law that goes beyond the limits of the authority granted to it by the Constitution, or because it infringes upon the inalienable rights of the citizens. Some maintain that the provision in the recent civil rights law forbidding racial discrimination in small, local hotels goes far beyond the authority to regulate interstate commerce granted to the federal government under the Constitution of the United States. Others claim that the Selective Service Law lacks authority. Although the government's power of induction has currently expired, this law still requires young men to register and be classified for military service. In times when the draft law is operative, many contend that it forces men to risk their lives against their will, and this demand is in conflict with the human right to life. When the law exceeds the authority of the government, it is no longer morally binding. In these cases, acts of civil disobedience are right.

Even if it is true that the burden of proof must be borne by the person who would break the law, the civil disobedient is often willing to accept this burden. The more common and plausible arguments used to justify acts of civil disobedience are that such acts are sometimes necessary to preserve the moral integrity of the citizen; that the individual citizen has a duty to combat immorality; that civil disobedience is a means of social progress; that there is often no practicable alternative for reform; and that the government sometimes exceeds its authority. None of these arguments proves, nor is intended to prove, that civil disobedience is always right. Everyone agrees that under normal circumstances every citizen ought to obey the law and use other means of protest. The civil disobedient's claim is a more modest one: that some acts of nonviolent illegal protest are right under certain circumstances.

REBUTTALS AND REJOINDERS

Which arguments are really weightier can be decided only after critical reexamination and reflective evaluation. It is necessary to see what objections can be made against each argument and how well, if at all, each objection can be countered. Let us take another look at three of the arguments cited.

Political Obligation

Civil disobedience is always wrong because it is always wrong to disobey the law. This argument assumes that one of the political obligations of every citizen, at least in a democracy, is to obey the law. Since civil disobedience violates this political duty, it is always wrong.

To this argument it can be objected that the citizen has no obligation to obey the law as such; that is, the mere existence of some statute imposes no obligation to obey upon the individual. No doubt the individual citizen ought to obey most laws, but this is not simply because they are laws. The individual's obligation to obey most laws is derived from the fortunate fact that they are very useful to society. Most laws promote the welfare of the members of society and, therefore, ought to be obeyed. But if some legislature, in ignorance or through malice, enacts some useless or harmful statute, the citizen has no moral obligation to obey this law.

In rejoinder, one can argue that this objection misinterprets the citizen's obligation to obey the law. This obligation is not founded upon the utility of the law, for then it would indeed cease whenever the law was useless. Actually, the obligation to obey the law comes from a sort of social contract. Of course, the citizen has not signed an explicit contract to henceforth and forever obey the laws of society. But by the very act of living in the society and accepting all the benefits made possible by its laws, the citizen has tacitly agreed to abide by those laws. This agreement remains binding no matter how useless or even harmful any particular law may be. The citizen always has an obligation to obey the law.

Not if the law is unjust, the civil disobedient will counter. An unjust law is one that conflicts with a higher law, the moral law. Whether this moral law is thought of as the commands of God or the principles of Nature or the dictates of Reason, it takes precedence over the law of society. When the two laws conflict, one ought to abide by the moral law even if this means breaking the law of the land. Obviously, it would be morally wrong to violate the moral law. Since an unjust law is inconsistent with the moral law, to obey an unjust law would be to do a morally wrong act. Since there can be no moral obligation to do what is morally wrong, there is no genuine political obligation to obey an unjust law.

The theological moralist might argue that even an unjust law is morally binding. We know this is so because in Romans 13:1 we read that God commands us to obey even unjust authorities. Paradoxical as this command may seem to our limited minds, it is our moral duty to obey the commands of God. His moral law allows no exceptions for unjust laws. Thus, every citizen ought always to obey the law.

To this religious defense of our obligation to obey the law, several replies are possible. But leaving aside the views of the atheist and the antitheological moralist, we must consider the possibility that we have misinterpreted the word of God. The religious legalism suggested in the Old Testament has been modified by the New Testament. No moral rule, including the command to obey civil authorities, is ever binding without exception. There are always unusual circumstances and unexpected conditions under which a moral rule that is usually valid ceases to hold. In such cases, conscience must guide the individual's action. The moral agent, and every citizen is also a moral agent, ought in the last analysis to obey his own conscience. When the law of society conflicts with the conscience of the individual, the individual no longer has any obligation to obey the law. The one and only duty of every citizen is to act conscientiously, for conscience is the voice of God within each person.

Perhaps, but even within the religious framework, the reliability of individual conscience is suspect. This is why all the important religions have relied on social institutions like the Church to interpret Holy Scripture and give moral guidance. Seen in the context of modern science, the conscience is even more dubious. Whether it is the voice of the father figure internalized or reflects the nonrational process of enculturation, it is far from an infallible source of knowledge of right and wrong. The manner in which the consciences of different individuals conflict shows that conscience cannot be trusted to reveal the truth about moral choices. Such conflict also shows that society cannot afford to allow each citizen to follow his own conscience, for then conflicting consciences would lead to social conflicts and, ultimately, social chaos. Society, for its very self-preservation, must have the right to demand obedience to its laws. This right of society to demand obedience implies a corresponding duty of its citizens to obey. Therefore, the individual ought always to obey the laws established by society, and civil disobedience is always wrong.

This is not the last word on the matter, of course. But before the complexities become even more confusing, we might view the issue of civil disobedience from another perspective by reexamining a different argument, one that favors civil disobedience.

A Means of Social Progress

Civil disobedience is sometimes right because in some circumstances it is a means of social progress. This is a utilitarian argument based on pragmatic considerations. What makes an act of civil disobedience right is its utility, the contribution it makes to the good of the citizens in society. The value of civil disobedience derives from the fact that it works, that it is, under certain circumstances, an effective technique of social change. Acts of civil disobedience by Martin Luther King and his followers reduced racial discrimination more rapidly and radically than alternative modes of action such as preaching in the churches or working within the established political parties. It is this practical effectiveness in changing society for the better that justifies some acts of nonviolent illegal protest.

One objection to this argument is that civil disobedience has only a specious efficacy. While it may appear to be a highly effective way to improve society, in reality it is an unreliable and inefficient political technique. A similar objection can be made to totalitarian methods of government. On the surface, they appear to be much more effective in promoting the public welfare than the slow, deliberate methods of democracy. After all, it took Mussolini to make the Italian trains run on time and Stalin to mechanize Russian agriculture. There is no doubt that totalitarian methods are more effective than democratic ones in one sense: they produce more results faster. But the purpose of government is not just to get results of any sort; it is to achieve a very special end—the happiness and freedom of the people. Totalitarian methods are not very well adapted to producing this particular result, because the goals of the dictator may not conform to those actually desired by most of the people, and the means used may well be destructive of popular freedom. When seen in the long run and in terms of their proper objective, totalitarian methods are really inefficient compared to slower but surer democratic methods. Similarly, civil disobedience has a specious effectiveness. It seems to produce desirable results much faster than the cumbersome methods of open discussion, political organization, and legal reform. But in a democracy the goals of civil disobedience are imposed upon the reluctant majority by the very small minority that engages in civil disobedience. Hence, these goals may or may not reflect the real needs of the people of the country as a whole. And even if the gains are real, they are precarious because they may be swept aside by the resentful majority at any moment. If the true goal is stable social welfare, a continuing good life for all the citizens, then civil disobedience is a much less effective mode of action than it seems at first glance.

The civil disobedient can, and probably should, accept this argument as revealing an important truth, but only part of the truth. It must be admitted that a courageous and conscientious act of civil disobedience, often accompanied by widespread publicity and commotion, may accomplish much less than it promises. Rocking the boat may be exciting, but it does not necessarily advance the ship of state. That this may be true must be admitted. That this is often true need not be denied. What can and must be denied is that this is always the case. Certainly, civil disobedience is a dangerous technique for achieving social change, and for some (not all) of the reasons that totalitarian methods are dangerous to the welfare of the people. Civil disobedience can all too easily be abused. But this does not prove that it cannot be an effective means of social progress when responsibly used by a self-disciplined leader with a moral purpose. In the right hands, civil disobedience is a politically useful and morally justified mode of action.

Not at all, the solid citizen may object. Unfortunately, the good intentions of the civil disobedient do not guarantee the goodness of the results of his action. The methods of civil disobedience are essentially self-defeating. No act of civil disobedience can achieve its goal because the nature of the means taken is inconsistent in practice with the intended result. One cannot, for example, defend civil rights through acts of civil disobedience, because such disobedience weakens our Constitution and the courts that define and uphold the civil rights recognized in our society. Again, civil disobedience cannot solve the problems of inferior education, unemployment, and deteriorating housing in our urban ghettos because such acts produce class conflicts and mob violence that exacerbate these very problems. The point of civil disobedience is to protest some social evil and thereby mobilize political forces to improve society. Unfortunately, the illegality and political coerciveness of the method of reform produce reactions of fear and anger that mobilize the political opposition. By its very nature, no act of civil disobedience can achieve its end; it is essentially self-defeating.

In an effort to rebut this objection, the civil disobedient may point out that this argument ignores one essential aspect of civil disobedience. Granted that every act of civil disobedience violates the law of the land and that this method of protest is chosen because it promises to put political pressure on the opposition. Nevertheless, it should not be forgotten that every such act is also nonviolent. It is this nonviolence that enables civil disobedience to minimize the very real dangers outlined in the above objection. Recent history gives evidence of solid accomplishments attained by this method—witness the liberation of India from British imperialism and the real, if limited, advance in civil rights in the South. Of course, the profound spirit of nonviolence required to make civil disobedience effective is possible only under the leadership of a morally inspired and restrained person like Mahatma Gandhi or Martin Luther King.

More than such a leader is required, it may be objected. Civil disobedience is a moral protest, and necessarily moral on at least two dimensions. Its central purpose is to protest some moral evil, and it achieves its purpose, if at all, by appealing to the moral standards of the citizens. Its goal is to inform the public of some injustice or inhumanity in society and to arouse public opposition to that evil, but its effectiveness in appealing to the public depends on the moral sensitivity and responsiveness of the citizens. The courageousness and conscientiousness of the act will have wide and deep appeal only if the general populace is itself deeply concerned about morality. Gandhi was able to exert political pressure on the British only because the British are a thoroughly civilized people with an abiding sense of fair play. Martin Luther King was able to mobilize support for his civil rights movement only because most people in the United States are more just and compassionate than the practice of racial discrimination suggests. Thus civil disobedience can be politically effective only where it is unnecessary. Civil disobedience can hope to achieve its aim only where the citizenry is open and responsive to moral values. And where the public is moral in this way, the same end could be achieved by open discussion and political organization without any violation of the law.

The civil disobedient may reply with a paradox: Sometimes the best way to get a person to listen to reason is by using nonrational, coercive means. One rather common method of morally educating the young is by spanking them. But what justifies this forceful method of education? Just how does a pain in the bottom produce moral insight in the head? In itself, it does not. Spanking can be an effective method of moral education only if it is a prelude to reasoning. It is not enough to spank the child; the child must be told why he or she has been spanked, what wrong he or she has done, and what makes a misdeed wrong. But in that case, why not reason with the child without resorting to spanking at all? Because the child will not listen to reason. He or she is too complacent to question this deed and too impatient to waste time pondering any considerations that might prove it a misdeed. Therefore, the nonrational method of spanking is sometimes a necessary preliminary to rational methods of moral education. Similarly, the public may be unwilling to listen to reason at times. People may be oblivious to some crying social evil. They may be too apathetic to pay attention to moral prophets protesting this evil. If they do attend briefly to some rational protest, they may be too prejudiced to take the moral arguments seriously. But civil disobedience is a form of protest that is difficult to ignore and hard to brush aside as mere rhetoric. Because it violates the law, it demands attention from society at large. Because it is a courageous commitment to action, it cannot be discounted as mere words. And the conscientiousness and self-discipline of civil disobedients may create a respect for their persons that carries over to a responsiveness to their message. Civil disobedience is only a preliminary to the entirely legal processes of public discussion and political reform, but it can be a necessary first step in a total course of action that achieves real social gains.

Perhaps, but at what price? If one wishes to evaluate civil disobedience fairly in utilitarian terms, in terms of the good achieved and evil rectified, one must also reckon up the harm done. The social goods purchased with the currency of civil disobedience may be bought at too high a price; the social cost is tremendous and too often ignored. Movements that employ civil disobedience as a political technique often become vehicles for infiltration by extremists and revolutionaries. The morally idealistic and socially responsible leaders of the movement are thus used as instruments by those whose motives and tactics are less scrupulous. This is a danger that can threaten our entire democratic way of life. Moreover, although civil disobedience is itself nonviolent, it very often results in mob violence, in the destruction of private and public property, and in the injury of innocent persons. Finally, just because it defies the law of the land, it brings about a spreading lawlessness that undermines the rule of law and order essential for social stability and justice. Even if civil disobedience should achieve its goal, the value of the goal is not worth the social costs of achieving it.

Lawlessness and Violence

This objection to the utilitarian justification of civil disobedience raises a third argument. The cogency of the argument that civil disobedience is sometimes right because it is an effective means of social progress hinges in part upon the soundness of the counterargument that civil disobedience is always wrong because it is a cause of lawlessness and violence. Since the charge that civil disobedience causes violence parallels the charge that it causes lawlessness, let us simplify our discussion by limiting our attention to the latter.

The charge to be examined, then, is that acts of civil disobedience cause lawlessness in society at large. Each such act serves as an example to many others to follow suit and violate the law of the land. The publicity that accompanies most acts of civil disobedience ensures that the example will be widely known. And the example will be widely imitated because there will be many circumstances in which one's personal inclination to violate some onerous or obnoxious law is reinforced by the prospect of public approval for apparently courageous and conscientious action.

In rejoinder, the civil disobedient will argue that this danger is more of a theoretical possibility than an actual danger. For better or worse, there are very few citizens in any society who are willing to take the personal risk involved in civil disobedience. To break the law is to expose oneself to all the penalties society inflicts upon the lawbreaker. Only a very courageous and conscientious person, or the criminal personality, will be prepared to take this risk. Most members of any society are neither moral heroes nor hardened criminals. Therefore, the example of the civil disobedient will not in fact produce any general lawlessness.

Even if an act of civil disobedience does not cause widespread violation of the law, it may be objected, still it inevitably weakens respect for the law in the civil disobedient and in those who support or approve of his or her act. To respect the law is to recognize its moral authority and, accordingly, to be prepared to abide by the law even when obedience is irksome. An act of civil disobedience expresses disrespect for the law because it rejects the authority of the violated statute. And each act of breaking the law weakens the disposition to obey the law in the future. Thus, civil disobedience both expresses and promotes an attitude of disrespect for the law.

It can be replied that this objection completely misinterprets the spirit of civil disobedience. Paradoxical as it may seem, acts of civil disobedience both express and enlarge respect for the law of the land. The central purpose of civil disobedience is to purify the law of injustice or immorality. Only someone who cares deeply about the law and recognizes its importance to society will endure the hardships attendant upon civil disobedience to improve the law in this way. Moreover, the civil disobedient usually accepts the legal punishments meted out by society for infraction of the law. This, too, shows that he or she accepts the authority of the law. The civil disobedient respects the law in caring enough to improve it and in accepting the penalties it inflicts.

In the eyes of the objector, this is a strange sort of respect indeed. To pick and choose between laws, to obey some and disobey others, is surely not to obey law as law. Each and every law is part of the law of our land; as such it commands our allegiance. No doubt the civil disobedient respects most laws, for he or she obeys most laws, but can hardly claim to respect the very law he or she is violating. True respect for the law as law requires accepting *every* law as morally binding just because it is the law.

If this is what is required by true respect for the law, and the civil disobedient would deny this, then respect for the law is not as fine as many imagine. To accept every law as morally binding just because it is law is to abdicate moral responsibility. The individual who does this is allowing the legislators in society, whoever they may be, to determine for him or her what is right or wrong. The great danger in modern society, with its mass media and pressures toward conformity, is widespread subservience and lack of integrity in its citizens. This danger is a threat, in particular, to any democratic way of life. Only if the individual is prepared to accept one's duties as a citizen, including the duty to criticize and oppose the government when conscience demands it, can democracy survive. Any doctrine that equates respect for the law with total subservience to the law is antithetical to the spirit of democracy.

The defender of law and order will counter that branding acceptance of the law as "total subservience" is misleading and unfair. What respect really amounts to is simply voluntary compliance with the law. Anyone tempted to embark on or support civil disobedience should first consider carefully the alternatives to voluntary compliance with the law. If the citizens in any society are unwilling to comply with the law of their own free will, then either the public officials must force them to comply or the law will not be obeyed. The former will require brutal enforcement of the law; the latter will produce social chaos. Since neither of these alternatives is morally acceptable, society as a whole and its individual citizens must set as their moral ideal willing obedience to every law.

The civil disobedient will reply that this objection oversimplifies the social situation. Of course neither brutal enforcement nor social chaos is morally acceptable, but the alternative need not be obedience to every law by every citizen on every occasion. For one thing, acceptance of the law is a matter of degree. The moral ideal of a free and stable society requires a general acceptance of the law. Most people must obey the law most of the time, and they must do this without the imposition of harsh legal penalties for disobedience. But general or widespread acceptance is entirely compatible with occasional acts of civil disobedience in exceptional circumstances. Accordingly, limited civil disobedience need not cause public lawlessness.

In addition, civil disobedience sometimes serves to promote general acceptance of the law. To see this we must probe beneath acceptance of the law to the motives or reasons for compliance. Blind habit may cause citizens to obey the law, and the threat of severe penalties may cause them to fear it, but respect for the law comes from recognizing that the law serves the public welfare in a just manner. Hence, one of the more common and potent causes of disrespect for the laws in any society is the existence of one or more laws generally recognized as unjust or immoral. It is when the public loses moral respect for the law that it refuses to accept it as morally binding. By removing the injustice or moral evil in the law, acts of civil disobedience preserve and strengthen, rather than threaten, general respect for and obedience to the law.

The specific moral problem under consideration in this chapter is whether civil disobedience is ever right in a democracy. The main arguments pro and con have been summarized, and three of these have been selected for reexamination. Amid claim and counterclaim, argument and rebuttal, the answer to this problem is not yet clear. To reach any definite and reasonable conclusion, one would have to think through each argument carefully and critically and then weigh the arguments against one another. Before embarking on this ambitious but important enterprise, the student may wish to know the author's position on the issue of civil disobedience.

CONDITIONAL CIVIL DISOBEDIENCE

I believe that civil disobedience is sometimes, although not often, right. This is not to deny that every citizen has an obligation to obey the law. I would not limit the citizen's obligation to obeying only good laws, alleging that useless or harmful laws are not morally binding. Every law, just because it is law, imposes some obligation upon the citizen. Each law is part and parcel of a *system* of laws adjudicated and enforced by an organized set of legal institutions. The benefits that any society derives from law depend on this total system of laws and not on this or that law in isolation. Since every law is part of this system of laws, one ought always to obey the law of one's land.

On the other hand, this obligation to obey the law is prima facie; that is, one ought always to obey the law *unless* some contrary moral consideration outweighs this obligation. When prima facie obligations conflict, one ought to do that act which fulfills the stronger obligation or obligations.* It is quite possible, then, to admit that one always has an obligation to obey the law and yet go on to assert that upon occasion this obligation is outweighed by a more stringent obligation to disobey. This is the case when the fabric of society is marred by a serious moral evil and when civil disobedience would be the most effective method of removing that evil.

Such cases are not common. It is not so much that serious moral evils seldom infect society as that civil disobedience is rarely an effective means of removing them. It seems to me that there are two rather different sets of circumstances under which civil disobedience can be an appropriate form

* This position was taken by W. D. Ross. See pages 34–36.

of action. First, when civil disobedience can create widespread support for moral reform simply by communicating the moral evil to the general public. This is sometimes the case when one or a few leaders in a moral cause engage in civil disobedience to dramatize the issue and win supporters. Civil disobedience is then a first step in a total effort, including discussion, propagandizing, and political organizing, to rectify a social wrong. Such an act of civil disobedience is most likely to be effective when the public is ignorant of the moral evil, when civil disobedience calls attention to some neglected injustice. It is imperative that the act of civil disobedience be widely publicized and that it take on a form that clearly indicates the object of moral protest. Moreover, it must be accompanied by a campaign of explanation and argument that communicates the facts to the public and gives them solid reasons to support moral reform and some indication of the political actions required to achieve this reform. Communicating the injustice will be to no avail, however, unless the moral sensibilities of the public are such that large numbers of citizens will recognize it as repugnant and care enough to make those sacrifices required to eliminate it from the body politic. When all these conditions are fulfilled, then civil disobedience is effective and, therefore, right. Once the moral evil has been communicated to the citizenry, however, continued acts of civil disobedience become increasingly ineffective. Reiteration does more to deaden interest and alienate potential allies than to reveal unsuspected evils and win adherents. Again, when the general public is unresponsive to the cause, or even hostile to it, merely communicating the moral evil is a useless exercise in illegal showmanship.

This brings us to the second set of circumstances in which civil disobedience can be an effective method of social progress. This is when it can exert massive political pressure on an apathetic and conservative society. In this case, civil disobedience must almost always be performed on a large scale and sustained over a considerable period of time. Each act of civil disobedience is right only because it is one of many acts that together force moral reform by a reluctant government. This sort of civil disobedience does not take place spontaneously or by accident: it requires political organization. There must be dedicated and self-disciplined leaders who can attract and control a very large number of followers. It also requires that the populace be somewhat sympathetic to the protest movement, or only apathetic toward it—but not resolutely opposed to it. Otherwise, the attempt by the minority, no matter how moral its purpose, to exert pressure on the majority will call up resistance ranging from sporadic yet massive violence to organized political opposition that will defeat the attempt at moral reform.

Since the two sets of conditions I have described are uncommon, civil disobedience is usually wrong; since such conditions do occasionally occur, I believe that civil disobedience is sometimes right.

STUDY QUESTIONS

1. Some additional arguments against civil disobedience are: (a) that the end never justifies the means; (b) that the citizen is bound by the decisions of his elected representatives who enact the law; (c) that the nature of a law as command excludes optional obedience; (d) that government ought to be the rule of laws and not men; and (e) that history shows that every illegal political process is worse than the admittedly slow legal procedures for change. Try to state each of these arguments fully and clearly so that its point becomes apparent.

2. Other arguments for civil disobedience are: (a) that it is a nonviolent release for social tensions that would otherwise burst forth in violence; (b) that it may be demanded by the conscience of the civil disobedient; (c) that no moral dictate like "obey the law" is binding without exception; and (d) that history shows that privileged groups do not give up their unfair advantages voluntarily. Try to expand and explain each of these arguments.

3. Assuming that every citizen does have an obligation to obey the law, what is the ground of this political obligation? *Why* does the citizen have a duty to obey the law? The arguments summarized in this chapter suggest that this is either because the law is socially useful or because the citizen has made a contract with society to obey. Which of these two theories is more satisfactory? Is there some other theory of the ground of political obligation that is more adequate than either of these?

4. Is the obligation to obey the law, if there is such, absolute or prima facie? That is, must a person always obey the law, or are there some cases in which the obligation to obey the law is outweighed by a stronger contrary obligation? Defend your answer.

5. It may be harder to justify civil disobedience in a democracy because the fact that the citizens participate in the process of legislation seems to create some special obligation to obey the laws that emerge from that process. Does participation really impose any such obligation? If so, why? If not, why does it seem to do so?

6. Another reason that it seems harder to justify civil disobedience in a democracy is that in any genuine democracy the procedures for changing any law or policy are always in the hands of the people. Does the fact that any actual democracy falls short of the democratic ideal completely nullify this consideration? Would civil disobedience ever be morally justified in a *perfect* democracy?

7. It is sometimes alleged that civil disobedience is unnecessary in our society because the Supreme Court traditionally defends the civil rights of all citizens. Is the factual assumption of this argument true? If true, would it be sufficient to justify the conclusion drawn? Are there injustices or moral evils in society that do not consist in the denial of civil rights?

8. What is respect for the law, anyway? Does such respect require obedience to the law always, usually, or not at all? Why?

9. Does respect for the law require that the lawbreaker accept the legal penalties for his violation of the law? Is there any reason why the civil disobedient ought not to try to evade or resist punishment for his act? Does his act cease to be an act of civil disobedience if he refuses to be punished for it?

10. Is an act of civil disobedience a crime? If not, why not? If so, can one really distinguish between the civil disobedient and the common criminal?

11. Precisely what is involved in universalizing an individual act of civil disobedience? It might be claimed that Martin Luther King's act of protest was wrong, because if all black people violated the law to protest injustices to their race, the consequences would be disastrous. Or it might be claimed that King's act was right, because if every black person of his moral and political stature did such acts, much good and little harm would follow. Anyway, since there is only one person in the world precisely like Martin Luther King, if every *such* person committed civil disobedience, the situation would be just the same as if King's act had not been universalized. Why does universalizability matter?

12. Civil disobedients often appeal to "the higher moral law" to justify their actions, but the logic of this appeal is obscure. Does this argument assume that there is *no obligation* to obey the immoral law, or that there is an *obligation to disobey* the law, or that there is an *obligation to fight evil*, even if this incidentally involves breaking the law?

13. In direct civil disobedience, the law being violated is itself the object of moral protest. In indirect civil disobedience, some other moral evil is being protested by breaking a law that is not itself objectionable. The act of protesting the Selective Service Act by burning one's draft card is direct civil disobedience. The act of protesting the draft law by mass demonstration even though the demonstrators have been denied a legally required permit is an example of indirect civil disobedience. Could the argument that civil disobedience is sometimes right because it preserves the agent's moral integrity be used to justify any act of indirect civil disobedience? If so, when and how? If not, does this weaken the force of this argument?

14. Does the argument that civil disobedience disassociates an individual from moral evil beg the point at issue? After all, *if* it is morally wrong to break the law, then civil disobedience does not disassociate a person from moral wrong. Or does it?

15. Is there really a duty to combat immorality? If so, why? Does the duty demand our using any and every possible means? If so, does the end justify the means? If not, does this duty justify using illegal means?

16. Under precisely what conditions is civil disobedience an effective means of social progress? Do these conditions make civil obedience unnecessary because they would enable legal means to work as well?

17. Consider the converse argument: Under normal conditions the legal procedures for removing injustice or changing an immoral policy are adequate. When legal procedures are not adequate, there is a small and powerless minority protesting in an unpopular cause. In this case, the civil disobedients will not have control of the mass media or political organizations to publicize and gain popular support for their cause. Without the cooperation of the media and the political parties, civil disobedience can accomplish nothing. Therefore, the only times when civil disobedience might be necessary are times when it is useless. Is this a telling argument? Why or why not?

18. What gives a government the authority to make this or that law? What is it to have such authority? Does such authority imply any obligation to obey the law? Why or why not?

19. Suppose that the civil disobedient denies the authority of the government in power to make or enforce any law at all. Could he still be a civil disobedient—or would he be a revolutionary? Why does it matter whether we draw this distinction sharply?

20. What reason is there to assert that, simply by living in a society and accepting the benefits of its laws, the citizen is making a tacit agreement to abide by its laws? Even if there is such a social contract, how can its precise terms be determined in the absence of any written document? Specifically, how can we tell whether the citizen agrees to abide by all the laws, or only the socially useful laws, or only laws that pay off for himself?

21. Why insist that civil disobedience be confined to nonviolent acts? Does nonviolence increase the political effectiveness of acts of protest by winning popular respect, or does it reduce effectiveness by exerting only limited pressure for reform?

22. How many of the arguments for or against civil disobedience could be applied to the issue of whether *violent* illegal acts of moral protest are ever right in a democracy? What additional considerations become relevant in moving from nonviolent action to violent acts?

23. How many of the arguments for or against *civil* disobedience can be applied to the issue of whether nonviolent *academic* disobedience is ever right in a college or university? How similar are the rules and regulations of an educational institution to the laws of society? Does the undemocratic nature of most academic institutions, where faculty and administrators impose rules on the students, change the nature of the moral issues involved?

24. When the author specifies two sets of conditions under which he believes that civil disobedience can be effective in improving society, he is implicitly distinguishing between civil disobedience as a mode of communication and civil disobedience as a form of political pressure. What conditions really are required for each form of civil disobedience to be effective? Do the different forms require different tactics on the part of the civil disobedient? Are these classifications mutually exclusive and collectively exhaustive?

BIBLIOGRAPHY

BEDAU, HUGO ADAMS, ED. *Civil Disobedience: Theory and Practice.* New York: Pegasus, 1969.

BICKEL, ALEXANDER M. *The Morality of Consent.* New Haven: Yale University Press, 1975.

COHEN, CARL. *Civil Disobedience: Conscience, Tactics, and the Law.* New York: Columbia University Press, 1971.

DICKINSON, JOHN. "A Working Theory of Sovereignty II." *Political Science Quarterly* 43 (1928): 32–63.

DOUGLAS, WILLIAM O. *Points of Rebellion.* New York: Vintage Press, 1970.

DWORKIN, RONALD. "A Theory of Civil Disobedience." In *Ethics and Social Justice,* edited by Howard E. Kiefer and Milton Munitz. New York: New York University Press, 1968.

FEINBERG, JOEL, "Civil Disobedience in the Modern World." *Humanities in Society* 2 (1979): 37–59.

FORTAS, ABE. *Concerning Dissent and Civil Disobedience.* New York: World Publishing Co., 1968.

HALL, ROBERT TOM. *Morality of Civil Disobedience.* New York: Harper & Row, 1971.

HATFIELD, MARK O. *Not Quite So Simple,* chap. 7. New York: Harper & Row, 1968.

KADISH, MORTIMER R., AND KADISH, SANFORD H. *Discretion to Disobey: A Study of Lawful Departures from Legal Rules.* Stanford: Stanford University Press, 1973.

KEETON, MORRIS. "The Morality of Civil Disobedience." *Texas Law Review* 43 (1964–65): 507–525.

LIEBMAN, MORRIS I. "Civil Disobedience—A Threat to Our Law Society." *American Criminal Law Quarterly* 3 (1964): 21–26.

The Monist 54 (October 1970) (issue on the topic "Legal Obligation and Civil Disobedience") 469–624.

MURPHY, JEFFRIE G., ED. *Civil Disobedience and Violence*. Belmont, Calif.: Wadsworth Publishing Co., 1971.

SINGER, PETER. *Democracy and Disobedience*. London: Oxford University Press, 1973.

VAN DEN HAAG, ERNEST. *Political Violence and Civil Disobedience*. New York: Harper & Row, 1972.

WASSERSTROM, RICHARD A. "The Obligation to Obey the Law." *UCLA Law Review* 10 (1963): 780–807.

WHITTAKER, CHARLES EVANS, AND COFFIN, WILLIAM SLOAN. *Law, Order, and Civil Disobedience*. Washington, D.C.: American Enterprise Institute, 1967.

WOOZLEY, A. D. *Law and Obedience: The Argument of Plato's "Crito."* London: Duckworth, 1979.

ZINN, HOWARD. *Disobedience and Democracy: Nine Fallacies on Law and Order*. New York: Random House, 1968.

2
RIGHT AND WRONG

*When right is maintained, human society
is preserved, but when it is neglected,
society is corrupted.*

Dante in *On Monarchy*

The issue of civil disobedience is, as we have seen, a debatable one. Moral philosophers and concerned citizens disagree on whether civil disobedience is ever right in a democracy, and each advances supporting arguments. In each argument, some consideration is presented that is supposed to prove that civil disobedience is sometimes right or always wrong. But what determines the rightness or wrongness of an act? Any attempt to assess critically the arguments given for or against civil disobedience necessarily raises this question. In this way, the specific moral problem "Is civil disobedience ever right in a democracy?" leads to the theoretical ethical problem "What makes an act right or wrong?"

This is an ethical problem, as opposed to a moral problem, because it concerns all kinds of acts, not just acts of civil disobedience. It is a theoretical problem because any fully developed answer would constitute an ethical theory. In this chapter, we will survey some of the more important answers philosophers have given to this question. But first, let us note that several of these answers have been implicit in the arguments for and against civil disobedience discussed in Chapter 1.

FROM MORAL ARGUMENTS TO ETHICAL THEORIES

One argument in favor of civil disobedience is that it is sometimes right because it is sometimes an effective means of social progress. Suppose it could be established that civil disobedience actually is a means of social progress. Why would this prove that it is right? Presumably because social progress is good or desirable, and it is right to produce good results. This argument offered in support of a specific moral conclusion, that civil disobedience is sometimes right, presupposes a general theory about what makes any act right—that it is the value produced that makes an act right.

One of the stronger counterarguments is that civil disobedience is always wrong because it is a cause of lawlessness and violence. Although this argument is intended to disprove the conclusion of the preceding one, the two arguments presuppose the same theory of obligation, the same theory of what makes an act right or wrong. Why should the alleged fact that civil disobedience is a cause of lawlessness and violence imply that it is wrong? Presumably because lawlessness and violence are bad or undesirable, and it is wrong to do acts that have bad consequences. Once more the appeal is to utility, the good or bad produced by the act. If utilitarianism is acceptable as an ethical theory, then these arguments are both valid. The moral problem of civil disobedience then hinges on which judgment of utility is correct, on whether civil disobedience really does improve society or actually harms it.

But perhaps utility is quite irrelevant to the rightness or wrongness of civil disobedience. Consider the argument that civil disobedience is sometimes right because the law or policy being protested is morally wrong. When fully developed, this argument alleges that the act of civil disobedience is somehow required by the higher law, the set of universal rules of right and wrong action that govern morality. Implicit in this argument is the theory that what makes an act right or wrong is conformity to moral law. If this is true, then considerations about the goods produced or evils resulting from the act would seem to have no bearing on its rightness.

Or consider the argument that civil disobedience is wrong because no act of civil disobedience can be universalized. Although some acts of civil disobedience may seem right when considered as individual acts, we recognize that no such act can be morally right because if everyone were to engage in civil disobedience under similar circumstances, the results would be disastrous. This argument presupposes that what makes an act right or wrong is whether or not it can be universalized. But this is a theory of obligation that, on the surface at least, is entirely different from either the utilitarian theory or the appeal to the higher moral law. To assess reliably the soundness of any argument about which acts are right, then, we must first decide which theory of right and wrong is correct.

THEORIES OF OBLIGATION

Philosophers have proposed many answers to the question "What makes an act right or wrong?" Their answers are usually called *theories of obligation*. It is generally assumed that one has a moral obligation to do the right act and to refrain from doing any wrong act. Accordingly, right-making and wrong-making characteristics, i.e., those factors that make any act right or wrong, are called the *grounds of obligation*. These factors are the reasons why one ought or ought not to do the contemplated act. The question "What makes an act right or wrong?" is then equivalent to the question "What are the grounds of obligation?" Let us look at some of the answers to this question.

The Mores

Every society has its own customs, certain ways of acting that are generally practiced. In our society, for example, it is the custom to sleep at night, eat with a knife and fork, and refrain from stealing. For some pattern of activity to be generally practiced it is not necessary that everyone always act in this manner; it is sufficient that most people act in this way most of the time. Some of these customs are socially sanctioned and others are not. Our society censures and punishes the thief, but it does not condemn and discipline the person who works at night and sleeps during the day. Those customs that are socially sanctioned are the mores.

William Graham Sumner, a cultural anthropologist, has maintained that it is mores that make an action right or wrong. The right act is the one that conforms to the mores of the agent's society; the act that violates the mores is wrong. Some acts, like tying our shoelaces into a bow, are neither morally right nor morally wrong because the mores do not govern them at all. The mores of any society are passed on from one generation to the next. Adults, particularly parents, try to teach the children to do certain things and to refrain from other sorts of action. Those who deviate from the expected patterns of behavior, adults as well as children, are subject to disapproval, blame, and various informal pressures or even legal punishments. Those who conform to the mores are approved, praised, and sometimes rewarded in obvious or subtle ways. Thus the mores in any society serve as standards of what is morally right and wrong.

One advantage of this theory is that it seems to explain the bindingness of obligation. We generally feel that we ought to do what is right and ought not to do what is wrong. What we ought to do is independent of personal inclinations, if not opposed to them. I ought to pay my debts, whether or not I feel so inclined; I ought not to beat my child, no matter how badly I want to retaliate for his rude remarks or misbehavior. We are not completely free to do as we wish; we are tied down by our obligations. Why is it that we feel morally bound in this way? The theory that the mores make an act right or wrong explains this feeling as a product of enculturation. Most individuals have been brought up to realize that if they violate the mores of society, they can expect to be censured or punished for those actions. We feel bound by right and wrong because we are apprehensive of the social sanctions supporting the mores. The ties that bind us to the right act are psychological ones. It is our fear of social censure and punishment that obliges us to do what is right and refrain from doing what is wrong.

One disadvantage of this theory is that it implies certain moral judgments that seem unacceptable to the morally sensitive and reflective person. In some societies, infanticide is still practiced; it is customary to kill any babies born after the family has reached a certain size. The theory that the mores make an act right or wrong implies that in some societies infanticide is right. But any reasonable person will recognize that this slaughter of helpless infants is morally wrong. Again, in the South before the Civil War the fugitive slave, if recaptured, was often maimed, frequently by chopping off one foot. This act of maiming a fugitive slave was customary and even sanctioned by society. Did that fact make this cruel and vindictive act morally right? The theory that the mores define right and wrong behavior implies that it did, but this implication seems clearly false. If this consequence of the theory really is false, then the theory must be mistaken, for any theory that implies false consequences is itself false.

I do not wish to suggest that this refutation is conclusive. Not only is this argument open to criticism, there are many other arguments, pro and con, that would have to be considered before one could reasonably accept or reject the view that it is the mores that make an act right or wrong.

The Law of God

Because the mores of any society seem open to moral condemnation, philosophers have looked for some higher standard of right and wrong. Many, perhaps inspired by the Old Testament, believe that they have found such a standard in the law of God. God's law is a system of universal rules of action, rules prescribing certain kinds of acts and proscribing other kinds, promulgated and enforced by God. God has made His will known to us and sanctions it with eternal rewards and punishments to be fixed on the Day of Judgment. The Ten Commandments are an example of the law of God, but philosophers need not accept these as a complete or final rendering of the Divine Will. Any act that conforms to the law of God is right; an act that violates God's law is wrong.

This theory also seems to explain the bindingness of obligation, but in a manner that allows merely human institutions to be subject to moral criticism. The law of God is enforced with eternal rewards and punishments, whether these are thought of as the traditional heaven and hell or as taking more subtle forms. These divine sanctions uphold the law of God in much the same way that social sanctions support the mores. We feel bound to obey the law of God because we fear that if we do not, we will suffer the consequences meted out to those who disobey our omniscient and omnipotent Creator. In this way, the theory that the law of God makes an act right or wrong seems able to explain why it is that we feel constrained to do what is right and not do what is wrong.

But suppose that God were to command adultery and murder? No one seriously supposes that God ever has or will command any such thing. No doubt He has willed the best of all possible laws and is too wise and kind to change His legislation. The question is simply what *would* be the case *if* God were to change His commands. Would adultery and murder then be right? If it really is the law of God that makes any act right or wrong, then if God were to change His law, acts that had been morally wrong would become morally right. But, it is argued, this implication cannot be accepted by any moral person, for it entails that there is nothing intrinsically wrong in even the most heinous acts. If acts of adultery and murder could become right simply by a change in the law of God, without any change in the acts themselves, this would mean that there is nothing in the nature of adultery or killing that makes such acts wrong. If this were true, then their prohibition by God would be entirely arbitrary and unjustified. To suggest this is both theological blasphemy, because it implies that God is an arbitrary dictator, and false moral theory, because it implies that under some circumstances adultery and murder would be morally right. The point of this objection is that whatever it is that makes an act right or wrong must be something *in* the act itself and not something external to it. To say that it is something outside the act, like the mores of society or the law of God, that makes it right or wrong seems morally perverse and theoretically absurd. It seems morally perverse to insinuate that there is nothing in the nature of adultery and murder that makes them wrong, that their being acts of betraying supreme trust and destroying human life has nothing to do with their wrongness. And it seems theoretically absurd to try to explain why this or that act is wrong in terms of something outside the act. It would be absurd to try to explain why I feel so hot by saying that my wife has a fever, and this absurdity is not lessened by the fact that I am married to the most divine of women. Whatever it may be that makes me feel hot must be something about me. Similarly, whatever it may be that makes an act wrong must be something about the act itself. Considerations like these have led some moral philosophers to conclude that what makes an act right or wrong must lie in the nature of that act.

One Characteristic of the Act

Why would it be wrong for me to chop up a beautiful woman on Friday the 13th? Not the unlucky date or the fact that her husband disapproves; nothing external to my act can make it wrong. According to this theory of obligation, rightness and wrongness depend on the intrinsic nature of the act. Moreover, it is always some one thing in the nature of an act that is right-making or wrong-making. Although any act has many characteristics, most of these are irrelevant to its moral status. It is not the fact that my victim is a female rather than a male, or that she is an adult rather than a child, or even that she is beautiful that makes my act of hacking her into pieces so very wrong. One and only one feature of my act, the fact that it is an act of killing a human being, makes it wrong. It is necessary to add, however, that the single right-making or wrong-making characteristic may be a very complex one. To be precise, one should say that what makes my act of exuberant self-expression wrong is the fact that it is an act of killing-a-human-being-neither-in-self-defense-nor-under-duress-of-circumstances. Simple or complex, it is always one characteristic of an act, a single aspect of its intrinsic nature, that determines whether it is right or wrong. This theory has been ably championed by moral philosophers like Samuel Clarke, an eighteenth-century rationalist and theologian.

One advantage of this theory is that it explains an important feature of rightness and wrongness: these are dependent or consequential characteristics. Some of the characteristics of any object or act are independent or constitutive: they constitute or make up its nature. Presumably each of these characteristics could be changed without affecting the others. Imagine a simple composition consisting of a blue circle on a square background of violet. The nature of the composition is constituted by the two shapes, the color of each, the size of each, and their arrangement. The color of the circle could be changed without any change in the size or the shape of the circle or square, or even in the color of the square. Or the arrangement of the composition could be changed by moving the blue circle slightly to the right or left in the violet background without changing any color or size or shape. The beauty of the composition is another thing. To change the colors or the sizes or the shapes or the arrangement is almost sure to affect the beauty of the composition, because this characteristic depends on the others. Beauty is a dependent or consequential characteristic; it is dependent on and a consequence of the other characteristics that constitute the nature of the thing. Similarly, rightness and wrongness are consequential or dependent characteristics. Whether an act is right or wrong depends on some other characteristic of the act—whether it is an act of telling the truth or killing a human being. This aspect of rightness and wrongness is taken into account by the theory that what makes an act right or wrong is one characteristic of the act itself.

But perhaps this answer to our question oversimplifies morality. It asserts that only one characteristic of any act makes it right or wrong, while in point of fact an act often has several morally relevant features. When a witness testifying in court answers a question truthfully, what makes his act right? In this case there are at least three right-making characteristics. The act is right because it is an act of telling the truth, because it is an act of abiding by the oath the witness swore upon taking the stand, and because it is an act of obeying the law requiring witnesses to tell the truth. These three characteristics do not coalesce to form one complex characteristic as happens in other cases. Killing-a-human-being-neither-in-self-defense-nor-under-duress-of-circumstances is a single complex characteristic because killing-a-human-being is the primary characteristic modified by not-in-self-defense and not-under-duress-of-circumstances. On the other hand, no one of the three characteristics of being truth-telling, oath-abiding, and law-obeying is more basic than the others. Each is independently relevant to the moral status of the act; that is, each would be right-making in the absence of the others. Moreover, none of the characteristics modifies another. To say that an act is oath-abiding is not to qualify the way in which it is truth-telling, and to say that it is law-abiding is not to say how it is oath-abiding.

The independence of the several features that make an act right or wrong is brought home to us in cases where obligations conflict. When a person is confronted with a situation that requires choosing between two acts that are incompatible in practice, each of which is morally binding, it becomes obvious that to pick out any single feature as the only one that is morally relevant is to oversimplify the situation. Imagine that a professor has promised to meet one of his students in his office at two o'clock in order to help the student with a term paper. As the professor walks back toward the campus after lunch, he comes upon a child just knocked down by a hit-and-run driver. His first impulse, of course, is to help the child, but then he remembers his promise to the student. He recognizes that he has a moral obligation to keep his promise to the student, but he is also very much aware of his obligation to help this child in distress. Given the situation, he cannot fulfill both obligations. If he gives the child first aid, gets him to his parents or a doctor, and reports the incident to the police, he will not arrive at his office until long after two o'clock. If he proceeds to his office and meets the student as he promised, he cannot also help the injured child. Which act is right? In practice, even a professor would not have to deliberate very long before choosing to help the child. Although practically simple, this example is theoretically interesting because it shows so clearly that more than one characteristic of an act may be morally relevant. The right act is surely to stay and help the child. In this act, the characteristic of being an act of aiding a person in distress is right-making, while being an act of breaking a promise is wrong-making. Only if the moral relevance of both characteristics is recognized can the conflict of obligations be explained. The theory that a single characteristic makes an act right or wrong seems to oversimplify morality in cases of converging obligations like that of the truthful witness, and in cases of conflicting obligations like that of the helpful professor. Some other theory is required to account for the complexities of moral choices.

One or More Characteristics of the Act

W. D. Ross, a twentieth-century British moral philosopher, has maintained that it is one or more characteristics of an act that make it right or wrong. Ross agrees with Clarke that what makes an act right or wrong is something about the nature of the act, something intrinsic to the act rather than external to it. He disagrees, however, with the view that it must be some single feature of the act that makes it right or wrong. There probably are acts with only one right-making or wrong-making characteristic, but typically each act will have several morally relevant characteristics. Whether an act is right or wrong depends on whether its right-making characteristics outweigh its wrong-making characteristics or vice versa. The professor's act of giving first aid to the child is right because, at least in this case, the characteristic of being an act of relieving distress outweighs the characteristic of being an act of breaking a promise. What the moral agent ought to do in any given situation is that act with the greatest balance of right-making over wrong-making characteristics.

There is another, and perhaps more common, way to state Ross' theory. Each right-making characteristic makes an act prima facie right; each wrong-making characteristic makes an act prima facie wrong. The fact that our humane professor broke his promise to the student did not make his act of aiding the injured child actually wrong, for he was breaking his promise in order to fulfill his more stringent obligation to help someone in distress. Still, it would be inappropriate to suggest that there is nothing wrong in breaking a promise even in this case. The professor will probably feel moral regret at breaking his promise and will feel a need to make amends to the student, perhaps by explaining the situation and arranging another meeting time as early as possible. Although the professor's act is not actually wrong, it is prima facie wrong. To say that an act is prima facie wrong is to say that it is actually wrong *unless* (as in this case) it has some right-making characteristic that outweighs any wrong-making characteristics. Correspondingly, to say that an act is prima facie right is to say that it is actually right unless its prima facie rightness is outweighed by its prima facie wrongness. As promise-breaking, the professor's act is prima facie wrong; as distress-relieving, it is prima facie right. It is actually right because the characteristic of being distress-relieving imposes a more stringent obligation than the characteristic of being promise-breaking. According to this theory, a moral agent ought always to do that act with the greatest balance of prima facie rightness over prima facie wrongness.

A strong point of this theory is that it remains faithful to three features of our reasoning about obligations. Whenever an act is judged right or wrong, the question "Why?" can always be asked. The reasons we typically give and accept as relevant are statements about the nature of the act in question. Moreover, in many if not most cases, several different reasons must be considered before any final conclusion can be drawn about the moral status of the act. All three features of our moral reasoning are explained by the theory that what makes an act right or wrong is one or more characteristics of the act.

1. One can always ask for reasons to justify any particular judgment of obligation, because rightness and wrongness are dependent or consequential characteristics derived from those other characteristics that constitute the nature of the act.
2. Any morally relevant consideration must be some statement about the act itself, not something external to it, because it is the nature of the act that makes it right or wrong.
3. There are usually several reasons to be considered, because it is one *or more* characteristics of the act that make it right or wrong.

But perhaps this theory does not take our moral reasoning far enough. Just as it makes sense to ask why some particular act is right or wrong, so it always seems meaningful and reasonable to ask why some *kind* of act is right or wrong. Just as the particular judgment, "The professor's act of helping the injured child is right" can and should be supported with the reason "because it is an act of relieving distress," so the judgment "all acts of relieving distress are prima facie right" needs to be justified by some reason should it be challenged. Ross, however, refuses to admit that any challenge is legitimate at this point. Since it is the characteristic of being distress-relieving that makes the professor's act right, there is no room left for any further question of why it is that distress-relieving acts are prima facie right. No possible answer would constitute a rational justification for the general principle of prima facie obligation. To argue "Acts of relieving distress are right because they are acts of relieving distress" will not do, because mere reiteration is circular reasoning and begs the issue. On the other hand, no other reason would do any better; to give some *other* reason why acts of relieving distress are right would be to insinuate, contrary to Ross' theory, that it is not the characteristic of being distress-relieving but some other characteristic mentioned in the reason that makes such acts right. In other words, to hold that an act is right or wrong because it is a certain kind of act rules out the question of why all acts of this kind are right. But this seems to terminate moral reasoning prematurely, for it does make good sense to ask for and to give reasons why any kind of act is right or wrong.

One plausible answer to the question of why certain kinds of acts are right and other kinds wrong is that the former are beneficial while the latter are harmful. To be beneficial is to do good or increase the goodness in the world; to be harmful is to do evil or increase the badness in existence. The crux of this answer is that it is the goodness or badness produced by the act that makes the act right or wrong. Any theory that holds that goodness is the only ultimate right-making characteristic and badness the only ultimate wrong-making characteristic is called a *teleological theory of obligation*. The defining mark of a teleological theory is that it claims that the *only* ground of obligation is the good produced or the bad prevented. By contrast, a *deontological theory of obligation* denies that the only basic reason why some act ought to be done is the value it brings into existence. Deontological theories of obligation take two forms. An extreme deontological theory claims that value is never an ultimate ground of obligation. A moderate deontological theory asserts that, while value is one ground of obligation, there are other grounds as well. William Graham Sumner is an example of an extreme deontological theorist because he holds that what makes an act right is not the good it brings into existence but its conformity to the mores of society. Ross maintains a moderate deontological theory because he claims that in addition to beneficiality, other characteristics such as being promise-keeping or truth-telling may make an act right. The next three theories we will discuss are all teleological theories of obligation; all assert that the rightness or wrongness of an act depends exclusively on goodness or badness produced.

The Agent's Welfare

Ethical egoism is the theory that what makes an act right or wrong is the agent's welfare. It is a teleological theory because it holds that the only ground of obligation is the good produced or bad prevented. The distinction between right and wrong action is grounded entirely in the good and bad brought into existence. Not everyone's good is relevant, however. What makes an act right or wrong is its impact on the agent's own welfare. Ultimately, the only reason why any person ought or ought not to do some specified act is that it will be beneficial or harmful to the individual's own interests. The difference, if any, that the act makes to the welfare of others is entirely irrelevant. Why, for example, is it wrong for one person to express annoyance by kicking another in the shins? Ultimately, not because the act of kicking will harm the other person by causing pain and injury, but because the kicker will be harmed when the victim (or some sympathetic spectator) retaliates. Ethical egoism is the theory that what anyone ought to do is always the act that is most beneficial to oneself. Plato seems to have held this theory, for in *The Republic* all the arguments he advances to show that one ought to act justly rest ultimately on the agent's own welfare. In our own time, Ayn Rand has made ethical egoism popular, particularly in her novels.

One advantage of ethical egoism is that it seems to explain why one ought to do what is right. A person does not always want to do what is right, and sometimes very much wants to do what is wrong. An individual may not wish to pay income taxes, or may feel inclined to lie in order to avoid an awkward situation. Whatever personal desires and inclinations are involved, the individual still believes in doing what is right and refraining from wrong action. But why? What reason is there to pay taxes and forego spending that money on oneself, or tell the truth when to do so is to cause oneself embarrassment and even shame? If ethical egoism is accepted, the answer is self-interest. The individual ought to pay taxes because that act will strengthen society and give it the means to provide the public services from which he benefits; the personal sacrifice required by not spending the tax money in other ways is more than made up by the individual's gain in security and enjoyment of public roads, parks, etc. The real reason a person ought not to lie is that, although lying may avoid some slight temporary embarrassment, it will result in feelings of insecurity and unhappiness, because in the future others will distrust the person who is deceitful. Thus, when a person's sense of duty is in conflict with personal desires, the question may arise, "Why should I do what is right and not do what is wrong?" The answer of ethical egoism is that the right act is to the long-term advantage of the agent and the wrong act harmful to the agent in the end. In moments of temptation, this seems the most satisfactory of all possible answers because it helps to overcome the conflict between desire and duty which prompted the question in the first place.

But is it true that duty and self-interest always coincide? Ethical egoism holds that the most advantageous act, the one that benefits the agent most, is always the right one. Reflection on a few examples makes this claim very dubious. It is very easy for a doctor to pocket payments for house calls without keeping any records of these odd bits of income. In the course of a year, these small payments add up to a sizeable sum of unreported income. It would be very easy for the doctor to cheat when filing income taxes and pay no tax on this additional income. The personal advantage to be derived from keeping this amount of money and spending it in other ways would be considerable; the disadvantage to the doctor from an impairment in governmental services caused by this small loss of public revenue would be infinitesimal. The chance that any harm would come to the doctor from the detection and punishment of this crime is very slight indeed. Surely the act that would contribute most to the doctor's own welfare is that of cheating on income taxes. Far from being morally right, as ethical egoism implies, this act is morally wrong because it is a violation of the law and an unfair attempt to evade the burdens that must be borne by all citizens if society, and the many benefits it confers, is to be sustained.

A college or university professor, to take another example, has many duties; among these are the duties of preparing lectures, holding classes, grading papers, and meeting individually with students to help them with their work. Let us suppose that a promising young assistant professor has agreed to read a paper at a forthcoming professional meeting but that, through no fault of her own, she has not found time to write the paper. What ought she to do now? Since salary, promotion, and professional standing depend in a very direct way on delivering and publishing papers, probably the most advantageous course of action would be for her to dismiss a few classes, devote very little time to preparing for the rest, postpone any grading of papers, and stay away from her office until she has completed the paper for the professional meeting. Although this act would pay off in terms of the agent's own welfare, it would be wrong for her to neglect her duties as a teacher in this way. If these examples have been judged correctly, it is not true that the only right-making characteristic is the agent's own welfare. It is sometimes wrong for one individual to benefit himself or herself at the expense of other members of society. This suggests that right and wrong are grounded in the welfare of all, not just the agent.

The Utility of the Act

Jeremy Bentham and G. E. Moore hold a position known as *act-utilitarianism*. It is called utilitarianism because it asserts that what makes an act right or wrong is utility or disutility; it is called *act*-utilitarianism because it asserts that it is the utility of the act itself that is morally relevant. On this view, an act is right or wrong depending on the degree to which it is useful or harmful. But what is it to be useful, anyway? Usefulness, or utility, consists in bringing value into existence; harmfulness, or disutility, consists in bringing disvalue into existence. Utilitarians disagree, however, about the nature of value and disvalue. Bentham believes that the only intrinsic good is pleasure. Moore rejects hedonism and claims that there are several distinct kinds of things that are good for their own sake, including beautiful objects and some virtuous acts, as well as pleasures. Whatever theory of value is given, the act-utilitarian maintains that one ought always to do that act which produces the most good or the least bad possible in the given situation. There is a tendency among utilitarians to think of utility entirely in terms of the consequences of an act, but this is not essential to the theory. A moral philosopher who believes that some acts are intrinsically good— quite apart from their consequences—can and should consider the intrinsic value of the act as well as its instrumental value when judging the utility of the act. Act-utilitarianism agrees with ethical egoism that the distinction between right and wrong action is grounded entirely in the value or disvalue brought into existence; this is why they are both teleological theories of obligation. But utilitarianism denies that only the welfare of the agent is morally relevant and asserts that everyone's good or bad must be considered in judging right and wrong actions.

One point in favor of act-utilitarianism is that it can give a plausible explanation as to why certain kinds of acts are right and others wrong. Why, for example, is it right to tell the truth and wrong to steal? To reply, as Ross does, that acts of telling the truth are right because of their "truthtellingness" and acts of stealing wrong because of their "stealingness" is not much of an explanation. Why does "truthtellingness" make an act right, and what is wrong with "stealingness"? The most obvious answer is that telling the truth is useful and stealing harmful. This is a very plausible explanation because a little reflection on the facts of human life assures us that it is useful to be able to rely on the truthfulness of others and that taking the property of others without their permission does cause insecurity, distrust, and retaliation. Therefore, there is considerable empirical evidence for the thesis that right acts are useful and wrong acts harmful. And while this might be a sheer coincidence, it seems much more likely that this is because the utility of certain acts makes them right and the disutility of other kinds of acts makes them wrong.

Further reflection, particularly reflection on exceptional cases, makes act-utilitarianism seem less plausible. Take the case of Robin Hood. He made a practice of stealing from the rich and sharing the proceeds with the poor. His acts of stealing did very little harm because those he robbed were seldom injured and because his victims were so wealthy that they hardly missed what was taken from them. His acts did considerable good because the poor used the money given to them to buy necessities like food, clothes, and shelter from which they benefited greatly. If what makes an act right or wrong is its utility or disutility, then the acts of Robin Hood must surely have been right. Yet any morally sensitive person recognizes that it is wrong to steal, whether the victim is rich or not.

Or take a case that strikes closer to home. One very serious problem in any college or university library is the theft or unauthorized borrowing of books and journals. It is not just that it costs large sums to replace stolen items; often these are out of print or very difficult to acquire. Even when the book or journal is eventually returned, other members of the campus community have been unable to use it for study or research in the meantime. In spite of expensive steps, such as hiring guards to search everyone leaving the library or installing special detection devices, it is virtually impossible to eliminate these selfish and irresponsible thefts by detecting and punishing the offenders. Suppose that some university administration decides, therefore, to frame a few students. The dean of the college can easily pick out a few students with poor grades who are probably on campus only because of their parents' insistence. For these students, suspension will probably be doing more good than harm because they are not profiting from their studies and will be much happier elsewhere. Moreover, this act of punishing the innocent will benefit the many students who remain on campus because it will act as a deterrent to the real culprits, many of whom will come to believe that the detection of library thefts is much more effective than in fact it is. And since those unjustly punished will be immediately sent off campus, they cannot remain to protest their innocence and agitate against the administration. Under these circumstances, this act of punishing the innocent would seem to do a great deal of good and very little harm. Accordingly, act-utilitarianism implies that it would be morally right. We can clearly see, however, that this implication of act-utilitarianism is false. It cannot be right to punish, much less to punish so severely, innocent students. Once more it appears that act-utilitarianism must be rejected because it implies unacceptable moral judgments.

The Utility of the Rule

Is there any way of avoiding such unacceptable implications without giving up the connection between rightness and utility? Several recent moral philosophers, including J. O. Urmson and Richard B. Brandt, have explored a theory called *rule-utilitarianism*. According to this theory, an act is right or wrong depending on whether it conforms to or violates a moral rule. A moral rule, in turn, is justified or unjustified depending on its utility or disutility. Presumably the moral ideal is to have that set of moral rules that maximizes utility for any given society. Although the acceptability of any moral rule depends entirely on its utility, it is completely inappropriate to apply the test of utility directly to an individual act in the way that act-utilitarianism does. The rightness or wrongness of any particular act is to be judged simply by whether it conforms to or violates a moral rule.

Suppose that when a policeman stops my car and asks me whether I saw the red light I just ran through, I try to avoid getting a traffic ticket by saying that I was watching a child running toward the curb so that I did not even notice the traffic light. Why is my act of lying wrong? Not because my individual act is harmful; I did not hit any child and my lie may save me from paying a fine. My act is wrong because it violates the moral rule prohibiting lying. One moral rule that is useful for any individual to accept and any society to sanction is the rule against lying. Most acts of lying are wrong because they violate this useful moral rule. Why, then, is my act of telling the hostess that I had a lovely time when in fact I was bored to tears not morally wrong? The reason why my little white lie is right is not because of its utility, although it does cause the hostess some modest happiness and spares her hurt feelings. The utility of the individual act is irrelevant to its rightness. What makes my little lie right is the fact that it conforms to one of the exceptions built into the rule against lying. The most useful rule for any society to have is not simply, "Acts of lying are always wrong" but something more like, "Lying is wrong except to save a human life or to spare hurt feelings over unimportant matters." Although most moral rules allow for exceptions in specified types of cases, no rule will be likely to contain very many exception clauses. A moral rule loses much of its practical value if it becomes so complex that it cannot be remembered and understood easily, or if its application in particular cases becomes so uncertain as to cause social dissension. Again, no moral rule will contain any qualification as broad as "except when lying would be useful," for this would weaken the rule so much that its utility would be impaired. Rule-utilitarianism, then, is the theory that one ought always to do that act which conforms to the most useful set of moral rules. This view is called utilitarianism because it does ground rightness in utility; it is called *rule*-utilitarianism because it is the utility of the rule, rather than the individual act, that makes the act right.

The obvious advantage of this theory, and the one that has probably attracted many recent philosophers to it, is that it seems to avoid the unacceptable implications of act-utilitarianism. To return to the case of Robin Hood, rule-utilitarianism does not justify stealing from the rich for the purpose of helping the poor. The most useful set of moral rules, at least for any society like ours, will contain a prohibition against stealing in order to preserve the institution of private property. This institution is a socially valuable one because it motivates individuals to exert themselves to produce as much wealth as possible in the expectation that they will profit from their exertions. This motivating power will be lessened to the degree that the individual's right to possess, use, and dispose of private property is impaired. This would be precisely the effect of qualifying the rule against stealing by allowing stealing from the wealthy. Who would endeavor to accumulate wealth under a system that allowed one's wealth to be taken away at any time? Since the most useful moral rule would not allow stealing from the wealthy, rule-utilitarianism does not justify the acts of Robin Hood.

Nor does rule-utilitarianism justify the act of punishing innocent students to serve as a frightening example to those who are stealing books and journals from a university library. One of the moral rules governing punishment, a socially useful institution, requires that those punished be guilty of some wrong act. It is quite possible that some individual acts of punishing the innocent under exceptional circumstances are socially useful. But this does not make these acts right, according to this theory, because the rightness of an act is determined, not by its utility, but by its conformity to a useful moral rule. The moral rule forbidding punishment of the innocent might possibly contain some such clause as "except to prevent social disaster," because a rule allowing this exception might be more useful than an unqualified rule against unjust punishment. But the rule will not contain any clause as broad as "except when unjust punishment would be useful," because this clause would allow a dangerous amount of discretion to remain in the hands of public authorities who might abuse their power in harmful ways. Thus, rule-utilitarianism does not seem to condone punishing the innocent in cases where act-utilitarianism implies that it would be morally right. Apparently, rule-utilitarianism does not commit one to false moral consequences.

Why, then, is not every moral philosopher a rule-utilitarian? To many philosophers this theory is inconsistent because it both accepts and rejects utility as the ultimate moral criterion. It holds that the right act in any given situation conforms to a moral rule which is part of a set of moral rules that maximizes utility. Now the obvious way for a set of moral rules to maximize utility is for the rules to require in each and every situation the act that produces more good or less bad than any other act possible under the circumstances. But if the set of moral rules requires the most useful act in every situation, then it will turn out to justify exactly the same acts, including stealing from the rich and punishing the innocent, that act-utilitarianism justifies. It would then lose its advantage over that more traditional form of utilitarianism. Presumably, then, the moral rules contemplated under rule-utilitarianism will sometimes require the agent to act in ways that do not maximize the utilities possible in the situation. It is at just this point that its critics charge rule-utilitarianism with inconsistency. On the one hand, rule-utilitarianism asserts that the justified set of moral rules is the set that will maximize utility. On the other hand, it asserts that the justified set of moral rules will require acts that do not maximize utility. Thus it appears both to accept and to reject utility as the ultimate standard of right action.

Universalizability

Immanuel Kant, an eighteenth-century German rationalist, maintained that what makes an act right is the universalizability of its maxim, and that the maxim of any wrong act is nonuniversalizable. Before one can even understand this theory, much less judge its adequacy, one must recognize that some maxim is implicit in every moral act. Doing something, in the morally relevant sense, involves more than bodily motion. When the doctor taps me just below the knee with a little hammer, my leg jerks. Although my leg swings upward, I do not do anything; my leg jerks, but I do not kick. This can be seen from the fact that I am not held morally responsible if my foot knocks the doctor's glasses off so that they break. When I kick my bridge partner under the table to protest a bad play, on the other hand, I have done something for which I am morally responsible.

Acting, in the moral sense, does not require deliberating in advance or even consciously choosing what to do, but it does require some awareness of what we are doing. The moral agent always has some awareness of what kind of act he or she is doing and in what circumstances he is doing it. For this reason, Kant argues, there is always some maxim implicit in every moral act. A maxim is simply a rule of action on which someone is or might be acting. When I kick my bridge partner under the table, I am acting on a rule or maxim something like "Whenever one's bridge partner loses points by playing stupidly and one can forcefully and even painfully call the partner's attention to it without fearing retaliation and without others noticing, then do so." According to Kant, my act is right or wrong depending on whether or not the maxim implicit in it can be universalized, can be accepted as a universal rule of action for every person to act on in every case where it is applicable. My act of kicking is morally wrong because, although I am willing enough to kick my bridge partners from time to time, I am not willing for them to kick me. For this reason, I am unwilling to see the rule of action implicit in my act universalized into "*Anyone* in a position to kick a bridge partner who has lost points by playing stupidly, without fear of retaliation or detection, ought *always* to do so."

According to Kant there are two very different ways in which a maxim may be nonuniversalizable. Some maxims become self-contradictory or internally inconsistent when made into universal moral laws. Others simply become unacceptable to any rational agent. When someone takes a few ears of corn from a neighbor's garden after dark, that person is acting on some such maxim as "Steal what you want when you can get away with it." It is all too easy for someone to act on this maxim; many of us do this from time to time. The professional thief may even adopt this maxim as a consistent rule of action. But it is impossible to universalize this maxim into a rule to be acted on by everyone in every situation. Suppose that *everyone* stole *whatever* he wanted *whenever* he could get away with it. Given the abundance of desirable goods and the limited police force, theft would become so prevalent that no one could rest secure in the possession of anything of value. This would destroy the right to possession essential to the institution of private property. But if there were no longer any social institution of private property, there could not be any act of stealing, because to steal is to take the property of another without permission. In this way, the rule "Everyone ought always to steal when safe" is internally inconsistent, for it prescribes the destruction of the social institution it presupposes.

In other cases a maxim becomes, not logically inconsistent, but only unacceptable when it is made into a universal law of action. Someone who refuses to come to the aid of another person in distress is acting on a maxim like "Do not help the needy when it would be inconvenient unless there is some real prospect of gain." There is nothing logically contradictory in making this maxim into the universal law of action "*No one* ought *ever* to help the needy when to do so would be inconvenient and there is no real prospect of gain." Still, this universal law of action cannot be accepted by any fully rational person. As reasonable individuals we realize that there will be occasions when we will be in dire need of help. Therefore, we cannot accept the universal principle that everyone, even those who will someday be in a position to help us, shall always refuse to help the needy. What makes any act wrong, then, is that its maxim cannot be made into a universal law of action binding on all persons without becoming either self-contradictory or unacceptable to reason. What makes any act morally right is that the maxim implicit in it is universalizable. Thus, universalizability is what makes any act right or wrong.

The strength of this theory lies in the way in which it seems to capture the essence of morality. To act morally seems to be to act on principle. What morality demands is not just that one tell the truth usually or whenever it is convenient; one does what is morally right only by always telling the truth. Conversely, it is morally wrong to make an exception of oneself. The student who cheats on an examination does not want other students to do the same; then there would be no real advantage gained in cheating. The student wants to remain an exception to the rule that everyone should abide by the principle of honesty. This exception clause seems to be precisely what makes this act of cheating morally wrong: the agent is unwilling to accept the maxim of the act as a universal principle of human action. Thus universalizability seems to be what distinguishes right from wrong.

But does universalizability really distinguish between right and wrong acts? Many philosophers argue that this criterion does not work because it is entirely lacking in content. This theory does not specify which kinds of acts are right and which are wrong. Instead, it holds that *any* kind of act is right provided its maxim can be made into a universal law of action. The difficulty is that every maxim can be universalized, or so it is claimed. There is not really any internal inconsistency in the universal law that everyone ought always to steal when it's safe to do so. To be sure, if this principle were consistently acted on, the security of private property would disappear. But there is no logical inconsistency in willing the destruction of this particular social institution. Again, even though no one in fact may accept the principle that everyone should always refrain from helping the needy, this does not prove that this principle could not be accepted. It is possible to imagine a person strong and confident enough to choose a course of complete self-reliance in a ruthlessly competitive world; for such a person, the opportunities for immediate and frequent gain would far outweigh the mere possibility of someday suffering from the system. If the possibility of making any rule of action into a universal law is always present, then no act can be declared wrong on the ground that its maxim is nonuniversalizable. If so, then universalizability provides no criterion for distinguishing right from wrong.

Respect for Persons

Kant also holds that it is respect for persons or the lack of it that makes an act right or wrong. He does not advance this as a separate theory; in his eyes, universalizability and respect for persons are two aspects of the same moral standard, although most other philosophers do not see it this way. On the theory that what makes an act right is respect for persons, the crucial factor in determining the moral status of any act is how the agent treats people. One ought always to treat people with respect, to treat them as ends-in-themselves and never as means only.

It is important to notice three things about this theory. First, it does not forbid treating people as means; what it forbids is treating people as *mere* means or means only. It is not wrong for a physician to use his patients as a means of earning a living provided the doctor also treats them as ends-in-themselves, as rational moral agents with goals of their own. It is not wrong to use a friend as a means to companionship and conversation as long as that friend is also respected as a person. Second, this theory requires that *all* people be treated as ends-in-themselves; the agent ought to respect his or her own humanity as well as that of other persons. A Kantian would probably argue that the act of murder is morally wrong because the killer is using the victim as a means to revenge or personal gain. Correspondingly, a Kantian might also argue that the act of suicide is wrong because the agent is using his own person as a means of escape from misery. Third, this theory requires that the moral agent treat all persons with respect, as ends-in-themselves. But just what does it mean to treat people as ends-in-themselves? It is not just a matter of considering a person's feelings or well-being. Conversely, using someone as a means is not just a matter of acting selfishly toward that person. The key notion is that of respecting a person *as a person*. Suppose that a father refuses to allow his son, who has recently obtained his driver's license, to borrow the family car for the senior dance. His act need not be selfish in the least; he may not have the slightest desire to use the car himself. His reason for refusing to give his son the car may be that he is concerned the boy might have a serious accident. The father knows that his son enjoys driving fast, that he will probably drink at the senior dance, and that he will probably invite one or two other couples to share the car. He is afraid that the result will be an accident that the son would regret for years. Although the father's refusal to allow his son to borrow the car is motivated by an unselfish concern for the son's welfare, it is still failing to treat the son as an end-in-himself because the father is not respecting his son as a person. Why does he refuse to lend the car? Simply because he does not believe that his son is rational enough to use it wisely. Therefore, he does not treat his son as a fully rational person, as a responsible moral agent free to make his own choices. To treat people as ends-in-themselves, then, is to respect their rationality, to leave them free to make their own choices. To treat people as mere means is to impose one's will upon them, to force them to do what one thinks best rather than what they think best. What makes an act right or wrong is respect for persons as rational moral agents. The right act is one that allows others freedom to choose for themselves. An act is wrong if it forces any human being, including the agent, to act against his own rational will.

One thing that can be said for this theory is that it recognizes the very special place that human beings have in morality. No doubt one ought to treat a cat with kindness and take good care of a useful animal like a farm horse. But a human being, say one's spouse, is more than another pet or useful animal around the house. It is not enough to be kind and attentive to the needs of one's wife or husband; one ought also to respect one's spouse as a person. Each person is a rational moral agent, a being capable of choosing and acting rationally. As such, every human being has a very special kind of value—moral value. A cat may be a very desirable pet and a horse a very useful worker, but only a human being can be morally good or evil. This moral value intrinsic to human nature gives each person an innate dignity. This human dignity in turn commands a very special sort of treatment. All human beings ought to be treated as ends-in-themselves, as moral agents with the capacity for rational choice. The theory that what makes an act right is respect for persons recognizes the unique moral status of human beings.

But perhaps it emphasizes the dignity of human beings at the expense of other morally significant features of life. Can one really hold that respect for persons is the only ground of obligation? Surely I have an obligation to feed my cat regularly, and clearly it would be wrong for me to beat my horse when he is too tired to pull the plow any longer. How does Kant's theory explain these moral obligations? Respect for persons does not seem involved in these cases at all, or if it is, it is not the central and most relevant feature of the situation. In addition to respect for human beings, morality demands consideration for all sentient beings. Any adequate theory of obligation must account for both these demands.

What makes an act right or wrong? In this chapter, we have considered very briefly nine answers to this ethical problem—the mores, the law of God, one characteristic of the act, one or more characteristics of the act, the agent's welfare, the utility of the act, the utility of the rule, universalizability, and respect for persons. Each of these answers, if fully developed, constitutes a theory of obligation. It is the task of the moral philosopher to weigh the advantages and disadvantages of each theory and decide which answer, everything considered, is most adequate.

ACT-UTILITARIANISM DEFENDED

My own position is that I would like to be an act-utilitarian. I say that I "would like to be" an act-utilitarian because I am far from confident that this theory of obligation can deal adequately with some of the hard cases presented to refute it. But before discussing the difficulties with this theory, let me explain why I find it attractive.

First, it seems to me that the correct theory of obligation must be some sort of teleological theory, a theory that grounds right and wrong in the good and bad brought into existence. This is because it always makes sense to ask of any act and of any kind of act, "Why is it right?" or "Why is it wrong?" Judgments of obligation, whether in particular cases or in classes of cases, are not self-evident, not known by some sort of intuition or direct revelation. They are always subject to challenge and require rational justification. Of the various reasons that might be given to support the judgment that some act is right or wrong, the most basic seems to be "because it is useful or harmful, because it brings good or bad into existence." That this reason is ultimate can be seen from the fact that the question "But why is it right to bring good things into the world?" does not demand an answer in the way that "But why is it right to tell the truth?" does. The correct theory of obligation, then, is one that grounds right and wrong in the good and bad brought into existence.

But which one, for there are several teleological theories of obligation. *Ethical egoism* holds that what makes an act right or wrong is the good or bad it creates for the moral agent himself. *Ethical altruism* claims that the ground of obligation is the good or bad produced for others, persons other than the agent doing the act. *Ethical elitism* alleges that what makes an act right or wrong is the benefit or harm it confers on members of some elite class or group of individuals. I reject all of these theories, and others like them, for the same reason: all pick out some limited class of goods and bads to serve as the ground of obligation. The difficulty is that no plausible reason can be given for limiting the ground of obligation in this way. Why my welfare rather than that of other people? Why the well-being of some elite class rather than that of all human beings? Since no cogent answer can be given to this question, all of these theories make an arbitrary and rationally unjustified distinction between those values that make an act right or wrong and those which are irrelevant. If it really is value and disvalue that makes an act right or wrong, then it is all value and disvalue that does so. Hence the only reasonable position to take is a universal teleological theory of obligation. The ground of obligation is all value and disvalue. Since animals as well as human beings can experience good and bad, one ought to consider all sentient creatures, not just human beings, in deciding what one ought to do.

The view I adopt, therefore, is that one ought always to do that act which brings more value or less disvalue into existence than any alternative act possible under the circumstances. This is act-utilitarianism, for it grounds the rightness of any act in *its* utility, its productiveness of value. Although I sincerely believe this theory and want to defend it rationally, I find myself uncertain as to its correctness. This is because of various hard cases, examples of acts that act-utilitarianism seems to imply are right when our moral judgment pronounces them wrong. The acts of a Robin Hood would seem to be justified by act-utilitarianism because such acts do relatively little harm to the rich and great good to the poor; nevertheless my conscience tells me that it is wrong to steal, even from the rich. Again, there are easily imaginable situations in which it would seem to be highly useful to punish innocent people in order to prevent even greater evils, but any such act strikes the moral judge as unjust and clearly wrong. In my own mind, certain acts of euthanasia present the hardest cases. I can see little value in keeping alive an elderly person suffering great pain from an incurable disease who has begged for a release from this hopeless misery. To kill this human being in some quick and painless manner would relieve unbearable agony, shorten the acute discomfort of loved ones who must watch this prolonged suffering, and preserve economic and medical resources that might be used to help others with hope of recovery. Surely acts of euthanasia sometimes do considerable good. Still, I find myself condemning the act of deliberately killing a human being, even when the motive is mercy. I *think* that euthanasia is sometimes right, but I *feel* intensely that it is wrong. My theory tells me that it is rationally justified, but my heart insists that it is callous and inhuman. Should I trust my ethical theory or my moral disapproval in particular cases?

Rule-utilitarianism is an attempt to have it both ways, to maintain a theory that grounds obligation in utility without coming into conflict with our moral sensibilities. I do not find this attempt successful, however. In order to deal with hard cases like that mentioned above, rule-utilitarianism must deny that utility or disutility is directly relevant to the rightness or wrongness of an act. Although the moral rule is to be judged by its utility, the individual act is not to be judged right or wrong because it is beneficial or harmful. Now if utility is a good enough reason to justify a moral rule, and the rule-utilitarian insists on this much, then I do not see why it is not a good reason for judging some act right. What is it about rules and acts that makes utility relevant to the former but irrelevant to the latter? I do not see how the rule-utilitarian can answer this question. Moreover, I do see, or think I see, that rule-utilitarianism is mistaken in what it denies. It denies that "because it brings value into existence" is a valid reason for "it is a right act" and that "because it does harm" is a good reason for saying "it is a wrong act." My reason tells me quite the opposite. I might be tempted by a theory that asserts that in addition to such utilitarian considerations, other considerations such as justice or consent are relevant to the moral rightness or wrongness of an act. But I cannot accept a theory that rejects the relevance of the best of all reasons for judging an act right or wrong.

How, then, can I deal with the hard cases that seem to refute act-utilitarianism? Since the point of each case lies in its specific description, each case must be considered carefully in its own terms. Sometimes the hard case can be shown to be compatible with act-utilitarianism after all. Although the act seems useful on first or even second glance, further reflection may reveal additional disutilities that explain why the act is morally wrong. This seems to me to be so in the Robin Hood case. It was wrong of Robin Hood to steal from the rich even though he distributed his ill-gotten gains to the poor. What makes his acts wrong is not simply that they deprived a few rich people of a small portion of their wealth. The indirect disutilities of these acts of stealing from the rich include the insecurity felt by many who were not in fact robbed, the wasted manpower used by society in trying to capture and punish Robin Hood, and the loss of the goods Robin Hood could have brought into existence had he lived his life in a more productive vocation.

The example of euthanasia, however, cannot be dealt with in this way. Try as I may, I honestly cannot discover great hidden disutilities in the act of killing an elderly person suffering greatly from an incurable illness, provided that certain safeguards like a written medical opinion by at least two doctors and a request by the patient are preserved. In this case I cannot find any way to reconcile my theory with my moral judgment. What I do in this case is to hold fast to act-utilitarianism and distrust my moral sense. I claim that my condemnation of such acts is an irrational disapproval, a condemnation that will change upon further reasoning about the act. Rejection of my moral sensibilities in this case is not, I trust, entirely arbitrary. For one thing, I have found in several past cases that moral judgments in conflict with considerations of utility were reversed by additional reasoning. For another, I cannot find in the description of the act in question any reason for my moral condemnation. That I feel its wrongness is clear, but I cannot state to myself any rational justification for my feeling. Hence, I discount this particular judgment as irrational.

I do not do so lightly or with great confidence. As long as my condemnation of euthanasia persists, there is a logical inconsistency between my ethical theory and my moral judgment in this case. This is not a satisfactory situation for a moral philosopher who wishes to find a rationally justified theory, for the truth can hardly contain inconsistent statements. This is why I originally said that I "would like to be" an act-utilitarian. I am far from sure that I can defend this position in the end. But I cling to it because it seems the most reasonable of all the answers to the question, "What makes an act right or wrong?"

As a moral philosopher I might refuse to commit myself and continue the search for the perfect answer, but as a practical man I cannot postpone my commitment. I must make decisions today and every day; and to be made rationally, these decisions must be grounded in the relevant considerations. But which considerations are relevant? What does make an act right or wrong? Until I know the answer to this theoretical ethical problem, I do not know which reasons to weigh when I am deliberating about my moral choices. Therefore, I commit myself, tentatively, to the most adequate theory I can find or formulate. If I am consistent, my theory of the grounds of obligation will be reflected in the stand I take on specific moral issues and the choices I make in particular situations. What reasons, for instance, did I give to defend my stand on the issue of civil disobedience? Were they all utilitarian considerations? Did they all appeal to the good produced or the harm done by individual acts of civil disobedience? If they did, I consistently applied my act-utilitarianism to that moral problem. The goal of the moral philosopher is to discover and formulate and defend with cogent arguments an ethical theory that can be applied consistently and with morally sound consequences to moral issues and individual decisions.

STUDY QUESTIONS

1. Is it *morally* wrong to eat peas with a knife or to burp in public? Why or why not? How, if at all, do the rules of etiquette in any society differ from its mores?

2. Is polygamy really wrong in our society, and right in other societies like those of Islamic countries? If so, how do you explain this difference? If not, why not?

3. Do changes in the mores of a society ever make acts that were wrong right or vice versa? Do the mores of any society ever get better or worse? Is there ever any such thing as the moral progress or moral deterioration of a society?

4. Is any act required by the mores ever morally wrong? If so, by what higher standard are the mores of a society to be judged?

5. Why does it seem better to many philosophers to have God rather than society serve as the moral standard? Is God more moral than society? Why or why not?

6. It has been said, "If God is dead, everything is permitted." Is it?

7. Does the question, "Would it be wrong to disobey God?" make sense? If not, why not? If so, how might this question be answered?

8. Are worshiping God and attending church moral obligations? Why or why not?

9. Is the ethic of love presented in the New Testament a repudiation of the legalistic morality of the Old Testament? Support your interpretation with textual evidence.

10. Is our current income tax law, which contains loopholes that allow many individuals with high incomes to get by with paying little or no tax, an unjust

law? If so, is it unjust by some higher law? What is the nature of this higher law and in what sense is it higher?

11. What connection is there between the theory that a single characteristic of the act makes it right or wrong and the view that morality requires acting on principle? Are there any universal principles of right and wrong that are true without exception?

12. How does one know whether some proposed moral principle is correct or not? Is there any rational way to resolve disagreements over moral principles? If so, how? If not, is every moral judgment arbitrary in the end?

13. Are conflicts of obligations real or only illusory? What reason might be given for saying that real duties never conflict? What evidence is there that duties do conflict? What theory of obligation best explains your position?

14. How can we distinguish between some characteristic intrinsic to the nature of an act and something external to the act? The inner spirit of an act is often contrasted with the external law. Is the spirit in which an act is done or the motive from which it is done really intrinsic rather than extrinsic to the act? Why or why not? Are the consequences of an act part of the act or external to it? Does it matter whether the consequences are intended or unintended? Does it matter whether the consequences are proximate or remote?

15. On the given occasion we might say that a certain person bent his finger *or* pulled the trigger *or* fired a gun *or* shot a man *or* killed a man *or* caused blood to gush out onto the new carpet. Are all of these descriptions of the same act or of different acts? If they all describe the same act, which of the possible descriptions gives the real nature of the act? If they describe different acts, how many acts can a person perform at once?

16. If several characteristics of an act are right-making or wrong-making, how does one know what one ought to do when these conflict? Do certain sorts of characteristics always outweigh others, or does it all depend on the individual case? Is it possible to generalize truthfully about right and wrong?

17. Ross claims that what one ought to do depends on the special relation in which the moral agent stands to other persons—relations like being a parent of, being a friend of, having made a promise to, or being the recipient of kindness from. Does his theory explain the moral relevance of such relations? Are these relations contained in the intrinsic nature of the act or external to it?

18. Does the situation in which an act is done have any bearing on whether it is right or wrong? If so, must we reject the view that the rightness or wrongness of an act depends on the intrinsic nature of the act? If not, is it as wrong to lie in a situation where lying saves a human life as where it merely saves the liar from embarrassment?

19. Is it rational for any individual to sacrifice his own welfare for the well-being of another person? If so, what reason is there to justify this self-sacrifice? If not, does morality require one to act irrationally at times?

20. Does each person have a right to preserve his own life? If so, does this right imply that one's own welfare takes precedence over the welfare of others in some way? If not, is it always wrong to kill in self-defense?

21. Must the ethical egoist hold that the welfare of others is entirely irrelevant to what one ought to do? Suppose that the agent's own welfare were causally dependent in some way upon the welfare of other people. Would the welfare of those others then be relevant to what the agent ought to do? Would the distinction between ethical egoism and ethical altruism then disappear?

22. Does the rightness or wrongness of an act depend on how much good or evil it brings into existence? Suppose I try to save a drowning child and succeed only in soaking my clothes. Have I done wrong because my act did no good and even harmed my clothes a little?

23. Does the welfare of *all* people really count *equally* in determining obligation? Suppose that I am in a situation where I could do something to make my mother happy or do something else to make some stranger slightly happier than my mother would be. Ought I really to do good to the stranger rather than to benefit my mother?

24. Is the utility of the act the only morally relevant factor? Would it be right for me to refuse to repay a debt on the grounds that I have some slightly better use for the money?

25. Does the distribution as well as the amount of value produced count? Suppose that one has to choose between an act that will give happiness to several virtuous people and an act that will give slightly more happiness to several wicked people. Which act would be right? If the former, what makes it right to do an act that is not the best one possible under the circumstances? If the latter, is justice morally irrelevant?

26. Does each society always have that set of moral rules that maximizes utility for that society? If so, how do you explain this extraordinary social wisdom? If not, do the moral rules cease to be morally binding?

27. In precisely what way are moral rules useful? Is it that acting in conformity to them is useful, or that having them enforced by society is useful, or that the individual's accepting them as guides to conduct is useful? What difference would it make to rule-utilitarianism whether one measured the utility of a rule by its conformity value or its enforcement value or its acceptance value?

28. Should the rule-utilitarian say that it is the rules actually accepted in any society *or* those rules that would be useful if they were accepted that determine what one ought to do? Suppose that one of the moral rules accepted in a moral agent's society is harmful rather than useful. Does the agent have any moral obligation to obey this rule while trying to get society to change it? If so, why? If not, are the rules of society irrelevant to our moral obligations?

29. Do moral rules ever conflict? If so, how might the rule-utilitarian deal with practical inconsistencies in a set of moral rules? If not, why not? How, if at all, might the rule-utilitarian construct a theory in order to ensure that conflicts between moral rules are either avoided or resolved in every case?

30. Must we be able to state some moral rules in words in order to know whether some act is right or wrong? If not, does this mean that moral rules are irrelevant to what we ought to do? Do we need to reflect on all the remote consequences of an act before we know whether it is right or wrong? If not, does this mean that consequences are irrelevant?

31. It is sometimes said that the theory of universalizability is just the golden rule dressed up in philosophical language. Is this so?

32. Would it be possible for some act to be wrong for this person to do now, but right for someone else to do *exactly* the same kind of act in *just* the same kind of situation? If not, why not? If so, does this imply that universalizability is at least a necessary condition of rightness?

33. Is the drafted soldier used as a mere means? What of the volunteer? Suppose he volunteers simply to avoid being drafted?

34. Do criminals forfeit the right to be treated as ends-in-themselves? If so, how

does the criminal forfeit the right? If not, is it wrong to force the criminal to go to jail unwillingly?

35. Are little children really rational moral agents? If so, is it wrong for parents to impose their will upon their children? If not, may one treat one's child as one would a pet?

36. Are mentally handicapped or severely retarded individuals really rational persons? If not, is there any reason to respect them as persons? What of the senile or the insane?

37. Why should one worry if one's ethical theory is not always consistent with one's moral judgments in particular cases? Is consistency all that important? Why or why not?

38. Should an ethical theory be accepted or rejected on the basis of its implications for particular cases, or should we judge particular cases on the basis of some universal theory? What reason might be given for holding that theory is more basic than particular moral judgments or vice versa? What do you consider to be the ultimate data from which the moral philosopher should reason?

39. What are the hardest cases you can imagine for the act-utilitarian to explain? How would you explain these cases?

40. Would it advance the welfare of all for every person to become an act-utilitarian? Would a person who believes that one need not keep a promise or tell the truth or help another in distress be as useful a member of society as a person who believes that one always ought, at least prima facie, to do these kinds of acts? If so, how? If not, does this disqualify act-utilitarianism as an adequate ethical theory?

BIBLIOGRAPHY

AQUINAS, SAINT THOMAS. *Summa Theologica*, I–II, Questions 90–97. In *Basic Writings of Saint Thomas Aquinas*, edited by Anton C. Pegis. New York: Random House, 1945.

BENTHAM, JEREMY. *An Introduction to the Principles of Morals and Legislation*, chap. 1, edited by J. H. Burns and H. L. A. Hart. London: Athlone Press, 1970.

BRANDT, RICHARD B. "Toward a Credible Form of Utilitarianism." In *Morality and the Language of Conduct*, edited by Hector-Neri Castaneda and George Nakhnikian, pp. 107–143. Detroit: Wayne State University Press, 1963.

CLARKE, SAMUEL. *Discourse Upon Natural Religion*. In *British Moralists*, edited by Lewis Amherst Selby-Bigge, vol. 2, pp. 3–34. New York: Dover Publications, 1965.

KANT, IMMANUEL. *Foundations of the Metaphysics of Morals*, 2d Section. In *Critique of Practical Reason and Other Writings in Moral Philosophy*, edited by Lewis W. Beck. Chicago: University of Chicago Press, 1949.

MOORE, GEORGE EDWARD. *Principia Ethica*, chap. 5. Cambridge, Eng.: Cambridge University Press, 1903.

OLD TESTAMENT: *Deuteronomy* 5:6–29.

OLD TESTAMENT: *Exodus* 20:1–21.

PLATO. *The Republic*, pp. 41–53, 301–320. Translated and edited by Francis Macdonald Cornford. New York: Oxford University Press, 1945.

RAND, AYN. "The Objectivist Ethics." In *The Virtue of Selfishness: A New Concept of Egoism*, pp. 13–55. New York: New American Library, 1961.

ROSS, WILLIAM DAVID. *The Right and the Good*, chap. 2. Oxford, Eng.: Clarendon Press, 1930.

SUMNER, WILLIAM GRAHAM. *Folkways*, pp. 2–38. Boston: Ginn and Co., 1906.

URMSON, J. O. "The Interpretation of the Moral Philosophy of J. S. Mill." *Philosophical Quarterly* 3 (1953):33–39.

3
GENETIC ENGINEERING

How beauteous mankind is! O brave new world that has such people in 't!

Shakespeare in *The Tempest*

It is clear that the general quality of the world's population is not very high, is beginning to deteriorate, and should and could be improved.

Julian Huxley in "The Future of Man—Evolutionary Aspects"

Although the morality of miscegenation is controversial (the very name condemns the practice), the cross-breeding of plants is generally taken for granted, and hybrid fruits and vegetables are valued for their flavor, color, and texture. The breeding of animals to incorporate or increase desired characteristics is uncontroversial and highly successful. Horses are bred for work, poodles for show, and swine to increase the yield of lean meat for food. Since most customers prefer white meat to dark, turkeys are now bred to have a shorter bone structure with heavier breast muscles, with the incidental advantage that they fit more easily into our ovens.

Eugenics—the production of fine offspring, especially human—has a long history in theory and practice. In *The Republic*, Plato pictured the ideal state as a class society in which the wise rule, the spirited defend the state in time of war and administer it in time of peace, and the workers perform the economic functions of production and distribution of goods and services. He proposed to arrange marriages and sexual intercourse so that the rulers and guardians would have additional opportunities to produce children in order to increase the levels of intelligence and spirit in future generations. Aldous Huxley, in his dystopia *Brave New World*, imagined a state in which Alphas, Betas, and Gammas are deliberately manufactured in controlled laboratories to produce the superhuman and subhuman beings needed to perform higher and lower functions, respectively, in the society. For decades, many couples who know that they are carriers of hemophilia have voluntarily abstained from having children in order not to pass on this disease to their male children, and recently some courts have ordered the compulsory sterilization of feeble-minded women in order to prevent them from giving birth. Traditional eugenics has been the practice of selecting biologically or psychologically superior parents; today we are able to select genes or even modify the genetic materials in human chromosomes. Thus, the development of the modern science of genetics together with the new technologies of reproduction and genetic surgery have brought genetic engineering into existence. Is this a blessing, or a curse in disguise?

DEFINING THE PROBLEM

Recent developments in science and medicine have made it possible for us to control the genetic inheritance of human offspring much more extensively and precisely than ever before. But before we embark enthusiastically on widespread use of these new biomedical technologies, we should pause to ask ourselves a serious moral question: "Is the genetic engineering of human beings desirable?" This is not the only question we could and should ask. Equally important are the questions: "Would the genetic engineering of human beings be morally wrong?" and "Should the genetic engineering of humans be legally prohibited?" But since the answers to these latter questions might depend upon whether this contemplated use of biomedical technology would, on balance, be beneficial or harmful, let us focus in this chapter upon the desirability of genetic engineering.

Originally, an engineer was one who constructed or operated engines, such as the steam engine. Today engineering is the activity of designing and constructing, or at least supervising the construction of, machinery, buildings, bridges, roads, etc. Genetic engineering, accordingly, is the activity of designing, constructing, or reconstructing the genetic code of a living organism. Sometimes the term is used in a narrower sense; Jonathan Glover, for example, defines genetic engineering as using enzymes to add to or subtract from a stretch of DNA. But I shall use the expression "genetic engineering" in its broader and more common sense because most of the moral problems raised by genetic surgery are also raised by other means of controlling the genetic code of human beings. However, I shall not be concerned with the genetic engineering of nonhuman organisms. It is when human lives are at stake that the potential benefits and harms of genetic engineering become morally relevant in our society.

It may be helpful to remind ourselves of a few of the forms that genetic engineering can and does take. This engineering can be done by selecting genetic materials to unite to form a new organism, by eliminating genetically defective products, or by reconstructing the genetic inheritance of the offspring. For example, if a husband knows that he is a carrier of a serious genetic defect, he may feel that it would be morally irresponsible for him to father a child who might inherit a devastating genetic disease. The couple might decide to have a child by artificial insemination from a donor. Or today even an unmarried woman can obtain sperm from the sperm bank in California to which several Nobel Prize winners have donated in the expectation that, when this sperm is introduced into her womb, she will become pregnant and give birth to a child with superior intelligence inherited, in part, from its unknown father. There is no medical reason why the genetic materials for a child need come from either parent. Now that in vitro fertilization is a moderately successful technique, ova could be collected from one female, sperm chosen from a sperm bank, these could be united in the laboratory, and the fertilized ovum implanted in a second woman who would then become pregnant and bear the child. However a child may have been conceived, it is now possible to test the fetus for a wide range of genetic defects by using amniocentesis or even newer techniques. In the event that a serious genetic disease is identified, most couples choose to have an abortion and thereby prevent the birth of a badly defective baby. In a very few cases, it is now possible to perform genetic surgery upon the fetus to remedy the genetic defect diagnosed before birth. As our knowledge of genetic structure and our techniques of gene splicing improve, it should be possible to reconstruct the genetic code of a human being in a wider range of cases and at a later stage of life.

The central question of this chapter is whether the widespread genetic engineering of human beings is desirable. This is a very different kind of question from the one we asked in Chapter 1. We are not asking whether genetic engineering is morally right or wrong. It is not a question of moral obligation, but of value. The question is whether, on balance, genetic engineering would be beneficial or harmful. No doubt there would be some good consequences if physicians were to try much more often than they do now to construct or reconstruct the genetic code of a human being to prevent the birth of a defective child or achieve the birth of improved offspring, but there would surely be some harmful consequences as well. Our problem is to try to identify the main sorts of benefits and harms that would come with genetic engineering and to weigh the values against the disvalues in order to judge whether, on balance, the practice of designing, constructing, and reconstructing the genetic code of human beings would be desirable. First let us look at the promised values we might hope to achieve in this way.

ALLEGED VALUES

Prevent Genetic Illness

Many of the most serious diseases arise, entirely or in part, from genetic causes. In some cases, anyone born with a specific chromosomal structure has or will develop the disease; in others, the tendency to develop the disease is inherited. The victims of these diseases frequently suffer a miserable fate. A baby born with polycystic kidneys or Tay-Sachs disease has no hope of a cure and can have no prospect of anything other than a very short and painful life. Patients suffering from cystic fibrosis used to have a life expectancy of about eight years. Today they can hope to live about twenty, provided they live a semi-isolated life to shelter them from respiratory infections; many must have fluids drained out of their lungs several times each day and must obtain prompt and frequent hospital treatment. One who has inherited Down's Syndrome or Huntington's Chorea may live to middle age or beyond, but the former can never develop normal psychological capacities and must forever be dependent upon family or even institutions for care; the latter will find his or her physical and psychological capacities beginning to degenerate in the prime of life. The suffering, both physical and psychological, that these genetic illnesses impose on patients is grievous. Moreover, their families often suffer greatly with them. It is a terrible thing to have one's hopes of a normal and happy baby crushed and to witness the misery of a loved one. Add to this the disruption in one's life caused by the need to provide special care for these patients and the financial burdens of the medical expenses, and the amount of harm genetic diseases cause to the families of the patients becomes immense. Genetic engineering might well prevent a significant portion of such inherited diseases and spare the patients and their families the pain, unhappiness, and other costs they now incur by selecting genetically sound materials before conception, aborting fetuses known to be genetically defective, and using genetic surgery to eliminate the genes that cause many genetic diseases later in life. Surely this would be of immense value to those who would otherwise inherit genetic diseases and to their families.

Halt Deterioration

Another promised value of genetic engineering is that it could halt, or at least retard, the deterioration of the gene pool. The gene pool consists of the sum total of the genes in the chromosomes of all the human beings now alive who are or will reach childbearing age. Obviously, it is from this genetic material, and from it alone, that new human beings can be conceived. Hence, the human gene pool at any given time will determine the fundamental biological characteristics of the human species in the future. Unfortunately, the quality of the gene pool has been deteriorating rapidly in the last few decades. This is due to two causes. Human beings today are exposed to considerably more radiation and absorb a much wider range of chemical substances than ever before. One consequence is an increasing rate of mutations in the genetic code of human beings. Since most mutations are biologically harmful, the long-term effects for human beings are dismal. Of course, mutations are not a new phenomenon; they have been an essential element in evolution from the beginning of life. But natural processes have tended to eliminate harmful mutations from the human gene pool because individuals afflicted by the most serious of them could not survive. Modern medicine, however, has transformed the survival of the fittest into the survival of fit and unfit alike. Consider diabetes as a familiar, but far from unique, example. For centuries infants born with a tendency to develop diabetes had a relatively poor life expectancy. Many of them became seriously ill and died before they reached the childbearing age. Women who did survive often could not conceive or would abort spontaneously. In these ways, nature cleansed the gene pool of the chromosomes that caused this lamentable illness. Today, however, infants born carrying the genetic structure that produces diabetes can expect a normal, or near normal, life span, and diabetic women can conceive and bear children almost as frequently as more healthy women. Therefore, the proportion of the gene pool that carries this inherited disease is constantly increasing. Since this is true for a wide variety of genetic defects, the prognosis for the human race is a rapidly accelerating incidence of genetically caused illnesses. Larger and larger proportions of our population will suffer from cystic fibrosis, muscular dystrophy, hemophilia, Huntington's Chorea, and other dreadful illnesses. In addition to the suffering imposed on patients and their families, as already noted, there will be potentially calamitous social consequences. Already a considerable proportion of the space in our hospitals and nursing homes is devoted to the care of those with genetic diseases; the proportion will steadily grow until we may be unable to provide adequate medical care for those with less debilitating but more remediable ailments. The proportion of the human population healthy enough to live productive lives will become progressively smaller and the proportion of helpless and hapless persons will grow ever larger. The inevitable consequence will be a rapidly declining standard of living for all human beings. The stakes are high. If anything could be done to stop the deterioration of the gene pool, it would be tremendously beneficial for future human beings. Genetic engineering is the only hope we have of achieving this immense value.

Provide Needed Individuals

We live in a rapidly changing society; to be sure, social change is an old story, but the rate of change has accelerated in this century. While individual initiative and a certain fierce courage were required in the days of pioneering, today's crowded cities need a less aggressive and more cooperative personality. In a single generation, the proportion of the working force doing hard manual labor has been halved and the proportion in highly skilled or intellectually demanding jobs has more than doubled. Everywhere we witness a growing number of social misfits, individuals who are incapable of finding a useful place in our society. The middle-aged workers made redundant by the new technologies and the functionally illiterate unable to find work are only the most obvious examples. It is not only that these individuals are nonproductive and a burden on society as well. They are condemned to live in poverty, in misery, and with little or no hope of a better future. As society changes, the kinds of individuals it needs, those who can live productively and happily within that society, also change. The possibility of producing individuals who can fit into modern society is limited, among other things, by their biological inheritance. Genetic engineering could be used to modify the genetic code of future generations so that they would be the sorts of people needed by their societies and not social misfits condemned to a useless and hopeless life. For example, genetic engineering might produce more intelligent and less aggressive offspring to fit the needs of a more scientific and urban society. This would be of great benefit to our society and to its members.

Improve Humans

It is not merely that the more intelligent person fits the needs of society better; he or she is capable of a more rewarding vocation or more satisfying activities. A physician or teacher experiences rewards denied to the janitor or ditch-digger; the pleasures of watching a fine production of *King Lear* or of discussing philosophy are richer and finer than those of watching most television programs or of drinking beer. But these intellectual pursuits are available only to those with considerable intelligence. More generally, the quality of one's life depends in large part upon one's physical and psychological characteristics, and these are genetically determined to a considerable degree. On a more basic level, the individual with a strong and healthy body is more likely to live a happy life than one with a crippled body or one plagued with illnesses. Genetic engineering provides the techniques to create superior human beings, at least biologically superior. In this way, it can indirectly improve the quality of human lives. Since in the end it is the quality of human lives that matters, this is the ultimate benefit anyone or anything could give to human beings. Genetic engineering might well increase human longevity, especially design human beings capable of remaining active and healthy much later in life. If its successes in the plant and animal worlds are any indication, it might also modify our genetic structure in ways that would confer resistance to certain diseases. In these and other ways, genetic engineering might bring into existence human beings capable of living much longer and happier lives.

Increase Knowledge

Genetic engineering would make important contributions to genetic theory and medical science. Although common sense knowledge arises primarily from everyday experience, modern science depends very heavily upon laboratory experiments to discover new truths and distinguish between true and false theories. The laboratory offers two great advantages over natural observations. For one thing, in the laboratory one or a few variables can be changed at a time in such a way as to identify the precise factors upon which natural processes and structural features depend. For another, laboratory instruments render observable things one cannot experience with the naked eye or unaided ear and can measure with precision variables that can only be estimated in nature. Both of these advantages would apply to genetic engineering. By introducing small and identifiable changes into the chromosomes of human beings it could identify with precision the crucial determining factors in the biological inheritance of human beings. And many of the techniques of genetic engineering, such as amniocentesis and in vitro fertilization, render observable and measurable what is naturally hidden in the mother's womb. Thus, the practice of genetic engineering would probably give us exciting new theoretical insights in biology and medicine. These would in turn enable us to develop new medical treatments and even new medical technologies that would be applicable to normal childbirth and the treatment of genetic illnesses in addition to improved genetic engineering in the future. One of the very considerable values of genetic engineering would be its contribution to biological and medical science, important in themselves and beneficial in their applications.

Advocates of the widespread genetic engineering of human beings argue that it would be beneficial in many ways. We have considered the most plausible and important of these alleged values. Genetic engineering might well be valuable because it would prevent genetic illness, halt the deterioration of the gene pool, produce individuals needed in our changing society, create improved human beings capable of living more satisfying lives, and increase our scientific knowledge. Before we can decide whether genetic engineering is desirable, however, we must balance these desirable prospects against any harms that might eventuate from the application of genetic engineering to human lives.

ALLEGED DISVALUES

Grave Abuse

Although genetic engineering could be used for desirable ends, in evil or merely irresponsible hands, it could equally be subject to great abuses. The recent history of amniocentesis and abortion reveals that in practice when we begin by eliminating only fetuses with a severe form of genetic defect, we then tend to eliminate for much less serious forms. Similarly, if abortion of unborn babies with the most devastating diseases, such as Tay-Sachs disease, is accepted by the medical profession, overanxious couples may choose to abort unborn babies with only some prospect of inheriting minor defects. Most hemophiliacs, for example, live rich, full lives, provided they take the proper precautions. What a waste it would be to deny them this opportunity. Even in the case of Down's Syndrome, there is serious debate about whether abortion is already abused. Although children with this defect can never grow up to be entirely normal, those with mild cases can achieve a considerable degree of independence and social interaction, and even the worst off are not miserable simply because their intellectual capacities have not developed far enough for them to understand their plight. Now that we know of hundreds of diseases that are genetically determined, the prospects for the abuse of genetic engineering by excessive and unnecessary abortions take on frightening proportions.

The danger of regrettable decisions by pregnant women might well tempt society to intervene, as it has in the recent Baby Doe cases. These were court cases in which the government sued to compel physicians to prolong the life of an infant born with serious genetic defects, even though the parents had refused to consent to such treatment. Moreover, genetic engineering can greatly reduce the incidence of the most serious genetic diseases and halt the deterioration of the gene pool only if it is practiced consistently on a very wide scale. Therefore, to be effective it must be controlled by the state. At the very least, this means government regulation with a consequent loss of valuable personal freedom and state intrusion into the intimate and personal decisions of conception, pregnancy, and childbirth. At worst, there could be something like the Nazi attempt to breed a "superior race" of pure Aryans even when this required genocide towards the entire Jewish population. Genetic engineering provides a medical weapon to those in power that is very hard to restrain. Decisions to use it are almost sure to be affected by racial and cultural stereotypes even if not by sheer malice. In Huxley's *Brave New World,* the state deliberately creates inferior human beings, the Betas and the Gammas, to fulfill society's need for lower classes to perform the more routine functions without having the intellect or imagination to resent and resist their lot. One reason that the genetic engineering of human beings is undesirable is that it would be almost impossible to prevent its misuse on either a personal or social scale.

Excessive Risk

Another reason to doubt the value of the genetic engineering of humans is that it may well be too dangerous to use even intelligently and with the best of intentions. The cumulative effect of individual choices, each innocent in itself, could be disastrous. Since it is possible to know the sex of an unborn baby and many couples in our society have a decided preference for male rather than female children, many couples might decide to abort female fetuses and try again. In the long run, this would upset the male–female ratio in our society in ways that would strain the social institution of monogamous marriage and produce a variety of other social dislocations. Even successful uses of genetic engineering would very probably have undesirable side-effects. Our experience with animal breeding shows that if we promote one attribute we tend to weaken others and produce a vulnerable and unbalanced species; for example, poodles bred for woolly coats have severe ear trouble. Many genes are *both* harmful and useful. Thus, the genetic code that is responsible for sickle cell anemia also confers a high resistance to malaria. Were we to effectively use genetic engineering to prevent this disease among African blacks, where it is prevalent, we would at the same time vastly increase their suffering from malaria, which is also common in most parts of Africa. If modern ecology shows us anything, it is that deliberate modifications of the natural balance at any point, however well intentioned, will create unanticipated problems at many other points. Our successes return to plague us at other times and in other places. Thus, genetic engineering is today, and will remain for some time, high-risk technology. Not every attempt to control the genetic structure of human offspring will succeed. Sometimes instead of producing an improved genetic code and a healthy human being, the result is a defective product, a seriously abnormal person. Since these are human beings we have engineered, we cannot simply dispose of them like defective watches or industrial wastes; we have to live with our mistakes. Some failures will lie hidden in the chromosomes of human offspring and be passed on to their children in turn. The deleterious consequences may not become evident for generations, by which time they may have spread to many individuals and be irreversible. The excessive risk inevitable in the genetic engineering of human beings makes its use undesirable.

Degrade Humanity

Human engineering would be very undesirable because it would undermine respect for human beings. The belief in the sanctity of each human life is essential for good will within a society and for worthwhile human interactions. If genetic engineering were to replace sexual intercourse on any large scale as the normal method of producing children, our attitudes toward human offspring would change for the worse. Human beings would become products to be designed and constructed, much as we now design and construct automobiles, watches, or radios. Kant argues that while any object has its price in terms of other objects for which one would be willing to exchange it, human beings have a dignity that makes each person irreplaceable and above all price. Respect for human beings as moral agents recognizes their personality and is basic to morality and humane personal relationships that contribute so much to the quality of our lives. Genetic engineering would change our attitude to human beings, causing us to think of them as products, objects to be valued for their usefulness, not respected for their humanity.

Essentially, genetic engineering is the application of quality control to human beings. Slightly defective products are sold in our stores as seconds and seriously defective products are discarded as failures. The genetic engineering of human beings would transfer these attitudes, quite appropriate to objects, to human offspring. It would stigmatize human beings suffering from genetic diseases or genetically defective in any way as inferior products, subnormal human beings. It would tend to create an expectation of biological perfection in prospective parents, an unrealistic expectation that would lead to harmful frustrations and an unwillingness to accept children for what they are. The lowering of self-respect in imperfect children, and we are all imperfect in many ways, would be dreadful. Thus, any widespread application of genetic engineering to human offspring would change our attitude from one that recognizes the dignity and value of each human individual to one that would degrade human beings to the level of mere objects, often imperfect ones at that.

Devalue Sexual Intercourse

Sexual intercourse is naturally both an act of love and of procreation, but genetic engineering would divorce love-making from baby-making. It would thereby deprive sexual intercourse of its natural significance. This is not to say that every act of intercourse should result in conception. But some acts do, and almost any could if contraceptive measures are not taken. The couple is well aware of the natural connection between sexual intercourse and procreation, and this awareness gives meaning to their sexual relations even when they do not expect to conceive a child. Sex becomes an emotional bond between them and a symbol of their union, past or future, in their child or children. Having a child is one of the most meaningful and important of human experiences; sharing a love for and care of a child is one of the strongest and most satisfying of human bonds. To sever the connection between intercourse and procreation would be to rob it of this significance, to trivialize it and reduce it to an intense but meaningless pastime. This would be a great loss of value in human life.

Strain Parent–Child Relationships

The genetic engineering of human offspring would impose intolerable stresses and strains upon the relationship between parent and child. The burden of parental responsibility for the biological inheritance of the child would become much heavier than it now is, and perhaps unbearable. Whether the parents had elected genetic engineering or deliberately decided not to do so, they would feel deeply guilty for the birth of a genetically defective child. The defective child would be aware that the parents had tried to engineer a perfect child and failed, or failed even to try to correct the inherited defect. Either way, the child would resent the fact that he or she must suffer for the failure of the parents. Parents who engage in "gene shopping" will have unrealistic hopes and a consequent unwillingness to accept anything but a near-perfect child. Rejected children will recognize their status and respond with mixed guilt and anger. No longer will inherited diseases or defects be regarded as due to divine providence or natural accident. They will be thought, and felt, to be preventable and subject to deliberate control. The resulting emotions parents feel for their children and children for their parents will change what could and should be a loving, accepting relationship into a strained and unsatisfactory, even painful, one.

The alleged values of the genetic engineering of human beings can be balanced, at least in number, with alleged disvalues. Many argue that were we to attempt to design, construct, and reconstruct the genetic codes of human beings, this would inevitably lead to grave abuse, excessive risk, degraded humanity, devalued sexual intercourse, and strained parent–child relationships. Before we attempt to assess the relative probability and importance of these promised benefits and threatened harms, let us look more closely at the relation between parent and child.

THE PARENT–CHILD RELATION

Whether the application of genetic engineering to the human race is a good or a bad thing will depend in large measure on whether it changes the relation between parents and their children for better or worse. But precisely what is this relationship? Clearly, it has many aspects. We should take note of these before considering the impact of genetic engineering upon them; most obviously:

1. The parent–child relation is a biological relation. While husband and wife are related by marriage, the parent and child are "blood relatives." We now know that what is crucial in this biological link between parent and child is genetic. The biological inheritance of the child is encoded in its chromosomes, which derive one-half of their genes from the biological mother and the other half from the biological father. This genetic relationship between parent and child is permanent, unless modified by genetic surgery, and of tremendous importance to the future of the child. The child normally has another temporary but also important biological relation with its mother, for the fetus cannot survive from the time of conception until delivery without being carried in the mother's womb. While this biological connection ceases at delivery, the child normally carries its genetic inheritance from conception until its death.

2. The parent–child relation is also a creative relation. That this is logically distinct from the biological relation is illustrated forcefully by the story of Pygmalion, a king of Cyprus who carved and then fell in love with the statue of a woman, Galatea, who was then brought to life by the Greek goddess Aphrodite. Pygmalion created Galatea, then, as a parent creates a child, but in this mythical case the creative relation does not coincide with any biological or genetic relation; Galatea was created out of stone rather than the genetic materials of the creator. Traditionally, it has been held that the parents created the child "out of their loins," so that it is "flesh of their flesh and blood of their blood." Thus, the creative relation has coincided with the biological one. With the introduction of the new reproductive technologies, however, the two are often severed, and the creative relation may become rather complex. When artificial insemination or artificial enovulation with donor is used, half of the genetic material is derived from someone other than husband or wife. With in vitro fertilization, a couple or even a single woman could use male sperm and female ova from banks to which genetically healthy individuals have donated. Who then is most accurately to be called the creator or creators of the child? Perhaps the couple or single woman who have decided to have the child in this way. But the medical team that carries out the new reproductive technology also plays a part in the creation of a new human life. At least, the parents can claim a central and indispensable role in the creation of the child. They, perhaps with help, created the child.

3. The parent–child relation is almost inevitably also a psychological relation. Parent and child are very much aware of and have feelings for each other. Much of the value of their relationship lies in or arises from this psychological dimension of their relation. Each experiences sights, sounds, smells, and tactile sensations of the other. Each has beliefs about the other. Often one will dream, or day-dream, of the other. The emotions each has toward the other include love, hate, often love–hate, admiration, anger, pride, and many more. For a parent, this psychological relation will begin before birth, for it grows steadily during pregnancy, and it may begin even before conception as the parent hopes (or fears) to have a child and begins to plan for parenthood. The exact content of this psychological relation between parent and child will vary greatly, but it is always richly present within the family. To some degree it is even there when parent and child do not live together on a daily basis.

The child living with a divorced parent may visit the other parent or, if not, see pictures of or wonder about him or her.

4. The parent–child relation is typically a family relation. The family is a social institution. Apparently every society has some such institution, although the forms it takes vary greatly from culture to culture. The nuclear family is the basic household unit of those who live together. It is structured by the roles that each member of the family plays. These are roles such as that of husband and wife, parent and child, breadwinner and homemaker, etc. Each role carries with it specific activities defined by what society expects of one playing that role. The role of the parent in our society is to care for the basic needs of the child, including at least protection from dangers and the provision of some education; the role of the child is to be cared for and increasingly to help the parents in family enterprises.

5. The parent–child relation is also a legal relation. In our society, as in most, the parent and child stand in very special legal relationships to each other. Most obviously, these consist of legal rights and duties. The parent has a legal duty not to neglect and not to abuse the child, along with the legal right to command the child and not be interfered with in his or her activities of caring for the child. The child has the legal duty to obey its parent and legal rights to be fed, clothed, protected, educated, etc., by its parent. But the legal relation is even more complex than this. The parent has the legal power of consenting to medical treatment for the child and a legal immunity from loss of custody without due process of law. This legal relation between parent and child is as important in practice as it is complex in constitution.

6. Finally, at least for our purposes, the parent–child relation is a moral relation. This moral relation is analogous to, but richer and more far-reaching than, the legal relation between them. Just as the parent has legal duties to care for and not abuse the child, so has he or she moral duties to care for and not abuse the child. But the parent may have moral duties to or regarding the child over and beyond those that are legally recognized. If I have promised to take my son to a Saint Louis Cardinals baseball game, for example, I have a moral obligation to do so even though my promise does not constitute a legally enforceable contract. And, probably, my daughter has a moral right to ask that I listen to her side of the story before I punish her, even though this is not included within her legal right to due process. The moral rights, duties, powers, and immunities of parent and child probably vary a good deal from family to family even within the same society, while the legal relation between parent and child is socially defined and much more nearly uniform within any given society.

Clearly, the parent–child relation is very complex. While it is correct English to speak or write of "the parent–child relation," it is essential for any accurate thinking or appropriate evaluation to distinguish the very different aspects of this relationship. At the very least, one needs to pay careful attention to the biological, creative, psychological, family, legal, and moral relations between any parent and his or her child. We are now prepared to consider some of the ways in which these aspects of the parent–child relation would probably be changed by genetic engineering were it to become widely practiced upon human beings.

Genetic engineering directly and necessarily changes the biological relation between at least one family parent and the child. If a couple decide to have a child by artificial insemination with a donor, then the father in the family is not the biological parent of the child. If it should happen that two people choose to have a child by in vitro fertilization using both sperm and ova obtained from medical banks, then the child they would take home from the hospital would not be genetically related to either of them. Even if a couple procreate a child out of their own loins, the biological relation to their child will be modified if genetic surgery is subsequently performed upon the fetus. So much is obvious. What is less obvious is whether any such change would be desirable or undesirable or neither.

In our society today, the biological relation between parent and child serves the very important function of locating responsibility for the child. Normally the biological father and mother play the roles of mother and father in a nuclear family within which they care for their child. Since human beings must go through a very long period of dependency before they can take care of themselves, it is obviously essential that someone should feed, clothe, protect, educate, and bring up the child. This nurture and care will take much time and energy and require financial resources as well. Who is to assume this responsibility for the child? In our society, it is expected that the biological parents will also be family parents. Moreover, the biological mother has the legal duty to care for the child, at least until alternative legal arrangements for custody are made, and the biological father has the legal duty to provide financial support for the child. That this legal duty is important for the child (and mother) is shown by the increasing number of paternity suits, often decided on the basis of biological evidence, as the number of illegitimate births and broken homes grows. Now genetic engineering would tend to sever the biological relation of parent to child from the family and legal, even the moral, relations. Who, then, would be expected to assume responsibility for the care of the child? It might be that new social institutions and legal arrangements could solve this problem satisfactorily. But if not, there would inevitably be disputes about who should bear the burdens of this responsibility and, in many cases, individuals would seek to evade their responsibilities for the child; thus the well-being of the child would suffer. It is difficult to make accurate and reliable predictions while biomedical technology and social institutions are changing rapidly, but at the very least there is a serious threat of the most undesirable consequences here.

Human beings care deeply about their biological relationships. Most couples deeply want a child "of their own," by which they mean one biologically related to themselves. Often either husband or wife will hesitate or even refuse to adopt a child because this would not be the same to them; it would not be "my" child. Adopted children, although they usually love their adoptive parents deeply, still wonder about their "real" or biological parents, and sometimes, later in life, wish to be reunited with them. I must confess that I do not understand very well why so many of us think and feel this way. Even granted the psychological importance of roots, it remains unclear why these must be biological roots in one's ancestors; even given the significance of having children to carry on the family, why must they be biologically related to one? One might imagine that these ways of thinking and feeling are outmoded in the modern world and should be eliminated, but I am not so sure. Whatever their origins and whatever their justification, or lack of it, they are extremely valuable in two ways. First, they give a great deal of meaning to human lives. No man or woman is an island, and one cannot live a rich, satisfying life without feeling close to other persons and identifying oneself as belonging to a larger family. Nor will it do to identify oneself with the larger human family, for this dilutes and weakens the love and loyalty that give significance to one's life. One's biological relations to one's parents and/or children are infused with psychological meaning that helps to give value to one's experiences throughout life. Second, because we care deeply about our biological relations to others, we tend to care about those to whom we are biologically related. Since parents care for their children psychologically, it is only natural that they should care for them in the sense of caring for their needs. Thus, the psychological dimension attached to the biological relation of parent to child serves as an underpinning for our willingness to accept the responsibilities that go with the family, legal, and moral relation of parent to child. Whether it is wisdom or superstition, the way we tend to think and feel about those biologically related to us is most valuable in assuring that they are neither neglected nor abused.

In *The Cynics' Calendar*, Addison Mizner quipped, "God gives us relatives; thank God, we can choose our friends." We do not always like, or love and admire, those to whom we are biologically related. We might even imagine that we could choose a better parent, more promising child, or more helpful sibling if only biological relationships were subject to our control. But the rapidly rising divorce rate, not to mention the frequencies of lovers' quarrels and broken friendships, suggests that it is a very good thing that we *cannot* choose our relatives. As long as the biological relation between parent and child is fixed and unchangeable, it gives stability and security to the relation of parent to child, of child to parent. A husband may divorce his wife, and thus run away from his responsibilities to her, but no father can divorce his child. He can, alas, abandon his child and refuse to fulfill his responsibilities for its well-being. But the biological father remains the biological father, so that the basis for family responsibilities together with legal and moral duties regarding the child remains forever. The child can run away from home, but he or she cannot thereby sever his or her biological relation to the parents. Thus, the biological relation provides a firm foundation upon which the other aspects of the parent–child relation can, and ideally should, be built. Genetic engineering would modify this biological relation and sever it from other aspects of the parent–child relation. If, as seems quite possible, this were to result in a loss of stability and security in this most important relationship, that would be harmful to parent and, above all, to the child.

I am neither social scientist nor prophet. I hesitate to predict just how genetic engineering would modify the biological relation of parent to child or precisely what the further implications of any such change would be. It seems very likely, however, that some modifications would be most undesirable because they would make it harder to locate who is to be held responsible for the care of the child, would undermine the valuable ways we now think and feel about those related biologically to us, and would make the family relation of parent to child less stable and secure.

While genetic engineering would directly and necessarily change the biological relation of parent to child, it would indirectly and incidentally, but perhaps importantly, change some other aspects of the parent–child relation as well. As one small example of this, let us consider briefly the likely impact of genetic engineering upon the psychological relation between parent and child. It has been argued, you will recall, that the genetic engineering of human beings is undesirable because it would strain the parent–child relation by imposing an unbearable burden of responsibility upon the parent and could cause any child born with genetic defects as a result of or in spite of attempted engineering to feel great resentment and anger at its parents. This prediction may well be true, but it is only part of the story. One must also remember that we cannot escape the psychological tensions that could arise between parent and child from feelings of guilt or resentment simply because the parents *abstained* from the application of genetic engineering. Both parent and child will know that new reproductive technologies and genetic surgery are now available so that, in the case of any child born genetically defective, the parent will feel guilt at *not* having used these means, and the child will feel resentment at having to suffer from defects that might have been avoided had they been used. Indeed, genetic illness infects the psychological relation between parent and child with even more strains. The parent of a child suffering such an illness lives under considerable financial pressures and often must deal with dislocated patterns of family activity because of the special care needed by such patients; these leave the parent less able to relate fully and lovingly with the child and sometimes produce parental feelings of resentment at the innocent child imposing such hardships upon the parent. The genetically ill child may have diminished capacities to understand its lamentable condition and is often too preoccupied with its own suffering to cooperate lovingly with the parent. An argument in favor of genetic engineering is that it can prevent genetic illness. To the degree that this is true, it can thereby prevent the psychological strains imposed upon the parent–

child relation by such illnesses. On balance, it seems that genetic engineering, if wisely used, would do as much or more to improve the psychological relation of parent and child as to injure it. The question remains, of course, as to when it is wise to use genetic engineering upon humans.

MY TENTATIVE CONCLUSION

The time has come for me to explain, and if possible to defend with cogent reasoning, my conclusion regarding the specific moral problem we have been exploring in this chapter. Is the widespread genetic engineering of human beings desirable? I believe that it would be beneficial, *provided* that it is chosen by the parent for reasons of negative eugenics. In my answer, I presuppose that the necessary technology is available and has been adequately tested. If the technology required to carry out the desired genetic engineering is not available, either because it has yet to be developed or because the medical resources lie out of reach of the parent or parents contemplating its use, then in practice the question of value becomes irrelevant. Until the needed sort of genetic engineering becomes possible, the value or disvalue of its use remains idle. If the technology is available, but its reliability has not been adequately established, then it is undesirable to use it on any widespread basis. At best, what should be done is to experiment in a very limited number of cases to further develop and test these means of controlling the biological inheritance of human offspring.

Granted my presuppositions, the application of genetic engineering to human beings would frequently be desirable. The reason is simply that it can and, wisely used, will prevent much genetic illness with all the evils such ailments bring with them. First and foremost is the very great suffering, often intense physical pain, and frustration and desperation of the patients afflicted with genetic illnesses. These range from severe illnesses at birth to conditions, such as diabetes or Huntington's disease, that normally develop only later in life. There are also the relatives and friends who suffer in sympathy with their loved ones. In addition, there are the great financial burdens imposed upon patients, their families, and the larger society. It is clearly desirable to eliminate illnesses and these associated evils.

At the same time, it seems to me that genetic engineering of human beings will be, on balance, beneficial only under two conditions. First, it must be chosen by the parents. I have in mind, of course, the parent or parents who will stand in the family relation to the child, those who will play the social role of parent within the family that will raise the child. It would be harmful, I believe, for genetic engineering to be imposed upon the parents by the state. This would mean too great a loss of personal freedom and too great an invasion of privacy. Nor should the decision to use genetic surgery be made by other individuals, such as physicians or hospital administrators, for much the same reasons. Let me add, however, that it is obviously desirable for expert medical personnel to advise any parent or parents considering genetic engineering for their child. There are several reasons why the personal choice of the parents involved will help to ensure the desirability of genetic engineering. Individual cases differ in any number of important ways, including genetic make-up, personality, financial resources, life plans, and fundamental moral and religious convictions. The parent or pair of parents are more likely to know what is relevant to their case than others, no matter how well intentioned the latter might be. Moreover, the parents involved are more likely to choose responsibly because it is they who must live with the consequences of the decision. Also, they will be more likely to accept and fulfill their responsibilities as parents if they have freely chosen to assume them. Finally, each parental decision will have a very limited effect, in contrast to the much larger impact of any societal decision that would affect large classes of parents. In this way, mistaken decisions would be less harmful and would tend to be cancelled out by wiser decisions of other parents.

A second condition needed to ensure the desirability of the genetic engineering of human beings is that it be limited to negative eugenics. Eugenics is the science of improving the population by control of inherited qualities. Positive eugenics is the effort to breed in or insert valuable genetic traits; negative eugenics is the effort to eliminate harmful ones. At first glance, it might seem that it would be desirable to practice both positive and negative eugenics, but this is not so. Primarily, this is because genetic engineering is a very high-risk technology. It is very difficult to predict precisely what the results of any genetic intervention will be, and unintended effects can be devastating to the individual and harmful to the human race. Therefore, as long as there is no urgent need to use genetic engineering, it is better to play it safe and do nothing. But where the parents are carriers of severe genetic defects, or where a fetus or infant has been diagnosed as having inherited a severe genetic illness, there is both more to gain and less to lose by attempting to remedy the situation with genetic engineering. There is more to gain because the prevention or elimination of the genetic illness would free the child and others from great evils; there is less to lose because when the situation is already very threatening or bad, any untoward result of genetic intervention will not transform an acceptable situation into a markedly worse one. Moreover, it is easier to identify and define a genetic defect than a genetic ideal; it is clear that Down's Syndrome is an illness, but most unclear just how high intelligence must be to make one a desirable human being. Finally, the required technology is more likely to be available and adequately tested when it is closely tied to some illness because medical science and practice focus attention primarily upon the diagnosis and treatment of human diseases.

My conclusion, therefore, is that genetic engineering of human beings is desirable provided that it is limited to cases where the family parent or parents choose it for reasons of negative eugenics. But can it be so limited? Many moral philosophers will try to refute my conclusion with what is called a "slippery slope" argument. Even granted that genetic engineering were desirable *if* it were so limited, the argument goes, it is undesirable to apply genetic engineering even under the conditions I specify because this would be only the first step onto a slippery slope that would cause us to slide downhill to more and more undesirable uses of genetic engineering. Unwise or irresponsible decisions by individual parents would lead to state intervention with the dangers of grave abuse and widespread negative consequences. Since the line between genetic defects and the lack of genetic excellence is vague and controversial, negative eugenics will inevitably lead to positive eugenics. Hence, it is undesirable to practice the genetic engineering of human beings in any form because the initiation of apparently desirable kinds of genetic engineering will lead to undesirable and eventually calamitous uses of genetic engineering.

In assessing the import of any slippery slope argument, there are two questions to bear in mind. How slippery is the slope? And how much is to be gained by venturing onto the top of the slope? Now, to my mind, the top of the slope I propose is not very slippery at all. Genetic engineering is and will remain very expensive for the foreseeable future, and procreation by sexual intercourse is much less bother and much more enjoyable than the newer reproductive technologies. If individual parents are given the choice, they will probably use too little rather than too much genetic engineering. There is, of course, the possibility of state intervention. But given the very personal nature of the choice involved, this danger is relatively slight in a democratic society such as ours. In other societies, the risk might be greater. Again, if we begin with genetic engineering to prevent or eliminate only the most severe genetic defects, it is unlikely that we will move to positive eugenics. What may well happen is that there will be some movement from the elimination of severe defects to attempts to prevent lesser defects. But where these attempts are successful, they will probably do as much good as evil. Where they prove to be failures, other parents will have been forewarned and will be less likely to continue such attempts. I do not intend to deny that any application of genetic engineering to human beings involves stepping onto a slippery slope, but I do not believe that the step I propose is onto a very slippery one.

Still, there is risk. Is it desirable to take the risk of beginning medical practices that might conceivably lead to most undesirable results? I believe it is. The incidence of genetic illness in our society is growing steadily, and the length of time that patients suffer from such diseases is increasing also. Paradoxically, both of these great evils are side-effects of the tremendous advances in medical science and treatment during the past few decades. Given the vast human misery and huge unnecessary financial burden imposed by genetic illnesses, it would be intolerable to do nothing. Where the prevention or elimination of these evils is possible, it is surely highly desirable. Since there is much to gain by stepping onto the slippery slope, let us do so. But let us constantly bear in mind the conditions under which genetic engineering would be desirable in order that we not slide too far downhill.

STUDY QUESTIONS

1. The author alleges that the moral issues posed by genetic engineering in the broad sense are essentially the same as those posed by genetic engineering in the narrower sense. Is this really true? What are the moral problems arising from genetic surgery or gene splicing? Are these the same problems that arise in the use of other ways of designing and controlling the genetic structure of human offspring, by, say, the new reproductive technologies?

2. It is sometimes said that artificial insemination from a donor amounts to adultery and is, therefore, morally wrong. Is this true? What is adultery, anyway?

3. Sometimes what is genetically inherited is not a genetic illness but a tendency to develop one. Would abortion be morally permissible, even required, if a fetus is identified as being disposed to develop a serious illness? Remember that in many cases the "defective" individual does not in fact acquire the illness toward which he or she is disposed. Would the percentage of instances in which the tendency is actualized make a crucial difference? If so, what would be the decisive percentage? If not, why not?

4. There are various ways one might try to prevent genetic illness—refrain from using ova or sperm that are coded for that defect, test the fetus and abort those found defective, perform genetic surgery to repair identified defects. What are the advantages and disadvantages of each of these methods? Are any of these methods always or usually undesirable? Why or why not?

5. Genetic illnesses impose suffering and hardship upon the patients, their families, and society more generally. Are all of these equally relevant to the moral imperative to prevent such illness? Why or why not?

6. Suppose that one engineers the genetic codes of Dick and Jane and others for the purpose of halting the deterioration of the human gene pool. Is this using individual human beings merely as a means of improving the human race? If so, is this morally wrong? If not, why not?

7. Would it be more accurate to say that halting the deterioration of the gene pool would benefit human beings *or* prevent catastrophic harm to human beings? Does such a distinction matter for deciding whether the genetic engineering of human beings is desirable? Does it matter for deciding whether it is morally permissible? Why?

8. One of the reasons why the gene pool is probably deteriorating so rapidly is the success of modern medicine in treating genetic diseases. If this deterioration is exceedingly bad, does this imply it would be desirable to withhold medical treatment from many individuals afflicted with or carrying genetic defects?

9. The characteristics of any human being are a function of both heredity and

environment. What *kinds* of characteristics determine whether some individual is needed by his or her society? Are these the sorts of characteristics that are entirely, or in large measure, genetically determined?

10. Given the rate of change in modern societies, how accurately and how long in advance can one reliably predict what sorts of individuals will be needed in a society? Does this bear on the desirability of genetic engineering?

11. What constitutes an improvement in human beings? For example, increased longevity might be an improvement if this longer life would be a healthy and happy one, but it could be most detrimental if it simply added years of incapacity, illness, and misery to our lives. What are the implications of this ambiguity for any practical program of genetic engineering?

12. Let us assume that there are a number of different ways in which genetic engineering could improve human offspring but that these could not all be achieved at the same time. What criteria should one use to decide which improvements should be attempted?

13. Limited and selective genetic engineering on an experimental basis might effectively increase knowledge, but any attempt to halt the deterioration of the gene pool would require widespread and systematic genetic engineering. Does this imply that we need to refine our question to distinguish between the desirability of experimental genetic engineering and the desirability of large-scale genetic engineering?

14. Some argue that genetic engineering is "subject to" grave abuse. Does this mean that it could be or that it will be abused? If the former, why worry about merely possible abuse as long as it is not actual? If the latter, what is the evidence that it will in fact be abused if introduced at all?

15. Granted the danger of abuse, many would argue that the solution is not to forbid genetic engineering but to regulate its use by law. How might this best be accomplished? Would such legal regulation be effective in preventing the misuse of genetic engineering? How can we know before we try?

16. Memories of the racist policies of Nazi Germany are called up to argue against any contemporary use of genetic engineering. Are horror stories of a totalitarian Nazi state really lessons for a democratic society dedicated to the moral ideals of liberty and equality?

17. It is said that genetic engineering imposes excessive risk. What makes a risk excessive? It might be reasonable for a parent to risk his or her life to save a child from a burning house, but not to risk life merely for the thrill of reckless driving. Granted that genetic engineering is risky, what reason is there to judge that risk excessive?

18. It is presumably undesirable to have to dispose of, or live with, defective fetuses or infants resulting from genetic engineering that fails. But it is also undesirable to have to dispose of, or live with, fetuses or infants that are genetically defective because we did not practice genetic engineering to avoid or cure these defects. Which of these alternatives is worse? Why? Is there any way we could avoid this hard choice? If so, how? If not, which should we choose?

19. Some argue that genetic engineering would improve humanity; others argue that it would degrade humanity. Are these two arguments diametrically opposed or do they appeal to very different kinds of consequences? Could one consistently hold that genetic engineering would *both* improve and degrade humanity? If so, how would one decide whether, on balance, it would be desirable or undesirable? If not, why not?

20. Precisely what is human dignity? Is it some characteristic intrinsic to human nature or does it consist in some attitude, perhaps respect, that others take toward a human being? Precisely how might genetic engineering damage human dignity? If it did, why would this be undesirable? Would it be more undesirable than the genetic diseases that might be prevented by genetic engineering?

21. Would genetic engineering in fact stigmatize human beings afflicted with genetic defects? Does a physician who diagnoses a genetic disease stigmatize the patient? If so, is the diagnosis of genetic diseases undesirable? If not, why is it that genetic engineering, unlike genetic diagnosis, does stigmatize?

22. What gives sexual intercourse its meaning for the couple engaging in it? Does all of its significance come from the expectation that this sexual act will procreate a child? Suppose that only a part of its meaning comes from the natural connection between sexual intercourse and procreation, how important is this part of its significance?

23. Distinguish carefully between the very different ways in which genetic engineering is alleged to strain the parent–child relationship. Are these all equally likely to occur in fact? Would they be equally undesirable if in fact they were to occur?

24. The parental responsibility for the genetic defects of a child resulting from genetic engineering is grave indeed, but so is the parental responsibility for the child whose defects might have been avoided had they chosen to use genetic engineering. Is there any way for contemporary parents to avoid responsibility for the genetic inheritance of their children? If so, how? If not, why not? Is there any way to reduce, if not avoid, this responsibility?

25. Is the common desire to have children "of one's own," with one's own genetic inheritance, an irrational and outmoded sentiment or a reasonable desire that our society ought to respect? Why?

26. Does the biological relation between parent and child impose any moral duties or confer any moral rights? Imagine that an unmarried woman gives up her baby for adoption two days after birth. If she later becomes wealthy, does she have any moral obligation to help pay for the baby's college education? If she later decides that she wants to bring up her child, does she have any right to demand that the adoptive parents return the child to her? Give reasons to support your answers to these difficult questions.

27. The author concludes that genetic engineering is desirable only if it is freely chosen by the parents. But in a number of recent "wrongful life" cases, medical malpractice cases in which an infant has sued a physician for wrongfully causing him or her to be born, the court has held that an infant has a right not be born defective. Is there really any such right? If so, ought society to compel parents to respect this right by using genetic engineering to avoid the birth of any infant suffering from serious genetic defects?

28. The author accepts negative eugenics but rejects positive eugenics. Can one accept the one and reject the other without self-contradiction? If so, is this a reasonable position to hold? Why or why not?

BIBLIOGRAPHY

BAYLES, MICHAEL D. *Reproductive Ethics*. Englewood Cliffs, N.J.: Prentice-Hall, 1984.
BUCKLEY, JOHN J., JR., ed. *Genetics Now: Ethical Issues in Genetic Research*. Washington, D.C.: University Press of America, 1978.

ELLISON, CRAIG W., ed. *Modifying Man.* Washington, D.C.: University Press of America, 1978.
ETZIONI, AMITAI. *Genetic Fix: The Next Technological Revolution.* New York: Harper & Row, 1975.
FLETCHER, JOSEPH. *Ethics of Genetic Control: Ending Reproductive Roulette.* Garden City, N.Y.: Doubleday, 1974.
GLOVER, JONATHAN. *What Sort of People Should There Be?* New York: Penguin, 1984.
GOODFIELD, JUNE. *Playing God: Genetic Engineering and the Manipulation of Life.* New York: Random House, 1977.
HILTON, BRUCE, et al. *Ethical Issues in Human Genetics: Genetic Counseling and the Use of Genetic Knowledge.* New York: Plenum Press, 1973.
LAPPÉ, MARC. *Genetics Politics: The Limits of Biological Control.* New York: Simon and Schuster, 1979.
LIPKIN, MACK, JR., AND ROWLEY, P. T., eds. *Genetic Responsibility: On Choosing Our Children's Genes.* New York: Plenum Press, 1974.
LUDMERER, KENNETH M. *Genetics and American Society.* Baltimore: Johns Hopkins University Press, 1972.
RAMSEY, PAUL. *Fabricated Man: The Ethics of Genetic Control.* New Haven: Yale University Press, 1970.
STABLEFORD, BRIAN. *Future Man: Brave New World or Genetic Nightmare?* New York: Crown, 1984.
TEICHLER-ZALLEN, DORIS, AND CLEMENTS, COLLEEN D., eds. *Science and Morality: New Directions in Bioethics.* Lexington, Mass.: Lexington Books, 1982.
WADE, NICHOLAS. *The Ultimate Experiments.* New York: Walker and Co., 1977.

4
THE GOOD

Abhor that which is evil; cleave to that which is good.

Men always love what is good or what they find good; it is in judging what is good that they go wrong.

J.-J. Rousseau in *The Social Contract*

We have been considering the debate between those who claim that the genetic engineering of humans is good and those who contend that it is bad. Each side can and does advance plausible arguments to support its conclusion. It is relevant here to point out that each of these arguments, whichever side of the issue it supports, presupposes some judgment of value. To argue that genetic engineering is good because it prevents illness or increases knowledge, for example, presupposes that preventing illness and increasing knowledge are good. On the other hand, to argue that genetic engineering is bad because it imposes risks or strains the parent–child relationship tacitly assumes that risk and a strained relation between parent and child are bad. The soundness of each argument, then, depends in part upon the correctness of the value judgment it takes for granted.

No value judgment is immune to challenge. One can always deny the truth of any evaluation or, more mildly, ask for reasons to accept its truth. One can ask, "Why is knowledge good?" or "Why is risk bad?" Notice that there are two very different answers that one might give to the first question. One might reply that knowledge is useful, that it can be applied in practice to increase human happiness, or that knowledge is good for its own sake, desirable quite apart from its consequences. Accordingly, many philosophers distinguish between extrinsic and intrinsic value. An object has extrinsic value when the ground of its value lies in its relation to some other thing of value; an object has intrinsic value when the ground of its value lies within the nature of the thing itself.

Moral philosophers have traditionally paid more attention to intrinsic value than to extrinsic value. One of the reasons is probably that judgments of extrinsic value are based upon and derived from judgments of intrinsic value. The nature of this dependence might be made a little clearer if we consider the evaluation of suicide. No one, I suppose, takes suicide to be desirable for its own sake, apart from its consequences. But sometimes a desperate person may still think suicide worthwhile. Why might someone in despair judge it good? Probably because it is a means to ending intolerable suffering, something judged very bad for its own sake. Such a person doubtless also regards suicide as a means to ending life, which is not deemed of any real value in itself. The person who believes suicide bad even in the worst of circumstances probably assumes very different judgments of intrinsic value to support that belief. Suffering is not considered so very bad in itself, while life, human existence, is judged to have tremendous value for its own sake. Thus disagreement about the extrinsic value or disvalue of suicide depends on more basic disagreements about the intrinsic value or disvalue of suffering and life. Each person derives conclusions about suicide from premises concerning the intrinsic value or disvalue of those other things connected with suicide. If the reason why anything has extrinsic value lies, by definition, in the value of one or more *other* things, then the rational justification of any judgment of extrinsic value must consist of evaluations of those other things themselves. And if those other things have only extrinsic value, then any evaluation of them must be derived from evaluations of still other things. In the end, however, all judgments of value must rest on judgments of intrinsic value, evaluations of things that have value for their own sake. Because these judgments of intrinsic value are logically fundamental, it is these which interest the philosopher most.

Moreover, if the moral philosopher could discover one or a few things that alone have intrinsic value, these things would then afford reasonable grounds for drawing conclusions about the value or disvalue of everything else. If it turned out, for example, that the only thing of intrinsic value is human happiness, then this would be the basis for evaluating people, pens, and drugs. Those people, pens, and drugs that increase human happiness would be good; those that destroy or lessen human happiness would be bad. To evaluate anything in the world we would have only to trace its connections with human happiness, or whatever else is judged intrinsically good. Since all extrinsic value is derived from intrinsic value, a knowledge of what is intrinsically good yields knowledge of extrinsic value as well.

For moral philosophers concerned with value, therefore, the key question is "What is intrinsically good?" The problem is to determine what kind or kinds of things are good, not just because they lead to other good things, but because of their own nature. The answer to this question, if systematically elaborated, constitutes a theory of value, or at least the core of such a theory.

Before going on to review a few of the more important theories of value, we might pause and reflect on the difference between theories of value and theories of obligation, some of which were treated in Chapter 2. One difference is that a theory of value must apply to a wide variety of things, while a theory of obligation applies only to actions. Only the acts of a moral agent can be right or wrong; but people and pens, dreams and paintings, jobs and experiences can be good or bad. A theory of obligation must explain what it is that makes any action right or wrong, the reason why one ought or ought not to do the act. A theory of value must explain what makes anything good or bad, the reason why it is desirable and worthy of pursuit or undesirable and to be avoided. Just as doing and desiring are distinct, so theories about the grounds of doing are distinct from theories about the rational grounds of desiring.

The two kinds of theory will nonetheless be connected in any complete moral philosophy or ethical system. Any teleological theory of obligation calls for some theory of value to complete it. Any theory that grounds the distinction between right and wrong in the difference between good and bad can be applied in practice only if it is accompanied by some theory about the nature of value and disvalue. Even a deontological theory of obligation, one that does not base obligation exclusively on value, will need to be supplemented with some view about what makes some things worthy of pursuit and others unworthy of human desire. The philosophical task, therefore, is not just to find a theory of obligation that seems correct and to find a theory of value that can be defended rationally. The task is to combine a theory of obligation and a theory of value into a systematic moral philosophy that will adequately answer every moral problem that can arise in human life. Having reached some tentative conclusions about right and wrong, let us try to answer the question, "What is intrinsically good?"

THEORIES OF VALUE

Pleasure

A perennially popular view is that pleasure is the good. This theory, called *hedonism*, has been defended by many philosophers including Epicurus in classical times and John Stuart Mill in the nineteenth century. Hedonism asserts that the only intrinsically good thing is pleasure and that the one thing that is intrinsically bad is pain. It does not deny, of course, that a great many things other than pleasure are good. Money, medicine, and people, to mention a very few, are certainly good. These things, however, are extrinsically rather than intrinsically good; they are of value only because in one way or another they lead to or cause pleasure. Money is good because with it we can buy things that are pleasant to contemplate or consume. Medicine is good because it dispels the pain of illness and allows us pleasures we can enjoy only when we are in good health. And good people are those whose actions bring pleasure to others. Careful examination of the tremendous variety of good things in our world shows that their value springs from a single source—pleasure. Everything that is desirable is either a pleasant experience or a cause of pleasant experiences. The one and only thing that is good for its own sake is pleasure.

One advantage of hedonism is that, of all the worthwhile things in our world, pleasure is the one that is most obviously good for its own sake. If one were to draw up a list of good things, pleasure would almost certainly be included on that list. We are all familiar with pleasures of various kinds, and we all prize them to a greater or lesser degree. Again, if one were to go through the list and cross off those items whose value seemed derived from their consequences, one would leave pleasure unexcised. Whatever it is that is intrinsically good must be good because of its own nature. Now it would be hard to deny that pleasure is good, although not so hard to deny that it is the greatest good in life. And if we ask ourselves *why* pleasure is good, we are not at all tempted to look to other things connected with it. The reason why pleasure is good lies in its very nature; pleasant experiences are prized just because they are pleasant and for no other reason. Ordinary and humble as pleasure may be compared to knowledge or virtue or power, at least it is clearly good for its own sake. Therefore, it is the most obvious candidate for the good, that which is intrinsically good.

Nevertheless, many philosophers reject this obvious answer as somehow degrading. What is pleasure, anyway? "Pleasure" is simply the name we give to certain feelings, like the feeling of satisfaction we get when we eat a tasty meal or the glow we feel inside when someone pays us a compliment. That pleasures are feelings is indicated both by the fact that we speak of "feeling pleasure" and by the fact that we cannot imagine what an unfelt pleasure would be. Now feelings are very different from ideas or images or judgments. The feeling of hunger is a pang of which one is conscious, and it is not to be confused with the idea of food or the image of a steak or the judgment that one's body is depleted. Ideas, images, and judgments all refer to something beyond themselves; one has an idea *of* something, an image *of* something, or a judgment *about* something. A feeling, on the other hand, is a self-contained state of consciousness that does not point to anything outside itself. Accordingly, having a feeling does not usually or necessarily involve intellect or imagination or conscience, but only that rudimentary form of consciousness human beings share with animals. It is for precisely this reason that hedonism is so often thought to be degrading. It finds the good, the ultimate goal of all human desire and striving, in mere feelings. It thereby excludes the higher faculties of intelligence and imagination from the good life and seems to imply that a human being should aim at no higher goal than animal sensations, for pigs and cattle presumably feel pleasure when they eat or lie in the sun just as human beings do. Those who reject the notion that all human goods can be reduced to mere feelings of pleasure seek some other answer to the question, "What is intrinsically good?"

The Object of Positive Interest

Ralph Barton Perry, a twentieth-century American philosopher, is probably the best known advocate of the interest theory of value. According to this theory, to be good is to be the object of positive interest. An interest is a mental state or disposition of being for or against something. Examples of such pro and con attitudes are desire and aversion, liking and disliking, love and hate, approval and disapproval, admiration and contempt. Interests go in pairs; in each pair the first is favorable toward its object and the second is unfavorable. Anything that is the object of a favorable interest, anything that is desired or liked or loved, is good; to be bad is simply to be disliked or hated or disapproved. The interest someone takes in something makes it good, confers value upon it. Thus, we do not desire steak because it is good; it is good because we desire it. There is no property of goodness in the steak to arouse our desire; there is only tenderness, juiciness, and meaty flavor in the steak. The steak becomes valuable when we want to have it and like to eat it. If, however, everyone were to lose all interest in steak, it would lose all its value.

This interest theory of value is a general theory of value. That is, it is supposed to explain all kinds of goodness and badness. To be good is to be the object of positive interest; to be bad is to be the object of negative interest. This definition covers both intrinsic and extrinsic value. To define intrinsic value, therefore, we must add some further qualification. To be intrinsically good is to be the object of positive interest for its own sake. Some things, like pleasure, we desire for their own sake, just because they are the kinds of things they are. Other things we desire or like or approve, not for their own sake, but for the sake of the other things they bring with them. Most of us desire medicine only for the sake of its curative effects upon us. We do not like the taste of medicine or admire the color and shape of pills; we want to take medication because we want to get rid of pain or discomfort and become well enough to return to active life. The things we desire or like or love only for the sake of their consequences or concomitants have extrinsic value. Intrinsic value consists in being the object of positive interest for its own sake.

In order to avoid misunderstanding, we must distinguish between the sense in which this theory of value is relativistic and the sense in which it is not. For something to be good it must be desired or liked or loved or admired or approved. Thus value consists in a relation between the valuable object and one or more persons who take an interest in that object. It follows that nothing is good or bad in itself; things are always good or bad *for* someone who takes an interest in them. Obviously, the very same thing can be good for one person and bad for another. I desire kippered herrings; I want to have them and like to eat them for breakfast. For me kippers are good. But kippers are bad for my son who dislikes their taste, detests their smell, and has a strong aversion to eating them. In this sense value is relative. Any object is good or bad relative to someone who takes an interest in it.

There is another sense, however, in which value is not relative. The truth or falsity of any value judgment is not relative to the judger. If my son thinks that kippers are bad for him and I firmly believe that they are good for him, we cannot both be correct. Thinking that something is good does not make it good, and believing that something is bad does not make it bad. Although value is always value *for* someone, whether or not the object does have value for that person is a matter of objective fact. If my son does not like or desire or want kippers, then my belief that they are good for him is just plain false. The existence or nonexistence of an interest, and consequently of the value conferred by that interest, is a matter of objective fact independent of anyone's opinion. The interest theory of value might be said to be a version of objective relativism. Value is relative to the valuer; in this sense good and bad are relative. But judgments of value are objectively true or false; in this sense values are objective.

One of the strong points of the interest theory of value is the way it can explain the variety of good things. We apply one and the same word, "good," to a wide variety of things. Moral philosophers have long sought some essence of goodness shared by all these heterogeneous things. But as we reflect on the diversity of things we call good, it is very hard to find anything they have in common that might explain their goodness. What, for example, do the pleasure of sipping wine and the bitter medicine one swallows reluctantly have in common to make them both good? What do a useful pen and a moving symphony share to give them their very different kinds of value? Is there any one property that explains the value of a thousand dollars and a person whose virtue is beyond all price? The more we look at good things in our mind's eye, the more diversity and less homogeneity we find. But what all good things have in common is the positive interest we take in them. We can desire or like or admire a wide variety of objects: wine and medicine, pens and symphonies, money and people. Hence, the interest theory of value can easily explain how such a wide variety of things can all be good.

Still, one may wonder whether positive interest really does confer value. Does desire, for example, always make its object good? Hard experience seems to teach us that the fact that something is desired does not guarantee that it is desirable. I may desire the ripe red apple sitting on the fruit vendor's cart. Perhaps I buy it and take it home, wanting to eat it all the time. After lunch I bite into it only to find it rotten and worm-infested inside. What are we to say of the apple? The interest theory of value implies that the apple was good from the moment I set eyes on it until that awful moment when I bit into it and lost all interest in it. Most of us would prefer to say that the apple was bad ever since it went rotten and became wormy. My misplaced desire for the apple does nothing to make it a good apple. Again, take the example of revenge. An angry person may intensely desire revenge. He certainly wants revenge and may even like it when he gets it. Does this make revenge good for him? Not necessarily. Revenge may bring harm to the avenger in the form of reprisals, unforeseen consequences or regretted actions. Many of us, alas, are irrational enough to want revenge even at such a price. Does our irrational wanting confer genuine value on revenge? In retrospect, in the cool hour of reason, we think not and regret our vengeance. If desire can be misplaced, if we can want something only to find out later that it was not worth wanting, then value cannot consist simply in being the object of positive interest.

These first two answers to our question, hedonism and the interest theory of value, are both naturalistic; they seek to explain value within a naturalistic metaphysics. Both theories locate value within our natural world and require no realities or categories that transcend nature in order to explain what makes things good or bad. Other moral philosophers have thought of good and bad in very different terms. Theologians usually explain good and bad in terms of God or the eternal soul. Such theories are supernatural because they assert the existence of realities that lie outside the world revealed by the natural sciences and use concepts that go beyond the natural in defining value. Let us consider next two theories of value that have usually been associated with theology.

The Vision of God

Saint Augustine, a fourth-century Christian theologian, argues that it is a mistake to seek the nature of goodness in the earthly things we ordinarily call good. Pleasure, money, power, and health are not real and genuine goods. For one thing, they are too precarious. Personal fortunes may be lost and power may be usurped, or an accident may rob a person of his health. It is foolish to prize things that may be taken away no matter what is done to protect or preserve them. Again, worldly goods never really do satisfy their possessor. We all know or have heard of very rich people who live unhappy and miserable lives. The libertine who lives a life of pleasure may find that existence empty and unsatisfying. The real good, the ultimate goal of human life, lies outside this world in heavenly salvation.

Heavenly bliss cannot be described in earthly terms. Since these are the only terms we fully understand, the most we can do is to hint at the nature of salvation by analogy with our present experiences. When one is saved, one draws near to God; one sees God "face to face." This vision of God is the only thing of real, intrinsic value. It cannot be taken away, for salvation is a state of eternal bliss. It satisfies one fully, for it is the final goal of all human striving. This vision of God is a state of heavenly bliss incomparably more satisfying than the worldly satisfactions with which we are familiar. It is some sort of direct experience of God in which the soul of the perceiver is transformed and a state of complete ecstasy is attained. This vision of God is the only thing worth pursuing for its own sake. Every other good is merely a means to this.

One thing that can be said for this theory is that it sets up a goal worthy of human effort. It would be hard to imagine anything better than heavenly bliss; if anything is genuinely good, surely this is. God is by very definition perfect, for only a perfect being could be divine, an object worthy of worship. Thus, God is completely perfect in every respect. It follows at once that the highest good for human beings would be to attain and possess God. But what could it be for a human being to attain or possess God? No mere human could literally become God as one might become a policeman or a philosopher. Nor could one own God as one owns books or other tangible things. The only possibility is that one "draw near" to God. What it means to attain or possess God is to see Him, to be directly aware of Him, and to feel at one with Him. Since God is perfect, this vision of God is the highest perfection in which human beings can participate.

But can a mere human being really participate in the perfection of God? Let us grant that the vision of God, if it were possible, would be complete bliss. Is any such vision possible? Can God, if He exists, be perceived at all through our limited human faculties? Worse yet, atheists deny and agnostics doubt the very existence of God; there can be no seeing where there is nothing to be seen. Perhaps the vision of God is an illusory goal of human endeavor. The fact that it would be perfect if it could be attained is small consolation if it is in fact unattainable. If anything we actually do attain has any real value, its goodness must be explained in some other way.

Love

Another theory of value associated with a long religious tradition, recently made popular by Christian moralists like Joseph Fletcher, is that the one thing of intrinsic value is love. Although love can be thought of naturalistically in terms borrowed from the science of psychology, the traditional paradigm of love has its source in a supernatural theology. The creation and preservation of the human race is an outpouring of the benevolent love of God, and the redemption of humanity by the sacrifice of Christ upon the cross is the supreme example of a loving act. According to this theory, love is the only thing that is good for its own sake, and the one thing that is intrinsically bad is hate.

To properly interpret this theory of value we must take care to distinguish two very different sorts of love. I just love hamburgers, particularly when broiled over charcoal. This sort of love, called *eros*, is a desire to possess something one lacks. My love of hamburgers springs from a lack or imperfection in me; my hunger expresses the depletion of nourishment in my body. The goal of my desire is possession. What I want is not simply that hamburgers exist or even that they prosper; my object is to get my hands on hamburgers and to devour them. I love to get *my* hands on hamburgers and to devour them *myself*. This sort of love is self-centered and very close to selfish. The love of God for humanity is a very different sort of love. God did not create human life because He hoped to gain something from His creation. Being perfect, God is lacking in nothing and needs nothing any mortal could possibly give. God's redemption of humanity by the sacrifice of Christ was not a selfish act; it was motivated by a selfless concern for the welfare of all human beings, even the most sinful. This sort of love is called *agape*. It does not spring from any lack in the lover, but from a selfless concern for the well-being of the loved object. It is this sort of love, agape, that is the one thing of intrinsic value. It is good for its own sake, and it makes all the other good things in the world worthwhile.

This theory of value does seem to recognize one important truth: love is the most precious of all things. When we reflect on the lives of friends and acquaintances and ask ourselves what really makes a human life good or bad, the answer seems to be love or the absence of love. Somehow money, pleasure and even health are no guarantee of happiness, nor is their absence any sure sign of misery. More than any other single factor, what determines the quality of a human life is the kind of personal relations that one has with one's family, friends, and associates. If these personal relations are transfused with love, one is happy. If these relations are characterized by hate, envy, or even cold indifference, one lives a hard and unsatisfying life. Ultimately, then, the good life depends on love more than on any other single thing. The theory that love is the only thing of intrinsic value can explain why it is that love is so central to the good life. If love is the ultimate source of all value, then of course it is love that gives value to our lives.

Some philosophers, however, charge that a logical fallacy lies in such reasoning. Let us grant, for the sake of the argument, that love is the most valuable of all things. Does it follow that its value is intrinsic? It might be that love is precious just because it is a means to happiness. The presence of love transforms human relations in such a way as to make those who love one another happy. The lack of love is the worst of evils because without love human beings cause each other untold pain and suffering. The fact that love is the greatest of values, the most precious of things, even if true, does not imply that love has any intrinsic value, much less that it is the only thing that is good for its own sake.

Virtue

Epictetus, a first-century Stoic, maintained that only virtue is intrinsically good. The essence of human nature, that which distinguishes humans from other kinds of beings and makes them what they are, is reason. Hence, human virtue or the specific excellence of human life is living according to reason. Each human being embodies a spark of the Divine Reason, and God is thought of as a cosmic Reason guiding the course of nature. Accordingly, virtue can be spoken of either as living according to reason or living according to nature. When the passions or emotions overpower human reason, then a person's acts are evil. Greed causes people to steal; lust causes them to commit adultery; and ambition leads them to betray those who trust them. Virtue requires that our reason master our passions. When reason subdues the emotions, a person can accept the course of nature as expressing a Divine Providence and do his duty in every situation.

Virtue is the only thing that is good for its own sake because ultimately it is the only thing that really matters in life. Other things like wealth, power, health, or life itself may seem to be important, but they are not. None of these things can guarantee that a person will be happy; neither is the absence of any of them sure to make a person miserable. Wealthy individuals are not always happy, and many of us have known someone who has lived happily in spite of poverty. Power brings with it the fear of attack and a mistrust of those who pretend to be friends, while people with no real power are often contented enough. Men and women with strength of will can be happy in sickness; those without will-power are often miserable in health. Even death is no real evil, as the example of Socrates calmly meeting his death shows. Death is made to appear terrible by the fear and cowardice of weak-willed individuals. The only thing that determines whether a person lives well or badly is whether he lives virtuously or not. Therefore, virtue is the only thing that is intrinsically good.

The theory that only virtue is intrinsically good is plausible because virtue does seem to be good for its own sake. A virtuous act appears to be good quite apart from its consequences. When a solder dies bravely in a good cause without completing his mission, his act, judged by its consequences, is a failure. We might say that his virtuous act "did not do any good," but we would not deny that his courageous act was good. Or suppose that a woman jumps into an icy river and tries to save a drowning child. The fact that she fails to reach the child in time does not prevent us from recognizing that she has done a very fine thing. She did not succeed in saving a human life, but her act was good in spite of its consequences (or lack of them) because it was a brave and conscientious act. Since virtuous acts may be good even when they have no worthwhile consequences, the value of virtue must be intrinsic.

Still, it seems to be an exaggeration to claim that only virtue is intrinsically good, that nothing else really matters in life. It may be true that nothing else can necessarily make the difference between perfect happiness and complete misery. But from the fact, if it is a fact, that nothing else makes all the difference to the value of one's life, it does not follow that nothing else makes any difference at all. Pleasures, for example, have a value just as real, if less exalted, as the value of virtuous acts. Pleasures, from the enjoyment of a fine meal to the satisfaction of having done one's duty, seem to be good for their own sake. If so, it is a mistake to claim that only virtue is intrinsically good.

Power

Friedrich Nietzsche, a nineteenth-century German Idealist, held that the intrinsically good thing is power. When he speaks of power, he does not mean sheer brute physical strength. The battering fullback and bruising tackle, at least if their stereotypes are accurate, are not Nietzsche's ideal of the powerful man. Nor does he mean political or economic power, although these are less wide of the mark. The powerful person may be a military leader like Napoleon or a business leader like J. P. Morgan, but Jesus, Socrates, and Wagner were also powerful personalities in their various ways. What Nietzsche has in mind might be called "psychological power"; it is that inner strength that characterizes a genuinely powerful personality. Psychological power is a complex thing. It involves strong emotions, great will-power, high intelligence, creative imagination, daring, and self-discipline. Powerful individuals will dream dreams so original that ordinary people can hardly understand them; they will dare to act out their dreams despite the mistrust and opposition of the crowd; and they will have the drive and discipline to carry through their schemes to the end. They may suffer in the process, but the deep satisfactions in the creative exercise of power far outweigh any incidental pains. The one thing of real, intrinsic value is power.

This is an appealing theory because there is a nobility in the life of power. Powerful personalities rise above common experience. They suffer more than most, but their joys are greater, too. The life of a powerful person has a depth, fullness, and richness we long for in our own. Notice our attitude toward tragedy. Why do we pay money to go and watch Antigone or Othello suffer? Perhaps because these powerful personalities reveal the highest that human life has to offer. In spite of their very real misfortunes, we are exalted by their example, for they show us dramatically that the powerful life is the best life to which a human being can aspire.

On the other hand, sheer power does not always seem good. Sometimes the exercise of power seems meaningless and pointless. Consider a business tycoon building up a huge commercial and industrial empire from almost nothing; only a powerful personality could accomplish this. Let us suppose also that this particular tycoon is not motivated by any concern for the general economy or for the welfare of his country. He or she is not even trying to provide pleasures, comforts, or security for the family. He or she just likes to engage in business dealings for their own sake. Thus divorced from all concern for consequences or larger purpose, the exercise of power seems to become trivial, meaningless, and pointless. At other times the life of power seems positively evil. Hitler had the power to dream huge dreams and to dominate those around him. Yet this powerful person devoted his energies to immoral purposes like subjugating Europe and exterminating the Jews. Power used in this way seems evil rather than good. There is real doubt, therefore, that power is always good for its own sake.

Self-Realization

Francis Herbert Bradley, a twentieth-century British Idealist, argued that the one thing that is intrinsically good is self-realization. The self, the individual living being, is not born complete and perfect. It grows and develops into a mature individual; or if it ceases to exercise its capacities, it begins to atrophy and deteriorate. The acorn either grows into a tall, healthy, leafy oak tree or it fails to achieve its natural end and rots or becomes a distorted, stunted tree. The good for any living thing is to actualize all its potentialities, to realize its own nature. Self-realization is the one thing good for its own sake.

What does this mean for a human being? Bradley assumes that the good, whatever it may be, must satisfy human desire. The trouble is that a human being has so many desires, not all of which can be satisfied together. The desire to eat and drink in large quantities conflicts with the desire to stay healthy. The desire to become rich or get good grades is incompatible with the desire to relax and enjoy the pleasures of loafing. Clearly, nothing is going to satisfy all these desires. Genuine satisfaction is possible only if one can modify one's desires so that they do not conflict. The ideal is to develop a coherent set of desires, a set that includes as many desires as possible in a harmonious fashion. In deciding whether abundant eating or robust health is more important, in deciding whether to live ambitiously or at a more leisurely pace, one is deciding what kind of person one wishes to become. It is by integrating one's desires that one becomes a self, an individual person. Thus, the realization of oneself is what makes real satisfaction possible. Ultimately, the only thing that matters in life is self-realization. It is this and this alone that is good for its own sake.

One consideration that argues for this theory of value is the fact that what is good for any living thing does seem to depend on the nature of that thing. Birds thrive in the air and drown in water; fish prosper in water and die in the air. What is of value to a human being may be worthless to an animal; even the most refined French poodle will derive little benefit or enjoyment from sitting through a performance of Molière's *Tartuffe*. The value of any object does seem to depend upon the kind of self for which it is valuable. One advantage of this theory is that it can easily explain why value is relative to species, why something of value to one species of living organism may be of no value or even harmful to another. If the good is self-realization, then the value of anything obviously depends upon the kind of self that is to be realized. Something that will contribute to the realization of one kind of self may not aid at all in the realization of some other sort of self.

A disadvantage of this theory is that it is hard to give content to it; that is, it is hard to use this theory to reach definite conclusions about the value or disvalue of any given object. The crucial difficulty lies in distinguishing between self-realization and self-deformation. How is one to know whether some modification or change in an individual is developing the potentialities inherent in its nature or distorting and frustrating its real nature? Does putting artificial fertilizers and extra water on a flower garden help the flowers to achieve their true flowerhood or does it turn them into unnaturally large deviants from the species? The Japanese prune their pine trees so that they take on unusual and interesting shapes. To our eye the result may look like a distorted and deformed tree, but to the Japanese gardener it may appear to be just what a pine tree should be. The same sort of difficulty arises in evaluating human goals. Do gourmets develop their human nature as their appetites for food and drink become more refined? Well, they certainly develop a capacity *in* human nature, but to many it is an aspect that is more animal than human. What, then, of the intellectual who becomes so immersed in books and ideas that all contact is lost with the concerns of the average person? It can be argued that the intellectual is realizing human nature by developing the highest human capacity, reason. But it can equally be argued that such a person is failing to develop many other genuine aspects of human nature. The theory that the good is self-realization is not very helpful unless it can tell us which changes or goals realize the true nature of the self and which are deviations from that nature. As it stands, this theory offers no clear criterion of value.

Several Irreducible Things

Traditionally moral philosophers have looked for *the* good. Although they have recognized that there are many different kinds of good things in our world, they have assumed that if one probes deep enough one will find that they all derive their value from some single, basic thing. William David Ross, a British moral philosopher, has challenged this assumption. Why take it for granted that one and only one thing is intrinsically good? Actually, there are several irreducible goods in this world.

Pleasure, at least if it is neither undeserved nor malicious, is obviously good for its own sake. But virtue is also good. A world with a given amount of pleasure in it would be less valuable than another world with the same amount of pleasure plus virtue. If adding virtue to a world makes it better, then virtue must have some real value. And since adding this amount of virtue does not, by hypothesis, increase the amount of pleasure in this world, this value must belong to the virtue itself, and not to any pleasant consequences that might result from virtuous acts. The same sort of argument shows that knowledge has intrinsic value, for adding knowledge to a world increases the value of that world. A fourth basic kind of good is the distribution of pleasure and pain according to virtue and vice. Let us compare two imaginary worlds. Each has the same amounts of pleasure and pain, virtue and vice; but in one world the virtuous enjoy the pleasure and the vicious suffer the pain, while in the other world the vicious enjoy the pleasure and the virtuous suffer the pain. Which is the better world? If the answer is that the former is the better world, this shows that the distribution of pleasure and pain according to desert is itself an additional good. Thus Ross concludes that there are four things that are intrinsically good— pleasure, virtue, knowledge, and the distribution of pleasure and pain according to virtue. These cannot be reduced to any single intrinsic good because they do not share any single good-making property. This theory can be labelled "axiological pluralism." *Axiology* is philosophical jargon for theory of value. This theory is axiological because it is a theory of value. It is a version of pluralism because it holds that several things are good for their own sake. In spite of its technical name, axiological pluralism is very close to common sense. Common sense, uncontaminated by philosophical speculation, would suggest that several different kinds of things are good for their own sake.

One strength of this theory is that it does seem to do justice to the variety of goods in our world. Everyone, of course, has to admit that many different kinds of things are valuable—automobiles, paintings, people, pleasant experiences, bitter medicines, technical skills, fine wines, good health, money, etc. Most theories of value, however, are forced to show that most of these things have only a derivative or borrowed value. Axiological monisms, theories that claim that only one thing is intrinsically good, are confronted with the task of showing that everything of value derives its goodness from a single source. Even imaginative philosophers find this no easy task. Since Ross asserts that there are four sources of value, he finds it much less difficult to trace the value of everything to something that is good for its own sake. In this way, axiological pluralism seems to account for the diversity of good things better than any axiological monism.

Nevertheless, axiological pluralism does seem to have one awkward consequence. It seems to imply that there are some important decisions for which it can offer no rational guidance. The crux of this theory is that there are several fundamentally different kinds of things that are intrinsically good. Imagine, for example, a situation that involves choosing between two of these. Suppose that one must choose whether to pursue the pleasure of sex at the loss of virtue or strive for virtue with the loss of pleasure. How could one decide which alternative is the greater good? If pleasure and virtue have no single good-making characteristic, then there seems to be no common denominator of value between them. If so, then their value is incommensurable; there is no single measure by which the value of pleasure gained or lost can be weighed against the value of virtue gained or lost. In this way axiological pluralism seems to imply that there is no rational basis for making judgments of comparative value in cases where the goods involved are of irreducibly different kinds. When faced with a choice between such radically diverse goods, axiological pluralism leaves us without any rational guidance. If one of the important functions of any theory of value is to provide a theoretical framework that will enable human beings to choose rationally between better and worse alternatives, then axiological pluralism cannot always perform this function.

Ethics is concerned with practice, with human decision and conduct. Many, if not all, decisions involve choosing between goals of action, objects worth striving for or to be avoided. For this reason, any intelligent decision requires the moral agent to evaluate the objects one might set up as goals of conduct. Accordingly, moral philosophers take as one of their tasks working out a theory of value—some theory that will explain just what it is that makes anything good or bad, desirable or undesirable. Objects with extrinsic value derive their goodness from other things that ultimately are good for their own sake. The fundamental theoretical question, therefore, is "What is intrinsically good?" We have glanced at eight answers to this general ethical question: pleasure, the object of positive interest, the vision of God, love, virtue, power, self-realization, and several irreducible things. Since moral philosophers dispute the relative merit of each of these answers, the student of philosophy cannot rest content with memorizing any one of these theories as the established truth. Instead, one must try to understand the various theories of value that have been advanced and ponder the arguments that can be given for and against each theory. If none of the traditional theories can withstand rational criticism, it will be necessary to modify some traditional theory or formulate some new answer that is more adequate.

AXIOLOGICAL PLURALISM AGAIN

When I reflect on various theories of value, I am strongly tempted to adopt hedonism. I agree with it that whatever it is that has intrinsic value must be something that is felt, something of which some mind is conscious. The good is, as Henry Sidgwick, a British moral philosopher, put it, desirable consciousness. Other things—physical objects, human beings, animals, actions, social institutions, or theories—have only extrinsic value; they are good or bad only as they make a difference to some experience. This experience need not be human. Presumably animals can feel pleasure and pain and, consequently, have desirable and undesirable experiences. Still, the only thing that is intrinsically good or bad is experience.

That experience is the only thing that is good for its own sake can be proved, I believe, from the fact that the question "Why?" always leads to and stops at experience. Whenever it is claimed that something is good or bad, one can always ask, "Why is it good?" or "Why is it bad?" It is always meaningful and legitimate to ask what reason a person has to justify a particular value judgment, what it is that makes the object good or bad. If one pushes this demand for the grounds of the value of anything other than an experience, sooner or later the reason why the object has value turns out to be that it produces or prevents some experience. Why is money good? Because we can buy food and medicine and paintings with it. Why is food good? Because we can eat it. Why is eating food good? Because eating food is an enjoyable experience and also nourishes the body. Why is nourishing the body good? Because it prevents the pangs of hunger, helps us to feel well, and enables us to engage in enjoyable activities. Why is medicine good? Because it is can cure disease. Why is curing disease good? Because it does away with the discomfort of illness and makes us feel better. Why are paintings good? Because we can look at them. Why is looking at paintings good? Because it is an enjoyable experience. In this way the question "Why?" always leads ultimately to experience. But suppose we persist and ask why the experiences of eating food, feeling well, and contemplating paintings are good? The appropriate answers seem to describe the nature of these experiences, not to point to any further consequences. Just as the question "Why?" leads to experience, so it stops at experience. The experience of eating food is good because the experience is pleasant; the experience of contemplating a painting is good because it is interesting and perhaps exciting.

It is at this point that I part company with hedonism. The hedonist maintains that the only characteristic that makes an experience intrinsically good is its pleasantness. I believe, on the contrary, that there are a great many very different characteristics that can make an experience good for its own sake. For the hedonist, paradigm cases of good experiences would seem to be the pleasures of eating, drinking, and sexual intercourse. That such pleasures are good can hardly be denied, nor need we doubt that they derive part of their intrinsic value from their pleasantness. But is it really true that none of their value is due to their other characteristics? Consider, for example, the experience of eating a tender, tasty, charcoal-broiled steak. One component of this experience is a feeling of pleasure or a glow of gratification. It would be a mistake, however, to infer from the fact that this pleasant component is good that the value of the total experience is derived from the pleasure alone, rather than from this pleasure together with some of the sensations that compose it. The taste of the meat, the charcoal-broiled smell, and the feeling of teeth sinking into tender flesh all contribute to the intrinsic value of the experience. Even when one considers only paradigm cases of pleasure, it seems an exaggeration to claim that the only thing that makes an experience desirable for its own sake is its pleasantness.

The case against hedonism becomes stronger when one turns to esthetic experiences. The experience of contemplating a painting or listening to a symphony can be, and often is, good for its own sake. But in reflecting on such experiences, it is hard to find in them any component that might properly be called "a pleasure." What a person is aware of in looking at a fine painting is an array of colors, shapes, textures, and a certain structure, all of which probably evoke certain images, emotions, and thoughts in the viewer. But the person absorbed in the work of art is not aware of any glow of gratification or identifiable feeling of pleasure. Again, the content of the experience of a disciplined yet moving performance of a symphony consists of musical tones, each with its pitch, intensity, and timbre, organized melodically and harmonically, and accompanied by the listener's emotions, and perhaps images and thoughts. If we speak of esthetic experiences as pleasant, this is probably not because we find any pleasure in them but because we are pleased to have them. The adjective "pleasant" describes a characteristic of our reaction to the experience and not a characteristic of the experience itself.

Finally, there seem to be some kinds of experience that are worth having for their own sake even though they are, if anything, unpleasant rather than pleasant. The experience of a June graduation can be, although it often is not, a very fine experience. The value of this experience is surely not derived from its consequences; it is hard to imagine a more useless way to spend an hour. One seldom learns anything from listening to the commencement speaker or gets a job by looking wise during the commencement exercise. Even the diploma, the only tangible reward, might more easily be obtained by mail than by attending a formal ceremony. Nor does it seem accurate to suggest that the value of the experience lies in the pleasure one feels. To be sure, one may experience an intense gratification upon receiving a diploma, and one may feel a diffuse glow of satisfaction through the occasion. But over and against these pleasures must be set the pains of sitting in those poorly-fitting chairs for an hour and the discomfort of sweltering in heavy black robes under the hot June sun. Measured from a purely hedonic standpoint, such an experience seems to me to be more unpleasant than pleasant. Yet it can be good for its own sake. Why? Because one can be aware of this hour of experience as the meaningful culmination of four years of aspiration and effort and as the beginning of a new life of greater independence, increased creativity, and heightened significance. The mistake of the hedonist is to look for the value of the experience in the way it feels. If the experience of graduation can be worthwhile, this is because it is meaningful, not because it is pleasant.

Another example is the experience of playing a hard game of football. This can be an intrinsically good experience, and in a paradoxical sort of way, the suffering the player goes through seems to make the experience better, not worse. Although a person can play football for the sake of winning or to make money, many play the game primarily for fun. This is to say that they play football because they find the playing good in itself and not because the playing derives some extrinsic value from its consequences. No doubt the playing is punctuated with pleasures. There are the several satisfactions of having delivered jolting blocks or having made clean tackles, and there may be a final glow of pleasure in winning the game. But what predominates in the experience of playing a hard game of football against worthy opponents is not these momentary thrills but a gradually increasing discomfort from sweat, dirty clothes, and bodily fatigue together with an increasing number of pains caused by various blows and bruises. If one thinks only of the pleasures and pains contained in the experience of a strenuous game of football, I contend that the verdict would often have to be negative because the pains outweigh the pleasures in many cases. But to judge the experience in terms of the balance of pleasures and pains is to conceive of value experience in too passive a manner. While pleasures come to a person from various causes and are simply felt by the individual who enjoys them, the value of many experiences lies in the awareness of doing something worthwhile and in the active interpretation of the significance of that action. The value lies in the experience of playing hard and in the interpreting that gives meaning to that experience. Once more, characteristics other than pleasantness make an experience good for its own sake.

My own view, therefore, is that many kinds of experience are intrinsically good. The only thing that can be either good or bad for its own sake is experience, human or nonhuman, and many different characteristics can make an experience desirable or undesirable. This theory is a version of axiological pluralism. It differs from Ross' version in limiting things of intrinsic value to experiences. It differs from Mill's hedonism in claiming that pleasantness is not the only good-making characteristic of an experience.

We began our search for a theory of value in the hope that such a theory would help us to solve the specific moral problem, "Is the genetic engineering of human beings desirable?" My theory, even if true, would not easily, much less automatically and unequivocally, provide an answer to this moral question. Still, it does tell us how to go about finding the answer. First, it tells us that genetic engineering is neither intrinsically good nor intrinsically bad. Genetic engineering in all its forms is an activity involving bodily movements and, typically, the manipulation of apparatus. Since genetic engineering is not itself an experience or set of experiences (although one may have experiences *of* genetic engineering), it is not the kind of thing that can be good or bad for its own sake. Whatever value or disvalue it may have must lie in its consequences.

This is hardly news. The arguments for and against genetic engineering appeal to its consequences; for example, that it will lead to abuses or prevent illness or strain the parent–child relationship. Obviously, to decide whether genetic engineering is desirable or undesirable we must determine which of these predicted results will in fact follow the use of genetic engineering on human beings. But my theory of value reminds us that we must do more. We must evaluate these consequences in terms of their impact upon experience. Is risk good because it adds zest to life, or is it bad because it often injures people in ways that cause them pain, frustration, and misery? Even granted that genetic engineering would reduce the meaningfulness of sexual intercourse, will this improve our sexual experiences by making them more innocent and carefree or reduce their value by trivializing them? Until a wide variety of questions about the ultimate consequences of genetic engineering for human experiences are answered, we cannot know with any confidence whether, in the end, genetic engineering is desirable or undesirable. My own theory implies that I have unfinished business, that I did not completely solve the problem posed in Chapter 3. Fortunately, it also points the direction in which continued investigation must go, toward the experiences that arise from the genetic engineering of human beings.

STUDY QUESTIONS

1. Suppose that someone asks why pleasure is good. What sort of answer could the hedonist give? Is this answer satisfactory? Why or why not?
2. Are all pleasures intrinsically good? What about the pleasure a small child gets from being rewarded for some act he or she did not actually do? What about the enjoyment a big bully gets in tormenting small children?
3. Hedonists have always tried to reply to the charge that their theory is degrading. One reply is that there are mental as well as bodily pleasures. Another is that there are exalted pleasures involving the higher faculties as well as the lower pleasures of mere feeling. Is either reply really adequate?
4. According to the interest theory of value, pleasure is good only because we desire and like it. Suppose someone became completely apathetic, perhaps as

a result of mental illness, and ceased to desire or like pleasure. Would pleasure lose its value for such a person? How do you know?

5. Imagine that a thirsty hiker sees a mountain stream and enjoys a drink of the water. He or she does not realize until becoming violently ill that the stream is polluted. Was the water good or was it bad before the pollution had its effect? Did it change its value when he or she changed his or her attitude toward it? How well can the interest theory of value explain this sort of situation?

6. Someone who holds the interest theory of value might say *either* that an object has extrinsic value when it is desired as a means *or* that it has extrinsic value when it is a means to some desired object. That is, the interest that confers extrinsic value might be either an interest in the means as means or an interest in the end to which the object with extrinsic value is a means. Which definition of extrinsic value would be theoretically preferable? Why?

7. Some argue that if God is perfect, then the vision of God must be bliss. But might not the vision of God be confusing, terrifying, and humiliating to finite creatures like ourselves? How would we discover whether the vision of God would be ecstasy or agony? If the latter, would this prove that this vision is bad or only that it is too good for mere human beings?

8. Does the pursuit of heavenly salvation require the rejection of all worldly "goods"? Why or why not? How might someone who holds that only the vision of God is intrinsically good explain the value of money, food, or books?

9. Those who hold that love is the good usually mean agape rather than eros. Would it be at all plausible to claim that eros is the source of all value? If so, what sort of a theory would this be? What would Ralph Barton Perry say of such a theory?

10. If love is intrinsically good, does the nature of the loved object make any difference to its value? Does it matter whether the person loved is virtuous or wicked? Does it matter whether the love is reciprocated? Why or why not?

11. It is sometimes alleged that all earthly "goods" are fleeting, precarious, and mixed with earthly "evils." Are these cogent reasons for denying intrinsic value to earthly things?

12. *Why* is love good? A few possible answers are that it feels good or that it transforms the lover's personality or that it improves personal relations. What do you think the true answer is? What sort of answer is required by the theory that only love is intrinsically good?

13. Whether virtue is really intrinsically good depends on the nature of virtue. Is Epictetus correct when he says that virtue consists in living according to reason? What kinds of examples make it plausible to claim that the passions are the enemy of virtue? What about emotions like brotherly love or righteous indignation? What is virtue, anyway?

14. Is the value of virtue really independent of its consequences? David Hume, the eighteenth-century British empiricist, claims that justice would lose its merit if it were to become useless. Would respecting the property of others lose its goodness if nature became so bountiful that everyone had more than enough or if nature were so niggardly that there was not enough food to keep everyone alive and healthy?

15. The Stoics argued that to be a slave is to be miserable and to be free is to be happy. Whether or not one has power, wealth, or health is not subject to the control of the individual. Hence, anyone who cares about these things lives enslaved to those who can give or withhold them. But whether or not one is

virtuous is entirely within one's own control. Thus a person who cares only about virtue lives a free and happy life. Does this argument, if its premises are true, really prove that virtue is the good? Is it true that the individual has more control over whether he is virtuous than over whether he is wealthy or healthy?

16. Can the virtuous person really be happy lacking fame, fortune, or even health? If so, does this prove these things valueless?

17. What would the person who believes that only virtue is intrinsically good say about the value of a ripe red apple or a useful pen?

18. Why is power good? Is it the mere existence of power or its possession or its exercise or its results that make it worthwhile? How do you know?

19. It has been argued that power is neither good nor bad in itself because it is good when used for some good purpose and bad when misused or abused. How might Nietzsche reply to this argument? Do you consider the argument or the reply stronger? Why?

20. The powerful personality seems to care very little about pleasures or pains, and the life of power often brings with it much suffering. If the life of power is really deep, rich, and rewarding, are we to say that suffering is good because it is necessary to the good life or that it is a necessary evil?

21. Are you ever tempted to change places with some character like Antigone or Othello? Why do we find ourselves elevated by watching a fine performance of a tragedy? Does this really tell us anything about the good?

22. Darwinian theory implies that in the natural process of evolution it is the fittest that survive. If human beings interfere in this natural process to help weaker and less fit individuals survive, the result could be the deterioration of the species. Is this a sound argument for the theory that power is the good? Why or why not?

23. Was Hitler really a powerful personality or a weak, sick person who managed to dominate those around him? By what criteria can one identify the genuinely powerful personality?

24. If self-realization is the good, how should parents bring up their children? Does parental guidance and restraint help the child develop most fully, or is the child's maximum self-development best achieved through self-expression unhindered by parental control? What evidence is there that sparing the rod really spoils the child *or* that authoritarian treatment really inhibits the fullest development of a child's capacities?

25. Is a college or university education a good thing? What, if anything, makes education worthwhile? Which of the theories of value we have studied best explains the value of education?

26. The ideal self to be realized depends on the nature of the self. Bradley thought of the self as an individual seeking to satisfy his *desires* as a member of a *society*. Aristotle thought of the self as striving to actualize its potential as a member of the *species* of *rational* animals. Which conception of the self is more adequate as a psychological theory of human nature? Which conception is more relevant to moral issues? Why?

27. Are human desires more relevant to the good (for human beings) than other aspects of human psychology like sense perceptions, beliefs, logical reasoning, or imaginative fantasy? If so, why? If not, why did Bradley emphasize desire so much?

28. Can there be individual self-realization apart from society? Why or why not? What does this imply about the good for human beings?

29. Aristotle believed that all individual human beings share some essential human nature. Is there anything all people have in common that makes them human? If so, does this imply that one should strive toward realizing some capacity shared with all other human beings, rather than developing some unique potential in oneself?

30. Is it the capacity to reason that distinguishes human beings from the other species of animals? If not, what does distinguish a person from an ape or a dog? To achieve self-realization, must a person develop all inherent capacities, even those shared with the lower animals? Or should a human being develop only the distinctive capacity of rationality?

31. Is a world with pleasure plus virtue really better than a world with an equal amount of pleasure but no virtue? How do you know? If so, does this imply that virtue is intrinsically good or only that it has some sort of value?

32. Do you think that Ross' list of intrinsically good things is complete? If not, what additional kinds of things are good for their own sake? Do you think that anything on his list lacks intrinsic value? How can someone defend the decision to include or exclude anything on such a list?

33. Is it really true that only experiences can be intrinsically good or bad? Imagine that by snapping your fingers you could bring into existence *either* a world filled with natural beauty (waterfalls, sunsets, mountains, flowers, etc.) but with no sentient beings to be conscious of this beauty, *or* a world filled with ugliness and filth (polluted air, rotting garbage, decaying urban ghettos, burnt-down forests, etc.) but again with no minds to be aware of this ugliness. Is this choice of no consequence because neither world has any value, or is one world better than the other—even if no mind is to experience the beauty of the one or the ugliness of the other? Does this thought experiment refute Mill and the author? Why or why not?

34. Does the question "Why?" really stop at experience? If asked why the experience of watching a performance of *Macbeth* or *Tartuffe* has value, one might describe the nature of the experience itself (the sounds were beautiful, the colors striking, and the images called up fascinating); or one might describe the consequences of the experience (one gains insight into human nature or one's mental health is improved by an emotional catharsis). Does this show that the value of experience is no more basic or ultimate than the value of physical objects? Why or why not?

35. Is the experience of playing a hard game of football ever *both* good for its own sake *and* more unpleasant than pleasant? How could you defend your answer?

BIBLIOGRAPHY

Aristotle. *Nicomachean Ethics,* Books 1 and 10. Any standard edition.
Augustine, Saint. *The City of God,* Book 22, chaps. 29–30. In *Basic Writings of Saint Augustine,* edited by Whitney J. Oates. New York: Random House, 1948.
Bradley, Francis Herbert. *Appearance and Reality,* 2d ed., chap. 25. Oxford, Eng.: Clarendon Press, 1930.
Epictetus. *Discourses,* Book 1, chaps. 1–4; Book 2, chaps. 8–10. In *Stoic and Epicurean Philosophers,* edited by Whitney J. Oates. New York: Random House, 1940.
Epicurus. "Letter to Menoeceus" and "Principal Doctrines." In *Stoic and Epicurean Philosophers,* edited by Whitney J. Oates. New York: Random House, 1940.

60148169

FLETCHER, JOSEPH. *Situation Ethics*, chap. 3. Philadelphia: The Westminster Press, 1966.

MILL, JOHN STUART. *Utilitarianism*, chap. 2. In *Utilitarianism, Liberty, and Representative Government*. New York: E. P. Dutton & Co., 1950.

NIETZSCHE, FRIEDRICH. *Genealogy of Morals*, first essay. Translated by Horace B. Samuel. New York: Russell & Russell Publishers, 1964.

PERRY, RALPH BARTON. *General Theory of Value*, chap. 5. Cambridge, Mass.: Harvard University Press, 1926.

ROSS, WILLIAM DAVID. *The Right and the Good*, chap. 5. Oxford, England: Clarendon Press, 1930.

SIDGWICK, HENRY. *The Methods of Ethics*. London: Macmillan and Co., 1907.

5
RAPE

I equate rape with someone throwing you up against a wall and tearing your liver and guts out of you. . . . Rape is worse than murder . . . and I'm disgusting.

A convicted rapist, quoted in Scully and Marolla, "Convicted Rapists' Vocabulary of Motive" © 1984 by The Society for the Study of Social Problems. Reprinted from *Social Problems,* Vol.31 No.5, June 1984, [pp. 530–544], by permission.

"Oh," she says, "the paper prints nothing but rapes. You know what a rape usually is? It's a woman who changed her mind afterward."

John Updike in *Rabbit Redux*
Copyright © 1971 by John Updike.
Published by Alfred A. Knopf.

Each year in the United States almost 30,000 persons are arrested and charged with forcible rape. Since only a small percentage of rapes are reported to the police and a minority of these reports result in legal action, it is very probable that at least half a million persons are raped in the United States each year. Leaving aside for the moment the most brutal cases, for example, where a full-grown man batters a young girl before forcing her to submit to sexual intercourse, or where a young man enters a nursing home and murders an elderly, weak woman before violating her, the experience of being raped is typically a devastating one. The sexual acts are almost always painful for the victim and often accompanied by the use or threat of deadly force. The victim is rendered helpless and degraded by being treated as a mere thing rather than as a person. Sexual intercourse, which can be so meaningful and rewarding, becomes disgusting, humiliating, even shameful. The victim feels used, dirtied, and rejected and is injured in body and soul. It is not merely the individuals raped who suffer—all women in our society are victimized by rape. From an early age, girls are taught the dangers of rape and the caution necessary to reduce one's chances of being raped. Women young and old know that no precautionary measures can ever completely eliminate the danger of rape, and they live in fear of the potential and unidentifiable rapist. This is why rape is sometimes said to be a form of terrorism by which males maintain their individual and social domination over females. One may well ask, "What kind of a person could impose such monstrous suffering upon another human being?" The philosopher will ask, "Are all rapists morally evil?"

DEFINING THE PROBLEM

This question, "Are all rapists morally evil?," is about the rapist, the person who rapes. Thus, the question we will address in this chapter is rather different from the ones we discussed in Chapters 1 and 3. Those specific moral problems concern kinds of actions—acts of civil disobedience or genetic engineering. This problem concerns one kind of agent—not the act, but the doer of the act. I propose that we define the rapist as anyone who actually rapes another person. This excludes the person who tries, but fails, to rape. It also excludes the individual who assists or encourages another to rape. I do not wish to suggest that these other classes of moral agents are without moral fault; I merely wish to distinguish those who actually commit a rape from others who are not rapists in this strict sense.

Our problem is to determine whether the rapist is morally evil. This is very different from wondering whether rape is morally wrong. We have already noted that it is a question of the correct moral assessment of the agent or person who does the act, not the act itself. To ask whether an action is morally right or wrong is to take up the viewpoint of someone deciding whether or not to do the act, the standpoint of someone deciding which of several alternative actions to perform. To ask whether an agent is morally good or evil is to take up the viewpoint of the observer deciding how to respond to the person who has done, or might do, the act—the standpoint of the moral judge trying to decide whether to approve or disapprove, praise or blame the agent. It is not a question about moral obligation, what one morally ought or ought not to do, but a question about moral value, whether the agent is good or evil. Still, the question we are asking here is quite different from the question we asked about genetic engineering in Chapter 3, or even the related question, "Is the genetic engineer beneficial or harmful?" To ask this latter question is to ask a question about the value of an agent, about his or her nonmoral value. Here we are posing the problem of the specifically moral value or disvalue of the rapist; we are asking whether the rapist is evil *as a moral agent*. Some rapists are no doubt very good liars, but this in no way makes them *morally* good; nor would the fact that some rapist is a very bad golfer have any bearing upon whether he is morally evil. Moral value is a very special sort of value depending entirely upon an agent's character, his or her virtue or vice.

The question we are asking is whether the rapist is always, in each and every instance, morally evil. Few moral philosophers doubt that most rapists are evil. The only serious question is whether there are some who are not evil. To suggest that perhaps some rapists are not evil is not to suggest that some may be virtuous. It may well be that some rapists are neither morally good nor morally evil simply because they are not responsible for their actions, for example, because they are feeble-minded or insane. Hence, our problem is to decide whether all rapists, or only some rapists, are wicked.

Unfortunately, our problem is not yet clearly defined. I have identified the rapist as the person who rapes. But precisely what is it for one person to rape another? My abridged but reliable dictionary informs me that "to rape" means "to force (a female) to submit to sexual intercourse." Let us assume that this report of contemporary English usage is accurate and seek to determine its precise significance.

Rape involves sexual intercourse. In its most narrow and strict sense, sexual intercourse is the insertion of a man's penis into a woman's vagina, often followed by ejaculation. In a broader but quite common and appropriate sense, the term "sexual intercourse" also includes the insertion of the penis into a female's anus or mouth and throat. This equally involves the penetration of the female's body by the male's penis and is often followed by ejaculation. The expressions "anal intercourse" and "oral intercourse" are often used, and many persons, both male and female, think of these as alternative (although not necessarily equally desirable) forms of sexual intercourse. By contrast, almost no one would think of calling kissing, even deep kissing, or fondling the breasts of a female, sexual intercourse. No doubt these are sexual activities, typically erotic in significance and feeling. But they are in a basically different category because they do not involve the genital organs. Sexual intercourse, then, is a form of sexual contact that involves the genital organ of at least one of the partners.

Fortunately, most sexual intercourse is not rape; it is rape only when one is forced "to submit" to it. To submit is to yield to the will of another. The dictionary notes that while "yield" has the widest sense of retreating from a position for any of a wide range of reasons, "submit" implies giving way out of necessity after opposing unsuccessfully. In paradigm cases of rape, there is a conflict of wills; the male wants to have sexual intercourse with the female, but the female is unwilling and resistant. The act of raping therefore involves more than having sexual intercourse; a necessary part of the rape is overcoming the resistance of the female. For this reason, many philosophers hold that statutory rape—sexual intercourse with a female under the age when she can give legally valid consent—is not really rape. In many instances of statutory rape, the male has no resistance to overcome; indeed, the young female may be eager to engage in sexual inter-course, even to the point of seducing the male. While reserving judgment on whether statutory rape is more or less evil than forcible rape, I would agree that it does not fit the sense of the verb "to rape" that I have in mind here. A more borderline case is that in which a male has sexual intercourse with an unconscious female, one who may be asleep, dead drunk, or even comatose. I would classify this as rape in the relevant sense. Although the female does not actually resist and then yield, neither does she willingly participate in the sexual intercourse. Often she would resist if she were conscious and able to do so. The male has his way with her by physically manipulating her body and in that sense at least is using physical force upon her.

In my discussion to this point, I have been speaking of rape as some-thing that a male does to a female. This presupposition is, I must admit, part and parcel of our everyday thinking and speaking. But notice that my dictionary defines the verb "to rape" as meaning "to force (a female) to submit to sexual intercourse." The parentheses indicate that this presuppo-sition, although generally taken for granted, is not part of the very mean-ing of that verb. As philosophers who should take ordinary language seri-ously but are not bound by it, we should ask whether this presupposition is justified. If Dick points a gun at Jane's head or holds a knife to her throat and forces her to submit to sexual intercourse, he clearly rapes her. Now suppose that Jane holds the gun or knife and forces Dick to submit to sexual intercourse. Is this not essentially the same kind of action and, therefore, equally rape? I think that it is. Some philosophers allege that my second example is purely imaginary and could never occur because it is physiologically or psychologically impossible. Sexual intercourse is possible only if the male can sustain an erection, and under the conditions de-scribed, Dick would be so terrified that he would be rendered impotent. Unfortunately, this is not true. There are recorded cases very similar to the one I describe. Moreover, psychologists inform us that in some males the excitement of danger, or even injury, is a powerful erotic stimulus. Finally, if one includes anal sex and oral sex within the notion of sexual inter-course, there is no compelling reason to presuppose that the victim of rape is always a female. Criminal statistics and newspaper reports remind us that homosexual rapes are far from uncommon, and that female rapists are not unknown. I propose, therefore, to omit the parenthetical presupposition from my definition of rape and to conceive of rape in nonsexist terms.

Accordingly, to rape is to force another to submit to sexual inter-course. All that remains, no mere trifle, is to explain what it is to force another to submit. To force someone to perform an action, in the strictest sense, is to compel that person to act by the use of force or coercion. Thus, a male uses force to compel a female to submit to sexual intercourse if he holds her down so that she cannot wriggle away or fend off his advances and forces her legs apart with his knees, or if he compels her to submit by hurting her with his fists, a club, or a knife. He uses coercion to compel his victim to submit if he threatens to kill her by shooting, stabbing, strangling or threatens to inflict grievous bodily injury upon her with a weapon. Not every use of force or coercion is compelling, however. If an overly ardent boyfriend gently pushes his companion's protective arm away from her loins, he has not compelled her to submit to his sexual advances; nor has a professor raped a coed if he threatens to reduce her grade from an A to a D unless she goes to bed with him. Strictly speaking, one person forces another to submit only if one obtains submission by means that permit no choice; that is, by the use of overpowering force or some irresistible threat. The victim is forced to submit only when she or he has been rendered helpless in some way and so cannot help but submit to sexual intercourse.

There are moral philosophers who define rape more broadly to include any and all sexual intercourse obtained by any form of coercion however slight, or without the free informed consent of the sexual partner. In this way they emphasize the evils of coercion and the importance of mutual consent in sexual relations. These are legitimate moral concerns. Nevertheless, I shall not follow their example. For one thing, this definition ignores the linguistic origins of the very term "to rape" and distorts an important part of what is implicit in contemporary usage. The verb is derived from the Latin verb "rapare" meaning to snatch or carry off by force. The famous rape of the Sabine women was an act of armed robbery rather than a sexual act, although the latter probably followed in due course. The connection between rape and force or violence remains to this day, both in our language and, alas, our experiences with this harsh reality. Moreover, this connection is morally crucial because it is central both to the very meaning of acts of rape and to the immense harm rape inflicts upon its victims. The rapist typically seeks to overpower his victim so that his will is in complete control and she is compelled to submit, and the victim finds being raped so terrifying and humiliating primarily because she is rendered completely helpless and manipulated like an object to be possessed and used. Lesser degrees of coercion, although morally objectionable, dilute or distort the full reprehensibility of rape. Therefore, I shall insist that the rapist is one who forces another to submit to sexual intercourse. Our problem is to determine whether the rapist is always, not just usually, morally evil.

CONDEMNATIONS

It is very natural for anyone familiar with the evils of rape to jump to the conclusion that the rapist is inevitably a morally evil person. And perhaps in the end this is the conclusion to which any informed and morally sensitive judge should come. But a moral philosopher will seek out reasons for such condemnation and will insist upon having grounds for any blame meted out to a moral agent. Many such condemnations are presented in the philosophical, legal, political, and social literature. Let us review the most important of these.

Lustful

Why does the rapist force the victim to submit to sexual intercourse? Obviously, or so it seems, because of an intense sex drive that is not gratified in other ways. Sexual desire is entirely natural and usually entirely innocent. In the normal human being, the desire for sexual intercourse is only one desire among many and is restrained by those other desires. My desire to possess my wife's body is qualified by my desire to please her and my desire not to endanger our mutual trust. Also, I desire more than the physical contact of our genitalia; I desire sexual *intercourse,* an interaction and communication with her of a sexual sort. Lust is an excessive and unrestrained sexual desire, and it is an animal or biological craving for merely physiological contact and gratification. This is why lust reduces the moral agent to the subhuman level and the lustful person is morally evil because he or she is acting like a brute animal. Since the rapist is lustful, dominated by lust, the rapist is morally evil.

Malicious

Scientific studies show that rape is often precipitated by some distressing event in the rapist's life—his wife has quarreled with him, his boss has fired him, or his girlfriend has jilted him. Rape is typically motivated by anger and hostility toward women, and the rapist desires to dominate, humiliate, and injure the victim. While the morally good person is motivated by benevolence, the desire to benefit others, the rapist acts from malice, the desire to injure and hurt another person. Such a malicious agent is morally evil.

Selfish

Whatever may motivate an individual rapist, the animal desire for sex or the hostile desire to hurt or some other desire, it is clear that the rapist cares only for the gratification of his (or her) own desires. That the victim is unwilling to have sexual intercourse with him (or her) and wants desperately to be left unmolested does little or nothing to restrain the rapist. To care only about one's own pleasures, interests, or welfare and not about those of others is selfish, and selfishness is surely a moral vice. Since the rapist is always selfish, he or she is always morally evil.

Cruel

If rape were merely inconvenient for the victim, it would be unreasonable to condemn the rapist so universally and so harshly. Alas, the horrors of rape are all too well documented. All but the very young, senile, or naive are aware of the danger of rape and fear it. When the sexual assault comes, the victim is typically terrified. Resistance invites only physical attack or the threat of grievous harm. The sexual intercourse is almost always painful. The awful recognition of one's helplessness is humiliating and the awareness of being used sexually often shaming. Unfortunately, the reactions of other persons—the police, one's family, one's friends—are often unsympathetic and even derogatory. Although the rapist may not fully appreciate the varied and immense suffering of the victim, he or she is well aware that the victim does suffer and is not restrained by this awareness. At the very least, the rapist is callous, cruel in disregarding the pain inflicted upon the victim. Often the rapist is sadistic, finding gratification in the pain and suffering of the victim. To be cruel is surely to be morally evil.

Unscrupulous

To be unscrupulous is to be without moral scruples, to be contemptuous of what is morally right. The morally good person will normally feel sexual desire and even intense anger upon occasion. But in the virtuous agent, these desires and impulses will be restrained by moral scruples. The morally good person will not treat others in ways that are morally wrong, especially when to do so would be to violate their fundamental moral rights. But the rapist deliberately chooses to mistreat the victim and does not scruple to violate the human rights to bodily integrity, privacy, and self-determination. What greater moral defect could there be in a moral agent than to be insensitive to and contemptuous of any and all moral standards? Since the rapist is always unscrupulous, the rapist is always morally evil.

Unjust

Rape is not merely a sexual assault by one individual upon another; it is an essential element in a social system of male domination. Rape is essentially an act of sexual conquest and thus expresses and reinforces the social norm of male power, domination, and superiority. The rapist forces his victim to submit out of fear and terrorizes potential victims so as to remind all women of their powerlessness, vulnerability, and inferiority in our sexist society. This systematic domination of males over females denies women equal liberty and opportunity and enables males to exploit females in many ways. Clearly, this system of male domination is grossly unjust. The rapist actively participates in this unjust system by his rape, helps to keep its victims in their place by terrorism, and takes advantage of his dominant position to enjoy the advantages of rape. Only an unjust person would participate in, reinforce, and take advantage of such a grossly unjust system. Therefore, all rapists are unjust and, since injustice is a vice, morally evil.

EXCUSES

One is tempted to condemn the rapist, every rapist, in the harshest terms; but excuses, even plausible excuses, are not hard to find in the literature of psychology, social work, and even moral philosophy. An excuse is a reason not to condemn or morally blame an agent, not necessarily a reason to praise or approve of him or her. It is also important to remember that the excuses we shall be considering are not imagined to apply to every rapist. There is a logical asymmetry between the arguments in the previous section and those in this. To prove that the rapist is always morally evil one must give some reason that applies to every rapist; to prove that the rapist is *not always* evil one need only give some reason that excuses some rapists, even if only a very few. We will describe here some of the excuses put forward.

Marital Rights

When a man and a woman marry, they enter into a marital contract or understanding that confers specific moral rights and duties upon each of them. The man agrees to become the breadwinner and to support his wife and family. Hence, the wife has a right to financial support and the husband has a correlative duty to support his wife. If a husband later decides that he would rather spend his wages on himself and not support his wife, she is acting within her rights if she forces him to perform his duty to her. Similarly, the husband acquires under the marriage contract a moral right to have sexual intercourse with his wife, and she has a correlative duty to serve him in this way. If she decides that she would rather not have sexual intercourse with him, he is entirely within his marital rights to force her to submit to sexual intercourse with him. To be sure, this is rape as I have defined it. But since no one is morally evil simply because he or she has exercised his or her moral rights, it is argued that the husband who rapes his own wife is not necessarily an evil person.

Seduction

Sometimes to say that one person forced another to submit to sexual intercourse is to tell only part, and the less important part, of the story. It would be like reporting that Jones beat Smith mercilessly. This might be true enough, but it might also be a morally misleading description of the situation. Perhaps Smith gratuitously insulted Jones, hit him several times, ridiculed him when Jones tried to leave rather than engage in physical combat. Finally, cornered and goaded into desperation, Jones fought back. Who is morally to blame for the injuries suffered by Smith? Smith himself is to blame because he started the fight and would not let Jones escape. Similarly, it is not uncommon for a girl or woman to encourage kissing and petting, to lead the male on, to arouse his sexual desires and encourage his hopes. If he then loses his self-control and forces her to submit to sexual intercourse, she has only herself to blame. She may be more naive than wicked, but at least one ought not to judge the rapist morally evil for responding so naturally to such powerful seduction.

It would be sexist to suggest that seductive provocation is an exclusively feminine trait. Among homosexuals, one male may seduce another and thereby provoke rape. Here, too, the argument goes, the seducer is sometimes more to blame than the rapist.

Unintentional

It is not what one does, but what one intends to do that makes one morally good or evil. Imagine that I am crossing an icy street one windy day alongside a little old lady. She begins to slip and I rush forward and reach out to prevent her from falling to the pavement. Unfortunately, my footing is uncertain and my reach mistimed so that my hand pushes her arm, causing her to fall and break her hip. Given her age, she may never walk again. I have harmed her dreadfully. But it would be unreasonable to judge me an evil person for trying to help her; my intention was good and entirely innocent. Now sometimes one person in fact forces another to submit to sexual intercourse unintentionally. I am not suggesting that one person rapes another without intending to have sexual intercourse with her or him. What I am suggesting is that the rapist's intention may be morally innocent because the rapist had no intention of *forcing* the other to *submit* to intercourse. For instance, a woman may have refused to have sex and may even have seemed to resist. But did she really mean "no"? In our society the male has long been expected to pursue and the female to resist—or pretend to resist—only to give in in the end. Some rapists say, and some psychologists confirm their affirmations, that they sincerely believed that their victims really wanted sexual intercourse with them and were merely pretending to be unwilling. If this is true, and this is a factual question rather than a moral one, then they did not intend to rape any more than I intended to cripple that little old lady. How, then, could these rapists be said to be morally evil?

Irresistible Impulse

Sometimes one cannot blame rapists for acting as they did because they were driven by an irresistible impulse. Sexual desire is one of the strongest drives in human nature. When one becomes thoroughly aroused sexually, there are times when one simply cannot restrain oneself, and when one acts on uncontrollable impulse—motivated by something one virtually cannot control—one is not morally responsible for one's actions. Compare the situation in which someone is driving on a highway at fifty or sixty miles an hour. When the driver notices a cluster of slow-moving vehicles ahead, he or she puts on the brakes only to discover that the brakes have failed. Driven by a built-up momentum, the car crashes into the car ahead seriously injuring several passengers. Grievous and undeniable as is the harm done, the driver is not therefore a morally evil person. Since the car was completely out of control, the driver literally could not have helped doing what he or she did and is not to blame morally. Similarly, the rapist driven by irresistible impulse is not morally to blame for what he or she could not help doing.

Unsound Mind

Only competent individuals, those in command of their rational and emotional faculties, are morally responsible for their actions. People who are not of sound mind are not properly blamed, or praised either, for what they do. Sometimes the rapist is not morally evil simply because he or she is not of sound mind. A few rapists are probably insane or feeble-minded. Some are surely sexual psychopaths, individuals who have displayed a more or less continuous pattern of sexual deviation and who are in such a state of mental aberration that they cannot refrain from committing sexual offenses. And then there are those rapists who are temporarily not of sound mind because they are under the influence of drugs or alcohol. Since some rapists are of unsound mind, and those who are not of sound mind are not morally responsible for their actions, some rapists are not morally evil.

ACT AND AGENT

When someone who is reasonably well informed and morally sensitive is asked or ponders whether every rapist is morally evil, the spontaneous reply is "yes, of course." Since there are excuses that can be offered by or on behalf of the rapist, one wonders why it seems so natural and reasonable to condemn rapists, and without exception. Perhaps many sense that rape is typically a monstrous wrong and imagine that anyone capable of such an act must be a moral monster; probably we all know enough about rape to recognize that it is morally wrong and suppose, on this basis, that the rapist is morally evil. But is this transition from act to agent a logical inference or merely an emotional association?

We have defined "the rapist" as the person who rapes. Hence, the moral agents whose virtue or vice is at issue here are identified simply by the act they commit. And we have defined the act of rape as the act of forcing another to submit to sexual intercourse. How is it possible to know whether a moral agent is morally good or morally evil, or neither, on the basis of knowing that he or she has done an act of a certain nature? Presumably the inference must involve at least two steps or aspects. From the nature of the act one must infer something about the agent who does or did that act. Then this something about the agent must imply that the agent is or is not morally evil. This sort of reasoning is typical of both condemnations and excuses. For example, from the fact that rape consists in forcing another to submit to sexual intercourse, one may infer that the agent is motivated by lust; then from the judgment that lust is a sinful motive, one may infer that the lustful agent is morally evil. On the other hand, from the fact that rape consists in forcing another to submit to sexual intercourse, sometimes in the face of determined resistance, one may infer that the rapist must be motivated by irresistible sexual desire; then from the judgment that one cannot be blamed for acting from an irresistible motive, one may conclude that the rapist is sometimes not morally evil. Let us examine the first step in the reasoning, the step from the nature of the act to some statement about the agent.

There seem to be three very different ways in which the nature of an act might be connected to some conclusion about the agent.

1. Act and agent might be logically connected by the very definition of the act done. For example, from the fact that Jones lied, one can validly infer that Jones intended to deceive the hearer or reader because "to lie" is defined as "to present false information with the intention of deceiving." But from the fact that Smith misled his or her hearer or reader, one cannot infer that the agent intended to deceive because the definition of "to mislead" makes no reference to the intention of the agent. Now from our definition of rape one can properly infer something about the rapist, that the agent used force or some irresistible threat and that the agent had sexual intercourse with the victim. However, it is not true by definition that the agent was motivated by lust or that his or her motive was irresistible.

2. Act and agent might be connected by some law of nature, some lawlike principle established by one of the sciences. Conceivably, it might be a law of human nature that the only impulse that motivates a human being to engage in sexual intercourse is the desire for sexual gratification or a lawlike principle of psychology that whenever one person forces another to submit, the former is motivated by hostility toward the latter. *If* some such scientific law were true, and known to be true, then one could infer something about the rapist from the nature of his or her action. It is not at all clear, however, that any of the condemnations or excuses we have summarized use this sort of reasoning. If they do, they can be clearly formulated and critically assessed only by making some such scientific principle explicit.

3. Act and agent might be connected by some empirical association that is not taken to be a lawlike statement. Observations and empirical reports of known rapists might tell us that they always, or at least often, have some characteristic in common. Psychologists or criminologists might discover that rapists generally have unusually strong sex drives, or are typically exceptionally hostile persons, or that most rapists are emotionally disturbed or have been using drugs. There may be no principle of human psychology to explain why this is so; this is merely a contingent correlation discovered by observation.

Still, this information might be taken for granted in some argument that infers something about the rapist from the nature of his or her act. When the argument takes this form, all one infers in the first instance from the nature of the act is that the agent is a rapist; this is true by definition, but it is not very informative. Any further information about the rapist is then derived from empirical generalizations about what has been found true of all, most, or some rapists. This seems the most plausible basis for knowing, or claiming to know, that all rapists are malicious or that some rapists are of unsound mind. There are ways, then, by which one can, often using additional factual premises, infer something about the agent from the nature of his or her act or acts.

Still, the second step in the argument remains unexplained. Let us reflect upon a couple of condemnations to see how information about the agent might imply that the agent is morally evil. Let us grant, for the sake of the argument, that every rapist is lustful, motivated to rape by lust. Since my dictionary defines lust as excessive sexual desire, and since this is regarded as sinful, this would seem to be adequate ground for condemning the rapist. But there are two difficulties in any inference from the sinfulness of the motive to the moral evil of the agent. For one thing, how does the evil motive render the agent morally evil? Is it simply *having* the evil motive that makes one evil or is it *acting on* the motive that makes one an evil agent? It would seem that morally good persons are sometimes tempted to act wrongly and that often it is evil motives that so tempt them. But the morally good person has the strength of character to resist such temptations and to do his or her duty in spite of any contrary inclinations. If so, merely having an evil motive does not prove one to be a morally evil agent. For instance, Jesus taught that "whosoever looketh on a woman to lust after her hath committed adultery with her already in his heart." No doubt, this is true. But how, if at all, does sinning in one's heart make one a morally evil agent? If one does not act out one's innermost desires, it is hard to see how they render one evil *as an agent*.

Another difficulty is understanding how one's motive for acting on a single occasion can be reliable evidence for the agent's moral character. I must confess that I am sometimes irritated. Indeed, I occasionally lose my temper over a trifling matter. But I am not an irritable person; for the most part I am patient and long suffering. Being moved to anger, especially by small matters, is most uncharacteristic of me; it is quite out of character. Now let us grant that some moral agent has been excited by lust to commit a rape. On this occasion, he or she has been motivated by excessive, even sinful, sexual desire. But does this imply that he or she is a lustful person, someone disposed to act on sexual desire? I do not see how. In fact, many psychological studies indicate that many rapists are undersexed, that they have less sexual drive than most persons. Whether or not this is true, the logical problem remains. How can information about the motive for any single act imply anything about the moral character of the agent?

In this respect, another plausible condemnation appears to be more promising. Let us suppose that we can show that all rapists are cruel. Now, to be cruel is to be "disposed to inflict violence, pain, or hardship and to find satisfaction in the suffering of others." Thus, cruelty is a disposition, a relatively stable character trait of the moral agent. In this respect, it is unlike lust or malice, motives upon which one may act on this or that occasion but which may be uncharacteristic of the agent. But now we are confronted with the opposite difficulty. Whereas before we had to explain how the motive of a single act of rape could imply anything about the character of the agent, now we need to explain how committing a single act of rape could prove that the agent is characteristically cruel. Still, since this problem lies within the first step of the argument, let us ignore it here. After all, we are here presupposing that the rapist is cruel.

Somehow we know that the rapist is cruel, and we recognize that the disposition of cruelty is a vice. Nevertheless, anyone's moral character is inevitably complex. Although no one individual can be both cruel and kind by disposition, he or she may well be cruel at the same time that he or she is courageous, honest, unselfish, and just. Might not these several virtues, especially if one possessed them to a high degree, more than outweigh a single, albeit a serious, vice? If one is to accurately judge the moral character of a person and condemn the agent as morally evil, it would seem that one should consider his or her virtues as well as vices and balance the one against the others. Of course, it may be that one need not do this. Just as an apple need not be rotten through and through to be a rotten apple, so it may be that any serious moral defect renders an agent morally evil. But one would like some explanation of why this is so. In the absence of some theory of moral value that would explain this to us, we cannot clearly see how the fact that the rapist is cruel necessarily implies that the rapist is an evil person, everything considered.

Telling a single lie does not prove that one is disposed to be dishonest, and a certain tendency to be dishonest on minor matters might be compatible with being a morally good—although hardly a morally perfect—person. Why should committing a single rape be different? Well, perhaps there are certain exceptional acts that test one's entire character. Perhaps raping someone or torturing someone just for fun is sufficient to demonstrate a thoroughly evil character, just as an act of great self-sacrifice might make one a moral saint or hero. I do not know that this is true, but sometimes a single action seems to take the measure of a man or woman. But we cannot know that this is true until we can explain how or why it is true. And until we have a more fully developed theory of moral value, we cannot be sure just how any condemnation can complete the two-step argument from the nature of rape to the moral evil of the rapist.

Excuses do more, or at least aim to do more, than raise questions about the condemnations of the rapist. They claim to rebut any argument from the act of rape to the moral evil of the rapist. The logic of excuses is various, and we cannot examine it all here. It may suffice to reflect upon a few examples and notice that excuses can counter condemnations in a number of very different ways. The examples, too, confront the same central problem of inferring a moral judgment of the rapist from the nature of the act of rape, but they have a somewhat easier time of it because all they need is something that will be true of some rapists and that will exonerate these from blame.

How, for example, is the appeal to marital rights supposed to excuse the husband who rapes his wife? Probably by reinterpreting or reassessing the moral import of his act. One very naturally, and perhaps correctly, thinks of rape as a harmful act in several serious ways and as violating the victim's moral rights. Thus, one has reason to judge any act of raping a woman to be morally wrong, and seriously so. But to think of rape as an act of exercising one's own moral rights is to radically reinterpret the action and to suggest that it is not morally wrong at all, or at the very least that is not very wrong. In this way, it destroys or weakens the basis for any condemnatory argument from the wrongness or badness of the act of rape to the moral evil of the agent.

To show that the rape was unintended is supposed to excuse the rapist in a very different way because it rebuts arguments from the act of rape to the moral character of the agent who rapes in quite another manner. To rape someone knowing that one is forcing her or him to submit to sexual intercourse against her or his will is to intentionally violate the moral rights to privacy and self-determination of the victim, and to rape someone knowing the harm one is doing to the victim is to act cruelly. But if one honestly does not know that one's actions have these features, then the fact that one rapes does not demonstrate that one is necessarily unscrupulous enough to violate rights or cruel enough to inflict such suffering and harm. In this way, the allegation that the rapist acted unintentionally might well block the inference from the wrongness or evil of the act to something in the agent, such as unscrupulousness or cruelty, that would in turn justify moral condemnation of the agent. We should note in passing, however, that Aristotle was probably wise to insist that the fact that an agent acted in ignorance of such facts blocks the inference to vice only on the presupposition that if the agent had known these things about his act, he would not have acted as he did. One sign of this is that the agent regrets the action upon discovering these facts. Rapists who feel no pangs of guilt or sorrow when they learn that they have unintentionally violated moral rights or harmed the victim are as evil as the person who acted knowingly and intentionally.

To assert that the rapist was or is of unsound mind rebuts the inference from the nature of the act of rape to the moral evil of the rapist in still a third way, at least if successful. Only a moral agent can be said to be morally good or evil. A bullet can kill a human being, but only the person who aimed the gun and pulled the trigger can be blamed morally for the murder. A dog might save his master's life, but no brute animal can be morally virtuous. A newborn infant and a senile man are not properly held morally responsible for what they do because neither is capable of acting in the morally relevant sense. Not every bit of overt behavior is a moral action. Imagine that I am having my annual medical checkup and the physician decides to test my reflexes. I cross my legs, the doctor hits my leg just below the knee, and nothing observable happens. The doctor bends closer to get a better look, hits my leg a bit more sharply, and my leg jerks up and knocks her glasses to the floor, breaking them. Morally speaking, I am not responsible for breaking those expensive glasses. I did not kick the doctor, my leg jerked. I did not *do* anything in the morally relevant sense. To act is to do something with some awareness of what one is doing and with the capacity to control what one does in the light of practical reasons. Only a being with the capacity to be conscious and rational can be a moral agent. If someone really is of unsound mind, that person is incapable of acting in the morally relevant sense and thus not, strictly speaking, a moral agent at all. This excuse, then, rebuts the inference from the nature of the act to the evil of the agent by showing that the rapist is not a moral agent and, therefore, not an appropriate subject for moral blame.

Both those who would condemn the rapist and those who would excuse him or her attempt to draw some conclusion about the moral character of the agent from the nature of the act he or she has done. Condemnations confront many difficulties in constructing a sound argument from the act of rape to the moral blameworthiness of the rapist. Various excuses try, and perhaps succeed, in rebutting such two-step arguments in various ways. The complexity of these arguments and counterarguments is bewildering. How on earth can one draw any reasonable conclusion at all?

A REASONED CONCLUSION

The question we are trying to answer in this chapter is this: Are all rapists morally evil? There are, of course, only two logically possible answers to this question, "yes, all" and "not all." The only way to decide which answer is more reasonable is to reflect upon and critically assess the reasons that can be given for each of these contrary conclusions. Fortunately, we are already familiar with the most plausible pro and con reasons, for the condemnations we have provide arguments for asserting that every rapist is morally evil, and the excuses we have reviewed give arguments for holding that some rapists are not evil. Let us, then, reexamine these condemnations and excuses, select those that seem to be sound arguments (that is, logically valid inferences from true premises), and try to reach some conclusion in the light of all, or at least the strongest, of these sound arguments.

I am inclined to dismiss the condemnations that assume that the rapist is always lustful or always malicious. For one thing, criminologists and psychologists who have made empirical studies of rape frequently conclude that those who commit rapes fall into a number of distinct, although overlapping, classes. Some rapists are seeking sexual gratification and disregard the wishes or welfare of their victims; for others, rape is an aggressive form of assault motivated by antagonism toward the victim or the group represented by the victim. Thus, although it is surely true that many rapists are lustful and many rapists are malicious, it is very doubtful that all rapists are motivated by either of these motives. To be sure, it is possible that all rapists are motivated by one or the other of these two motives, but I know of no reason to assume that these two motives exhaust the motives to rape. For another thing, I do not understand how ascribing some motive to a single act can imply that the agent is morally evil. Precisely what is the connection between a motive for an act and the moral character of the person? Even granted that the motive is an evil one, which could be denied, how does the evil of the motive render the person as a moral agent evil?

In this respect, the arguments that the rapist is always evil because he or she is cruel or selfish are on stronger ground. Cruelty and selfishness are very probably moral vices, while sexual desire and hostility may or may not be morally vicious. Nevertheless, I very much doubt that *all* rapists are cruel. No doubt most rapists intentionally harm their victims, and those motivated by malice take satisfaction in the suffering of those they rape. But psychological studies suggest that some rapists honestly do not realize how, or how much, they are inflicting harm and others regret the suffering they cause at the same time that they cause their victims to suffer. It seems to me that most, but not all, rapists can be said to be cruel persons and, hence, morally evil agents.

The assertion that all rapists, every rapist without exception, are selfish strikes me as more probable. I have deliberately defined rape so as to exclude subtle or weak forms of coercion. To rape is to force another to submit to sexual intercourse. To force someone to do something is to use force or some threat of grievous harm; to submit is to give way to an alien will out of necessity. Any rapist who is at all aware of what he or she is doing must sense that the victim does not wish to be raped and that he or she is imposing his or her wishes upon the reluctant victim. This would seem to be a paradigm case of selfish action, the action of a person who cares only about his or her own wishes or interests and is not concerned with the welfare of others. Since I am neither a psychoanalyst nor a clinical psychologist, I am very hesitant to generalize about rapists. Still, I think that the universal condemnation of rapists on the ground that they are selfish should be taken more seriously than the condemnations grounded on lustfulness, maliciousness, or even cruelty.

I am also impressed by the argument that all rapists are morally evil because they are unscrupulous, or at least if "unscrupulous" is interpreted broadly. To be unscrupulous, you will recall, is to be without scruples, contemptuous of what is right or wrong. Now surely most rapists realize that what they are doing is morally wrong; yet they rape anyway. To so act is to be unscrupulous in the narrow sense of being contemptuous of moral standards, whether these standards be the constraints of moral duty or the demands of the moral rights of others. But there seem to be a few rapists who genuinely do not recognize that they are doing something that violates the rights of the victim and that they morally ought not to do. Does this moral blindness excuse them? I think not. Although they are not contemptuous of what is morally right or obligatory, they are unscrupulous in the broader sense of being without scruples. Their very failure to realize that harming others gratuitously and causing others to suffer for their own selfish purposes is morally wrong reveals a moral defect in their character. The morally good person is one who is sensitive to and caring for others, one who perceives what is morally required of him or her because one is morally mature.

In short, I think it very unlikely that all rapists without exception are either lustful or malicious or even cruel. One can, it seems to me, make a much stronger case for holding that all rapists are selfish and unscrupulous. Although I am very hesitant to accept any universal generalization about rapists, I am willing to grant these assertions for the moment. What I will question is whether selfishness and unscrupulousness necessarily render the agent morally evil. But first I wish to pose another question. Are these two vices, if granted, any adequate measure of the moral evil we should ascribe to the rapist? After all, the confidence man (or woman) is typically selfish and unscrupulous, but we do not judge him (or her) to be *very* evil. In fact, we tend to admire anyone who has sufficient intelligence, imagination, and grace to succeed at playing the confidence game. We condemn the rapist much more harshly. Is our moral blame reasonable? If so, can it be grounded on nothing more than selfishness and unscrupulousness?

To begin with, it is important to bear in mind that our condemnation of the rapist need not always be so limited. Although there is reason to doubt that every rapist is lustful and malicious and cruel, there is abundant evidence to show that many are. The literature on rape is replete with horror stories, especially reports of vicious men inflicting great suffering upon helpless women and girls. These rapists, and there are many of them, are malicious and cruel, and their moral character is surely much more evil than that of the typical confidence man.

More important, I believe, is the fact that moral vices admit of degrees. A man might be selfish about the little things, like serving himself the largest helping of steak, yet unselfishly limit his recreation or spending-money to ensure that his wife can pursue a career or his children can attend the best schools. A woman may lie in conversation about her age, but be scrupulously honest in applying for a passport. To charge the rapist with selfishness and unscrupulousness is to condemn him or her very harshly because he or she is held to be selfish and unscrupulous about something that is very important. Forcible rape is a sexual assault. Although the wrongness of rape is not captured by defining it as sexual intercourse without consent, it is a very special sort of assault just because it is sexual. Sexual intercourse is very important in human life, both because it plays a central role in the social institution of the family and because of its significance in some of the more intimate personal relationships that fundamentally affect the life of an individual. For these reasons, sexual intercourse is charged with emotion and filled with meaning. This meaning of sexual intercourse is part and parcel of what the rapist does and what the victim suffers. Therefore, any rapist who does not care about what he or she is doing to the victim is very selfish indeed, and any rapist who is contemptuous of or even insensitive to the moral demands imposed by sexual intercourse is highly unscrupulous. Therefore, these condemnations, given the nature and importance of rape, are grounds for blaming the rapist severely.

There are, however, those who attempt to rebut such condemnations by advancing excuses. It is high time to review these and decide whether any of them do absolve the rapist, at least some rapists, from moral censure. It is unnecessary to prove that any rapist is morally good; these arguments need only support the weaker conclusion that the rapist is not always evil. I do not believe that the appeal to marital rights does even this much. No husband's moral right that may impose duties upon a wife is an unlimited right, and I can imagine no reason for holding that a husband has a moral right to have his wife submit to sexual intercourse with him whenever he chooses and without regard to circumstances, especially her wishes. Even if he did have such a moral right, what are we to think of a husband who insists upon exercising his rights when his wife is not merely reluctant but resists until forced to submit to his selfish will? There are some occasions when only an evil person will exercise his rights, as we sometimes see in melodramas in which the wicked banker forecloses on the mortgage of a helpless widow just hours before she receives the money to repay him. The appeal to marital rights is no excuse at all.

I am more sympathetic to the rapist who pleads, "But I was seduced." To be sure, this excuse is often proffered when it is entirely out of place. The woman who dresses so as to be sexually attractive or the hitchhiker who accepts a ride after her car has broken down on the highway is not "inviting" sexual intercourse, much less "asking to be raped." But there are occasions, probably atypical, when the victim of a rape has made the first sexual advance and encouraged sexual intimacies short of intercourse in a way that at the very least suggests a willingness to go all the way; indeed, sometimes the victim will consent to intercourse only to resist at the last moment. On such occasions, it seems to me that rapist and victim must share the blame. Thus, seduction may well be a mitigating circumstance, a factor that reduces somewhat the wickedness of the rapist. (This is applicable to lesbian and homosexual rapes as well as male–female rapes.) But to admit that the victim might share the blame with the rapist is not to assert or imply that the rapist is blameless; it is quite compatible with insisting that by far the larger share of the blame belongs to the rapist. Therefore, the plea that one was seduced occasionally mitigates the censure, but never excuses the rapist.

Can one ever rape unintentionally? The standard excuse is that the rapist sometimes, not very often, really does not know that he or she is forcing the victim to submit to sexual intercourse because he or she sincerely believes that the victim is only pretending to resist and really wants sex. Since I have excluded minor threats and slight coercion from my definition of rape, it is hard to imagine circumstances when one could rape unintentionally. Still, some psychologists report cases where this might be true. Even then, however, I am unwilling to admit that such ignorance completely excuses the rapist, for there seems to be culpable ignorance. Sometimes when one acts in ignorance, one ought to have known better. It seems to me that there must be something irresponsible and morally insensitive about any person who could rape another without realizing, at least dimly, what one is doing. Surely, this is a moral defect in the rapist.

I am quite willing to admit that one cannot properly be held morally responsible for something one could not help doing. If one really has no choice, then one is not to blame for what one does. But I do not believe that any psychologically normal person cannot help raping. Whatever the impulse to rape, whether sexual desire or anger, it is not literally irresistible. Any normal person can, if only he or she will, resist even the strongest impulses. To deny this is to undermine moral responsibility and the appropriateness of moral praise or blame in any instance. Only in the case of someone who is psychologically abnormal in some way might a rapist be driven by an irresistible impulse. But then this excuse collapses into the next, and last, one.

There are rapists—I hazard no guess as to how many—who are of unsound mind. Some of these may be permanently mentally defective or semi-permanently insane in such a way that they are incapable of any moral decision to rape or not to rape. Others may be temporarily emotionally disturbed, or drunk, or under the influence of drugs. (For becoming drunk or for taking drugs one may certainly be responsible, but those are actions or a series of actions that are also not identical to the actions said to arise *from* the substance abuse. In legal cases there may be complications like this that we cannot discuss here.) Such persons are not moral agents in the full and strict sense because their psychological incapacities render them unable to act in the morally relevant sense of initiating behavior in the light of practical reasons. Persons of unsound mind are not morally responsible for what they do; it is inappropriate to blame or praise them for their actions. If any of these persons are morally evil, it is not because they are rapists, not because they have forced another to submit to sexual intercourse. For this reason, if for no other, I believe that not all rapists are morally evil. Some rapists are not morally evil because they are of unsound mind and, therefore, not morally responsible agents.

To deny that all rapists are morally evil is not, I hope, to fail to take rape seriously or to suggest that somehow rapists are not so evil. Many rapists are malicious agents and as such vicious people. Most rapists are selfish and unscrupulous and, given the significance of sexual intercourse in human life and the importance of the moral norms regulating sexual conduct, morally evil to a high degree. One can and should recognize that there are excuses that mitigate condemnation or absolve some rapists while at the same time insisting that strong moral condemnation of most rapists is reasonable and just.

STUDY QUESTIONS

1. The author's definition of rape is only one of many. Another is "Rape is any sexual intimacy forced on one person by another." This at least has the advantage of simplicity. What other advantages and disadvantages does it have as defining the sort of act we might most usefully discuss in this chapter?

2. The model penal code defines the crime of rape in terms of "a male who has sexual intercourse with a female." Is there any reason to define rape in such a way that all rapists are male and all victims of rape female? Are you convinced by the author's reasons for rejecting this sort of a definition?

3. The model penal code defines rape as involving sexual intercourse "with a female not his wife." Obviously husbands sometimes do force their wives to submit to sexual intercourse. Is there any reason to define rape so that such acts are not a crime? Should moral philosophers and legislators define rape in the same way or do their different purposes call for quite different definitions of rape?

4. According to the model penal code, rape is a lesser offense if the victim was a voluntary social companion of the rapist and had previously permitted him sexual liberties. Do such circumstances really make a difference in evaluating the immorality of rape? Should they make a difference in the law? Why or why not?

5. According to the model penal code, sexual intercourse includes intercourse per os or per anus, with some penetration, however slight. Some states, however, define rape in terms of vaginal intercourse and sodomy in terms of intercourse per os or per anus. Is there any reason to differentiate between forms of intercourse to define two distinct crimes in this manner? If so, does the reason imply any significant moral difference?

6. Traditionally, sexual intercourse has been defined in terms of the insertion of the penis in the vagina. Is there any strong reason to define rape in terms of this more narrow definition? Is this essentially different from anal or oral

intercourse because only in this way does the female become pregnant? Or because only this mode of intercourse is sacred to God or reserved for marriage?

7. Lust is almost by definition evil, but sexual desire is not. Is there really any basis for this difference in our language? Can you describe in psychological terms the difference between lust and mere sexual desire? If so, how does this psychological difference imply any moral difference? If not, must one reject the argument that the rapist is evil because he or she is lustful?

8. Lust is supposed to be a merely animal desire. But is not sexual desire always a physiologically conditioned animal desire? If so, does this show that lust is not evil or that sexual desire is just as evil as lust?

9. Does maliciousness necessarily make a person morally evil? Suppose that I am a malicious person who desires to harm several of my acquaintances but that I am so ineffectual that I never manage to injure anyone. Is there any reason to blame me morally when I have actually done no harm?

10. Imagine that when a rapist is charged with maliciousness, he replies that he is not motivated by any desire to harm or injure others; he is merely indifferent to the welfare of his victims. Would this reply defend him from any allegation of being morally evil or would it implicitly condemn him morally? Why?

11. We sometimes speak of people as selfish and sometimes as self-centered. What is the difference? Are both selfishness and self-centeredness vices? Why or why not?

12. Suppose that an act of rape in fact imposes great suffering upon the victim, and perhaps on others also, but let us imagine that the rapist is completely unaware of the suffering he is causing. Would it follow that the rapist is not cruel? Would it follow that the suffering he is causing does nothing to show that he is morally evil? Explain.

13. Rapists sometimes argue that they have done no harm by reporting that eventually the victim relaxed and enjoyed it. Is this sort of report ever in fact true? If true, would it excuse the rapist? Why or why not?

14. An agent may be unscrupulous either in acting contrary to his or her scruples, that is, feeling that an act is wrong but doing it anyway, or in acting without scruples, that is, doing a wrong act without feeling any compunction. Is the moral agent to be judged evil in both cases? If so, are these two sorts of unscrupulousness equally evil? If not, why not?

15. One might compare a sexist system of male domination over females with a racist system of white ownership of black slaves. Given that the social institution of slavery is unjust and that any society that maintains and sanctions slavery is unjust, does it follow that each individual slave owner is unjust? Precisely how does participation in an unjust social system make one, or show one, to be an unjust individual?

16. Imagine a slave-holder who sincerely believes that slavery is just because he really believes that blacks are naturally inferior to whites. Imagine also that he consistently tries, within the limits of the social system, to treat his slaves fairly. Would that slave-holder necessarily be an unjust person? If so, why? If not, could there be any analogous sort of rapist?

17. Suppose that an individual rapist is entirely unaware of the role that rape plays in the systematic domination of males over females and that his motivation for raping is a personal desire for sex. Would he be absolved of any charge of being unjust? Why or why not?

18. Does a husband really have a moral right that his wife have sexual intercourse with him whenever he so desires? If so, what is the ground or reason for this right? If not, must we also deny that the wife has a moral right to be financially supported by her husband?

19. Is it really true that no one is morally evil by virtue of exercising his or her moral rights? Are there some rights that one ought not to exercise, at least under some circumstances? Reflect upon the moral character of the banker, often portrayed in melodramas, who forecloses his mortgage on the poor widow's farm knowing that the next day she will receive enough money to pay off her debt.

20. Suppose that seductive provocation sometimes leads to rape. Does this fact show that it is the person raped rather than the rapist who is morally to blame? Does it show that the rapist is less evil than would be the case in an unprovoked rape? Does it show that both the rapist and the raped are equally to blame? What, if anything, does it imply?

21. A mitigating circumstance is one that makes some act or some agent less guilty or less evil than would be the case were this circumstance not present. Is seductive provocation a mitigating circumstance in a case of rape? If so, how can any circumstance reduce the blame without completely excusing the act? If not, what would be a mitigating circumstance, if any?

22. Suppose that occasionally some rapist sincerely believes that his victim is merely pretending to resist and that he is not really forcing her to submit to sexual intercourse. Would this make him morally innocent? Why might it be what one intends to do, rather than what one actually does, that should determine whether an agent is morally good or evil?

23. Is it ever in fact true that one person rapes another unintentionally? Recall that the author defines rape narrowly so that it necessarily involves the use of force or coercion that is *compelling*. How, if at all, does this bear on the argument that the rapist is sometimes not evil because he sometimes acts unintentionally?

24. Are any impulses really irresistible? How does one know? Let us grant that some rapists are driven by an irresistible impulse, say uncontrollable sexual desire or passionate anger. Would this excuse the rapist? Might one argue that a morally good person would not have such an irresistible impulse? Explain.

25. Individuals seem to differ in their ability to resist impulses such as sexual desire, greed, or anger. Does this show that these impulses are weaker in some persons than in others or that some persons have more will-power than others or both or neither? What conclusions should one draw about whether the inability to resist some impulse excuses a moral agent who gives in to it?

26. Does the fact that someone is of unsound mind prove that that person is not morally evil, even when he or she does an act that would show normal agents to be evil? Why or why not?

27. Are rapists any more, or any less, likely than murderers or thieves or arsonists to be of unsound mind? What does your answer imply about the moral culpability of these various classes of wrongdoers?

28. One may be of unsound mind because one is insane or emotionally disturbed or, to give a very different sort of condition, because one is intoxicated with alcohol or drugs. Do these two sorts of unsoundness of mind excuse one equally and in the same way? Why or why not?

29. Someone might argue that the individual who rapes while drunk is not morally responsible for the rape but *is* responsible for getting drunk. Is this true? If so, would this entirely rebut the argument that drunk rapists are not morally evil because they are of unsound mind?

30. Some sociologists and social psychologists hold that males are trained from childhood to separate sexual desire from caring or loving and to regard females as sexual objects. Is this true? If true, does it show that it is society and not the rapist that is morally to blame for the evils of rape? Explain.

31. Rapists often portray themselves as decent persons who have made a serious mistake. They allege that they are basically good, kind, family men and conscientious citizens who merely gave in to temptation on this one occasion. Are some rapists really "nice guys" on the whole? If so, does this show that some rapists are not morally evil? If not, why not?

32. Pick the condemnation or excuse which you consider most plausible. Explain clearly and in detail the logic of the argument from the nature of the act of rape to the moral character of the agent. Is the logical structure of this argument typical or do various condemnations and excuses argue in logically different ways?

33. It seems appropriate to condemn the typical act of rape as a very serious wrong. Does it follow that we ought to condemn the typical rapist as morally evil to a high degree? Why or why not?

34. What is it about rape that leads us to conclude that rape is morally very wrong? Is this conclusion rationally justified? Are these features of rape captured in the author's definition of rape? Should they be included in the very definition of the act? Why or why not?

BIBLIOGRAPHY

AMIR, MENACHEM. *Patterns in Forcible Rape.* Chicago: University of Chicago Press, 1971.
AQUINAS, THOMAS. *Summa Theologica.* Vol. 43, p. 249 (2:2, question 154, article 12). New York: Blackfriars-McGraw-Hill, 1968.
BENEKE, TIMOTHY. *Men on Rape.* New York: St. Martin's Press, 1982.
BROWNMILLER, SUSAN. *Against Our Will.* New York: Simon and Schuster, 1974.
BURGESS, ANN W., AND HOLMSTROM, LYNDA L. *Rape: Victims of Crisis.* Bowie, Md.: R. J. Brady, 1974.
CURLEY, E. M. "Excusing Rape." *Philosophy & Public Affairs* 5 (1976): 325–360.
DE SADE, MARQUIS. *The Complete Justine, Philosophy in the Bedroom, and Other Writings.* Translated by Richard Seaver and Austin Wainhouse, pp. 318–326. New York: Grove Press, 1965.
GEBHARD, PAUL H. ET AL. *Sex Offenders: An Analysis of Types.* New York: Harper & Row, 1965.
GOLDBERG, JACOB A, AND ROSAMUND, W. *Girls on City Streets: A Study of 1400 Cases of Rape.* New York: Foundation Books, 1935.
GROTH, A. NICHOLAS. *Men Who Rape.* New York: Plenum Press, 1979.
KARPMAN, BENJAMIN. *The Sexual Offender and His Offense.* New York: Julian Press, 1954.
MCDONALD, JOHN MARSHALL. *Rape: Offenders and Their Victims.* Springfield, Ill.: Charles C. Thomas, 1971.
MEDEA, ANDREA, AND THOMPSON, KATHLEEN. *Against Rape.* New York: Noonday, 1974.
RUSSELL, DIANA. *The Politics of Rape.* New York: Stein & Day, 1975.
RUSSELL, DIANA. *Sexual Exploitation.* Beverly Hills: Sage Publications, 1984.
SCHWENDINGER, JULIA R, AND SCHWENDINGER, HERMAN. *Rape and Inequality.* Beverly Hills: Sage Publications, 1983.

SCULLY, DIANA, AND MAROLLA, JOSEPH. "Convicted Rapists' Vocabulary of Motive: Excuses and Justifications," *Social Problems* 31 (1984): 530–542.
SCULLY, DIANA, AND MAROLLA, JOSEPH. "Riding the Bull at Gilley's: Convicted Rapists Describe the Rewards of Rape," *Social Problems* 32 (1985): 251–262.
VETTERLING-BRAGGIN, MARY; ELLISTON, FREDERICK A.; AND ENGLISH, JANE, eds. *Feminism and Philosophy,* pp. 309–376. Totowa, N.J.: Littlefield, Adams & Co., 1981.

6
MORAL VALUE

*Public virtue cannot exist in a nation
without private, and public virtue is the
only foundation of republics.*

John Adams in letter to Mary Warren,
April 16, 1776

*If he does really think that there is no
distinction between virtue and vice, why
sir, when he leaves our houses let us
count our spoons.*

Samuel Johnson in Boswell's
Life of Johnson.

The arguments used to establish any specific moral conclusion require two sorts of premises: statements of facts and statements of ethical principles. Accordingly, disagreement over some specific moral conclusion may result either from disagreement about the facts of the case or from disagreement about which ethical theory is correct. For example, people often disagree about whether the rapist is always morally evil just because they disagree about the facts. Some excuse many rapists because they believe that they are mentally ill and therefore acting compulsively, while others believe that rapists could have spared their victims had they chosen to do so. People may also disagree about whether the rapist is always morally evil because they have different conceptions of virtue and vice. Those who conceive of virtue in terms of unselfish love will almost certainly condemn the rapist as lacking in compassion for his victim while those who are convinced that virtue consists in nobility might see the rapist as the powerful personality, conceived as Nietzsche conceived of him (as we will see), wrongly condemned by the weak who are motivated by the ignoble sentiments of resentment, fear, and envy. Here, as elsewhere, in attempting to think through a specific moral problem, one is inevitably forced to wrestle with some more general ethical problem. Thus, "Are all rapists morally evil?" inevitably leads to the question "What makes an agent morally good or evil?"

This question is twice removed from a question we have already considered, "What makes an act morally right or wrong?" Obviously it concerns agents rather than their acts. An agent is simply any person who acts or is capable of acting. It also concerns value rather than obligation. We are asking what makes an agent virtuous or wicked, not what makes an act right or wrong. To ask what makes a person virtuous or wicked is to inquire into the grounds of moral approval or disapproval, the reasons why praising or condemning the agent would be rationally justified. But to ask what makes an act right or wrong is to inquire after the grounds of choice, the reasons why doing or not doing the act would be rationally justified. A judgment of moral value expresses the standpoint of a moral observer reacting to an agent with the sentiment of moral approval or disapproval. A judgment of obligation takes up the standpoint of an agent choosing to do or not do some action. Thus, our question about what makes an agent morally good poses a problem of evaluation rather than a problem of deciding what one ought to do.

Nevertheless, it is a significantly different problem from the one posed by the question "What is the good?" Asking what makes an agent *morally* good or evil is not at all the same as asking what makes someone good or bad in some generic, nonmoral sense. Am I good or bad? Well, I am a good teacher, a good public speaker, a mediocre typist, and a very bad golfer; but none of these makes me morally good or evil because specifically moral value is a very special sort of value. Only a moral agent can be morally good or evil. Primarily and in the strict sense, it is human beings who can be said to be virtuous or wicked. If there are angels who carry out the orders of God or occasionally, like Satan, rebel against God, then they are also morally good or evil. But presumably watches or dogs, even good watches or dogs, cannot meaningfully be said to be morally good or evil simply because they are not moral agents. Moreover, to speak of an agent as morally good or evil is to evaluate that agent *as* a moral agent, not as a teacher, typist, or golfer. If someone is highly successful in swindling little old ladies by virtue of his cleverness, imagination, and ingratiating personality, he can correctly be called "a good confidence man," but not "a good person." Thus the question "What makes someone *morally* good?" comes down to "What makes an agent *as* a moral agent good?" Several answers to this question, several theories of moral value, are worthy of attention.

THEORIES OF MORAL VALUE

Righteousness

As one might expect, our religious heritage contains several theories of moral value. One traditional conception of virtue is suggested by many passages in the Old Testament. Virtue consists in righteousness, in submission to the will of God. The righteous agent is the person who acts in obedience to the commands of God. More than accidental or grudging conformity to the Divine Law is required to confer moral value; one must obey intentionally, fully accepting God's will. The unrighteous agent is the person who defies or rejects the will of God. Wickedness springs from that sinful pride in which one puts one's own desires and judgment before those of God; in pride one violates the Divine Law, or at best submits to it resentfully and reluctantly. The Old Testament tells us that the righteous man bows down before God; he is not stiff-necked. He or she accepts and gladly obeys the will of the Creator. The morally good agent is the person who acts in willing submission to God; the morally evil agent is the person who disobeys, or longs to disobey, God out of sinful pride.

On behalf of this theory of virtue it can be argued that it recognizes the perfection of God. God is by definition the Divine Being. Inscrutable as God's nature may be to the finite human mind, at least God's divinity implies that the Creator is omnipotent, omniscient, and all-good. It is only reasonable to obey the will of an omniscient and omnipotent God, for He or She will know whether or not we obey and has the power to determine our eternal destiny for better or worse. Again, an all-good being deserves willing obedience. Only a selfish or self-centered person would refuse to submit to the Divine Will. Surely there can be no higher or better standard of moral value than the morally perfect being that is God.

On the other hand, this theory seems to condemn some persons unfairly. If virtue consists in willing obedience to God, then any moral agent who fails to submit to God's will is entirely lacking in moral value. This seems unduly harsh, for it implies that heathens, who fail to obey the will of God simply because they have not heard the Gospel preached, are wicked no matter how loving and conscientious their acts may be. Again, what about atheists who do not act in willing submission to the will of God because they do not believe in the existence of any Divine Being? The atheist may well be mistaken in denying the existence of God, but his or her intellectual error hardly seems an adequate ground for impugning his or her moral character. Submission to the will of God, even if reasonable and desirable, does not seem necessary to the moral goodness of a person. Surely the heathen or atheist who lives a loving, courageous, and conscientious life is virtuous even though he or she is not, strictly speaking, righteous.

Love

Some people contend that while the Old Testament teaches an ethics of law, the New Testament preaches an ethics of love. While the former claims that what makes an act right is conformity to the law of God and what makes an agent morally good is righteousness, the latter grounds morality upon love. In Chapter 4, we discussed the view of Joseph Fletcher that the only thing of intrinsic value is love. In this chapter we will consider the related but different view that it is love that makes an agent virtuous.

Paul Ramsey, a contemporary Christian moralist, contends that love is the ground of moral value. What determines the moral value of an agent is not his or her conformity to some external law, whether that of God or society, but the inner spirit in which he or she acts. All agents motivated primarily by love are virtuous, and agents who act in an unloving spirit are wicked. The love to which Ramsey refers is Christian love rather than mere desire or possessive love; it is agape rather than eros. Agape is a selfless concern for the well-being of its object, springing from the perfection of the one who loves. Eros is a self-centered desire to possess some object, springing from some lack or need in the lover. Christian love takes all humankind for its object, for it recognizes that all human beings are created in the image of God. In this way, the love of one's neighbor is tied to the love of God. The supreme example of a loving act is the action of Christ in sacrificing himself for all humanity from a pure and outgoing compassion. Any agent motivated by a love like this is morally good; any unloving agent is evil. Although this theory of moral value has usually been advanced by Christian philosophers, it could be proposed outside of any religious framework. It would be quite possible for someone to hold that love is the source of all virtue without thinking of love in specifically Christian terms.

One line of reasoning that could lead to this theory of virtue begins with reflection on the various forms of vice. In examining a wide variety of vices, one may be struck by the fact that each is unloving in one way or another. Persons motivated by hate, selfishness, envy, or callousness are surely morally evil, and it is hard to think of examples of wicked persons who are not motivated by some form of unlovingness. If moral evil does always spring from a lack of love, then presumably the universal antidote to vice is love. This supports the conclusion that it is love that makes any agent morally good.

But does love really guarantee moral goodness? To many moralists it appears that loving persons can, upon occasion, do evil acts precisely because of their love or concern for others. A wealthy person might be filled with pity for the unemployed in his or her community so that he or she gives them financial support for long periods of time. Although the agent is motivated by love, he or she might well undermine the character of those who receive charity by making them less self-reliant or even lazy. Surely it cannot be virtuous to act in ways that weaken the moral fiber of fellow human beings. Or, to take a very different example, suppose that someone takes part in a riot out of compassion for the inhabitants of an urban ghetto. This person destroys property and may even injure innocent bystanders, but is motivated by sympathy and compassion for the victims of our urban society. Many people would judge that the love expressed in this agent's action is not sufficient to outweigh the fact that it is intentionally harmful and thus morally irresponsible. Apparently not all loving agents are morally good.

A Disposition To Choose Rationally

Turning from our Judeo-Christian heritage to ancient Greek philosophy, it is only natural to think first of Aristotle, whose treatment of virtue is the starting place for so many contemporary discussions. Like Plato, Aristotle had a very broad conception of virtue. The virtue of anything is its specific excellence, that which makes anything good of its species. Thus, the virtue of a knife is to cut easily and cleanly, and the virtue of a watch is whatever it is that makes it keep accurate time. Human virtue, then, will depend upon what defines the human species. Since human beings are like the other animals in having physical bodies, the capacities of nutrition and reproduction, and the capacities of sensation, desire, and motivation, none of these define human nature. What is distinctive and essential to a human being is rationality, the capacity to reason. Hence, the virtue of a human consists in rationality; and moral virtue is the disposition to choose rationally. An occasional rational choice does not make anyone morally good; to be virtuous one must be disposed to choose rationally, one must usually or habitually choose rationally. Now the paradigms of rational action lie in the skills, such as cobbling or medicine. In choosing the thickness or texture of the sole of a shoe, the rational cobbler will avoid a piece of leather that is so thick that it will not bend easily or so thin that it will wear out quickly. In prescribing a medicine, the rational physician will not choose either a potentially dangerous overdose or an ineffective underdose. The rationality of any choice, accordingly, consists in avoiding either of two extremes; practical reason consists in choosing the mean. This is why Aristotle maintains that moral virtue is a disposition to choose the mean.

Even if one finds Aristotle's doctrine of the mean unhelpful or mistaken as a criterion for rational action, one may wish to preserve the essential insight in his theory of moral virtue. Aristotle takes it for granted that moral virtue must be displayed in right action. To be sure, a morally good person might occasionally act wrongly, but surely the virtuous person must be disposed to do what is right and must habitually refrain from wrong action. It is hard to see how this presupposition could reasonably be denied. The goodness of an agent *as* an *agent* must somehow lie in the morality of his or her *actions*. Aristotle's theory provides a very plausible explanation of the necessary connection between virtue and obligation. Since the right action is the alternative in any choice situation supported with the weight of practical reasons, the balance of reasons for acting over reasons against acting in this manner, then the disposition of any agent to choose rationally will ensure that most of the time that agent will choose the right act. In this way, the moral goodness of the agent will necessarily be expressed in the moral rightness of action.

Aristotle not only gives us a general theory of moral virtue together with a plausible argument to establish it, he also provides a detailed and illuminating characterization of the specific virtues, such as generosity, justice, or courage. One may well wonder, however, whether he has correctly identified what it is that makes these dispositions morally good. According to his theory, it is the rationality of any disposition to choose that makes it virtuous, that renders it worthy of our moral approval and praise; conversely, it is the irrationality of any disposition that explains why it is a vice. But is it really a lack of reason, rather than the absence of pity or compassion, that we morally condemn in the cruel person? And is it really the disposition to choose rationally that we morally approve in the courageous soldier or firefighter? One test of the philosophical adequacy of any general theory of moral goodness is its ability to explain our pretheoretical judgments of virtue or vice. Many persons would conclude that Aristotle's theory cannot pass this test.

Conscientiousness

Immanuel Kant, one of the greatest of modern philosophers, also grounded virtue on practical reason, but in a very different manner. According to Kant, moral obligations are imposed by the categorical imperative—the commands of pure reason. The good will (the morally good agent) responds to the dictates of reason with the purely rational motive of respect for the moral law. Kant concludes that it is conscientiousness, the sense of duty, that makes an agent morally good. Every agent motivated by a sense of duty is virtuous; when one's sense of duty is overcome by some conflicting desire or inclination, one is morally evil. A conscientious agent is one who is motivated by the sense of duty, the agent who does what he or she believes is the right thing to do because it is what is morally required of one. Although we ordinarily speak of the sense of duty as the desire to do what is right just because it is right, it is not a desire of the same sort as the desire for fame or food or happiness. Kant calls these desires "inclinations" and holds that they are feelings based on the empirical nature of human beings. The sense of duty, on the other hand, is a purely rational respect for the moral law entirely independent of our sensations or feelings. In spite of being grounded in reason rather than feeling, the sense of duty is an emotion that can move one to action. When this motive prevails, the agent is virtuous; when this motive is overcome by some contrary inclination, the agent is wicked. This theory implies that the student who refrains from cheating on an examination because he or she believes that one ought to be honest is morally good; the student who refrains from cheating simply out of habit is neither good nor evil; and the student whose sense of duty is overcome by the desire for a good grade so that he or she cheats is morally evil.

One strength of this theory is that it can explain the specifically moral character of virtuous persons. A painting of the good Samaritan helping the injured man can be beautiful or powerful but not virtuous. The dog that remains faithful to its master and protects him from violent attack is a good dog, but no brute animal can literally be virtuous. The moral value that people have is a very special sort of value, very different from esthetic, instrumental, economic, or utility value. But precisely what is it that gives virtue its specifically moral character? According to Kant, what makes an agent virtuous is his or her conscientiousness, the fact that the sense of duty prevails in his or her actions. The sense of duty is a specifically moral motive—in fact, the only specifically moral motive—because its very nature consists in a respect for the moral law and a desire to do what is morally right simply because one has a moral duty to do so. The nature of conscientiousness explains what is specifically moral about virtue. And since only moral agents are capable of acting conscientiously, of choosing to act from a sense of duty, this theory also explains why it is that only moral agents can possess this very special sort of value.

One weakness of this theory is that conscientiousness does not seem to guarantee that the agent will be virtuous. Consider the churchmen who participated in the thirteenth-century Inquisition by burning heretics at the stake. These Roman Catholics were often motivated by a deep and sincere sense of religious duty, but they were, nevertheless, very intolerant and cruel. Or consider those Nazis, perhaps the minority, who herded Jews into concentration camps, led them into gas chambers, and buried mounds of corpses because they really believed that they had a moral obligation to preserve the purity of the superior Aryan race. Such examples seem to indicate that the sense of duty can be so misguided that conscientiousness may not be sufficient to make an agent morally good.

The Human Constitution

Another conception of virtue is that what makes an agent morally good is his or her conformity to the human constitution. The constitution of anything consists in the elements that make it up together with the relations in which these elements stand. If we were to describe the constitution of our federal government, for example, we would have to mention the elements that make it up—the legislature (composed of the House of Representatives and the Senate), the administration (composed of the president, the vice-president, the cabinet, and the various departments and bureaus), and the judiciary (composed of the Supreme Court, the circuit courts, and the district courts). Such a list of parts would not, however, describe fully the constitution of our government; to do this we must also specify the relations of authority between these various parts. We must mention the fact that the president has the authority to veto legislation but that the legislature can override that veto with a two-thirds vote in each house; the fact that the president appoints judges to the Supreme Court, but only with the advice and consent of the Senate; the fact that the courts have the authority to declare acts of Congress unconstitutional; and other facts about the relations between the parts of our government.

Similarly, the human constitution consists of various elements standing in relations of authority. A human being has many particular passions, such as the appetite for food, for sex, for wealth, for revenge, etc. These appetites are called "particular passions" because each is directed toward some particular kind of object, and only that kind of object will satisfy this particular appetite. Thirst is satisfied when one obtains some liquid to drink but not when one gets a peanut butter sandwich or a new pair of shoes. In addition to many particular passions, human nature contains two general passions—self-love and benevolence. Self-love is the desire for the satisfaction of one's own particular passions; benevolence is the desire for the satisfaction of other people's particular passions. These are general passions in that the object desired is the satisfaction of *any* and *all* of the particular appetites. While the desire for food is directed at food alone, self-love may be gratified by the satisfaction derived from eating, drinking, becoming famous, or obtaining the object of any of the other particular passions. Finally, human nature contains the element of conscience. Conscience is that faculty by which we feel rational approval or disapproval of actions or agents.

To complete the description of the human constitution, it is necessary only to add the relations between these elements. The general passions have authority over the particular passions, and conscience has authority over both the particular and the general passions. This implies that when thirst and self-love conflict—for example—when a thirsty person wants to drink from a stream known to be dangerously polluted, self-love rather than thirst ought to control that person's action. Again, when conscience conflicts with self-love or any other passion or set of passions, one ought to overcome these passions and act as one's conscience dictates. This view of human nature, and the conception of moral value grounded in it, was advocated by Joseph Butler, an Anglican bishop of the eighteenth century. He held that any agent who conforms to the human constitution is morally good and that any agent who violates that constitution is morally evil.

One strength of this theory is that it does recognize something of the complexity of human nature. It does not reduce a human being to a purely rational will or, at the other extreme, to a brute animal with nothing but feelings and desires. Not only does it admit that a human being is made up of many parts, but it also sees that these various parts stand in complicated relations to one another. Its moral ideal tries to include all of these aspects of human nature. As a consequence, its conception of virtue does not require the moral agent to try to suppress or eliminate some basic part of himself or herself. This is a considerable advantage in any philosophy of moral practice because any ideal that demands the denial of any essential part of human nature is bound to be unrealistic and impossible to live up to for actual human beings.

Nevertheless, this very effort to be all-inclusive leads to a serious difficulty for this theory. This theory declares, you will remember, that the virtuous agent is one who is in conformity with human nature, while the wicked agent is one who violates human nature. But how could any human being possibly fail to conform to human nature? Even the most evil act springs from some motive or motives in the agent; and if the agent is a human being, then the act must spring from something in human nature. Unless there is some flaw in this line of reasoning, the theory that virtue consists in conformity to human nature implies that every human being is morally good. This is a reductio ad absurdum of the theory because it is obvious that many moral agents are morally evil and, as we say, all too human.

Good Dispositions

The contemporary British philosopher G. J. Warnock recognizes the imperfections in human nature and builds his moral theory around them. He argues that the general object of morality is to contribute, by way of the actions of rational beings, to the amelioration of the human predicament, of that which causes much avoidable human suffering. The human predicament results from a number of diverse limiting factors—limited resources, limited information, limited intelligence, limited rationality, and limited sympathies. As a consequence, human needs are often unmet and human beings are often harmed, or at least not helped when they are in distress. Of the limitations that constitute the human predicament, the most important are internal to human nature. Thus, the limitations in human sympathies frequently lead one person to harm another, to refrain from helping others when they need help, to discriminate against those outside the restricted sphere of one's concern, or to deceive others. If the human predicament is to be ameliorated, people must acquire good dispositions—some readiness to voluntarily do desirable actions which most humans are not naturally disposed to do and similarly a readiness voluntarily not to do damaging actions. Warnock's notion of a disposition is like Aristotle's in that it refers to a tendency to act in some specific manner, but it adds the proviso that one is ready to do so willingly and without the need of any social compulsion. The fundamental moral virtues are (at least): non-maleficence, beneficence, fairness, and non-deception—the good dispositions that tend to counteract the four harmful tendencies that spring from the limited sympathies in human nature. Accordingly, what makes an agent morally good is a good disposition, a readiness to act voluntarily in ways that overcome the limitation of human sympathies and whose exercise is primarily good for persons other than the agent.

An advantage of this theory is that it can explain in a plausible way just how the moral virtues differ from our moral obligations. Warnock suggests that they differ in two essential respects. While obligations are kinds of *actions* that one ought to do, virtues are dispositions of the *agent* that it would be good for one to have. Again, while an obligation is a kind of act society would be morally justified in *compelling* one to do, a virtue is a readiness to act *voluntarily* and without any threat of social sanctions for a failure to do so. Since moral virtues and moral obligations, such as honesty and truthtelling, are often confused, a theory that can explain just how they differ while both being morally relevant has much to recommend it.

Some moral philosophers will decide to reject this theory, however, because it does not fit some of the traditional paradigms of moral virtue. Philosophers from Plato and Aristotle to the present day have generally thought that courage is a moral virtue. But it does not seem to be a disposition that counteracts some limitation in human sympathies. The human frailty that it overcomes is fear or loss of nerve. Again, temperance has traditionally been believed to be one of the most important moral virtues. But this virtue overcomes excessive appetites rather than limited concern for the welfare of others. Examples such as these suggest that Warnock has recognized too narrow a range of good dispositions in his theory of moral value.

Good Intentions

It is quite natural to imagine that the person who does good is good and that the person who acts in harmful ways is evil. Accordingly, a woman who gives food to the poor is thought to be virtuous because she benefits them, and the man who poisons the candy he gives out on Halloween is evil because of the harmful consequences of his actions. But this simple correlation between the moral value of an agent and the nonmoral value of the consequences of his or her actions does not always hold good. Suppose, for example, that I am hiking along a highway and come upon the victim of an automobile accident. This unfortunate person is slumped unconscious over the steering wheel in his smashed car. Knowing enough first aid to be aware of the danger of further injuring the victim, I feel along his bones as well as I can to determine whether any of them are broken. Finding no evidence of a fracture, I lift him out of the car, place him on the ground, and treat him for shock. Unfortunately, his backbone had indeed been fractured in the accident so that my act of moving him causes a nerve in his spinal column to be severed, rendering him permanently paralyzed from the waist down. Assuming that he would not have died from shock or suffered greater injury by being left in the car until the ambulance arrived, I have clearly done an act with very harmful consequences. But would we say that, acting on my knowledge of first aid and motivated by compassion as I was, I was morally evil and deserved blame? I think not.

If the agent is not always to blame for unintended harm, most likely the agent does not deserve moral praise for doing good unintentionally either. This suggests that what makes an agent morally good or evil is good or bad intentions. An agent is virtuous when he or she intends to benefit people by his or her actions; a wicked person is the one whose intention is to harm people. When a woman jumps into a chilly river and tries without success to save a drowning child, she is not wicked because she merely muddied and soaked her clothes without actually doing any good; she is virtuous because she intended to save a human life. Again, if the gun misfires when a jealous husband attempts to kill his wife, he is not blameless merely because he did no harm; he is wicked because he intended to do great harm. The moral value of an agent, then, depends entirely upon his or her intentions. A contemporary philosopher who has defended this theory of moral value is W. H. F. Barnes. The morally good agent is the one who intends to bring about good results; the morally evil agent is the one who intends to harm people.

This theory of moral value is attractive in part because it seems to provide a fair basis for moral praise or blame. Although we would not always be justified in blaming a person for doing something that accidentally harms another, it does seem reasonable to blame him or her if he or she intentionally brings about bad consequences. Accidental or inadvertent harm is no evidence of vice, but to deliberately harm someone, except under duress of circumstances, seems a clear indication of wickedness. What more plausible way of explaining this difference than to hold that what makes an agent morally good or evil is good or bad intentions?

Still, this theory may not quite capture the essence of virtue and vice. Although it seems too harsh to blame the agent for any and all bad consequences that may result from an action, it seems too lenient to restrict blame to intended consequences only. Suppose a hunter accidentally kills his hunting partner while cleaning his rifle. Should we consider him blameless because he did not intend to kill his fellow hunter? Probably not. The hunter should have known his gun was loaded. Or suppose that, while driving along the highway one-handed and deep in conversation with someone in the back seat of his car, a driver hits and maims a pedestrian. No doubt he did not intentionally run down the person, but he is still at fault morally because he ought to have been more careful. Thus, although the intention of the agent is clearly relevant to his or her moral value, other factors also appear to be relevant. Precisely what these various factors have in common and why they make someone morally good or evil remains to be explained.

Useful Personality Traits

The morally good person is the person "of good character." But just what is one's character and precisely what makes one's character good? One's character consists of one's various personality traits. If asked to describe the character of a friend, one might describe him as "irritable but friendly, honest but a bit lazy." A personality trait is something characteristic of the person, a fairly stable disposition to respond in specific ways to certain sorts of situations. We wouldn't say that a man is irritable just because he loses his temper once or occasionally; but if he often loses his temper and regularly becomes angry, even at minor irritations, then he has the trait of irritability. Again, we do not judge a person lazy for taking a nap on a hot day or doing very little during a two-week vacation. But a person who habitually naps, loafs, and takes it easy and very seldom works long or hard is judged lazy. The traits that determine moral value are personality traits. Physical or bodily features like strength or litheness are irrelevant to virtue or vice. Not all personality traits count either. In most theories, traits like enthusiasm or imagination are also irrelevant to specifically moral value. Which personality traits, then, do make an agent morally good?

David Hume, the eighteenth-century Scottish philosopher, held that virtue consists in useful personality traits. The way he put it was that the virtues are qualities of mind that are useful or agreeable to the possessor or others. But if utility is defined broadly as the characteristic of bringing value into existence, and if it is assumed that whatever is agreeable is valuable, then this amounts to a utilitarian theory of virtue. Notice that this is not the theory most commonly called "utilitarianism," for that is a theory about what makes an act right or wrong, while Hume's theory is about what makes an agent good or evil. Generosity, for example, is a very useful personality trait because it motivates people to act in ways that make others happy or relieves their distress. Cowardice is a vice because it is a harmful personality trait that causes people to act in ways that endanger others in time of crisis, or it may cause someone to fail to act in urgent situations where the well-being of the agent or others is threatened. Put in the form of a general theory, Hume's view is that an agent with predominantly useful personality traits is morally good and an agent with predominantly harmful personality traits is morally evil.

One advantage of this theory is that it can explain the importance we attach to virtue and vice. Most of us want deeply to be morally good persons and feel shame when we discover some moral defect in our character. Most parents spend a great deal of time and energy trying to mold the character of their children. Society, in various formal and informal ways, encourages virtue and discourages vice. Why all this fuss and bother? We are greatly concerned about virtue because the moral value of an agent is tied to social welfare. The morally good agent has personality traits that motivate him or her to act in beneficial ways; the morally evil agent has harmful personality traits. Thus, the difference between virtue and vice in an agent makes a significant difference to the well-being or to the ill of the members of the society in which he or she lives and acts usefully or harmfully. It is for this reason that society and the individuals who make it up care about moral value.

One disadvantage of this theory is that it seems unable to explain the specifically moral character of virtue or vice. Hume's theory is supposed to tell us what makes an agent morally good. Now *moral* value is a very special kind of value, and it calls forth a very special attitude in the observer or judge. A reliable watchdog may be a very useful animal if it barks whenever intruders are about and fights off attackers upon occasion. Hence, one may reasonably desire to possess such a dog and the owner may well feel pleased and even proud of the dog. Although she or he may ordinarily speak of the dog as "reliable" and "brave," we don't usually go so far as to characterize it as "courageous" or to ascribe moral virtue to it in any literal sense. Only moral agents, beings capable of deliberation and rational choice, can be *morally* good or evil. Moral value is a very special sort of value, and it commands the very special sort of response of moral approval and respect. The merely useful seems to lack the peculiar elevation or dignity of the specifically moral. Hume lists among the useful personality traits wit and cheerfulness, but these hardly seem to be paradigms of moral virtues, even if they are, in his phrase, aspects of "personal merit." Whatever it is that makes an agent morally good, it must be something worthy of our moral respect.

Noble Personality Traits

Friedrich Nietzsche maintained that human beings fall into two classes—the masters and the slaves, the powerful and the weak. By the masters he does not necessarily mean those who happen to have power in a particular society at a particular time, for many of these people are ignoble. The true master class is composed of those natural aristocrats whose powerful personalities raise them above the common herd of humanity. Certain personality traits are characteristic of the master and set him apart from the masses. He is possessed of deep feelings, strong drives, unusual imagination, great daring, high intelligence, and self-discipline. It is personality traits such as these that enable the natural nobleman to undertake and carry through profoundly original and dangerous grand projects in politics, business, science, or art. Any agent who possesses these noble personality traits is morally good; any agent who lacks these is ignoble and morally bad. Nietzsche agreed with Hume that character consists of personality traits, but he rejected vehemently the notion that mere utility defines the morally valuable traits. It is not those traits that are useful in increasing the happiness for the masses, but those personality traits characteristic of the master, the natural aristocrat with the powerful personality, that make an agent morally good.

One strength of this theory is that it seems to explain why it is that virtue commands not just our liking and desire, but our admiration and respect. There is a greatness about the strong personality, the natural nobleman, to which we respond with just these feelings of admiration and respect. The power of Napoleon did not consist primarily in the number of men he happened to have in his army. It lay in his imaginative strategy, his daring when crucial decisions were to be made, and his commanding personality that drew men to him and made them obey him unquestioningly. Socrates was much more than a very clever thinker and debater. He dared to reject every comfortable falsehood and face the condemnation of his society. His dedication to the pursuit of truth was complete and left no stray impulses to distract him from his life's work. Wagner was a musical innovator who put the stamp of his personality upon the music of his time, a music that merged powerful passions and large conceptions into a controlled art form. When we contemplate powerful individuals like these, we respond with much more than mere liking and a desire to imitate them; we feel profound admiration and respect. The most natural explanation of why we respond with the same sentiments to virtuous agents is that the morally good person is the one who possesses noble personality traits.

Some moral philosophers argue, on the other hand, that far from explaining our specifically moral feelings, Nietzsche's theory outrages the sensibilities of any truly moral person. Perhaps the powerful personality does command our admiration and respect, but not our *moral* admiration. Nor is there anything specifically moral about the respect we may have for the great scholar who takes no stand and is oblivious to all the pressing moral issues of the day. The appropriate response to virtue or vice, on the other hand, is the specifically moral attitude of approval or disapproval. On this score, it is emphatically not true that we typically approve of the powerful personality or of the acts that reveal such personality traits. In fact, the powerful personality may be morally reprehensible. The charismatic, ruthless military leader dedicated to a misguided cause, like exterminating a helpless people, may be a born master yet a moral monster. The impressive teacher who molds students into his or her own image regardless of their own interests, needs, or talents is doubtless a powerful personality, but his or her virtue is very much in doubt. If the noble personality traits are those characteristic of the powerful personality, as Nietzsche believed, the theory that defines moral value in terms of noble personality traits appears to do violence to our specifically moral sentiments of approval and disapproval.

The central question of this chapter has been "What makes an agent morally good or evil?" We have briefly examined nine different replies to this ethical question—righteousness, love, a disposition to choose rationally, conscientiousness, the human constitution, good dispositions, good intentions, useful personality traits, and noble personality traits. Although we have been able to learn something important from each of these theories of moral value, none has been entirely convincing. Can we discover a more adequate answer to our central question?

HUME REVISED

Of all the theories of moral value we have surveyed, Hume's theory strikes me as closest to the truth. For one thing, he has identified correctly the genus of virtue and vice, the generic sort of thing that makes any agent morally good or evil. We ascribe virtue or vice to the person, not to his body or her intellect alone. And although we are rightly sceptical of inner virtue that never expresses itself in observable action, we do not judge an agent to be morally good or evil on the basis of occasional and uncharacteristic actions. Hence, moral value consists in personality traits, fairly stable tendencies or dispositions to respond in specific ways to certain sorts of situations. These responses of the person are not limited to overt behavior; they express the entire personality. This is obvious in the case of kindness, which involves feeling pity for misfortune or joy in the happiness of others and thinking about how others feel or prosper or suffer (thoughtfulness, as we say) in addition to performing acts of kindness. It is equally true, although less obvious, of a virtue such as justice. To be sure, the just person characteristically treats others justly, but it requires more than this to confer moral value upon the agent. The genuinely just person cares about fairness, willingly makes personal sacrifices to avoid or eliminate injustice, and notices discrimination where others are too insensitive to see it. I agree with Hume, therefore, that it is personality traits that make an agent morally good or evil.

But what is it that distinguishes those personality traits that are specifically moral from those, like curiosity, that are not? And within the class of morally relevant personality traits, precisely what distinguishes the virtues from the vices? Hume's answer is utility. The virtues are the useful personality traits, and the vices are the harmful ones. As far as this goes, this seems to me to be the correct answer. If we examine the paradigms of virtue and vice, we find this utilitarian theory of moral value confirmed. Surely honesty is a very useful personality trait, for it keeps others from being harmfully misled by one's assertions and makes one trustworthy enough to ensure the success of important cooperative projects. Just as surely, cruelty is very harmful in that it causes agents to refrain from aiding those in distress or reducing their suffering, and it causes unnecessary misery since cruel agents act in injurious ways. It is not merely that the virtues happen to be useful; they are virtues *because* they are useful. The utility of a personality trait makes it good, and the fact that a personality trait is harmful is a cogent reason for judging it to be evil. Thus, Hume's theory both explains and justifies our considered judgments of moral value.

Moreover, the lack of social utility, and in extreme cases the harmfulness of alleged virtues, are cogent reasons for concluding that they are "false virtues." Hume waxes eloquent on this point.

> Celibacy, fasting, penance, mortification, self-denial, humility, silence, solitude, and the whole train of monkish virtues; for what reason are they everywhere rejected by men of sense, but because they serve to no manner of purpose; neither advance a man's fortune in the world, nor render him a more valuable member of society; neither qualify him for the entertainment of company, nor increase his power of self-enjoyment? (*Enquiry*, p. 270)

It might be thought that Hume is begging the question by rejecting these traditional religious "virtues" by arguing that they are completely useless personality traits, but this is not entirely true. If the traditional theological presuppositions were true, these traits would be genuine virtues because they would then be useful in that they would lead to the salvation of one's soul and indirectly by one's example lead others to eternal bliss. The theologian may, of course, be correct in believing that a personal God controls our destinies and that the personality traits he or she recommends are really valuable. But if they are in fact useless, as Hume maintains, then their lack of utility is an excellent reason for denying their moral value. It seems to me that a utilitarian theory of moral value is on the right track.

Still, Hume's theory does not go far enough. There is a tremendous variety of useful or harmful personality traits, not all of which are relevant to the moral value or disvalue of their possessor. Hume lists as prime examples of the virtues such qualities as cleanliness, cheerfulness, wit, tranquility, and ingenuity. Granted that these are elements of personal merit, they are not specifically moral personality traits. Why did Hume refuse to limit virtue to those excellences of the agent that are moral in the narrow and strict sense? Probably because he failed to notice the social dimension in our concept of morals. It is no accident, I believe, that the word "moral" is derived from "mores" and our word "ethics" from "ethos." Our concept of the moral was originally derived from, and remains tied to, our understanding of positive morality. Positive morality consists of norms or standards for conduct and character that are generally accepted in a society, internalized by the members of the society through enculturation, and imposed upon the individual by various forms of informal social pressure or promotion. Morals, like morality, also consist of norms for conduct and character. Moral norms are not the conventional standards that happen to be accepted by society, but rationally justified standards—ultimately practical reasons. Moral reasons are, however, a very special sort of reasons; they are dual-aspect reasons. By this I mean that they are not only reasons to guide the decisions of an individual moral agent, but also reasons to direct the practices of a society. This is why morals, like positive morality, are essentially social.

Accordingly, I propose to remedy the crucial defect in Hume's theory of moral value by adding a further condition that recognizes the social dimension of morals. The virtues are personality traits that it is useful for agents to possess *and* useful for society to nurture; the vices are personality traits that it is harmful for agents to have and useful for society to eradicate. Thus, the fact that someone is honest is a reason for ascribing moral value to him or her. Since it is a specifically moral reason, it is a dual-aspect reason. That the agent's personality trait is one of honesty is a reason for the agent to remain honest and, if possible, become even more honest *and* a reason for the agent's society to nurture his or her honesty. But what is it about honesty that makes it the sort of trait that an agent should strive to possess and a society seek to nurture? It is because it is useful to acquire and possess honesty and useful for society to form the agent's character in this way. The utility of the agent's being honest is derived from the fact that this personality trait will be expressed in useful actions of the agent. The utility of the society's activities of nurturing honesty in the agent is derived only in part from the usefulness of the honest agent's actions, for it also depends on the effectiveness of this sort of character formation by the community and the probability that the agent would not become honest without such social intervention. Hume was mistaken to include cleanliness among the virtues because its social utility is not great enough to justify the costs of social intervention in character formation. Intelligence is important enough to justify such intervention, but it is not effectively increased in the individual by the praise of any chance member of society when one possesses it or reproach by the community when any agent acts stupidly. In this way, Hume's catalogue of virtues can be narrowed down to the specifically moral personality traits by insisting that a virtue is a personality trait that is both useful to have and useful for society to nurture.

How does, or ought, society to form and reform the character of the moral agents that are its members? Moral education is primarily and for the most part carried out by informal means. This is to say that there is no specific community organization or specialized set of officials charged with nurturing virtue or eradicating vice in the *moral* sense. Any or every member of the society feels and acts in ways that mold, for better or worse, the character of those who make up the society. No doubt parents and teachers play a leading role, but friends, acquaintances, and even strangers do their share also. Since we care about how others think and feel about us, the mere admiration or contempt of family and friends plays a part in cultivating virtue and weeding out vice. When these are expressed verbally in praise for those who possess useful personality traits and reproach for those who have vices, moral education becomes more overt, deliberate, and effective. Stories, traditional or contemporary, often hold up virtuous models for hearers to imitate or examples of wickedness for readers to avoid. Sermons and shorter pronouncements are often patently or subtly didactic. Society honors virtue with titles, prestige, even privileges, while the evil character is dishonored both privately and publicly. Respectable persons shun those who are seen as the most evil agents. It is no accident that the psychological genesis of the feeling of shame is often said to lie in the fear of abandonment and the withdrawal of love, in contrast to guilt, which is more clearly allied to fear of punishment. Moral education involves more than instilling habits of action; it includes eliciting and molding feelings, especially pride and shame, and ways of thinking, such as paying attention to what is morally relevant and not forgetting one's responsibilities. This probably explains why it is not reasonable for society to try to force its members to be virtuous even though it is appropriate to try to compel someone to do his or her duty. The threat of sanctions is often effective in constraining someone to act in the required manner, but usually ineffective in causing the agent to think and feel in the desired way. It also explains why the legal system is only occasionally and secondarily an instrument by which society cultivates virtue and eradicates vice.

My view is that what makes an agent morally good or evil is a pair of utilities. More explicitly, what makes an agent morally good is the possession of the virtues, those personality traits that it is useful for agents to have and useful for society to nurture by informal means. What makes an agent morally evil is the possession of vices, those personality traits that it is harmful for agents to have *and* useful for society to eradicate. It seems to me that this theory retains the advantages of Hume's theory of moral value while, unlike his theory, it manages to explain what it is that makes a virtue or vice specifically moral.

At the start of this chapter I suggested that one needs a theory of moral value in order to assess the validity of arguments for specific conclusions about virtue or vice. One test of the adequacy of an ethical theory is its ability to help one resolve moral problems. Let us see whether my theory can pass this test by investigating briefly its ability to distinguish between valid and invalid arguments for the conclusion that all rapists are morally evil. One argument for this conclusion is that the rapist is always selfish; another, that he or she is always cruel. If these premises are true, and to show this one would need to do more than show that most rapists are selfish or cruel, these arguments are sound. Selfishness and cruelty are prime examples of vices according to my theory because they are very harmful personality traits that it is useful for society to seek to eradicate. Although my theory is not the only one that implies that selfishness and cruelty are vices, it does this as cogently as any and more convincingly than some.

Another argument we surveyed in the previous chapter is that the rapist is always evil because he or she is always lustful. Now there is serious doubt that most rapists are motivated by lust; there is considerable psychological evidence to support the view that rape is typically an act of violence and motivated primarily by angry frustration or hatred rather than sexual desire. But let us suppose that the rapist is always lustful. Would this prove that he or she is always morally evil? Not directly. Lust, defined by my dictionary as sensuous appetite or passionate desire, is not in and of itself a vice. Sexual desire, no matter how intense, is a motive rather than a personality trait. It is not typically very harmful, nor would it be useful for society to try to eradicate the sex drive from human nature. Thus, the argument as it stands is invalid because its premise is irrelevant to its conclusion. Nevertheless, it may point to a different and more cogent argument. In what way might a lustful or lascivious person be morally evil? He or she might be lacking in self-control. It is not lust or sexual desire that sometimes makes a person evil, but the lack of sufficient self-discipline to restrain that sensuous appetite and keep it from leading one to wrongful action, such as rape. Now my theory can explain why the lack of self-control would be a valid reason for concluding that the rapist is morally evil. Self-control or self-discipline, traditionally called temperance, is a moral virtue because it is a useful personality trait and one that it is useful for a society to cultivate in its members. In this way, a theory of moral value can help one to transform an invalid argument with a misleading premise into an illuminating and possibly sound argument. Although ethical theories are farther removed from decision and practice than specific moral conclusions, ethics is still a practical discipline because it does function in practical reasoning and help to establish conclusions about how we ought to act and what sort of persons we ought to become.

STUDY QUESTIONS

1. The author defines specifically moral value in terms of the value of a person *as* a moral agent. This suggests that only agents can have moral value. But we also speak of actions, desires or motives, and corporate bodies, such as a government or business enterprise, as good or evil. Are we speaking of moral value here? If so, is the meaning of such expressions somehow derivative from our evaluation of moral agents? If so, how? If not, what do we mean when we speak of a virtuous act, evil desire, or immoral corporation?

2. W. D. Ross writes mainly of morally good or bad actions and argues that the moral value of an action depends upon its motive. One might adopt his theory and then add that the morally good (or evil) agent is one who does

morally good (or evil) actions. Which is primary and which derivative—the moral value of agents or of actions? Why?

3. Some have defined righteousness as the willing obedience to the will of God. Now suppose that someone disobeys the will of God unintentionally, sincerely believing that he or she is doing what God commands. Should we judge the agent wicked because he or she violates the will of God or morally good because he or she was entirely willing to obey the Divine Will? What reason is there to answer in one way rather than the other?

4. Righteousness consists in submission to the will of God. Kant argued that moral virtue requires autonomy, that the moral agent decide for himself or herself which moral laws to obey and not allow another will to impose moral principles upon one. Do you believe that virtue depends upon submission to an external law or upon the autonomous choice of one's own moral principles? Why? Are the two necessarily incompatible?

5. What do we mean when we speak of conscientiousness or love as motives? The word "motive" suggests that there are little things inside or next to the self that push or pull (move) the person to act. Are motives really causes of this sort? Are motives one class of reasons, a person's reasons for doing an act? How, if at all, are motives related to personality traits? What, for example, is the connection between the motive of compassion and the trait of being compassionate?

6. At one point, Jesus condemned, not only the act of committing adultery, but the very lusting after another's spouse. Is it as wicked to commit adultery in one's imagination or heart as to commit it in one's neighbor's bed? Why?

7. Some people claimed that wartime acts of napalming Vietnamese villages were inhumane. *If* this is so, does it prove that the soldier doing this act under orders from a superior officer is morally evil? If so, is this because the soldier is lacking in love or conscientiousness? If not, does this imply that an individual is never morally responsible for any act done on the orders of someone in authority?

8. We sometimes say that a parent is "too kind" to his child. Do we mean that he fails to discipline the child because he loves the child too much or that he fails to discipline the child because his feeling for his child is not genuine love? Can one ever be *too* loving?

9. Does true love require that one turn the other cheek? Is it wicked to respond with anger to someone who picks a fight? Is it humanly possible for us to love someone who hates us? If not, can a person be morally condemned for failing to do the impossible?

10. Imagine that someone generally acts without love but not in hate. Does this absence of love automatically make the person wicked or only devoid of virtue and therefore morally neither good nor evil? Does the failure to love another indicate a callousness in the agent? If so, is this true in all or only some instances? If not, just what is the difference between callousness and the lack of love?

11. It is sometimes argued that virtue requires more than love; it demands carefulness, insight, and responsibility. If true, does this show that love is not a necessary condition of moral value? Could it be argued that love is a sufficient condition of moral value because carefulness, insight, and responsibility are not additional conditions of virtue but really parts or aspects of love?

12. The view that the virtue of anything is its specific excellence has a long and honorable philosophical history. But to modern ears it sounds strange to say

that the virtue of a knife is to cut easily and cleanly or that a pen that writes legibly and without blotting is a virtuous pen. Is the specific excellence of something really virtue in the *moral* sense of "virtue"? If the excellence of a knife as knife or pen as pen is not genuinely moral virtue, is the excellence of a human being as human being specifically moral virtue? If so, why? If not, is there any reason to believe that moral virtue depends on human nature?

13. Is the cool, clever, calculating safe-cracker morally good or evil? His reason seems in firm control of his feelings and actions. Can it be shown that he is really irrational in some way? If so, how? If not, must we reject the theory that the virtuous person is the rational one?

14. Usually we respect a person when he or she conscientiously does some act that he or she believes is morally required even though we may consider it morally wrong. Is this moral respect for a misguided conscience morally appropriate? Does it matter how badly misguided the conscience of another is? That is, are there some acts so very wrong that we should not respect the person whose conscience commands him or her to do them?

15. Kant seemed to think that the ordinary person knows well enough what is right and what is wrong; the moral problem is not to know what is right but to do it in the face of conflicting desires and inclinations. Is the conscience of the individual reliable? If so, how can one account for disagreement about what is morally right in many situations? If not, is there any reason to value conscientious action?

16. Some contemporary psychologists explain the conscience of the individual by the internalization of the norms generally accepted and sanctioned in his or her society. Some theologians, traditional and contemporary, believe that one's conscience is the word of God. What *is* conscience, anyway? Do the psychological origins of conscience have any bearing on the question of whether moral value lies in conscientiousness? Explain.

17. Observation of the human species suggests that it is human nature to eat when hungry. Is such an act virtuous? If so, what is it about such an act that makes it morally good? If not, does this show that virtue does not consist in conformity to human nature?

18. Evolution suggests that human beings are essentially similar to other animals. If the difference between a human being and an ape or dog is really one of degree, should we say that apes and dogs can be morally good or evil, but to a lesser degree than human beings? If not, what is it that distinguishes humans from brute animals and enables them to be virtuous or wicked?

19. Butler claims that when desire for revenge conflicts with self-love, self-love ought to prevail. Is this so? How can it be proved to be so? Butler claims that conscience has authority over both general and particular passions. Do you agree? Why or why not?

20. Butler holds that virtue consists in conformity to human nature; Warnock holds that virtue lies in having dispositions that overcome the limited sympathies in human nature. Why this difference? Is it because they have different conceptions of human nature or because they view the relation between human nature and morality differently?

21. Warnock points to several things that contribute to the human predicament and argues that the purpose of morality is to overcome or ameliorate this predicament. Still, he defines moral value in terms of only one of the factors that contribute to the human predicament. Is this limitation an advantage or a disadvantage of his theory of virtue? Why?

22. Consider three acts—an unintended homicide, an intentional homicide, and

an attempted but unsuccessful homicide. Which is the most wicked and which the least? Is there any additional information about any of the three acts that would be relevant to determining the degree of virtue or vice?

23. What is an intention, anyway? Is it a state of mind in the agent, perhaps just before or while he or she is doing the act?

24. It seems clear that we normally condemn a person morally for doing great harm, unless under duress of circumstances. What is less clear is why the harm done is taken to be evidence of moral evil. Is it because the very bad *consequences* directly make the agent evil? Or is it because we assume that the agent must have known that harm would result and thus must have *intended* the bad consequences? Or is it because a harmful act gives evidence of some evil *motive* like callousness or selfishness? Or is there some other explanation of why we normally disapprove the person who does great harm? Whichever explanation you think most plausible, explain why you think it better than the alternatives.

25. Is intelligence a useful personality trait? Does the fact that one person is more intelligent than another make that person morally better? Wisdom is one of the traditional virtues. Is wisdom really a moral virtue or is the tradition mistaken on this point? Is wisdom identical with intelligence?

26. The theory that the morally good person is the one with useful personality traits is an appeal to utility as the ground of moral value. Act-utilitarianism is also an appeal to utility, but as the ground of obligation. Is utility more plausible as a ground of virtue or of obligation? Why?

27. Sometimes Nietzsche writes as though he is rejecting the distinction between moral good or evil, derived from the slave morality, in favor of the nonmoral distinction between good and bad, characteristic of the thinking of the master class. On what grounds might one decide whether Nietzsche is really rejecting the very notion of moral virtue or proposing an alternative theory of moral value?

28. Suppose that we dropped the expressions "virtue" and "morally good" together with all synonyms and antonyms from our language. Would we find ourselves unable to say anything that really matters? What difference would it make to our practical life if we stopped making judgments of moral value? Explain and defend your reply.

29. "Morally good" and "morally evil" are sometimes defined in terms of that which is morally praiseworthy or blameworthy. Now moral praise and blame seem to be expressions of the speaker's moral attitudes of approval and disapproval. Are we always justified in blaming a person, in *expressing* our disapproval, when we are justified in feeling disapproval, or are there occasions when we ought not to express our feelings because the act we disapprove is none of our business or because public condemnation may have harmful consequences? If it is not always appropriate to blame what it is appropriate to disapprove, should moral value be defined in terms of approval and disapproval or praise and blame, or neither? Why?

BIBLIOGRAPHY

ARISTOTLE. *Nichomachean Ethics.* Books 2–5. Translated by David Ross; revised by J. L. Ackrill and J. O. Urmson. Oxford: Oxford University Press, 1980.

BARNES, W. H. F. "Intention, Motive, and Responsibility." *Aristotelian Society* 19 (1945): 230–248.

BUTLER, JOSEPH. *Sermons,* Preface and first three sermons. In *British Moralists,* vol. I, edited by Lewis Amherst Selby-Bigge. Oxford: Clarendon Press, 1897.

HUME, DAVID. *Enquiry Concerning the Principles of Morals,* Section 9. In *Hume's Enquiries,* edited by Lewis Amherst Selby-Bigge. Oxford: Clarendon Press, 1902.

KANT, IMMANUEL. *Foundations of the Metaphysics of Morals,* First Section. In *Critique of Practical Reason and Other Writings in Moral Philosophy,* edited and translated by Lewis W. Beck. Chicago: University of Chicago Press, 1949.

NIETZSCHE, FRIEDRICH. *Beyond Good and Evil,* chaps. 5 and 9. Translated by Helen Zimmern. New York: Russell & Russell Publishers, 1964.

OLD TESTAMENT: 5–11 *Deuteronomy.* 9:4–14, 10:12–20.

RAMSEY, PAUL. *Basic Christian Ethics,* chap. 2. New York: Charles Scribner's Sons, 1950.

WARNOCK, G. J. *The Object of Morality,* chap. 6. London: Methuen & Co., 1971.

7
ABORTION

Whether or not to have an abortion is a medical question to be decided like all other medical questions by the patient and her doctor.

Harriet F. Pilpel in "The Abortion Crisis"

Abortion is a moral, not a medical, problem. To be sure, the procedure is surgical; but this makes abortion no more a medical problem than the use of the electric chair makes capital punishment a problem of electrical engineering.

Thomas Szasz in "The Ethics of Abortion"

One of the moral issues currently being fought out in Congress and state legislatures is whether abortion should be legally permitted. Just as liberals have been challenging the morality of our traditionally restrictive abortion legislation for years, so conservatives are now objecting on moral grounds to the permissive nature of the 1973 Supreme Court decision in *Roe* v. *Wade* declaring most state antiabortion laws unconstitutional.

DEFINING THE PROBLEM

Abortion may best be defined as the intentional termination of pregnancy by inducing the loss of the fetus. Not every termination of pregnancy constitutes an act of abortion; the more usual, and happy, termination is the delivery of a live, healthy infant. Again, a surgical procedure that accidentally and unintentionally causes the death of the fetus does not count as abortion. Only those acts that intentionally end pregnancy by inducing the loss of the fetus are properly classed as abortions. So-called "spontaneous abortions" or miscarriages are not really acts at all in any moral or legal sense; they are simply physiological processes in the mother's body that happen to destroy the fetus.

147

During the last century every state in our country passed legislation prohibiting abortion. To this highly restrictive legislation there has been only one exception: a doctor was legally permitted to induce the loss of the fetus when considered medical judgment indicated that an abortion was necessary to save the life—not just the health but the very life—of the mother. Although doctors, hospital authorities, and the courts generally interpreted this exception very broadly, it still covered only a small fraction of the cases in which pregnant women demanded abortions and many doctors and civic leaders thought abortions ought to be granted.

Several years ago a few state legislatures decided to permit therapeutic abortion. An abortion is classified as therapeutic when it meets one or more of the following conditions: It is necessary either to preserve the physical or mental health of the mother, or to prevent the birth of a child that would probably be severely handicapped, or to terminate a pregnancy resulting from a criminal act like rape or incest. Such legislation partly solved one serious problem. In the few states permitting therapeutic abortion, doctors were no longer confronted with the cruel dilemma of either refusing to give a pregnant woman the medical treatment considered necessary or performing an illegal abortion. However, such compromise legislation did not satisfy the moral sense of the citizens. Conservatives refused to accept the law and continued to work politically for the repeal of "legalized murder." Liberals regarded the restriction of abortion to therapeutic cases as arbitrary and discriminatory and continued to press for abortion on demand.

Subsequently a very few states, led by New York, legalized abortion on demand. Abortion on demand is abortion whenever the pregnant woman, on the advice of her chosen doctor, requests that an abortion be performed. The law may still regulate the act of abortion; it may require that the abortion be performed by a licensed physician in an adequately equipped hospital or clinic, for example. But otherwise it permits the pregnant woman to have an abortion whenever she wishes without requiring her to give any reasons to justify her demand. Action in the state legislatures did not, however, settle the moral question of whether abortion on demand *ought* to be permitted by law. Most states refused to follow the lead of New York, and even in that state the legislature later voted to repeal the liberalized abortion law and was defeated only by the governor's veto.

In January of 1973 the focus of debate shifted from the state legislatures to the federal courts. In the cases of *Roe* v. *Wade* and *Doe* v. *Bolton* the Supreme Court of the United States declared unconstitutional all state laws that prohibit abortion during the first six months of pregnancy or regulate the physician's practice of abortion during the first three months of pregnancy. Although it seems unlikely that the Supreme Court will reverse its 7–2 decision in the foreseeable future, several constitutional amendments have been proposed that would limit abortions or return the power to regulate abortions to the states. Whatever the outcome of this political and legal battle, the moral issue remains a live one: Should abortion on demand be legally permitted?

REASONS FOR PERMISSIVE LEGISLATION

Many arguments have been advanced to show that the law ought not to prohibit abortion, even when the life of the mother is not at stake. Seven of these arguments deserve particular attention.

The Health of the Mother

If abortion is justified in order to preserve the life of the mother, why is it not also justified to preserve her health? After all, how valuable is life without health? Pregnancy sometimes does threaten the physical health of a woman. Under certain circumstances, such as a serious heart condition or severe diabetes, the added stress and strain imposed on the physical organism by the embryo may complicate an illness or disorder to the point where the health of the pregnant woman is endangered. As medical science advances, the threat is more often to the mental than to the physical health of the mother. If a woman is emotionally unstable, the continuation of pregnancy may precipitate an emotional breakdown. Women who are already under great stress from household burdens, career responsibilities, or economic hardship may find the prospect of caring for a child, or one more child, just too much to bear. Restrictive abortion laws do great harm to countless women by contributing to the destruction of their physical or mental health. The law ought to protect rather than endanger the health of the citizens. Therefore, abortion ought to be legally permitted so that women whose health is threatened by pregnancy may, should they and their doctors deem it advisable, have the medical care necessary to preserve their health.

Handicapped Children

It is unfair to require severely handicapped children to be born, but restrictive abortion laws do just that. Many babies born to women who took the drug thalidomide, for example, were born with no arms or legs. Such grossly deformed infants have almost no chance of happiness in life. When a woman is exposed to German measles during the early weeks of pregnancy, her child may be born with irremediable brain damage. Such a mentally handicapped child can never grow up to live anything like a normal life. In addition to such cases of physiological damage, children may be born with or develop severe emotional handicaps that incapacitate them for normal or happy life. Unwanted and rejected children often become schizoid, so torn apart emotionally that they must remain in an institution throughout their entire lives. It is unfair for the law to require such children to be born, for to do so condemns them, through no fault and by no choice of their own, to live abnormal and miserable lives. Abortion ought to be legally permitted so that the law will not unjustly penalize these children by forcing them to be born so severely handicapped that they have no chance for happiness.

Criminal Acts

Unfortunately, it is not uncommon for a woman to become pregnant through some criminal act of intercourse, as when a woman is assaulted and raped or a mere child has incestuous relations. These women and young girls are already victims of crime; it is cruel and unjust for the law to victimize them a second time by forcing them to bear unwanted children. Justice requires that as far as possible the undesirable consequences of criminal sexual acts should be prevented or undone. Punishing the criminal may also be required by justice, but it does no good to his victim. Abortion should be legally permitted so that women and very young girls who become pregnant through some criminal sexual act may terminate the pregnancy forced upon them against their will.

Discrimination

Restrictive abortion laws are unjust because they discriminate unfairly against certain groups of citizens. Statistical studies show, for example, that black women have much less chance of obtaining a legal abortion than white women. Welfare patients have much less chance than private patients. Unmarried women are denied the access to abortion that is available to married women. And women who can afford to travel can obtain abortions in other states or countries with more permissive laws, while others with fewer financial resources cannot. Whatever the intent of restrictive state abortion laws, in practice such legislation imposes much narrower limits on certain groups in our population than on other more fortunate groups. Justice requires that all citizens receive equal protection under the law. Abortion ought to be legalized in order to do away with discriminatory practices that result from restrictive legislation.

Illegal Abortions

Women who are determined to obtain an abortion will do so in spite of antiabortion laws. Restrictive abortion laws drive millions of women into seeking criminal abortions or attempting self-abortions. Criminal abortions are dangerous from a purely medical point of view. Some, although by no means all, criminal abortionists are unskilled in surgical techniques and ill-trained in medicine; these unscrupulous abortionists often operate under extremely unhygienic conditions. Even the most skillful and conscientious abortionists, since they are denied access to hospital facilities, must operate with very limited equipment and assistance. If everything goes smoothly, this may not matter; if unexpected complications arise, the health or life of the mother may be jeopardized. Since criminal operations must be kept secret, facilities for aftercare must be kept to a minimum. As a result, postoperative care, so necessary to prevent complications and to detect and deal with those that do occur, is minimal or nonexistent. Many women develop serious infections during or after illegal abortions. A considerable number become incapable of bearing children in the future; some even lose their lives.

If criminal abortions are less than safe, self-abortions are more than perilous. A great many attempts at self-abortion are ineffective. In themselves, such futile attempts may do no damage, but they are indirectly harmful because they delay the time of actual abortion until the later months of pregnancy when abortion, even under the best of conditions, is much less safe than during the early weeks. Agents of self-abortion that are strong enough to be effective, such as corrosive acids or sharp instruments, are very likely to do severe injury to the mother's physical organism. And when complications arise, the average woman knows too little about medicine to help herself or even to realize that she is in urgent need of medical assistance. All in all, illegal abortions constituted a major cause of maternal death before 1973, estimated as high as five or ten thousand women a year. The number of women who became infertile or seriously ill through illegal abortions was much, much greater. Restrictive abortion laws, however well-intentioned, that cause this great harm by driving women into seeking illegal abortions are morally unjustifiable. Abortion ought to be legally permitted in order to reduce the damage done by illegal abortions.

Overpopulation

One of the vital issues facing our world today is overpopulation. We are using up our natural resources at a tremendous rate so that maintaining our standard of living is becoming increasingly arduous and will soon be impossible. Even with impressive advances in agriculture, food production is falling behind population growth so that a large portion of humanity is today undernourished, and tomorrow starvation will face the majority. The increasing density of population is complicating the problems of preserving the physical and mental health of the world population, and the pollution that threatens to make our planet uninhabitable is mainly due to the number of people our industry is trying to support. It is morally imperative that every measure be used to curtail the population explosion. The obvious measure is the use of effective means of contraception. But where such means are not used or are ineffective, contraception should be supplemented by abortion. This does not imply abortion in every pregnancy; the elimination of human life is not necessary to avoid overpopulation. Abortion ought to be legally permitted, however, as one means of limiting the birthrate and helping to solve the problem of overpopulation.

The Right to Privacy

Any law prohibiting an abortion requested by a pregnant woman on the advice of her physician necessarily violates the fundamental legal and natural right to privacy. It intrudes upon the private relation of the pregnant woman and her physician, a relation that is and ought to be privileged and confidential. It invades the private relation of the mother to the father, one of the most intimate and personal of all human relations. And it interferes with the woman's private decision whether to bear a child, a profoundly personal decision. In these three ways any legal prohibition of abortion violates the right to privacy. Not only is this right recognized by the Constitution of the United States, it is one of the basic human rights. Every human being has an inviolable right to privacy because privacy is essential to the integrity of the individual moral agent, to the precious personal relationships of love and friendship, and to that individuality or uniqueness that makes each of us an individual person. Since only abortion on demand is consistent with the right to privacy, abortion on demand ought to be legally permitted.

Of the many arguments advanced in favor of permitting abortion on demand, we have summarized seven: The law ought to make available whatever medical care is necessary to preserve the physical and mental health of pregnant women. It is unfair to force severely handicapped children to be born. It is unjust to require the victims of criminal sexual acts to bear any children that might result. Restrictive abortion laws are unjust because they discriminate against certain groups of citizens. Abortion on demand ought to be legally permitted in order to prevent the illness, infertility, and even death of women who would otherwise resort to illegal abortions or self-abortions. Abortion is one means that should be used to solve the problem of overpopulation. And any prohibition of abortion is a violation of the right to privacy.

REASONS FOR RESTRICTIVE LEGISLATION

There are, of course, many concerned citizens who object strenuously to abortion on demand. They argue that our traditionally restrictive legislation ought to be reinstated by an amendment to the Constitution or by some other means. They, too, advance several arguments to support this position.

Harm to the Mother

Abortion, therapeutic or otherwise, is not as safe as some would have us believe; it is often harmful to the mother. Postabortion complications, like infection or infertility, are very common, and the possibility of death is not insignificant. Even higher is the incidence of psychological aftereffects. The woman who undergoes an abortion is often frustrated because deep down she really wants to bear her child and care for it. Hostility to men often arises, causing obvious marital stress, because the woman comes to feel that the abortion is forced upon her and performed by the males who surround her and dominate her life. Feelings of guilt are very frequent and very disturbing. Such psychological aftereffects may be brief and mild or they may be persistent and intense. It is not uncommon for a nervous breakdown or emotional disintegration to be precipitated by the experience of undergoing an abortion. The law should not permit acts as harmful as abortion.

Better Alternatives

Those who advocate legally permitting abortion are performing an important service to society, for they are pointing out genuine social problems to which solutions are imperative. But the answer is not abortion on demand, for there are other and more desirable ways to solve these problems. Much better than taking a human life would be preventing conception in the first place. Effective contraceptives are available. A wider dissemination of information about contraceptive techniques and a more responsible use of contraceptive devices would prevent most of the pregnancies that now occasion abortion. The problem of illegitimate and unwanted babies is a real and urgent one. But far better than killing these innocent babies before they are born would be arranging for their adoption so that they could live happy lives themselves and give joy to couples that may be unable to have children of their own. Severely handicapped children now impose almost unendurable burdens on their parents and have little chance for happiness in life. It must be admitted that nothing we can do will transform such children into normal human beings. Still, if the state provided adequate facilities for their care, with all the special equipment and trained personnel this would entail, even severely handicapped children need not live miserable lives, and their unfortunate parents need not shoulder the burden of their care. This solution is surely far better than killing all those embryos that might possibly be born handicapped in order to prevent the birth of that small percentage that would actually be born with severe physical or emotional handicaps. Abortion on demand ought not to be legally permitted because there are better ways to deal with the social problems it is intended to solve.

Promiscuity

Abortion on demand ought not to be legally permitted because it is a precedent that encourages sexual promiscuity. Sexual desire is easily aroused and very persistent, both within and outside of marriage. Society cannot safely allow its expression, however, between sexual partners who are not married without doing serious damage to the socially important institution of the family. Two factors that help to restrain and control the promiscuous expression of sexual desire are the fear of pregnancy and the dread of social condemnation. Legalized abortion weakens both forms of social control. Obviously the fear of pregnancy is less when abortion is readily available to solve the problems arising from an unexpected and unwelcome pregnancy. And the dread of social condemnation is lessened also, because legally permitting abortions amounts to a liberalization by society of its code of conduct governing sex. Since sexual promiscuity is socially harmful and since legalized abortion encourages sexual promiscuity, abortion on demand ought not to be legally permitted.

Murder

The act of intentionally taking a human life is murder. Since abortion is the intentional termination of pregnancy by inducing the loss of the fetus, and the fetus is a living human being, any act of abortion is an act of murder. Murder is one of the most immoral of acts and is always wrong. Such great moral wrongs should be legally prohibited and severely punished when they are committed. Since abortion is murder and ought to be legally prohibited, it obviously ought not to be permitted legally.

Dangerous Precedent

Legalizing abortion on demand is a dangerous precedent because it leads to heinous acts like infanticide, euthanasia, and eugenic murder. When the abortion laws are liberalized, the immediate result is a considerable increase in the number of socially accepted abortions. These acts of taking human life serve as examples to others and encourage them to take human life in similar situations. If it is permissible to kill an unborn child on the mere possibility that the infant may be handicapped, surely, it will be thought, it must be entirely proper to kill a child who is born actually handicapped. If the life of a human being is no longer held sacred by society, as witnessed by the intentional killing of the human embryo, then why not mercifully put some senile person or someone incurably ill out of his or her misery? Once society legally permits the deliberate taking of human life in any form, it is only a step to killing human beings deemed to be inferior in order to improve the human species. Thus an indirect result of legalized abortion is to encourage acts of infanticide, euthanasia, and eugenic murder. Permissive abortion laws make the killing of a human fetus an exception to the moral principle that all human life is sacred; this is a dangerous precedent that can lead to outrageously immoral acts of murder. Since the law ought not to encourage heinous acts like these, abortion on demand ought not to be legally permitted.

The Rights of the Unborn

One of the prime functions of law is to protect and enhance the rights of the citizens. No law should violate any basic human right or allow such violation by anyone in society. Abortion on demand ought not to be allowed because it infringes upon the basic rights of the unborn citizen. Under present law, the unborn child has certain rights like the right to inherit property or the right to compensation for damages. Suppose, for example, that a husband dies, leaving a pregnant wife and two children. His will specifies that half his property shall go to his wife and the other half shall be divided between his children. It will not do legally for each of the living children to receive one-fourth of the inheritance, for this denies the legally recognized right of the unborn child to its share of the father's property. Again, suppose that a pregnant woman is knocked down by a passing automobile so that, while she is not seriously injured herself, her child is consequently born deformed. The child can sue in the courts for due compensation. These legal rights are a social recognition of basic human rights the law exists to protect. Similarly, laws that forbid abortion would protect the fetus's right to life. Since the law ought not to allow any basic human right to be infringed and since abortion infringes the right to life of the unborn child, abortion ought not to be legally permitted.

At least six strong arguments can be given against legally permitting abortion on demand. Abortion is physically and psychologically harmful to the mother. There are more desirable ways to solve the social problems to which abortion is addressed. Legalized abortion on demand encourages sexual promiscuity and thereby undermines the social institution of the family. Abortion, therapeutic or on demand, is murder. Permitting abortion on demand is a dangerous precedent that can lead to highly immoral acts. Abortion infringes the right to life of the unborn child. These arguments, and others, are used to establish the conclusion that abortion on demand should not be legally permitted.

RETHINKING ONE ARGUMENT

The issue of whether abortion on demand should be legally permitted is probably the most complex of all the specific moral problems discussed in this book. Its complexity is revealed in two ways. There seem to be more cogent pro and con arguments on this issue than on any of the other issues; the few included in this text are only a sample of those commonly used. Again, several of these arguments, taken individually, are highly complicated in that many considerations must be weighed before one can finally assess their logical force. We can cut through this complexity and illustrate it at the same time by limiting our critical reexamination to an extended discussion of a single argument. This limitation is not intended to imply or suggest that no other argument is worthy of extended criticism; rather it is meant to be an example of the sort of rethinking that needs to be done for every argument used in debating this moral issue.

An apparently simple and compelling argument against legally permitting abortion on demand is that abortion is murder. Since murder, the intentional taking of a human life, is clearly and terribly wrong, it ought to be prohibited by law. Under no circumstances should the law permit acts as immoral as murder. This argument raises many ethical problems including the questions "Why is murder morally wrong?" and "Ought the law to prohibit immoral acts?" But let us ignore all of these related ethical problems and concentrate on a single question: "Is abortion really murder?"

At first glance, the answer must be in the affirmative. Murder is usually defined as the act of intentionally taking a human life. Since abortion is the intentional termination of pregnancy by inducing the loss of the fetus, abortion is necessarily an intentional act. And since "the loss of the fetus" clearly refers to the loss of life of a human fetus, abortion must be the act of taking a human life. By very definition, then, all acts of abortion seem to be acts of murder. On second glance, the answer is less obvious. It seems entirely meaningful to assert, as some moralists do, that some exceptional acts of intentionally taking a human life are morally justified, and it seems inappropriate to label justified acts of killing "murder." This suggests that the proper definition of murder is "an unjustified act of intentionally taking a human life." If this definition is accepted, there seem to be three main ways in which the charge that abortion is murder can be countered. The proabortionist can claim that abortion is a justifiable exception to the general rule that taking a human life is wrong; or that killing an organism is not murder until that physical organism has acquired a human soul; or that the human fetus fails to satisfy other less speculative criteria of humanness. Let us examine each of these lines of criticism in turn.

Morally Justified Exceptions

Not every act of intentionally taking a human life is murder because there are morally justified exceptions to the general rule that it is morally wrong to take a human life. (1) A person is morally justified, for example, in killing in self-defense. If a thief attacks me in a way to threaten my very life, I have a right to resist his attack even to the point of killing him. Since killing in self-defense is morally justified, it cannot properly be condemned as murder. Now the fetus is attacking the mother; in many cases its continued presence threatens her life or limb. Hence, it is not murder for her to kill the fetus in self-defense.

In reply it can be argued that at most this would justify self-abortion. The doctor who performs an abortion is not acting in *self*-defense. Again, how broad is the right to kill in self-defense? Granted that one may properly kill to preserve one's very life, may one kill to protect one's limb or one's pocketbook? If all that is granted is the right to defend one's life, this justifies only abortions to preserve the life of the mother, not abortion on demand or even therapeutic abortion. The crucial reply, however, is that the analogy between the fetus and the thief does not hold. One has the right to kill the thief in self-defense because the thief is engaging in unlawful conduct or using unlawful force. But the fetus is not engaging in conduct, unlawful or otherwise. The fetus is passive and performs no act at all in any morally or legally relevant sense. Nor is the fetus using unlawful force against the mother. It is not easy to see how abortion can be justified as an act of killing in self-defense.

There are, however, other exceptions to the general rule that taking a human life is wrong. Common law has long recognized that (2) it is not morally wrong, and thus not murder, to kill under duress of circumstances. Killing under duress of circumstances implies that the act is made necessary by the fact that it is the only way to avoid an even greater evil. Thus the captain of a ship may throw part or all of his cargo overboard in a violent storm if this is the only way to save his ship and the lives of its crew. The policeman may shoot a sniper, although he is not killing in self-defense, if this is the only way to save the lives of innocent passersby. Analogously, abortion might be justified as killing under duress of circumstances when abortion is the only way to avoid even greater evils.

The usual reply to this criticism is that abortion just does not avoid any greater evils. The direct and intended consequence of abortion is the loss of the fetus, the death of an unborn but living human being. What greater evil is there than the loss of a human life? Abortion might prevent the physical or mental illness of the mother, but illness is not a greater evil than death. Nor is the birth of a handicapped child or a child conceived through rape really worse than the deliberate cold-blooded killing of an unborn human being. Abortion cannot be justified as an act of killing under duress of circumstances because the circumstances under which it is performed do not threaten any evil greater than that of taking the most precious of all things, a human life.

The critic of the argument that abortion should not be legally permitted because it is murder can still fall back on one more exception to the general rule that taking a human life is wrong. (3) It is not always wrong to kill indirectly. This criticism relies on the principle of double effect: when an act produces two effects, one good and the other bad, the agent may intend the good and permit the bad, provided the amount of good is greater than the amount of bad. Consider, for example, the act of amputating a limb. The surgeon's act has two effects: it saves the patient's life and at the same time cripples him. This act of operating on a person with a gangrenous leg is not wrong on account of the harm it does because the badness of the crippling is outweighed by the greater value of saving the patient's life. The act is fully right, however, only on the condition that the surgeon *intend* to save the patient's life and only *permit* the crippling. That is, the doctor's purpose must be to achieve the good, not to bring about the bad. The bad effect is accepted only because it is an inevitable consequence of the greater good at which the surgeon aims. If the surgeon were to operate on a patient he hated in order to cripple him, incidentally saving the patient's life in the process, his act would not be morally right because the evil done would be a direct rather than indirect effect of the operation. The advocate of abortion can appeal to this principle of double effect. An act of abortion normally has two consequences: it preserves the health of the mother or prevents the birth of a severely handicapped child *and* it destroys the life of the fetus. This act is justified because the goodness of the mother's health or of the prevention of the birth of a miserably handicapped child is greater than the badness of the loss of life of a fetus that is not yet a conscious human being. Moreover the surgeon who performs the abortion does so for the sake of the good effect, not for the sake of the bad. He permits the bad only because it is an incidental and unavoidable consequence of achieving the greater good. Since abortion can be morally justified by the principle of double effect, it is not properly condemned as an act of murder.

In reply to this criticism, the moral philosopher who wishes to argue that abortion is murder can point out that the principle of double effect does not really apply to this case. This principle justifies an act of doing harm only on two conditions—that the act also do a greater good and that the agent intend the good rather than the bad. But, it can be argued, although abortion does have good consequences, the good it achieves does not outweigh the bad done. Human life is the most precious of all things.

Hence, the bad effect of destroying the life of the embryo is far greater, not less, than the good effect of preserving the mother's health or preventing the misery of a handicapped child. Again, the principle of double effect requires that the direct and intended effect of the act be good; the bad effect must be only an indirect and unintended consequence. But in the case of abortion, the intent is to induce the loss of the fetus; this bad effect is the surgeon's purpose and aim in performing the operation. It would appear that one cannot use the principle of double effect to justify abortion as an exception to the general rule that taking human life is murder.

This line of criticism seems to have come to an end. It began with the contention of the opponent of abortion that this act ought not to be permitted by law because it is an act of murder. The critic tried to show that although an act of intentionally killing a human being is usually murder, abortion belongs to one of the classes of exceptions in which the act of taking a human life is morally justified and, therefore, not properly condemned as murder. One possible basis for excepting abortion from the general condemnation of acts of murder is the principle that an individual has a right to kill in self-defense; another is that a person may kill under duress of circumstances; a third is that a bad effect may be permitted provided the agent intends a greater good. The moralist who insists that abortion is really murder can object to each of these bases for justifying abortion. Whether such objections are devastating is left to the judgment of the reader. Let us now pursue a second, very different, line of reasoning based on theological arguments.

The Human Soul

It seems clear that the act of abortion is an act of killing. But does this necessarily make it an act of murder? The act of swatting a fly or even slaughtering a cow is not murder. What makes the act of killing a human being any different? One view is that a human being is vastly different from an animal because, while an animal is merely a physical organism, a human being has a soul as well as a body. It is the presence of an immortal soul in the human body that makes killing that physical organism the morally heinous act of murder. But when does the human body acquire its soul? If there is some period during which the fetus does not possess a soul, then during this period abortion would not be murder. This possibility opens up a second distinct line of criticism of the argument that abortion ought not to be legally permitted because it is murder.

The critic may begin by reminding us of the traditional definition of soul as the principle of life; the human soul is whatever it is that makes the human organism alive. Now what is it to be alive? Living beings differ from inanimate objects in two significant ways. A living being is conscious of its environment; even the lowly amoeba is aware that some bits of matter it touches are food to be engulfed and others indigestible items to be rejected. Higher forms of animal life have higher forms of consciousness, with sense perception and reason at the top. By contrast, a stone or a table is not aware of what is going on around it. Again, a living organism moves itself, while an inanimate object must be moved by something outside of itself. A bear wanders about in the woods, seeking food and avoiding danger; a book must be pushed or pulled or carried if it is to move at all. Thus the two criteria for whether a body has a soul are consciousness and self-motion. It is not easy to know when the fetus becomes aware of its environment, but there is an identifiable time when it gains self-motion. The fetus acquires its soul approximately mid-term in the pregnancy at the moment of quickening, at the moment when it first begins to kick and squirm in the womb. It follows that before this time the fetus is merely an animal organism without any human soul. Hence, abortion, which is normally performed well before mid-term, is not murder at all.

The moralist who argues that abortion should not be legally permitted because it is murder is unlikely to accept this objection. He may well reply that self-motion in the limited sense of locomotion or overt bodily movement is an inadequate criterion of life. The fetus has obviously been alive for a long time before the moment of quickening, for it has been assimilating food and growing from the moment of conception. Since these processes are at least as reliable signs of life as locomotion, the fetus has been alive from its conception. If soul really is to be defined as the principle of life in an organism, as the critic assumes, then it follows that the human fetus has a soul from the beginning. Even before mid-term in the pregnancy, abortion is murdering a human being.

At this point the critic may refine his position by making some distinctions. The human soul is a complex thing having a number of levels. The vegetative soul is the faculty of assimilating food and reproducing; it is the level of soul human beings share with other animals and with plants. The sensitive soul is the faculty expressed in sensation, imagination, desire, and bodily motions; all animals, including human beings, possess a sensitive soul, but plants lack this level of soul. Finally, the rational soul is the capacity to think and choose intelligently. Only the human soul has all three levels— vegetative, sensitive, and rational. These must not be thought of as three separate souls somehow fastened together to make a human soul; they are three sets of capacities united in a single soul. A human being does not have more souls than an animal or a plant; it is just that the human soul has capacities the lower levels of soul lack. The obvious fact that the fetus assimilates food and grows from conception does show that it has a soul from the beginning, but not that it has a rational soul. The problem then is to determine precisely when the fetus acquires its rational soul. Obviously not at conception, for at that moment it is nothing like a human organism and, hence, not ready to take on a fully human soul. At conception the fetus acquires only a vegetative soul. It is the function of this soul to give biological life to the fetus and to enable it to develop into an animal. As the fetus grows it is gradually transformed from an amorphous bit of tissue into an organism made up of distinguishable parts interacting systematically in such a way as to sustain and complement one another. At this point the sensitive soul is added to the vegetative soul and the fetus becomes aware of its environment in the most rudimentary fashion. Finally, the fetus takes on something like the form of the human body and it is ready to acquire the rational soul that distinguishes human beings from the rest of the animals. The male fetus becomes a rational animal on about the fortieth day after conception, the female about the eightieth day. Abortion is, therefore, not murder if it is performed before the fortieth day, or the eightieth day if the embryo is female. Before this time killing the embryo is not murder because it is not killing a fully human being, a human organism with a rational soul.

Despite its roots in the theology of Saint Thomas Aquinas and its venerable history in canon law, this criticism of the view that abortion need not be murder is not sacrosanct. The assumption that lies behind this theory of successive infusions of three distinct levels of soul is that the zygote, the fertilized ovum, is a formless bit of matter. Only after this amorphous bit of matter has been organized into an orderly and formed body with something like the shape of an adult human is it capable of receiving the rational soul that distinguishes human from brute animals. The obvious reply is that advances in biology show clearly that even the zygote is no chaotic mass. Ovum and sperm may each be only a single cell, but each has a complex internal genetic structure. And from their first union at conception, the resulting being is an organism, a structured living being. Moreover, there is no obvious connection between having two arms and two legs and having the capacity to reason. Although it is quite plausible to argue that the human fetus cannot acquire a sensitive soul until it has formed eyes and ears, there seems no reason to argue that it cannot receive its capacity to reason until it has taken on a recognizable human shape. Finally, the period of forty days for the male and eighty days for the female is purely arbitrary. Since there is no compelling reason to select any one day rather than another for the infusion of the rational soul, the only reasonable position to take is that the human embryo has a fully human soul from the very beginning. Hence, abortion, no matter how early in pregnancy, is necessarily the murder of a human being.

Perhaps. This forthright position appears at once biologically informed, logically consistent, and morally elevated. But it has at least one unfortunate theological implication. Since baptism is required for any assurance of salvation, it implies that many human souls are denied salvation through no fault of their own. Obviously quite a few pregnant women die unexpectedly, precipitating the loss of the fetus before there is any opportunity to baptize the fetus doomed to death. Less obvious is the fact that one out of three fertilized ova fails to develop normally. If it is really true that each of these ova has a human soul from conception, then it follows that each of these human beings dies without the means of salvation. This seems so harsh a Divine Providence that most theologians would wish to reconsider the view that the ovum acquires a human soul at the moment of conception.

Before we leave the theologian trying to work out a consistent view that will not imply blasphemy, let us remind ourselves of the point at issue. The original argument was that abortion on demand ought not to be legally permitted because abortion is murder. What makes this surgical procedure murder is supposed to be that it is killing a physical organism possessed of an immortal soul. This suggests a line of criticism by which it is claimed that, at least during the early months when abortion is most common, the human fetus does not have a fully human soul. Reasons can be given for picking some stage of development—the moment of quickening or the time when the fetus comes to resemble the normal human body—as the time when a fully human soul is acquired. The moralist can defend the argument that abortion is murder by rejecting these times as arbitrary and asserting that the only reasonable time to select for the infusion of soul is the moment of conception. Like any assertion on the relation between body and soul, this position is not without difficulties of its own, including the question of salvation through baptism. Instead of wrestling with these difficulties, let us turn to a third distinct line of criticism.

Defining a Person

The central issue is whether abortion is murder. Presumably it is not murder if the aborted fetus is not a human being. Attempts to decide this issue by determining whether or not the fetus possesses an immortal human soul ended in theological tangles. Let us, therefore, try to find some less speculative criteria to determine whether or not the fetus really is a human being.

1.   The proabortion critic can contend that the fetus is not a human being on the ground that it is not a *separate* organism. However a person may be defined theologically, an individual person must at least be an entity other than the mother. The fetus, however, is not yet separated from the mother; it is still part of the mother's flesh. No doubt it is a living bit of flesh, but so is the mole on the tip of her nose. Just as it is not murder to remove a mole, particularly if there is reason to think it malignant, so it is not murder to remove a bit of organic matter from inside a mother's womb, particularly if this minor operation is required to preserve the health of the mother. Since abortion is not taking the life of a separate organism, it is not killing an individual human being.
       The moralist who contends that abortion is murder will not let his

argument be refuted so easily. He will deny that the fetus is a part of the mother rather than a separate organism. Admittedly, it lives within the mother's body, but it has all the defining marks of a biological organism; it has structural complexity, functional perfection, and a regulatory mechanism. The fetus is made up of different parts that are related to one another in definite ways. Each of its various parts functions so that the total activity of the fetus maintains life and even promotes growth. Finally, the total activity and the functioning of the parts are controlled in such a way that the fetus maintains a homeostasis. What reason remains, therefore, to allege that the fetus is not a separate organism?

2. The critic may admit that the fetus is, although attached to the mother, in some sense separate from her. But need it follow that the fetus is an additional human being, over and beyond the mother? No, because the fetus is not a *distinct* organism. In this criticism, the focus is not on the separation between mother and child but on the distinctness of the child. The fetus is not a human being different from the parent organism because it lacks any distinctive characteristics to distinguish it from the mother. It is not just that the fetus is living in its mother's body or that it is attached physically to that body; there are no distinct properties to make its flesh and blood different from the flesh and blood that make up the maternal organism.

   The reply suggested by biological investigation is that there is indeed something to distinguish the fetus from every part of the mother's organism. From the moment of conception, the genetic inheritance of the fetus is complete. It is not that the zygote begins with the mother's genetic structure which gradually changes into a different genetic code. Rather, the fetus has a new and distinct genetic structure derived from that of both parents but identical with neither. Biologically speaking, a new and distinct human organism comes into existence at conception. Hence, abortion is necessarily the destruction of an individual human life and, consequently, murder.

3. Undaunted, the critic can return to the attack and maintain that the fetus is not an individual human being because it is not an *independent* being. The fetus should not be thought of as a human being in its own right, as opposed to the parent organism, until it is viable and self-sustaining. This does not mean that the fetus must literally be able to supply its own needs before it is taken to be genuinely human, or even that it be born into the world at the natural termination of pregnancy. But it requires at least that the organism be capable, given reasonable care, of surviving without the mother. It is a well-established medical fact that the fetus lacks viability until late in pregnancy. The fetus should not be considered a human being, with its own moral claim upon life, until it acquires its own capacity to remain alive outside the mother's body. Before this time, abortion is not murder because it is not killing an independent human being.

   In reply, those who condemn abortion may claim that to ask biological independence is to ask too much. The newborn child is a completely dependent being. Normally it depends upon its mother for food, warmth, and protection. Without this maternal care it could not live for more than a few days at best. To be sure, other adults can assume this maternal responsibility. But this does not reduce the dependence of the infant; its dependence is merely transferred to another person. Unless one is prepared to hold that very young children may be killed without remorse, one cannot use independence as a criterion for defining murder. Completely dependent as it is, the fetus is still a human being.

4. At this point the difference between the biological point of view and the moral point of view begins to emerge. A human being may be defined in strictly biological terms, using the biological definition of a separate organism or the genetic theory of inheritance. But the moral issue of what distinguishes murder from justifiable killing is not a purely biological problem. Whether or not the fetus is a human being in the biological sense, it can be argued that it is not a human being in the moral sense because it lacks those characteristics that give moral worth to a human being. The human fetus is not yet *conscious*, is far from being a *rational agent*, and lacks all *personality*. Since it lacks precisely those features that lend dignity to a human being, it is not a human being in the morally relevant sense. Until it acquires these morally relevant characteristics, it is not fully human. Before that time, abortion is not really murder.

The moralist who regards abortion as murder can make one last move. It is true, for all we know, that the human fetus lacks consciousness, the power of rational choice, and personality. Are we, therefore, to consider it lower than the animals since they at least possess consciousness? Not at all. Just as the child in all his innocence has a moral dignity because he is potentially an adult rational person, so the fetus is more precious than any brute animal because it possesses something no animal can have—the capacity to grow into a conscious and conscientious person. The fetus is potentially conscious, potentially a rational agent, and potentially a personality. For this reason it should be respected as a human being. To kill such a being is murder.

One of the strongest arguments against legally permitting abortion rests on the premise that to kill the human fetus is murder. Is this premise true? We have not decided this crucial question. But perhaps we have carried the objections and replies to this argument far enough to show that the question is a complicated one and that a wide variety of arguments can be advanced on each side of the issue.

A CASE FOR ABORTION ON DEMAND

While I cannot pretend to have carried my critical assessment of the various arguments through to the end, it seems to me that the most compelling argument against legally permitting abortion is that abortion is murder. If abortion were murder, then this would be a very strong reason indeed for prohibiting it by law. My own view, however, is that abortion is not murder. Why not? The charge of murder cannot be refuted by contending that abortion is justifiable killing and, therefore, one of the classes of exceptions to the general rule that the intentional killing of a human being is morally wrong. For reasons outlined in the previous section, acts of abortion do not really fall under the right to kill in self-defense or under the right to kill under duress of circumstances or under the principle of double effect. If abortion is not murder, it is because the embryo it kills is not a human being.

My problem, and I cannot honestly claim to have solved it, is to explain precisely why the embryo, conceived by human parents and naturally endowed with the capacity to grow into a mature human being, is not itself a human being. I must admit that biologically it is a human being. From the standpoint of genetics and the theory of living organisms, the vital dividing line between parent and child is the moment of conception. Before conception there exist only ovum and sperm—neither of which is a human being. After conception there exists a new human being, a living organism with a unique genetic inheritance that will control its future growth and biological life as a human being. From the moral standpoint, on the other hand, the embryo is not a human being, not a person to be treated with the respect due to a moral agent. Why not? Because the embryo lacks the morally relevant characteristics of consciousness and the capacity for rational choice. The infant also lacks the capacity for rational choice, but I would not wish to deny that the infant is a human being and that to kill a newborn child is to commit homicide. Presumably the reason that the infant deserves to be respected as a person in its own right is that, while it lacks the characteristics of a mature moral agent, the infant already possesses the potentiality to acquire them by normal development. But does not the embryo also have the potentiality to develop into a mature moral agent? Why is the moment of birth, or possibly the time when the embryo becomes independently viable, the morally crucial moment that distinguishes nonhuman embryo from human being? Probably the answer lies in the degree of similarity between infant and mature adult contrasted with the degree of dissimilarity between embryo and mature moral agent. I have not been able to explain, however, exactly which characteristics are the morally relevant ones here or why the time of birth is more significant morally than any other time in the development from zygote to human adult. While I continue to search for an adequate explanation of this difference, I continue to believe, subject to correction in the light of further evidence, that abortion is not murder because the embryo is not, morally speaking, a human being.

If the embryo is not a human being, then one cannot justify the prohibition of abortion by an appeal to the rights of the unborn child. The fetus, at least during the first six months of pregnancy before it becomes viable, is not an unborn *child* in the full moral sense of a "very young person." Since it is not a human being, it can possess no human rights. Accordingly, abortion, although it does cause the death of the fetus, does not violate its natural right to life because only a person can have natural rights.

In *Roe* v. *Wade* the Supreme Court declared that the word "person" as used in the Constitution does not include the unborn. Accordingly, the fetus does not now have any legal right to life in our country. This does not, of course, settle the question of whether such a right ought to be recognized in our law. If I am correct in denying that the fetus is a human being in the morally relevant sense, then no appeal to its natural right to life can require its legal right to life. I am not convinced that it is necessary to recognize the fetus as a legal person in order to retain many of the so-called "rights of the unborn child" in our body of laws. All that is necessary is to recognize that the child, once born, is a person legally competent to inherit property or sue for damages on the basis of events that took place before it became a person. If the fetus is not a person in the moral sense and if it is not necessary to admit that it is a person in the legal sense, it cannot, therefore, be argued that permitting abortion on demand would violate any natural human right or any legal right of the "unborn child."

Can one argue any more cogently that abortion on demand ought to be legally permitted because prohibiting abortion violates the right to privacy? My doubts about this line of reasoning center around three questions brought to mind by the recent Supreme Court decision in *Roe* v. *Wade* and *Doe* v. *Bolton*. (1) *Whose* privacy is violated by any law prohibiting abortion on demand? Many passages in Justice Blackmun's argument suggest that it is the privacy of the pregnant woman and her physician. Now the patient–physician relation is and ought to be privileged in the law. The doctor ought not to be required, or even permitted, to make public anything learned about a patient in the course of consultation or treatment. But it is not clear that this sort of privacy is really involved in the abortion issue. Would prohibiting abortion somehow intrude on the confidential nature of the doctor–patient relation? Would it publicize the patient's desire to have an abortion in a way that allowing abortion on demand would not? More likely the sort of privacy at stake here is the privacy of the decision to have an abortion and the act of carrying out that decision. The medical decision as to what treatment is most desirable for a given patient is said to be a private one to be made solely by the patient and her doctor. Is the medical decision really private in some sense that excludes all legal regulation? This would imply that a statute prohibiting euthanasia by a doctor at his patient's request is a morally unjustified invasion of the privacy of the physician–patient relation. Again, suppose that after obtaining the patient's permission to proceed with treatment, the physician kills the patient by operating incompetently or administering an overdose of drugs. Is a law permitting the next of kin to sue for malpractice an immoral violation of the privacy of the patient–physician relation? In short, although I am convinced that the patient–physician relation is private in some sense that requires it to be legally privileged in order to preserve its confidentiality, I am not convinced that it is private in any sense that necessarily makes the legal regulation of medical treatment morally unjustified.

But perhaps it is the privacy of the mother and father that is invaded by any law prohibiting abortion on demand. In *Griswold* v. *Connecticut,* the Supreme Court declared a statute prohibiting the use of contraceptives unconstitutional on the grounds that it violated "the intimate relation of husband and wife." No doubt the privacy of the precious personal relation of wife and husband ought to be respected, but this could be done by permitting only married women to have abortions. To justify abortion on demand, abortion whenever any woman, married or unmarried, requests it, requires some other ground. The biological facts of life remind us that every pregnant mother has had sexual relations with the father. The sexual relation between male and female is surely an intimate one with a real claim to privacy. But a statute prohibiting abortion does not in any direct or obvious way require any observation of, prying into, or interference with the purely sexual relations between mother and father. In fact, the pregnant woman seeking an abortion may have broken off sexual relations with the father several weeks before she demands an abortion. How can the privacy of a past relation be the moral basis for legally allowing the woman to have an abortion now? Between the socially sanctioned relation of marriage and the biological relation of sex, stands the precious personal relation of love. This, too, is an intimate relationship that demands privacy for its growth and preservation. But it does not seem that it is the privacy of lovers that requires abortion on demand. If the argument were based upon the privacy of love, then only loving couples could demand an abortion. Yet it may be precisely because the pregnant woman does not stand in any loving relation to her casual "lover" or her legally constituted husband that an abortion is called for in her case. Again, if it were the privacy of lovers that required abortion on demand, then both lovers would have an equal right to demand an abortion, and a pregnant woman would have no such right without the consent of her lover.

If an argument for abortion on demand is to be grounded on the right to privacy, then it must be the privacy of the pregnant woman that is morally and legally relevant. The crucial premise for this argument was articulated by the Supreme Court in *Eisenstadt* v. *Baird*: "If the right to privacy means anything, it is the right of the *individual,* married or single, to be free from unwarranted governmental intrusion into matters so fundamentally affecting a person as the decision whether to bear or beget a child." The central issue is whether abortion on demand is morally required by the pregnant woman's right to privacy.

The resolution of this issue obviously depends on the content of the right to privacy. Granted that there is a right to privacy, just what does this right consist in? This is the second question that the recent Supreme Court decisions leave unanswered in my mind. (2) How is the right to privacy to be *defined?* Although Justice Blackmun refers to passages in the Constitution that presumably imply the right to privacy and cites many previous decisions in which the right to privacy was mentioned or affirmed, he nowhere defines the nature or content of this fundamental constitutional right. This may be entirely proper for a judge acting within a common-law system, but it is not sufficient for a philosopher trying to render his reasoning articulate and clear. The problem is to generalize about the various kinds of acts that seem to respect or violate the right to privacy in order to define some sphere of privacy that ought not to be invaded by public officials or private citizens. English judges have refused to recognize, and the British Parliament has refused to create, any general legal right to privacy. Their reasoning has been that although there are several limited spheres of privacy that ought to be protected by law, such as the privacy of the home from unwarranted searches and seizures or the privacy of one's mail from interception and publication, these limited spheres do not share any common feature of privacy that deserves moral respect and legal protection. The law of the United States, on the other hand, has explicitly recognized a general constitutional right to privacy at least since the case of *Griswold* v. *Connecticut* in 1965. However, lawyers in this country have often complained that this fundamental right remains poorly defined and indeterminate in content.

Leaving the definition of the legal right to privacy to the courts, the legislatures, and the lawyers, let us turn to the human right to privacy that is basic to any moral argument about what the law ought to be. Precisely what is this sphere of privacy to which every person has a basic human right? The paradigm cases suggest that the right to privacy prohibits others from seeking, storing, or communicating knowledge of an individual without his consent. This right is violated by the peeping Tom, the person who reads someone else's mail without permission, the credit rating company that retains outdated or unreliable information in its files, the university that keeps detailed files on the personal lives of its students, the doctor who gossips about the medical histories of his patients, and the newspaper that publishes stories about the romantic affairs and sexual indiscretions of local notables. But there are other invasions of privacy that do not seem to fall within this definition at all. The practical joker or disgruntled student who repeatedly dials my number late at night only to hang up just when I answer my phone is surely invading my privacy even though he is not seeking, storing, or communicating information about me. The manufacturer who allows his factory to emit a noxious smell that permeates my yard and penetrates into my closed house is violating the privacy of my home. The religious proselytizer who approaches me on the street to sell or even give me a pamphlet I do not want is also invading my privacy. Here the right to privacy implies that others should not intrude into one's experience or introduce objectionable things into one's immediate environment. But the right to privacy central to the debate over abortion is of still another sort. It is the right that others shall not interfere with one's personal decisions. It is this right, if it is a right, that parents violate when they force, or try to force, their child to be confirmed against his will. It is this right that a high school violates when it refuses to allow male students to wear long hair or female students to wear jeans. The institution of arranged marriages is morally objectionable in large measure just because it infringes upon the right of each person to decide whom to marry. It appears that there are at least three different kinds of privacy to which the individual does, or may, have a right.

To speak of *"the* right to privacy" is to presuppose that these three sorts of cases share some common essence of being private. But precisely what is this general sphere of privacy that always demands moral respect? This general privacy is not clearly defined in American law, nor have I found any philosophical definition that seems to cover all the various cases adequately. This does not prove, of course, that there is no such definition. But until we have that definition, we cannot know the content of any alleged right to privacy. And until we know what is and what is not contained in the right to privacy, we cannot know whether or not a law prohibiting abortion on demand invades the right to privacy.

But what does this matter? If we cannot define any general right to privacy, we can simply stop talking about *the* right to privacy. Instead, we will assert the existence of several natural rights to privacy, at least the three I have defined in the previous paragraph. We can then argue that abortion on demand is morally required because to legally prohibit a woman from having an abortion is to violate her human right to make a purely private decision. We can use this argument provided we can define this more specific right to make private decisions. The crucial problem here is to define "a private decision" in such a way that it is clear both that the pregnant woman's decision whether to have an abortion is a purely private one and that every person always has a right to make purely private decisions without any outside interference.

This leads to my last question about the appeal to privacy. (3) What is a purely private decision? One suggestion is that a purely private decision is one that belongs to a single individual. It is his or her decision, and it ought not to be obstructed by any other person or institution. It is the decider's private property, as it were. But does the abortion decision belong to the pregnant woman in the same way that her purse or her watch belongs to her? Probably what is literally meant here is that only the pregnant woman has the right to make the abortion decision and that no one else has any right to interfere in the making or carrying out of that decision. If this is what is meant by a purely private decision, then obviously everyone always does have a right to make purely private decisions because a purely private decision is by definition one that the individual person has a right to make. But on this interpretation the right to privacy turns out to be a tautologous and empty right; it is the right to make every decision one has a right to make. It can no longer be argued that the pregnant woman has a right to make the abortion decision *because* this is a private decision. To call the abortion decision private is simply to assert that the woman has a right to make it, not to give any evidence or ground for this alleged right.

Let us, therefore, try to find some less trivial definition of a purely private decision that will enable us to argue that the pregnant woman ought to be allowed to make the abortion decision just because it is a purely private one. In *Eisenstadt* v. *Baird* the court declared that a private decision is one that "fundamentally affects a person." Normally, at least, the abortion decision is private in this sense. The decision to terminate a pregnancy or to bear a child usually affects the life of the pregnant woman in very basic ways. But do decisions that fundamentally affect a person belong to that person alone if they also fundamentally affect other persons? Does one always have a right to make any decision that fundamentally affects oneself? My decision whether or not to murder my wife and children is one that fundamentally affects me. Would it be morally wrong, therefore, for the law to prohibit me from making and carrying out this tempting decision? It would seem that the law may prohibit an individual from acting as he chooses whenever his action would seriously harm other individuals.

Accordingly, some philosophers, including John Stuart Mill, have defined a purely private decision as one that would not harm anyone other than the decider. On this interpretation, what makes a decision private is not that it profoundly affects the decider but that it does not affect anyone else. But the decision to have an abortion is not a purely private decision in this sense, for it does affect others for better or worse. Even granted, as I have argued, that the fetus is not a person to be affected in any way, the father who will or will not have a child and often previous children by the same couple who will or will not have a sibling will be affected by the mother's decision.

It seems to me that the most plausible definition of a purely private decision lies between the last two interpretations. A purely private decision is one that affects the life of one person much more than it affects the lives of any or all other persons. This definition is broad enough to cover momentous decisions, like the choice of a vocation in life, that will profoundly affect the life of the person pursuing that vocation but will affect other persons more indirectly and less profoundly. It also covers more trivial decisions, like the decision whether to dye one's hair, that are private because they affect others even less than they affect the person whose hair is or is not to be dyed. Moreover I believe, although I am not sure how to prove my belief, that an individual does always have a right to make any decision that is purely private in this sense.

Finally, I am entirely willing to admit that the abortion decision is almost always one that affects the life of the pregnant woman much more than it affects the lives of any other persons. But there is one morally significant class of cases that seems to be an exception—cases in which a pregnant woman has to decide whether or not to bear a child that will very probably be severely handicapped. The hardest examples to include under this definition of a purely private decision seem to be the decisions of pregnant women whose fetuses have been diagnosed by amniocentesis to be seriously defective genetically. Suppose that one of these women already has one or more children or could easily have children at some later time and that, although she very much wants to bear the child she now carries, she would not be emotionally shattered by having an abortion. Suppose further that there is compelling evidence that the fetus would be born as a horribly deformed, a terminally ill, or a seriously disabled child. Now if the woman decides to have an abortion, obviously her decision will affect her life much more than the life of the unborn child simply because the child will not be born. But if she decides not to have an abortion, then it seems to me that her decision will affect her child much more horribly than her own life—recognizing that the loving mother will also be terribly hurt. In this case, I do not believe that the pregnant woman's decision whether *or not* to have an abortion is a purely private one in the sense that it affects her life much more than any other life or lives. Nor can I think of any other definition of "a purely private decision" that would cover every instance of the abortion decision.

Therefore, I am not prepared to argue that abortion on demand ought to be legally permitted because prohibiting abortion always violates the right to privacy. I can find no definition of "*the* right to privacy" that is general enough to cover all the kinds of privacy to which one seems to have a right, nor can I define "a private decision" in a way to show that a pregnant woman always has a right to have an abortion. If one is to appeal to the rights of the pregnant woman, and such an appeal is surely right and proper, one may have to appeal to other rights. I am convinced that the pregnant woman does have a natural right to have an abortion. What I am not convinced of is that this right is grounded in her right to privacy. Until my three questions about the right to privacy are answered more satisfactorily, I must base my conclusion on other reasons.

The most direct and compelling argument for abortion on demand is that this would eliminate illegal abortions. Where restrictive laws against abortion exist, they are markedly ineffective in preventing pregnant women from obtaining abortions. In part, this is because of the difficulty in enforcing such laws. In part, it is because of the determination of many women to have abortions and the willingness of many doctors to perform abortions. What restrictive abortion laws do succeed in doing, if this can be called success, is to force many women to resort to illegal abortions—either self-abortions or abortions performed by criminal abortionists. The physical and psychological harm inflicted by illegal abortions would be hard to exaggerate. Abortion on demand ought to be legally permitted in order to avoid this great social harm.

Unless, of course, permissive legislation would cause even more harm than restrictive legislation. None of the arguments to show that this is so are very convincing. Abortion performed during the early months, when most women demand it, is a relatively safe medical procedure. Any statistics that can be quoted concerning the medical complications arising from abortion can be matched with statistics of the infections, physical injuries, and even maternal deaths caused by continuing pregnancies. The danger that the mother will have a nervous breakdown or emotional disorder precipitated by an abortion has been greatly exaggerated. Instances of serious mental disturbance have been rare in cases of legal abortion, and they have not even been frequent among women who have resorted to illegal abortions. The emotional strain upon a woman who is forced, against her wishes, to bear and raise a child is usually far greater than the psychological stress upon a woman who is permitted to have an abortion at her own request. When one considers every aspect of the health and happiness of the mother and her family, it seems that in a very large number of cases the entire family is better off for an abortion. Even in those few cases where the woman's decision to have an abortion may be unwise, permitting her to make this very personal and important decision probably does much less harm than forcing her to bear the child against her will. Although I am not sure that the abortion decision is a purely private one, I am firmly convinced that any legal interference with it causes terrible harm and accomplishes nothing of value. Therefore, I conclude that abortion on demand ought to be legally permitted in our society.

STUDY QUESTIONS

1. Additional reasons given for legalizing abortion are: (a) that an unenforceable law creates disrespect for the legal system of a society; (b) that a woman's right to control her own body is absolute; (c) that it is hypocritical of society to glorify sex and then punish promiscuity; (d) that restrictive abortion laws force doctors either to commit illegal acts or to act against their medical judgment; and (e) that the law ought not to impose religious dogmas upon those citizens who are not believers. Can you expand each of these arguments sufficiently to show its assumptions and its logical structure?

2. Additional arguments against legally permitting abortion on demand are: (a) that the destruction of life ought not to be part of the role of the doctor as doctor; (b) that only God has the right to determine human life or death; and (c) that easy abortion undermines human character by increasing callousness and decreasing the capacity to face life. Can you formulate each of these arguments fully, clearly and succinctly?

3. Which of all the arguments for abortion do you consider the strongest? Why? Which of all the arguments against abortion do you take to have the most logical force? Why?

4. Is it reasonable to sacrifice the health of the mother, who is a mature person living in personal interaction with other human beings, for the sake of the life

of the fetus, which is unborn and only potentially a developed personality? Is it reasonable to sacrifice the life of the child for the mere health of the mother?

5. It can be argued that life is more valuable than health because life is a necessary condition of any and all values, while health is only one of many values. On the other hand, it can be argued that mere life has no great value because an unhappy and miserable life is worse than nonexistence. Considering these and other arguments, should one conclude that life is more valuable than mere health or that health is more valuable than mere life?

6. Does a normal human fetus have the right to be born? If so, what gives it that right? Does a malformed or defective human fetus have a right not to be born? If so, on what grounds?

7. Certainly a mentally defective or physically deformed child has much less chance of living a happy life than a normal child. But is it true that such a child is doomed to live a miserable life?

8. Somewhere between twenty and thirty percent of the children whose mothers have German measles before the twelfth week of pregnancy are born with congenital abnormalities. Is it right to force these children, who did not choose their unhappy existence, to be born? Is it right to kill the seventy to eighty percent who would have been born healthy and normal in order to prevent the birth of the abnormal minority?

9. In addition to physiological handicaps like bodily deformity and brain damage, the proponents of abortion often appeal to emotional handicaps. They claim that unwanted and rejected children often become emotionally disturbed and tend to develop schizophrenia or become criminals. Are physiological and emotional handicaps equally valid grounds for abortion? Why or why not?

10. Is it fair to penalize the innocent victim of assault and rape by forcing her to bear an unwanted child? Is it fair to make a second victim of the innocent child? How does one decide what justice requires in this situation?

11. Do all illegal sexual acts constitute equally valid ground for therapeutic abortion? Can an adult woman be thought of as the involuntary victim of an act of incestuous intercourse between consenting adults? Does it change the situation if the female is a mere child? Why, if the child has expressed consent and not resisted or complained? Why not, if a mere child does not understand fully what she is doing?

12. On what grounds, if any, is the law morally justified in prohibiting certain kinds of sexual intercourse? Do these same grounds justify abortion if the law has been disobeyed and pregnancy resulted? Why or why not?

13. If the fact that restrictive abortion laws result in discrimination against certain groups of citizens is a valid reason to repeal these prohibitions against abortion, then the fact that our present laws against murder and rape tend in practice to discriminate against blacks, who are much more likely than whites to be convicted and punished under these laws, must be a valid reason to repeal our laws against murder and rape. Are we to conclude that we actually ought to repeal our laws against murder and rape *or* that the argument from discrimination is not cogent?

14. An argument against the constitutionality of any law that discriminates against any group of citizens can be based upon the Fourteenth Amendment that guarantees "equal protection of the laws." But what *moral justification*, if

any, is there for requiring equal protection or equal opportunity or equal benefit from any law?

15. Does abortion on demand actually contribute significantly to the control of population? Suppose that the use of contraceptive techniques was a more effective means to population control than it now is. Would this make abortion unnecessary or even less desirable? Suppose that abortion were murder. Would the good end of population control justify the use of this evil means? Does the end ever justify the means? If so, why not here? If not, what does rationally justify the use of some chosen means to reach a desired end?

16. Whose privacy, if anyone's, is violated by a law prohibiting abortion? Is it the privacy of the pregnant woman and her doctor, or of the mother and father, or simply that of the individual pregnant woman? Just how does a law prohibiting abortion violate this person's privacy?

17. What is privacy? How would you define the sphere of or spheres of privacy that ought to be respected by others? On what grounds would you affirm or deny a human right to privacy? Can you see any good reason to create and protect a general legal right to privacy?

18. Suppose it is claimed that each individual has a right against interference in making and carrying out purely private decisions. How should a purely private decision be defined? Should this claimed right be taken to be a special case of some general right to privacy or of the general right to liberty or of the general right to property or what?

19. Suppose it is granted that any prohibition of abortion on demand does violate the right to privacy of the pregnant woman but it is denied that this right is absolute or unlimited. What kind of reason is sufficient to override a prima facie human right? Can the state violate the human rights of its citizens whenever it happens to be useful to do so? If so, do human rights really constitute any moral limitation upon restrictive legislation? If not, are utilitarian considerations entirely irrelevant to the justification of limiting the rights of individuals?

20. Are illegal abortions really as dangerous as is alleged? If so, does this constitute a reason for legally permitting abortion? Does not a woman who insists on obtaining an illegal abortion do so at her own initiative and, consequently, at her own risk? Speeding and reckless driving are also highly dangerous. Does this constitute a reason for legalizing speeding and reckless driving?

21. It is alleged that abortion, whether therapeutic or not, is harmful to the mother. Should the law protect its citizens by prohibiting medical treatment that is dangerous to the patient or should the choice of treatment be left up to the judgment of the doctor and the patient? On what grounds, if any, is it morally justified for the law to control the production and sale of food and drugs? Do or do not these same grounds apply to the legal control of medical treatment?

22. Supposing that some kind of legal control of medical practice is desirable, would it be better to prohibit in advance certain kinds of medical treatment *or* to leave the doctor free to treat as he sees fit but to indict those later found guilty of malpractice? Is the inflexibility of the former method of control worse than the uncertainty of punishment in the latter?

23. It is argued that more effective contraception, easier adoption of unwanted babies, and state care of the handicapped are more desirable alternatives to abortion. For whom is each alternative desirable? Suppose abortion were more desirable for the mother but the alternatives more desirable for other members of society. Whose "desirables" should determine the law?

24. Suppose that effective contraceptive techniques were available but were not used. Should abortion be prohibited on the grounds that the mother is responsible for her sexual actions, or should abortion be allowed on the grounds that this would reduce the harmful consequences of her past act of intercourse? Should the law take notice of the motive, such as religious scruples or carelessness or impatience, that caused the mother to refrain from using contraceptives?

25. Is adoption really any solution to the problem of unwanted babies? After all, the child is sure to learn sooner or later that he is adopted. Does the adoption of unwanted babies solve any other personal or social problems beyond freeing the natural parents of the necessity of caring for the unwanted baby and protecting the child from parental rejection?

26. Does legalized abortion on demand really encourage sexual promiscuity, either premarital or extramarital? Is the fear of pregnancy a significant controlling factor in this age of contraceptive devices? Is dread of social condemnation a genuine controlling factor in this permissive and impersonal age?

27. Granted that pregnancy is the natural result of sexual intercourse, is there any essential connection between the legal control of sex and the legal control of abortion? That is, if there are good reasons for restrictive or permissive legislation in one of these two areas, does it follow that there should be correspondingly restrictive or permissive legislation in the other? Why or why not?

28. Does the assertion that abortion is murder count against *all* abortions or only against therapeutic abortions or abortions on demand? Why? Assuming that abortion really is murder and hence morally wrong, is this a reason for prohibiting it legally? Perhaps the proper business of the law is to advance social utility and not to enforce morality. How, if at all, is the morality or immorality of an act relevant to whether it should be legally permitted or prohibited?

29. It is probably morally wrong for anyone to intentionally hurt the feelings of another, at least under normal circumstances, or for a parent to continually discriminate against one child in favor of another. Should these acts be legally forbidden? Why or why not? What does your conclusion imply about whether abortion ought to be illegal?

30. Another way of putting the question is this: What justifies society in interfering with the actions of the individual citizens? Does this something, whatever it is, justify the legal prohibition of abortion? On what principle does one distinguish between purely private matters and matters of legitimate public concern and control?

31. Does legalized abortion in fact cause any significant increase in the number of acts of infanticide, euthanasia, and eugenic murder? Are there really lots of people who want to do such acts and have been held back only or primarily because of the law? Does changing the law change people's motives in such a way as to multiply such acts? Explain carefully what kind of evidence you use to reach your conclusion.

32. Does legalized abortion *require* for its *justification* an appeal to general principles that would equally justify acts of infanticide, euthanasia and eugenic murder? If so, what are these principles? How can one know that these are the only principles that would justify legally permitting abortion?

33. Consider again the argument that legalized abortion on demand is a dangerous precedent. Does this argument claim that legalized abortion actually causes an increased number of acts of infanticide, euthanasia and eugenic

murder? Or does this argument claim that any possible justification of legalized abortion would also justify such heinous acts? Which way of interpreting
the argument makes it more cogent and compelling?

34. Are infanticide, euthanasia, and eugenic murder really heinous? Always or
     only usually? How do you know?

35. Exactly what right or rights of the unborn does abortion violate? Is the
     argument that abortion violates the legal right to life a valid argument in view
     of the 1973 Supreme Court decision? Does this argument not disappear as
     soon as the law is changed to do away with this right? Is there any good
     reason to try to reinstate this legal right? Is there some human right to life
     that exists independently of the law? Does the human fetus possess this right
     just as an adult human being does? Why or why not?

36. Does the wrongness of killing a human being depend upon the fact that a
     human being, unlike a mere animal, has a soul? If so, just what is a soul? Is
     there any way of knowing when the human organism acquires its soul?

37. Is the view that abortion is not murder until the fetus has acquired the third
     and highest level of soul simply too speculative to be taken seriously? Does the
     wrongness of killing a human being depend in any way upon the fact that a
     human being has the capacity to reason? Is there any justification for saying
     that the fetus becomes a human being in the moral sense only when it has
     grown to the point where it resembles the normal human organism?

38. Why is it that deliberately killing an adult human being is usually morally
     wrong? Why is it that it is usually wrong to kill a child? Explain why these
     same reasons do or do not show that it is usually morally wrong to kill a
     human fetus.

39. Do illegal abortions really cause such immense harm as the author claims? If
     so, is this a reason for legally permitting abortion *on demand*? Could not illegal
     abortions be made virtually unnecessary by the less morally objectionable
     practice of legally permitting *therapeutic* abortions? Would or would not al-
     most every woman who demanded an abortion be able to obtain a therapeutic
     abortion? What evidence do you have for your prediction?

40. Assuming that legally permitting abortion on demand does eliminate the
     harmful consequences of illegal abortions, does it at the same time cause
     some other serious social harm? If so, what desirable consequences does it
     have? Are these great enough to outweigh the bad consequences of criminal
     abortions?

41. Considering critically all the pro and con arguments, do you believe that
     abortion on demand ought or ought not be permitted by law? How would
     you defend your answer?

42. Suppose that the question were changed to "Should *therapeutic* abortion be
     legally permitted?" Would the same arguments apply or are different pro
     and con considerations relevant to this somewhat different question? Do you
     think that it would be easier or harder to morally justify permitting therapeu-
     tic abortion? Why?

BIBLIOGRAPHY

BONDESON, WILLIAM B. ET AL., eds. *Abortion and the Status of the Fetus.* Dordrecht: Reidel, 1983.
BRODY, BARUCH. *Abortion and the Sanctity of Human Life: A Philosophical View.* Cambridge, Mass.:
   MIT Press, 1975.

CALLAHAN, DANIEL J. *Abortion: Law, Choice, and Morality.* New York: Macmillan, 1970.

COHEN, MARSHALL; NAGEL, THOMAS; AND SCANLON, THOMAS, eds. *The Rights and Wrongs of Abortion.* Princeton: Princeton University Press, 1974.

FEINBERG, JOEL, ed. *The Problem of Abortion.* 2nd ed. Belmont, Cal.: Wadsworth Publishing Co., 1984.

GRANFIELD, DAVID. *The Abortion Decision.* Garden City, N.Y.: Doubleday & Co., 1969.

HARRISON, BEVERLY W. *Our Right to Choose: Toward a New Ethic of Abortion.* Boston: Beacon Press, 1983.

LADER, LAWRENCE. *Abortion.* Indianapolis: The Bobbs-Merrill Co., 1966.

NOONAN, JOHN T., ed. *The Morality of Abortion: Legal and Historical Perspectives.* Cambridge, Mass.: Harvard University Press, 1970.

NOONAN, JOHN T. *A Private Choice: Abortion in America in the Seventies.* New York: Free Press, 1979.

PERKINS, ROBERT, ed. *Abortion: Pro and Con.* Cambridge, Mass.: Schenkman Publishing Co., 1974.

Roe v. Wade. United States Reports, 410 (1973): 113–178.

SAINT JOHN-STEVAS, NORMAN. *The Right to Life.* New York: Holt, Rinehart and Winston, 1964.

SMITH, DAVID T., ed. *Abortion and the Law.* Cleveland: The Press of Case Western Reserve University, 1967.

SUMNER, L. W. *Abortion and Moral Theory.* Princeton, N.J.: Princeton University Press, 1981.

TOOLEY, MICHAEL. *Abortion and Infanticide.* New York: Oxford University Press, 1983.

WALTER, DAVID F., AND BUTLER, DOUGLAS J., eds. *Abortion, Society, and the Law.* Cleveland: The Press of Case Western Reserve University, 1973.

8
THE END OF THE LAW

*The Law of God, which we call the moral
law, must alone be the scope, and rule,
and end of all laws.*

John Calvin in *Institutes of the
Christian Religion*

*Morality cannot be legislated, but
behavior can be regulated. Judicial
decrees may not change the heart, but
they can restrain the heartless.*   -

Martin Luther King, Jr., in *Strength to Love*
Copyright © 1963 by Martin Luther King,
     Jr. Used by permission of Joan Daves.

The specific moral problem of whether abortion on demand ought to be
legally permitted provides a wealth of fascinating material for discussion,
but the issue is of more than intellectual and pedagogical moment. The
legalization of abortion is currently being debated in Congress and in many
state legislatures and political campaigns. By the very arguments they use,
both proponents and opponents of legalized abortion presuppose some
standard of the adequacy of the law. Reformers claim that restrictive abortion laws are a failure because they cause great social evils like psychological
harm to the mother, unwanted children, or dangerous illegal abortions.
Conservatives contend that permissive abortion laws are even worse because the law ought to prohibit immoral acts like murder. But which arguments appeal to the proper or relevant standards? What sort of considerations really show some law to be a success or a failure? This all depends on
the end or the purpose of the law. If the proper purpose of the law is to
carry out the will of God, then the legislator and the citizen should judge
the law in terms of the commands of God. If the end of the law should be
the increase of human happiness, then more mundane arguments are
logically valid and morally decisive. Before one can finally resolve any
specific moral problems concerning the law, one must answer the theoretical ethical question "What should be the end of the law?"

The law is more than this or that statute considered by itself. The law of the land is the entire legal system in force in that political territory. The legal system consists at least of statutes enacted by the legislative body, court decisions accepted as setting legal precedents, customs and principles recognized by the courts as legally binding, and the various legal institutions that determine and apply legal principles and decisions. Any individual statute or legal rule is to be judged in terms of its contribution to this entire legal system; *this* law is to be judged in terms of *the* law. The "end" of the law is the goal, aim, or purpose of the law. An end is something one aims at, some goal one intends to achieve by one's endeavors. Presumably the legal system has, or ought to have, some end in view, some goal toward which it is striving. The law is to be judged adequate or inadequate, good or bad, successful or unsuccessful according to whether or not it manages to attain its end. As moral philosophers, however, we cannot remain content with the actual purpose or goal which the law happens to pursue. Our concern is with the proper or best or rationally justified end or goal. We do not ask "What is the actual purpose of the legal system?" but "What should be the end of the law?"

THEORIES OF THE PURPOSE OF THE LAW

Peace

Thomas Hobbes, a seventeenth-century English philosopher, believed that the end of the law ought to be peace. The natural condition of the human race is a war of every man against every man. In a state of nature (that is, a state of anarchy with no legal system or political organization), there would be continual open conflict between individuals in which each person would use fraud and force to impose his will on others. Universal quarrel and combat would arise from three sources in human nature. The desire for possessions would lead to competition for desired objects. The fear of anticipated attack would lead each person to try to attack his or her competitors first. And egotism would lead each individual to try to force others to accord him honor and glory. In this state of nature, life would be "solitary, poor, nasty, brutish, and short." The purpose of society should be to prevent this miserable condition of total warfare; the end of the law should be peace. The legal system, consisting in the commands of the sovereign enforced by the courts, restrains the greed and egotism of individuals, provides security from fear of constant attack, and brings order out of chaos. The happy result is peace, the absence of fighting between individuals and at least a minimal security of life, limb, and property. Maintaining peace should be the end or goal of the law.

It can be said for this theory that it is very realistic. It recognizes the harsh realities of human nature. Too often philosophers idealize human nature and offer unworkable theories of the law that fail to apply to human beings as they really are. Hobbes has seen that people are selfish, cunning, and egotistical and has framed a legal philosophy to fit these facts. Moreover, he has faced the hard fact that peace is a necessary goal for every society. No society can exist without peace, for in a state of open warfare between its members there is not even that minimal social order requisite for maintaining any form of social institution. Finally, the members of any society must have peace if they are to live well—or even long. If peace is necessary for the existence of any society and for human life, then surely peace should be the goal of the law.

On the other hand, it can be replied that peace, even though it may be a necessary minimal goal, is hardly a sufficient goal for society or for humanity. The proper goal for society is not mere existence, but the sort of social existence that makes possible a good life for its members. If any society fails to provide a worthwhile life for its members, there is no longer any real reason to keep it in existence. Accordingly, any society and any legal system should aim at something higher than peace. Peace is a purely negative goal consisting in the absence of war or open conflict. Surely there must be some higher goal than this at which the law should aim.

Morality

Cicero, an ancient Roman Stoic, found this "something higher" in morality. The end of the law should be morality. The natural, and therefore proper, purpose of human law is to promote moral action by commanding morally right conduct and forbidding morally wrong acts. The distinction between right and wrong is not conventional, not merely the product of the mores of a society or the beliefs of human beings. The moral law is built into the nature of things. It is a natural law in which the divine Reason of God commands acts that ought to be done and forbids acts that ought not to be done. Human virtue consists in living according to Nature or according to Reason—that is, according to the divine Reason dwelling within Nature. Each person embodies a spark of the divine Reason that inclines toward virtue and right conduct, but he or she also has appetites and emotions that lead that person astray. The purpose of the law of any society ought to be to encourage and enforce morality by requiring morally right acts and prohibiting morally wrong acts. Thus the human law ought to require all citizens to pay their debts and tell the truth because these are commanded by the law of nature. Conversely, the law of society ought to prohibit murder and rape because these acts are forbidden by the law of nature.

If we grant Cicero's conception of morality, then his thesis that morality should be the end of the law seems very strong indeed. Cicero conceives of that natural law that defines morality as the highest Reason implanted in

Nature, commanding what ought to be done and forbidding the opposite. The essential point here is that it is reason that determines what is morally right and wrong; the moral law consists of rational commands and prohibitions. If this is so, then it would seem to follow that any law that deviated from the moral law must be irrational and, therefore, rationally unjustified. If reason dictates paying one's debts, for example, then surely any legal system that did not command citizens to pay their debts must fall short of reason and be without rational justification. Similarly, if the rational law of nature forbids murder, then it must be reasonable for the law of society to forbid murder also. In short, once it is granted that the moral law is the law of reason, then it seems to follow that the only rational end the human law could have would be to coincide with morality.

Plausible as this line of reasoning is, it can be challenged. No doubt morality constitutes a standard by which the law of any society may be judged. But does this really mean that the law should aim at requiring every morally right act and prohibiting every morally wrong one? It is wrong, as any parent can plainly see, for a child to treat his mother or father with disrespect. We must not leap to the conclusion, however, that the child's act of sassing his mother should be made illegal. For one thing, any such law is probably unenforceable, and unenforceable laws on the books tend to undermine respect for the law. For another thing, any attempt to enforce such a law would destroy the privacy of the family, a very precious value in any society. Or, to take another example, it is probably true that cigarette smoking is bad for one's health. It is also plausible to hold that people ought not to impair their health. Still, it may be that the act of smoking, although wrong, ought not to be prohibited by law. As long as the man who smokes does not injure others by carelessly setting their property on fire or blowing cigarette smoke in their faces, it is his business whether or not he smokes. Each person, it can be claimed, has a right to live his or her own life as he or she sees fit just as long as he or she does not thereby harm other people. The individual's right to freedom has as much moral justification as the authority of law. Some laws that forbid the individual to act irrationally would invade that individual's natural right to live his own life as he chooses. Thus some wrong acts should not be made illegal. If this is so, the end of the law ought not to be as simple as requiring morally right conduct and prohibiting morally wrong acts.

Natural Rights

The Declaration of Independence, reflecting the political philosophy of John Locke, maintains that the end of the law should be to secure the natural rights of the citizens. Every citizen has many legal rights, such as the right to vote or the right to a prescribed minimum wage, created and protected by the legal system of his society. But every human being also has certain natural rights, certain rights that exist whether or not they are recognized by society. God the Creator has given each human being inalienable rights of life, liberty, property, and the pursuit of happiness. Each person possesses these rights by nature, independently of any legal system or social convention. Nothing that can be done by any human being, no matter how powerful, can take away these God-given rights. Still, the enjoyment of these natural rights is precarious, for tyrannical governments may invade one's liberty, or immoral individuals may steal one's property. The purpose of any government and of its laws ought to be to preserve and protect the natural rights of every member of society. The law should prohibit murder and theft in order to secure the individual's rights to life and property. The law should not censor the free speech of its citizens, for to do so would be to infringe upon their natural right to liberty. The end of the law should be to secure the natural rights of the citizens.

It is not hard to construct an argument for this theory. Natural rights are of tremendous value to each human being; life, liberty, and property are essential for the good life. A person can hardly live well without life, and life without freedom or property would hardly be living well. Since life, liberty, and property are all precious and can be taken from an individual at any time against his will, it is crucial for his welfare that his right to retain and enjoy these things be preserved and protected. Now governments are made for men, not men for governments. Any government ought to serve its citizens and improve their lives, not exploit and injure them. Hence, any government ought to do everything it can to preserve the natural rights that are required to enable its citizens to live the good life. If the two premises of this argument are accepted, and surely they are very plausible, then its conclusion would be hard to deny. And a corollary of this conclusion seems to be that the end of the law should be to secure the natural rights of the citizens.

Many moral philosophers reply that this cannot be the end of the law because there are no natural rights to be secured. No doubt every citizen has many rights, but these are all legal rights, rights created and protected by the law. These rights, however, do not constitute any goal outside of the legal system at which it should or even can aim. The theory under consideration presupposes that in addition to having legal rights, every citizen possesses certain natural rights, certain rights that are completely independent of the law or any other social convention. Many philosophers believe that this presupposition is untenable because it contains an implicit contradiction. The notion of natural right is self-contradictory because a right is essentially social and what is social cannot be natural in the sense of being independent of society. A right is essentially a claim, something that can be obtained upon legitimate demand. I have a right to free speech and a right to be paid for my work. This means that if anyone tries to prevent me from speaking, I can get a judge or a policeman to cause him to cease and desist from interfering with my speech. If my employer refuses to pay me at the end of the month, I can go to court and force him to pay. Since a right is a claim, every right necessarily involves some process of claiming, some procedure by which a person can demand and obtain whatever it is he has a right to. And this process of claiming is an empty gesture unless there are officials in society who will hear the demand and enforce the claim. Thus a proper understanding of rights reveals that they could not exist unrecognized by society. Since a right is a claim that can be made by an individual and is enforced by society, there can be no natural rights, rights the individual possesses independently of society and its legal system. And since there are no natural rights, it cannot be the end of the law to secure the natural rights of the citizens.

The Common Good

Although it is easy to argue that the rights of the citizen depend for their very existence upon recognition by society, it would be hard to prove that the citizen can enjoy goods or suffer evils only when these are recognized by society. But to say that human welfare exists independently of society and its legal system is not to deny that the law affects human welfare greatly for good or ill. This suggests that the purpose of the law is to promote the public welfare. Saint Thomas Aquinas, the thirteenth-century Catholic theologian, asserted that the end of the law should be the common good.* The law is, or ought to be, directed toward the good; its goal should be to produce as much good or as little evil as possible. But whose good should it promote? Aquinas held that the law should pursue the common good. The common good is contrasted with any private good. My fame or fortune is my private good, my personal interest not shared by the other members of my society. Similarly, the special interests of the rulers, those who hold political power in society, constitute their private good. The common good consists in the welfare of all the citizens, the good of each and every member of the society. The common good is also contrasted with the good of humanity. Those who are not members of this society do not form part of the group whose welfare should be furthered by the law. The common good is composed of the welfare of all the citizens of the society— and not those outside the society. The law of any society should aim at this common good.

What this theory amounts to is ethical egoism translated from individual to social terms. Ethical egoism is the theory that each moral agent ought always to do that act that benefits himself or herself most; each act is to be judged right or wrong by its impact on the good of the agent. According to this view, it would be irrational for an agent to sacrifice his or her total well-

---

* Jean-Jacques Rousseau held a somewhat different but equally influential conception of the common good.

being for the sake of some partial good, as when one "cuts off one's nose to spite one's face." It would be equally irrational for an agent to sacrifice his or her own welfare for the sake of the good of other people, as when one gives to charity with no prospect of personal benefit. Analogously, the theory that the end of the law should be the common good maintains that the legal system of any society ought to be directed toward the welfare of the citizens of that society. It is equally irrational to sacrifice the good of all to the private good and to sacrifice the good of the citizens to the welfare of noncitizens. Since each society ought to pursue its own good, the law should aim at the common good of that society.

This conclusion can be supported by an appeal to the dictates of reason. The fundamental law of reason is, as Thomas Aquinas pointed out, to pursue good and shun evil. It would not be rational for a person to set any other goal of conduct. Surely it would be irrational to strive to attain some evil, and there could hardly be a reason to exert oneself to possess something without any value at all. It seems to be self-evident that the good is the goal of rational endeavor. But whose good should the law of society pursue? If the law aims at some private good, it is benefiting some individuals in society at the expense of other members of the same society. But all the individuals that make up a society are equally members of that society. Hence, the society *as society* could have no reason to prefer the good of some of its members over that of other members. Since it would be irrational to discriminate between the individuals within a society without some valid purpose, reason dictates that society as society should pursue the good of all its members alike—that is, pursue the common good. Reason, then, dictates pursuit of the good and impartiality between the members of the society. From these two dictates it seems to follow that the law of any society ought to set as its goal the common good, the good of all its citizens.

But should the law ignore the good of noncitizens? Granted that the law ought to aim at the common good rather than the private good of some powerful individual or interest group, the effects that the law has on human beings outside the society seem relevant also. Suppose, for example, that legislators or citizens are trying to decide what the immigration law of the society ought to be. Obviously, they must consider the public welfare most seriously. They should consider the society's need for persons with useful talents or skills as well as the potential burden on its welfare agencies if uneducated or diseased persons are allowed to come into the country. But are these the only relevant considerations? Traditionally our country has believed that it ought to frame its immigration laws so as to provide a haven for people fleeing from religious persecution abroad. It can be argued that we ought to make some special provision for the immigration of political refugees from tyrannical governments. Perhaps some allowance should be made in the law for the admission of people from overpopulated or underdeveloped lands. The needs and desires of noncitizens should not cause the legislators to lose sight of the common good, but neither should an exclusive preoccupation with the well-being of its own citizens cause the legislators to ignore the crying needs of other human beings. This line of reasoning, if accepted, suggests that the end of the law should be broader than the common good of its citizens.

The Good of Humanity

The end of the law should be the good of all humankind; the legal system of any society ought to aim at promoting the welfare of all human beings, citizens and noncitizens alike. This seems to have been the position of Jeremy Bentham, the English political philosopher and reformer. It will be worth our while to ponder ambiguities in his *Principles of Morals and Legislation* because they illustrate his struggle with a serious moral dilemma. On one point Bentham never wavers: the law, and presumably every particular law also, is to be judged in terms of its utility. The utility of anything is its tendency to produce good consequences or prevent bad ones. Since Bentham believed that intrinsic goodness and badness belong only to pleasure and pain, he equated utility with the tendency to increase human happiness or decrease human misery. But is the law of any society to be judged by its utility for the members of that society or its utility for all human beings? On this point Bentham's language is unclear. He often refers to the interest of the community. This suggests that he would judge the law of any society in terms of the welfare of the citizens of that society. If so, he agrees with Aquinas that the end of the law should be the common good. But this position is, as we have seen, the legal analogue of ethical egoism; it holds that each society ought to pursue its own good. Now Bentham clearly wishes to be a utilitarian in moral theory. He holds that the moral agent ought to do the act that produces more good or less harm *for everyone affected* than any alternative act possible under the circumstances. The utility by which he would measure the morality of any act is the tendency of that act to increase the happiness of any human being. The social analogue of act-utilitarianism is the theory that the end of the law should be the good of all humanity. Since Bentham is an act-utilitarian in ethics, one would expect him to advocate this same universal utility in his political theory. This expectation is confirmed by his treatment of the hedonic calculus, the method for measuring utility, in which he defines the extent of an act as the number of persons who are affected by it. Since an act, or the law, can affect people other than those who are members of the given society, it seems to follow that the welfare of noncitizens as well as citizens must be considered in calculating utility.

On this interpretation, then, Bentham held that the end of the law should be the good of all human beings. For practical purposes, this will often amount to no more than the common good, the welfare of all the members of the society, because the law will not have any impact on those outside the society. But whenever the law does affect people outside the society, their welfare must be considered also. The goal of any legal system should be to increase the happiness of all human beings. This position follows logically from the standard of the greatest happiness of the greatest number. The purpose of the law should be to increase human happiness without regard for whose happiness it may be; every person, not just every citizen, is to count for one and no more than one. The law should aim equally at the well-being of all people.

A strength of this theory is that it can be supported by a general theory of obligation; it seems to be a logical consequence of of act-utilitarianism. If every moral agent ought always to do the act that maximizes value for everyone, then it follows that legislators and citizens ought to work for laws that promote the welfare of all human beings. A corollary would seem to be that the end of the law should be to increase the good of humanity. It is no coincidence that utilitarians like Bentham and Mill held that the standard by which the legal system and any law within it ought to be measured is utility, the happiness of all human beings. It is the strength of their legal theory that it is not ad hoc and groundless; it can be supported by an appeal to a more basic ethical theory. The logical connection between philosophy of law and ethical theory is philosophically important because the goal of any philosopher is to work out a system of theories. The philosopher wants more than a collection of principles. He wants these theories to fit together in such a way that one helps to explain another and each helps to support the others. Thus there is a philosophical advantage in a system that contains these two coherent principles; that the end of the law should be the good of humanity and that one ought always to do the act that maximizes good in the world. Until some alternative ethical principle can be proposed to justify some other end for the law, legal utilitarianism is not to be rejected lightly.

Nevertheless, many philosophers believe that it must be rejected in the end. Legal utilitarianism is the view that the end of the law should be the good of humanity. This means not only that the law ought to promote the well-being of every human being, but that the good of every human being is equally relevant to what the law should be. But is it morally right for the legislator to be equally concerned with the good of citizen and noncitizen? If the welfare of noncitizens is put on a par with that of citizens, this seems to imply that the United States ought to relax its immigration laws to allow very large numbers of immigrants from despotic societies, underdeveloped countries, and overpopulated lands to enter our country. To do so would seriously lower the standard of living of most of the citizens of this country, but this harm would probably be outweighed by the decrease in suffering and the increase in happiness of those who were admitted, provided only that immigration were halted before complete social breakdown took place. Although utilitarianism seems to dictate this lenient immigration policy, a consideration of the duty of a legislator argues against it. The legislator does not stand in the same morally significant relation to all human beings. Or, to be more precise, in addition to being a potential benefactor to all human beings, the lawmaker has the special duty of representing the citizens of a society. Hence, the legislator has a special obligation to his constituents, an obligation that requires giving priority to their welfare in framing the laws of the society. The legislator ought not to consider the welfare of noncitizens on a par with the welfare of citizens because he stands in a special moral relation to the citizen; the citizen has entrusted him with the legislative authority. Hence, it is the duty of the legislator *as legislator* to consider the welfare of the citizens first and foremost. As a private moral agent, he may treat all human beings equally; as an elected representative of the citizens, he ought to be guided by the welfare of the citizens he is representing. This suggests that the proper goal of the law is not the good of all people but the good of the society.

Freedom

When a utilitarian looks at the law, he quite naturally judges it in terms of its utility, its tendency to increase the amount of value people can enjoy. Looked at from a different moral perspective, the law can be judged in terms of a very different ideal. Immanuel Kant, the eighteenth-century German philosopher, maintained that one ought to treat all persons as ends-in-themselves. One ought not to impose one's will upon another human being but leave each person free to live his own life as he chooses. This suggests that the end of the law should be freedom.

Quite logically, Kant asserted this position in his legal philosophy. The freedom Kant had in mind is the moral freedom of each human being to choose between alternatives and to express his or her will in action unrestricted by any other human beings. Every person has practical reason, the ability to decide rationally between alternative courses of action. Accordingly, each person should be respected—that is, allowed by all other persons to exercise reason and decide for himself or herself how to live. Freedom requires more than free will, the ability to choose between alternatives; it requires being able to carry out one's will in action. One is not free whenever one has to act against one's will; the opposite of freedom is coercion. It is not only brute force that limits individual freedom, as when someone is chained to a post or carried out of the room kicking and screaming. Coercion may take the form of threats of force, as when the bandit holds a gun to someone's head, or even hindrances to action, as when black citizens are required to pass special tests before being allowed to vote. The purpose of the law ought to be to maximize the freedom of every individual and to minimize coercion within society.

One of the reasons that Kant's legal theory is so attractive is that it projects a high social ideal. The society he defines is one in which every adult person is free to decide what to do with his or her own life and in which people do not impose their will upon others. This sort of society seems highly desirable, for what human being does not prize liberty and object to being forced against his will to act or refrain from acting? This free society also seems to be required by morality, for the responsibility involved in obligation and virtue presupposes that the moral agent has the freedom to choose for himself or herself. Thus, a bank president would not be held morally responsible for unlocking the safe if he or she did so against his will and only because his or her very life was threatened. A society in which each individual has complete moral freedom and in which no person is subject to the coercion of any alien will is an ideal worthy of human striving. Since the law can harmonize the conflicting wills of individuals, the end of the law should be the individual freedom that would make the ideal society possible.

But is the law an effective means of maximizing human freedom? Some philosophers argue that there is an inconsistency in Kant's theory. There is probably no logical contradiction in the assertion that the end of the law should be freedom, but there seems to be a practical contradiction between the nature of the means used and the end pursued. Freedom, as this theory conceives it, consists in the absence of coercion. A person is free whenever he or she can choose and act without being forced to go against his or her own will by any other person. The means to achieve this uncoerced freedom is supposed to be the law. But coercion seems to be central to the very nature of the law. The law is imposed on the citizens by some legislative authority, and obedience is enforced by legal sanctions. Those who disobey the law are punished, and the fear of punishment is a powerful motive in causing citizens to be law-abiding. But if the citizens are forced to obey the law, whether they wish to do so or not, the law is necessarily a limitation upon their freedom. Since the law is by nature coercive, it would seem an inappropriate means to use to achieve human freedom, at least as long as freedom is thought of as the opposite of coercion. It can be argued that it is no more rational to use the law as a means to achieving human freedom than it would be to use germs as a means to achieving human health.

Justice

It would be much harder to argue that the law is an inappropriate means to use to achieve justice. However, we must not lose sight of the fact that the word "justice" is used in both a broad and a narrow sense. In its broader sense, justice includes all of morality. But if the word is used this broadly, then to say that the end of the law should be justice is simply to repeat the theory that the end of the law should be morality; and in fact, Cicero does often speak of justice as the end of the law. We have a distinct legal theory requiring separate discussion, however, only if the word "justice" is used more narrowly so that it refers to only one part of morality. Clearly the word is often used in this qualified sense. Traditionally justice was thought to be only one of the virtues; morality also included the virtues of wisdom, temperance, courage, and perhaps others. An act of gluttony is morally wrong, but it is not unjust in the sense in which an act of giving the best grades to the prettiest coeds or excluding blacks from a fraternity is unjust.

Sir John Salmond, the recent British jurist, held that the end of the law should be justice, in this restricted sense of the word. The nature of justice can be seen most clearly in its opposite; injustice is the charge leveled against persons, acts, or rules that treat anyone unfairly. Accordingly, the defining concept in justice is that of fairness. Fairness seems to have two aspects. It requires that one treat like cases alike; justice implies an impartiality that rules out both favoritism and vindictiveness. But justice requires more than treating similar cases similarly. It would be unfair to give the lowest grades to the best students and the highest grades to the poorest students, even if this were done uniformly in every case. Fairness requires that each case be treated as it deserves. "To each his own" is one traditional formula for justice; it means that each person should be treated according to individual merit. These two aspects of justice are nicely pictured in the figure of justice as a blindfolded woman holding a balance scale. Justice is blindfolded so that she will be unable to do favors for her friends or injury to her personal enemies. The scales enable her to give out equal amounts of good for good or evil for evil according to the desert of each person judged.

The law, then, should achieve justice or fairness. It is not only that the rules embodied in the law should be fair and that they should be applied fairly by the courts. The law should ensure that the state deals fairly with each citizen and that the individual citizens deal fairly with one another. Within the administration of justice, one can distinguish between distributive and corrective justice. The former concerns the fair distribution of burdens or benefits among the citizens. Tax laws, for example, should be equal in some sense, either exacting the same amount of money from each citizen or imposing an equal degree of financial sacrifice upon each. Again, Social Security payments should be fair, treating equally all citizens who have contributed equally or who stand in equal need of help. Corrective justice concerns equalizing the balance of goods and evils when this balance has been disturbed by unjust actions. If a criminal has done serious harm to some member of society, then it is only fair that he or she be punished, that he or she suffer an equal amount of harm. Or if an innocent person has been punished, it is only fair that that person receive some balancing compensation from society. The law of any society ought to aim at ensuring distributive and corrective justice in that society.

One strength of this legal theory is that justice seems a singularly appropriate end for the law to pursue. While there are many worthwhile goals that the law might strive to achieve, justice by its very nature seems the most fitting end of the law. The law consists of those rules of conduct society imposes upon its members to regulate their interactions. Its natural province is the interaction of people in society rather than the personal life of each individual. Now many values, both moral and nonmoral, seem to be individual rather than social concerns. It is only natural for each person to pursue pleasure, but it does not much matter to society what form this pleasure takes as long as it does no harm to the other members of society. Intemperance and imprudence may well be moral vices, but what does this matter to society as long as they affect only the life of the individual? Injustice is another matter. Justice is the part of morality that concerns how one individual treats others. By its very nature, the unfair treatment of one person by another is more than an individual matter. Since justice and injustice apply to the interactions between people, they are social in their very essence. Since the law consists of the rules society imposes to regulate the interactions between its members and since justice is that part of morality that deals with the interaction between persons, justice would seem to be the right and proper end of the law.

A serious difficulty with the view that the end of the law should be justice is that there seem to be no criteria of justice. A criterion is some test or measure by which something can be judged. We can use litmus paper to test the presence of acid in a solution and measure the degree of temperature with a thermometer, but by what standard can we judge justice or injustice? Some moralists contend that the graduated income tax is unjust because it requires those who work hardest and earn the most to pay more taxes than the lazier or less skillful workers with less income. Others object to the flat or uniform income tax on the grounds that it imposes more hardship on the person with a low income than the person with a high income who can more easily afford to give up the specified percentage of earnings. Again, is capital punishment a fair treatment of the murderer, who has taken one life and so deserves to lose his own, or is it cruel and unusual punishment that is too harsh to be fitting for any human being? Desert is no criterion of justice; it is only justice under a different name. Unfortunately, the notions of treating similar cases similarly and treating a person as he deserves are so vague and indefinite that reasonable people frequently disagree about their application. Since there are no clearly identifiable criteria by which the presence or absence of justice can be recognized, justice cannot serve as an end of human endeavor. The difficulty is that an end is supposed to be a goal, something that gives direction to striving and to action. But an indefinite end fails to give direction because it does not distinguish between success and failure, between what it is to achieve the goal and what it is to fail. The theory that the end of the law should be justice is of no more practical help than the suggestion that one look for buried treasure somewhere or other. There is no end to a search like that.

We have considered seven different theories as to what the end of the law should be. The end might be maintaining the peace, enforcing morality, preserving natural rights, promoting the common good, increasing the good of humanity, protecting freedom, or advancing justice. Each of these ends seems worthy of pursuit, but which of them ought the law to take as its goal?

THE GOOD OF ALL SENTIENT BEINGS

My own position is that the end of the law should be the good. I believe that Aquinas and Bentham began their search on the right foot. The fundamental practical imperative of reason is to pursue good and shun evil; the good, that which has value, is the only rational goal of action. It is true by definition that no other end is worth pursuing. It is a truth going beyond definition that one ought always to desire, choose, and strive for the good. This fundamental rational imperative is formulated in act-utilitarianism as a theory of obligation, and I infer that the analogous position is reasonable in legal theory. Although I cannot offer a proof of my conclusion, I can explain why I accept it. Given any actual or proposed law, it is both meaningful and legitimate to ask, "Why should or should not this be the law?" To this question, the reply "because it would do good" or "because it would do harm" seems a relevant answer. Moreover, this answer seems ultimate because there is no room left for the question "But why should we pursue the good?" or "But why should we try to avoid harm?" Now, there are other relevant replies to the question why some particular law should or should not be part of the law, but none of these other replies is ultimate. For example, the argument "This statute ought to be enacted because it would increase human liberty" is cogent enough, but the question remains: "Why ought we to promote human liberty?" Since value judgments are the ultimate grounds for legislation and legal reform, the end of the law should be the good.

But whose good should the law pursue? It is here that Aquinas and Bentham part company, and I disagree with both. Aquinas held that, since the law is an instrument of society, the end of the law should be the good of the members of the legislating society. The difficulty with this theory is that it distinguishes between the good that ought to be pursued, that of the citizens, and the good that ought not to be pursued, the good of all noncitizens. What rational ground can be given for this distinction? I can conceive of no ground that would justify this discrimination. Quite the contrary. If "because it is good" is a valid reason why the law should promote the health or wealth of the citizens, then "because it is good" must equally be a cogent reason why the law should promote the health or wealth of noncitizens. If the end of the law is the good, then the only relevant consideration is the good that the law might achieve or frustrate, not who will possess this good. This suggests that the end of the law should be the good of all human beings, but this does not go quite far enough. Human beings are not the only kind of beings who can possess good or bad; at least the higher animals are capable of enjoying pleasures and suffering pains. Ultimately, the good consists of value experiences—experiences that are good or bad, desirable or undesirable for their own sake. Presumably all sentient creatures are capable of having value experiences. Hence, the good encompasses the lives of more than human beings. This insistence upon the good of nonhuman creatures is no idle philosophical quibble, for it makes a practical difference to the law. It is the basis for legislation prohibiting cruelty to animals, for example. If the act-utilitarianism with which Bentham began is carried to its logical conclusion, it implies that the end of the law should be the good of all, the desirable experiences of all sentient creatures. Being logical, this is the conclusion I draw.

Having drawn this conclusion, I am immediately confronted with a further, somewhat awkward, implication. That the end of the law should be the good of *all* implies, given the fact that what is best for the numbers of a society does not always coincide with what is best for those who are not members of that society, that sometimes the legislator ought to sacrifice the welfare of the citizens to the welfare of those who are not members of the society. This seems to conflict with the duty of a legislator. Some philosophers suggest that the society for which the laws are made could have no reason to sacrifice its good for the good of others. This suggestion is, I believe, false. The society may have the best of all possible reasons; in some cases, the good of those outside the society is greater than the social good to be sacrificed. In other cases, this will not be true. Where this is not true, it would not be rational to sacrifice the welfare of the members of the society for the sake of the lesser good of those outside the society. Reason does not require, or even allow, every social sacrifice. The end of the law should be the greatest good of all, citizens and noncitizens alike.

But is this position really acceptable? It seems to imply sacrifices that, to be quite honest, no reasonable citizen of this country would accept. Given the widespread malnutrition and even starvation in the world about us, this position seems to imply that the United States ought to collect taxes from its citizens in order to buy up as much foodstuffs as our country can produce and distribute this to the needy throughout the world. No doubt this policy would be immediately beneficial to some of our citizens, the farmers and ranchers and food processors. But it would place an exceedingly heavy burden of taxation upon all the citizens. Even the food producers who profited initially would have to give up most of their gain in increased taxes and higher food prices. Should our law really exact this price from our citizens? If not, my theory seems to be refuted. With some hesitation, I suggest that the policy apparently implied by my theory does not really follow from it. The reason is not that distributing food to the needy throughout the world would do so much harm to the citizens of the United States, but that it would do much less good to the needy noncitizens than one at first imagines. The immediate consequence of this policy would be to reduce hunger and malnutrition and to promote health and happiness on a large scale. Before long, however, this highly beneficial result would probably be followed by less happy consequences, primarily the birth of innumerable additional human beings. The population would probably increase until the old problems of malnutrition and starvation returned, but on a larger scale. The moral of this tale is not that the United States, or any other relatively wealthy country, has no moral obligation to use its resources to improve the lot of those who live in less fortunate countries. The moral is that not every sacrifice that seems reasonable is reasonable in the end. Some sacrifices of national interest are reasonable, and these ought to be made for the sake of the good of all. But such reasonable sacrifices, just because they are reasonable, do not constitute any refutation of my theory.

One other objection, at least, deserves some consideration. My view is that the end of the law should be the good of all. Accordingly, I reject all of the other theories discussed earlier in this chapter. But is it reasonable to reject all of those fine ends? Do I really wish to maintain that the end of the law ought not to include justice or liberty? I do not wish to maintain this, not do I believe that I am compelled to do so. Justice and liberty are entirely proper ends of the law because they are so valuable. Although neither has intrinsic value, both contribute immensely to human happiness. It is because they are so very good that justice and liberty ought to be ends of the law. But this does not require me to modify my theory and admit that there are reasonable ends the law ought to pursue in addition to the good of all. The good of all incorporates all valuable ends, including justice and liberty, by virtue of their value. These many ends are derivative, however; they should be pursued by the law because of their value. The single ultimate end of the law should be the good of all, the desirable consciousness of all sentient creatures. At least, subject to critical questioning, this is my conclusion.

STUDY QUESTIONS

1. We speak of the laws as good or bad, just or unjust, right or wrong, justified or unjustified, legitimate or illegitimate. Are these pairs of terms synonymous

or does each mark a different distinction? If they express different sorts of moral judgments, are different standards required for each? What sort of moral judgment of the law seems to you to be the most important?

2. The law consists of particular laws, mostly statutes, together with common-law principles, previous court decisions, and various legal institutions. Can the law, the entire legal system, be judged by the same standards one would use in judging some particular law? Can a single law be judged morally apart from its place in the entire legal system?

3. In order to find some standard by which to judge the law and the particular laws it contains, we asked, "What should be the end of the law?" Does this way of putting the question prejudice our search for moral standards? After all, it takes up a teleological viewpoint, for it looks for ends or goals by which to judge the law. But might there not be moral standards that are independent of ends or goals? Why or why not?

4. Precisely what is peace? Is peace simply the absence of war? And does war consist in armed conflict between groups *or* any and all armed conflict *or* any conflict using force *or* any conflict whether or not force is used? How are security and order each related to peace?

5. Are human beings as selfish and egotistical as Hobbes claims? If not, does this undermine his conception of the proper goal of the law? If human nature is as Hobbes claims, does this justify his conclusion that the end of the law should be peace?

6. Peace seems to be a minimal goal at which the law might aim. One person might argue that a minimal goal is necessary and fundamental and therefore the most important goal. Another might argue that a minimal goal is much less than a maximal goal and thus not very important. Does either of these arguments have real cogency? Explain why you take each to be a strong or a weak argument.

7. Suppose it is granted that there is some sort of a moral law, some set of moral principles specifying which sorts of acts are right and which are wrong. Should the law of society duplicate this moral law in every respect? Is there any inconsistency in trying to force someone to be moral? Is the morality of an act entirely irrelevant to whether or not it should be illegal?

8. What reasons, if any, are there to believe that the moral law is natural, that it is not artificial or imposed by society? Are there any reasons to believe that moral laws are conventional or the products of human beings? Try to decide which set of reasons is more compelling.

9. Suppose that it is granted that there are some sort of nonartificial standards of moral right or wrong. Is there any reason to think of these as moral *laws*? In precisely what sense are moral principles lawlike?

10. The natural law is often referred to as "the higher law." What reason is there to believe that the natural law is higher than the law of society, that when the two conflict one ought to obey the natural law of morality and disobey statute law? Could one admit that there is a natural law but claim that it is lower than the law of society, and that one ought to obey the civil authorities rather than the natural law?

11. It is sometimes argued that the natural law theory is the only alternative to moral nihilism with respect to the law, that to deny the natural law theory is to imply that there is *no* moral standard *independent* of the law by which it could be judged immoral. Is this argument sound? What sorts of moral standards might there be that would not be versions of natural law?

12. Cicero thought of the moral law as the commands of a Divine Reason in the nature of things. What other ways of thinking of the moral law seem plausible? Would these other ways make it easier or harder to hold that the end of the law should be morality?

13. Is there some point at which legal intervention would be an invasion of the individual's right to freedom? If so, on what grounds can one distinguish between proper and improper legal intervention? On which side of the dividing line does morality lie?

14. What connection, if any, is there between an appeal to natural law and an appeal to natural rights? Are natural rights that set of legal rights grounded in natural law? If not, just what are natural rights and what is their ground? Could there be a body of natural law that provided for no natural rights at all? In thinking through these questions, reflect on the relation between statute law and the rights created by legal statute.

15. Suppose that it is granted that rights are essentially social in the limited sense that they could not exist outside of and apart from society. Does it follow logically that rights are created by society or that a specific right must be recognized by a society to be real in it? Explain your answer. Suppose that it is further granted that rights are created by society. Does it follow logically that all rights are legal rights? Could there be socially recognized rights that somehow exist outside the legal system of a society?

16. Human rights are usually defined as rights that all human beings possess just because they are human beings; that is, human rights must belong to every human being because such rights are grounded in human nature. Are there any such rights? What evidence, if any, is there to support the claim that human rights do or do not exist?

17. Could there be a society in which there were no individual rights at all? In precisely what ways would that society differ from ours? What, if anything, of value would be lacking in such a society?

18. Traditionally, it was believed that natural rights were given to the individual by God. If natural rights did not come from God, what might be their source? Would a philosopher who wished to defend a theory of natural rights do well to base his theory upon a theology or would he do better to ground his theory on something other than his conception of God? Why?

19. Suppose that it is granted that something, such as liberty or property, is extremely valuable to human beings. Does it follow that human beings ought to have a legal right to this thing? Does it follow that they actually do have a natural right to it? If not, from what would such conclusions follow?

20. Is the common good simply the sum or aggregate of the goods of every individual member of the society or does it consist of those goods shared by all the citizens? Does the state or society as a whole have any goods or interests independent of the goods of its members? Try to see what arguments can be given on each side of these issues and what difference it makes when it comes to judging particular laws as justified or unjustified.

21. Traditionally, Marxists have seen the law as an instrument by which the class in power exploits the other classes for its selfish interests. They hold that in fact the end of the law is not the common good but the good of the rulers. On what grounds, if any, might someone argue that the good of the rulers ought to be the end of the law? On what grounds might one argue that this ought not to be the end of the law?

22. If the end of the law is the common good rather than the private good of any

individual or interest group within society, then it seems to follow that some-times it will not be in the interest of the individual citizen to obey the law. Does this really follow logically? If so, does this undermine the individual's moral obligation to obey the law of society?

23. Does the analogy between ethical egoism and the theory that the end of the law should be the common good hold up in every respect or does it break down somewhere? Are societies subject to the same moral obligations as individuals or is there some reason to hold that societies are not subject to all the constraints of personal morality? Is there any inconsistency in holding both that the individual ought to act to promote the welfare of other individuals and that the society ought to concern itself exclusively with its own welfare?

24. Suppose that we distinguish between the legislator as public official with a duty to advance the common good and the legislator as private moral agent who ought to do what is morally right. Suppose, further, that some proposed law seems clearly required by the common good but morally wrong on other grounds. How ought the legislator to vote?

25. Must one choose between saying that the welfare of noncitizens is completely irrelevant to the moral judgment of the law and saying that the welfare of noncitizens counts equally with the welfare of citizens? Might there be some theory that gives priority to the welfare of citizens but allows some weight to that of noncitizens? If so, precisely how could this theory be formulated? On what rational basis could one decide how much weight to ascribe to the welfare of each group?

26. Suppose that the legislator's opinion of what law will best promote the common good differs from the opinion of the public as measured in a public opinion poll or in a recent popular vote. Should the legislator vote according to his own best judgment or according to the wishes of the public whose common good he is supposed to promote? Why?

27. Does the theory that the end of the law should be the good of humanity really follow logically from utilitarianism? Remember that act-utilitarianism is a theory about what makes an *act* right or wrong and that the law, as such, is not an act but a system containing rules, principles, precedents, and institutions. Can we even speak of the law or of a particular law as right or wrong in the same sense that we speak of an act as right or wrong?

28. In theory of obligation, there is a distinction between act-utilitarianism and rule-utilitarianism. Is there an analogous distinction between theories concerning the proper end of the law? Why or why not? Should one distinguish between judging a particular law in terms of its utility and judging a particular law in terms of the utility of the legal system of which it is a part? Should one distinguish between the utility of a particular law and the utility of some general kind or sort of law? Why or why not?

29. Does the theory that the end of the law should be the good of humanity, if accepted, serve to justify the welfare state in domestic politics and intervention abroad? If so, is this a strength or weakness in the theory? If not, why not?

30. What is freedom? Is it the negative freedom *from* external coercion or hindrances, or is it the positive freedom *to* act in specific ways and achieve desired goals? Has Kant grasped the real nature of freedom?

31. Is freedom of any great value to human beings? Why or why not? Is it of less value to emotionally disturbed or ignorant persons than to normal and informed persons? Is freedom intrinsically good or only a means to the good?

32. Does the fact that the law is enforced by legal sanctions limit or reduce the freedom of those who live under the rule of law? If so, is this limitation on freedom worthwhile or not? If not, how are freedom and coercion compatible?

33. Does it make any moral difference whether the people who must live under the law freely consent to it? Why is consent important? Does it have any practical impact on the content of the law? Does it affect the obligation to obey the law? Does the consent of the people exist only when each and every citizen has an opportunity to vote on the law?

34. Kant might argue that the law is not an inappropriate means to use to achieve human freedom because the law uses coercion to prevent an even greater loss of freedom. For example, the murderer is forced to stay in jail against his will in order to protect his potential victims from having their freedom destroyed by his potentially coercive acts. Is this line of argument really convincing in the end?

35. What is justice, anyway? Do the notions of impartiality and desert really capture the essence of justice? Are these notions so hopelessly vague as to rob justice of applicability in judging the law?

36. It almost seems as though justice is a purely negative standard. It is easy to think of cases where we would claim that some law ought to be repealed because it is unjust but hard to think of cases where we would argue that it ought to be enacted or kept on the books if it had nothing but justice to recommend it. If this is so, what does it reveal about the way in which justice functions as a moral standard of the law?

37. Can a just law be applied unjustly? Some people argue that it is fair enough to require literacy as a prerequisite to voting; there is nothing unjust in the literacy test itself. What has been unjust is the way it has been administered in some parts of the South where even illiterate whites were allowed to pass the test while many blacks failed the test without regard for their ability to read. Explain why you do or do not believe that one can distinguish between the justice of the content of a law and the justice of its application. Is persistent and systematic injustice in application of the law any reason to judge the law morally wrong or undesirable?

38. Can an unjust law be legislated justly? Suppose that there is full and fair hearing of all sides of the question, that all duly elected representatives are allowed to vote freely, and that they enact some arbitrary or unfair statute. Explain why you do or do not believe that one can distinguish between the procedural justice of the legislative process and the substantive justice of the product of the legislative process. Is procedural injustice any reason to judge the law enacted morally objectionable? Meditate two slogans: "no taxation without representation" and "one man one vote."

39. Let us consider these alleged distinctions by considering the draft law as it functioned during the Vietnam War. The law might be judged substantively unjust because to conscript a man for combat duty violates his right to life. It might be judged unjust in application because blacks bore a disproportionate burden of dangerous front-line duty in Vietnam. It might be judged procedurally unjust because the eighteen-year-olds drafted under it had no vote in passing the law. Do you consider each of these arguments cogent? Are all three kinds of injustice, if established, equally relevant to a moral assessment of the draft law?

40. Should the law really concern itself with the good of noncitizens and even animals? After all, neither noncitizens nor animals are members of the society

making the law or are governed by the law once it is made. On what grounds, then, is their welfare relevant to the law?

41.   Does the United States really have an obligation to sacrifice its own welfare for the greater good of other peoples? Is there any limit to the sacrifice that might be morally required of this country? Suppose that national security were so undermined that pursuing the good of all meant that the United States could not continue to exist as a viable state. Is any state morally required to commit national suicide?

42.   Are peace, freedom, and justice proper ends of the law only because they are parts of or conditions of the good? Would it be philosophically more adequate to have a theory embracing several ends of the law? If so, would this be a deontological rather than a teleological theory of the law?

BIBLIOGRAPHY

AQUINAS, SAINT THOMAS. *Summa Theologica,* I–II, Question 90, Articles 1 and 2; Question 92, Article 1; Question 95, Articles 3 and 4. In *Basic Writings of Saint Thomas Aquinas,* vol. 2, edited by Anton C. Pegis. New York: Random House, 1945.

BENTHAM, JEREMY. *An Introduction to the Principles of Morals and Legislation,* chaps. 1 and 4. Edited by J. H. Burns and H. L. A. Hart. London: Athlone Press, 1970.

CICERO. *De Legibus,* Book I, Sections VI–X; Book II, Sections IV–V. In *De Re Publica, De Legibus.* Cambridge, Mass.: Harvard University Press, Loeb Classical Library, 1928.

HART, H. L. A. *Concept of Law.* Oxford, Eng.: Clarendon Press, 1961.

HOBBES, THOMAS. *Leviathan,* chaps. 13, 17, and 26. New York: E. P. Dutton & Co., 1950.

KANT, IMMANUEL: "Introduction to the Metaphysics of Morals" and "Introduction to the Elements of Justice." In *The Metaphysical Elements of Justice,* translated by John Ladd. Indianapolis: The Bobbs-Merrill Co., 1965.

LOCKE, JOHN. *Treatise of Civil Government,* chaps. 2 and 9. In *Treatise of Civil Government and a Letter Concerning Toleration,* edited by Charles L. Sherman. New York: Appleton-Century-Crofts, 1937.

RAWLS, JOHN *A Theory of Justice.* Cambridge, Mass.: Belknap Press of Harvard University Press, 1971.

ROUSSEAU, JEAN-JACQUES. *Social Contract.* In *The Social Contract, and Discourses.* Translated by G. D. H. Cole. New York: E. P. Dutton & Co., 1950.

SALMOND, SIR JOHN WILLIAM. *Jurisprudence,* 12th ed., pp. 60–65. Edited by P. J. Fitzgerald. London: Sweet & Maxwell, 1966.

9
PREFERENTIAL ADMISSIONS

Preference by race is malign; its malignity has no clearer or more fitting name than racism.

Carl Cohen in "Race and the Constitution." Copyright © 1975, The Nation Magazine/The Nation Company, Inc.

I would admit that it is perhaps an individual injustice. But it might be necessary in order to overcome an historic group injustice or series of group injustices.

Andrew Young in *Atlanta Journal and Constitution* of September 22, 1974

There was a time when it was illegal in many states for educational institutions to ask any applicant for admission to specify his or her race or to supply a photograph. The fear, all too amply justified by past experience, was that such devices would be used to discriminate against black and other minority applicants. Unfortunately, history showed that this policy of official neutrality did not result in a proportionate representation of blacks among the students of colleges, universities, and professional schools. As a consequence, the law was reformed and it is now required that any institution of higher education receiving federal funds maintain an affirmative action program that will, among other things, take special measures to seek out qualified black applicants and to ensure that their applications receive especially careful and sympathetic consideration. Many schools now give preferential treatment to black applicants in their admissions procedures.

In 1973, Alan Bakke applied for admission to the Medical School of the University of California at Davis. He was denied admission, even though some of the minority students admitted had lower MCAT scores and lesser GPSs than his. The Medical School had set aside sixteen places out of one hundred reserved for minority students. Bakke sued, claiming that the University's preferential admissions procedure unconstitutionally discriminated against him. On June 28, 1978, the United States Supreme

Court ordered Bakke admitted to the Medical School. It held that the use of such fixed minority quotas in the admissions process was unconstitutional, but it did not rule out every reference to race in admissions criteria. Thus, the legality of preferential admissions remains ambiguous. The morality or immorality of preferential admissions is even more debatable.

OUR MORAL PROBLEM

Although there are many questions a moral philosopher will wish to ask about preferential admissions, especially those based on racial grounds, any careful thinker will insist upon distinguishing between these questions in order to avoid confusion. It will best serve our present purposes to address a single question: "Do blacks have a moral right to preferential admissions?"

In this context, the word "blacks" refers to black Americans, members of our society of Negro lineage. It would only confuse the issue to include African or Caribbean blacks at this point, for many of the crucial arguments appeal to the history of black slavery and the more recent racial discrimination in our country. Still, our question is not limited to black *applicants* because it may be that black Americans who have not applied for admission to some college or professional school have a right to preferential treatment in the *pre*application stages of their admissions programs— for example, in the mailing of information or the assignment of admissions officers to the schools they will visit to recruit applicants. Presumably, any reasonable answer to our question will have important implications for other minority groups, such as Hispanics, and even for women. But it will simplify exposition and argument here to limit our attention to black Americans.

We are asking of these persons whether they really do have a frequently asserted and almost as often denied moral right. Let us postpone any full discussion of the meaning of the expression "a right" until the next chapter. We should note in passing, however, that when we speak of rights we sometimes refer to rights of action and at other times to rights of recipience. When I assert my right to dress as I please or to gamble away my hard-earned income, I am asserting a right of action, a right to engage in some sort of action that others might well find objectionable. But when I claim my right to be paid by Washington University, I am claiming a right of recipience, a right to receive some sort of treatment by another. Therefore, my right to recipience, if genuine, implies a correlative duty on the part of the one against whom my right holds. The alleged right to preferential admissions is of this sort. What is claimed is the right of American blacks to receive preferential treatment by colleges, universities, and professional schools. If this right is genuine, it implies a correlative duty of these institutions to treat blacks preferentially.

Since this is a course in moral philosophy and ethical theory, we are asking whether blacks have a *moral* right to preferential admissions. What was directly at issue in the *Bakke* case was whether blacks have a legal right to preferential admissions, specifically a legal right to have sixteen places reserved for them in the entering class of students at the Medical School of the University of California at Davis. This legal issue is not our present concern, nor is it one that anyone but a lawyer could answer with any confidence. Our problem is to decide whether black Americans have a moral right to preferential admissions.

Precisely what does one mean by preferential admissions? Exactly what is the content of this moral right supposed to be? What is claimed is the right to be treated preferentially, specifically more favorably than whites, in the admissions procedures of an American college, university, or professional school. For example, the cutoff point on test scores, that point below which applications will be rejected out-of-hand and without any consideration of the letters of reference or the applicant's essay, might be set at a lower score for blacks than for whites. Or a black applicant might be given an opportunity to rewrite a sample essay while a white applicant might be given no such second chance. No one alleges, of course, that blacks have a moral right to every sort of preferential treatment in admissions. Of course, a totally unqualified black has no right to be accepted in spite of pitifully low test scores and dismal letters of reference. What is to be considered is whether black Americans have a right to receive more limited sorts of preferential treatment in the admissions procedures of American institutions of higher education.

One word of caution is urgently needed at this point. Preferential treatment must not be confused with affirmative action. While very few who understand these issues deny that blacks have a right to affirmative action, a great many well-informed and morally sensitive philosophers deny that they have any right to preferential admissions. The expression "affirmative action" comes from United States labor law. An employer who is found to have engaged in unfair labor practices can be ordered by the National Labor Relations Board or by a court of law to cease and desist from such unfair practices. That is, the employer could be required to engage in negative action, acting in such a way as *not* to treat labor unfairly. But sometimes the employer may be ordered to take positive measures to ensure that such unfair practices do not reoccur or even to make amends for past unfair practices; for example, to set up an appeals system to hear complaints from aggrieved workers. This would be affirmative action, doing something rather than refraining from doing something. Now in the admissions procedure of an academic institution it might be possible to reduce, or even eliminate, racial discrimination by affirmative actions of a racially neutral or nonpreferential sort. Suppose, for example, that a predominantly white professional school solicits applications mainly by word of mouth through its former graduates. Since the vast majority of its graduates are white, and consequently the young students with whom they come in contact will tend to be white, the result will be a predominantly white applicant pool and, selecting the best of these, very little opportunity for qualified and interested blacks to be admitted. If the professional school takes affirmative action by initiating a series of advertisements in big city newspapers and nationally circulated magazines, it might well provide interested blacks with a much greater opportunity to be admitted without giving them more favorable treatment than whites at all. To treat blacks preferentially would be to go beyond affirmative action; it would be to give them some sort of advantage over whites in the application process.

Our question "Do blacks have a moral right to preferential admissions?" is deliberately formulated in the present tense. It is a question about the rights of blacks now, at this time in the history of our country. Many of those who defend such a right do so on the grounds that black Americans have suffered from the heritage of slavery and the disadvantages of racial discrimination in our society. Preferential admissions is often thought of as a remedy for these past injustices and as a means to a more perfect society without racial prejudice. It is thought that it is a temporary measure morally required at this time in American history but to be discarded at a later date. We may or may not wish to accept this viewpoint in the end. But it will be well to begin here, for the urgency of the problem we are deliberating and the plausibility of the claim that blacks do have a right to preferential admissions arise from the circumstances under which blacks must live in America today.

REASONS TO AFFIRM

It is easy enough to claim a right, any right at all. One simply says that one has the right, perhaps in a loud or demanding voice. But not every alleged right is genuine, for one's claim may be entirely without grounds, or at least lacking in sufficient grounds. Before we decide that blacks really do have a moral right to preferential admissions, we need to inquire into the reasons one might have for affirming the existence of this controversial right. There are, or seem to be, several.

Remedial Justice

One who has been wrongly injured has a moral right to a remedy. For example, if Smith beats up Jones without justification or damages Jones' car by driving recklessly, then Jones has a moral right that Smith pay the consequent hospital bills or whatever it costs to repair the car. Like Jones, blacks in our society have been wrongly injured by whites. For centuries they were enslaved throughout much of the United States. Even after the

Civil War and their emancipation, they were unjustly segregated and relegated to a subservient position in our society by Jim Crow legislation. Even today, black Americans are wronged by racial discrimination in housing, education, and employment. Hence, blacks have a moral right to a remedy for the injuries they have wrongly suffered. Preferential admissions would be an appropriate remedy, or at least part of that remedy, because it would enable young blacks to enter the mainstream of American life and to overcome the injuries whites have inflicted upon them.

Unjust Enrichment

One difficulty with the appeal to remedial justice is that much, probably most, of the injuries wrongfully inflicted upon American blacks took place decades, even centuries ago. Why should contemporary whites, especially those who do not engage in racial discrimination and may even have worked politically for their equal rights, owe contemporary blacks any remedy? It may well be possible to evade this difficulty by recognizing the fundamental principle of natural justice that anyone who has been benefited at the expense of another without sufficient ground ought to restore such benefit to the person at whose expense it was received. Suppose, for example, that the property line between two farms is marked by a stream. Gradual silting of the old stream bed together with a spring flood moves the stream into a new location so that farmer West now has one additional acre of land and farmer East one acre less. Since farmer West has no moral or legal ground for his or her enrichment, farmer West did not purchase or inherit the valuable acre of rich farmland, farmer East has a right that farmer West restore the acre, or its value. Now past injustices to blacks continue to have consequences in their inferior housing, inadequate education in inner city or rural schools, and their lower quality of life. Even white Americans who have not actively discriminated against blacks have enjoyed educational and economic benefits derived from the past, and perhaps present, injustices perpetrated by others. Moreover, contemporary whites have no ground or justification for being thus enriched, for they have not earned it by any extraordinary services to blacks, at whose expense they have been relatively advantaged. Therefore, contemporary blacks have a right that the whites unjustly enriched at their expense restore to them what they have lost. Preferential admissions to colleges, universities, and professional schools would restore to blacks many of the educational benefits, and indirectly other economic benefits, they have lost to whites. Therefore, blacks have a moral right to preferential admissions.

Reparations Owed

Both the principle of remedial justice and the principle of unjust enrichment are individualistic. One who has been wrongfully injured has a right to a remedy from the one who has wronged him or her, and anyone who has been enriched without ground has a duty to restore such enrichment to the one at whose expense one has been unjustly enriched. But it is exceedingly difficult to know which individual blacks have been wronged by which whites or which whites have been enriched at the expense of exactly which individual blacks. Thus, the application of these moral principles to any decision to accept or reject this or that applicant, whether black or white, is highly problematic. Moral philosophers therefore sometimes appeal to group rights rather than the right of an individual black. The language used is most frequently that of reparations.

In ordinary language, "reparations" simply means repairs; for example, reparations to a deteriorating medieval cathedral. In more technical legal terminology, reparations (always in the plural) are simply compensation payable in money, labor, or goods by one nation to another for wartime damage done to civilians and their property. Notice that no effort is made to determine which soldier has wounded which civilian or which bombardier has released the bomb that destroyed the row of homes; it is the nation as a whole that owes reparations to the other nation as a collective entity. Since the purpose of reparations is, as the very word implies, to repair the damage done in the past war, presumably the recipient nation is expected to allocate what it receives to its citizens by some fair procedure. Hence, indirectly individual civilians who have suffered wartime damages have a right to receive their share of the total reparations paid.

By analogy, in "The Black Manifesto," adopted by the National Black Economic Development Conference on April 26, 1969, the black people as a people demanded of the white Christian churches and Jewish synagogues collectively $500 million in reparations owed because of their participation in the system of American capitalism that had, allegedly, done so much damage to innocent blacks. As a precedent, they cited the $820 million that Germany paid Israel for the resettlement of 500,000 Jews dislocated and injured by Nazi persecution. This sort of reasoning, if valid, might well be extended to preferential admissions. American whites as a group owe American blacks as a group reparations for the damages done to innocent blacks by past slavery, Jim Crow legislation, and continuing racial discrimination. Since whites owe this debt to blacks, blacks have a right that whites pay them reparations owed. Reparations can take many forms; for example, after a war, compensation may take the form of labor or goods instead of money. An appropriate form for reparations to take in the present case would be preferential admissions to American (predominantly white) colleges, universities, and professional schools because this would be the most effective way to repair the damage done to blacks in our country over the past decades. Therefore, blacks collectively have a right to programs of preferential admissions and individual blacks have a derivative right to their share of preferential treatment under such programs.

Distributive Justice

Justice demands that the institutions of any society, such as its legal and economic systems, distribute benefits and burdens fairly among the members of that society. Thus, it would be unjust to assess real estate taxes without any regard to the value of the property being taxed. Similarly, each citizen has a moral right to a fair share of the benefits distributed by the legal, educational, and economic systems of their society. But black Americans receive less than their fair share of such benefits. Statistical studies and informal observation clearly show that they generally attend inferior schools, have a higher infant mortality rate, and a lower level of medical care, live in less desirable housing, and have much lower per capita incomes than American whites. Preferential admissions to colleges, universities, and professional schools would help greatly to distribute goods and services more justly because of the importance of higher education in gaining employment opportunities and the income derived from one's work. Thus, the right of blacks to a fair share of the benefits distributed in our society implies a derivative right to preferential admissions as a means to the enjoyment of this fundamental moral right.

Equal Opportunity

One of the fundamental human rights, one of the basic moral rights each and every human being has *as* a human being, is the right to equal opportunity. There is no right to equal wealth or success or happiness, only a right to an equal chance to achieve these things for oneself. This is why the Declaration of Independence asserted, not the right to happiness, but the right to the pursuit of happiness. Now blacks in our society have much less opportunity than white Americans. Since their unequal opportunity is in large measure a consequence of the educational disadvantages under which blacks suffer, preferential admissions would tend to equalize the opportunity of blacks. It would tend to equalize educational opportunity directly by its very nature, and since economic opportunity depends so heavily upon education in our society, it would tend also to equalize other sorts of opportunity indirectly. Since blacks have a human right to equal opportunity, they have a moral right to preferential admissions to enable them to enjoy opportunity equal to that of whites in our society.

REASONS TO DENY

Although these arguments in support of the claim that black Americans have a moral right to preferential admissions persuade many moral philosophers, academic administrators, and private citizens, many others find them unconvincing. They, too, have their arguments. Were this not so, the moral problem we are considering would not be debated in practice or interesting in theory. Let us now survey briefly a few of the reasons put forward by those who would deny that blacks have a moral right to preferential admissions.

Reverse Discrimination

To give preferential treatment to black applicants in the competition for a place in the class of students entering a college, university, or professional school is necessarily to disadvantage white applicants for one of the limited number of places in that class. And to give preference to black applicants *because* they are black is necessarily to treat white applicants adversely merely because they are white. This is racial discrimination, albeit its victims belong to the Caucasian rather than the Negro race. But racial discrimination is morally wrong, whoever its victims may be. There can be no moral right to what is morally wrong. Therefore, blacks cannot have any moral right to preferential admissions.

Inequitable Treatment

Justice requires that similar cases be treated similarly. For example, two students who submit papers that are equally well researched, argued, and written should receive the same grade; and two individuals convicted of the same crime under the same aggravating and extenuating circumstances should receive the same penalty. It is inequitable, and therefore unjust, to treat cases that are similar in all relevant respects unequally. But any policy of preferential admissions for blacks will, if effective, surely result in inequitable treatment, for in some instances it will result in the admission of a black applicant coupled with the rejection of a white applicant with similar credentials. No black can have any moral right that would imply such inequitable treatment of a white candidate similar in all relevant respects. Therefore, black Americans cannot have any moral right to preferential admissions.

Unfair Consideration

Each applicant has a moral right to be considered on his or her merits. Any just admission procedure, one that respects the rights of black and white applicants alike, will base the decision to admit or reject any candidate purely upon his or her qualifications. What qualifies someone to be a student in a college, university, or professional school will be such things as previous academic achievements, native intelligence and imagination, intellectual interests, academic motivation, persistence, etc. The color of one's skin does not qualify one, or disqualify one either, to pursue a course of studies in an institution of higher education. Thus, to consider the race of any applicant in the admissions procedure is to violate the right to fair consideration of the competing applicants. More specifically, preferential admissions for blacks would violate the right to fair consideration of whites. No black applicant can have a moral right that academic institutions thus violate the moral rights of white applicants. Therefore, black Americans can have no moral right to preferential admissions.

Unfair Burden

Black Americans may well have a right to a remedy from our society, or its white members, for the injustices they have suffered. But far from being an appropriate remedy, preferential admissions would be a morally impermissible means to achieve social justice. It would compensate blacks by admitting them, at least some of them, to academic institutions to which they would not be admitted without such preferential treatment. But in this process, some white applicants who would have been admitted to these institutions, were there no preferential treatment of blacks, will be rejected. It is unfair that these few rejected whites should have to bear the entire burden of remedying the wrongful injuries inflicted by our entire society, or at least the majority of its white population. Justice demands some more equitable way of distributing the burdens of compensating American blacks for the widespread wrongs done to them by many individuals over a long period of time. Blacks can have no moral right to preferential admissions because this would impose an unfair, and therefore morally intolerable, burden upon a few arbitrarily chosen whites who would be injured thereby.

Unjust Confiscation

The places in the entering class of any college, university, or professional school belong to that academic institution. To be admitted to an academic institution is to be given the right to use its facilities and resources by attending classes, living in dormitories, doing research in its libraries and laboratories, and playing on its athletic fields. These rights belong to the institution because these resources are their property by gift or inheritance or by their management of their endowment and earned income. Their property right in these resources gives them the moral right to give, or to withhold, the use of these resources just as my ownership of my house gives me the right to give, or refuse to give, one of my friends access to my premises. To hold that blacks have a right to preferential admissions would be to imply that academic institutions are not free to give or refuse to give places in their student bodies as they freely choose because it implies that academic institutions are morally obligated or morally bound to give preference to black applicants whether they wish to or not. This limitation on the free use of their property amounts to unjust confiscation. Confiscation is the taking of private property for public use, especially by way of a penalty. For example, the city might seize my car because I have persistently refused to pay fines for illegal parking, or it might take away my home because I persist in using it as a house of prostitution. In the present case, preferential admissions would be taking away part of the academic institution's freedom to use its property as it sees fit, and thereby taking a portion of that property right, to pay society's debt to American blacks who have allegedly been wronged by our society. But it is unjust confiscation because the penalty is imposed upon the college, university, or professional school that is not even alleged to be the culprit. Since academic institutions have a basic moral right to give places in their classes to whomever they wish, a right that is part and parcel of their ownership of their resources, and since the highly debatable right to preferential admissions would be incompatible with this right because it would require unjust confiscation, blacks cannot have any real right to preferential admissions.

JUSTICE

The case for a moral right of black Americans to preferential admissions appeals primarily to considerations of justice, most obviously the arguments from remedial justice, distributive justice, and unjust enrichment. But the moral demands of justice do not seem to be entirely on one side of this controversial issue, for one appeal to justice can be countered with another. For example, the argument that preferential admissions would be an appropriate means to achieve distributive justice in our society by increasing the benefits enjoyed by black Americans can be countered with the argument that preferential admissions distributes the burdens unjustly because it imposes an unfair burden upon those few white applicants rejected as a consequence. Again, the appeal to remedial justice to show that preferential admissions would satisfy the moral right to a remedy of blacks who have been wrongly injured in our society can be met with the reply that there can be no moral right to remedy wrongs by unjustly confiscating the property of the colleges, universities, and professional schools who have earned, inherited, or been given the resources they now own. How can we measure one appeal to justice against another? Perhaps we could do so if only we had some general theory of justice that would provide some common denominator of these various species of justice.

Aristotle, a Greek philosopher who lived in the fourth century B.C., proposed a general theory of justice that is applicable to various species of justice. What is essential to justice in all its forms is equality. In remedial justice what is required is the equality of the wrongful injury and the remedy provided. The wrongdoer has gained by inflicting an injury upon the victim. To restore the moral equilibrium, the wrongful gain must be taken away from the person who acted unjustly and restored to the victim so that he or she is returned to his or her rightful position. In distributive justice, what is required is an equality of the ratios between benefits distributed and the merits of the recipients. For example, in grading examinations, the student who demonstrated twice as much knowledge and understanding of the subject should receive twice as good a grade. In exchange, justice demands that the value given equal the value received. A fair price for a book would be one such that the value to the seller of the money received would equal the value of the book to the purchaser. Accordingly, it is equality that, in different ways, determines justice in remedying wrongs, distributing benefits, and economic transactions.

Why equality? That is, what is the essential connection between equality and justice? Perhaps it is that justice or fairness requires impartiality and that injustice consists primarily in favoritism or bias. This conception is vividly portrayed in the picture of Justice as a blindfolded lady holding a set of scales. She is blindfolded so that she cannot recognize her friends or enemies and accord them undue favors or treat them with undue harshness; her scales are needed to balance equal amounts of injury with remedy or equal ratios between rewards (or punishments) and merits (or vices). Hence, the traditional formula that justice consists in treating similar cases similarly. Presumably what is morally wrong with racial discrimination is that persons who are similar in all morally relevant respects are treated differently, whites better and blacks worse, merely because of race. Justice demands equal treatment of blacks and whites.

But equality is only half the story. The traditional formula, more fully stated, is that justice consists in treating similar cases similarly and dissimilar cases differently. For example, just wages consist in equal pay for equal work, but higher pay for more or better work. It would certainly be unjust to discriminate against a black worker by giving him or her less pay for work equal to that of a higher-paid white; in this case justice does consist in equality. But it would be unjust also to give equal pay to black and white alike if the black performs more and better work than the white, for this would be another form of favoritism or partiality toward whites. Although Aristotle rightly insisted that impartiality is essential to justice, his definition of justice in terms of equality fails to make clear precisely what justice requires in particular situations.

William Frankena, a contemporary moral philosopher, has proposed a modified Aristotelian theory. Justice consists in the equal treatment of all persons except as inequality is required by just-making reasons. A just-making or justicizing reason is a very special sort of justifying reason. It is alleged that certain universities set aside a certain number of places in their freshman classes for applicants from families wealthy enough to donate huge sums of money to the university. Given the great amount of good that a university can do with large educational resources, the fact that John

Jones comes from a very wealthy family might be a reason to justify a decision to admit him even if his academic credentials are weak, but it does not at all show that admitting him is just. But to point out that Susan Smith's SAT scores were exceptionally high is a just-making reason; it is a consideration that does tend to show that the decision to admit her rather than some applicant with lower scores is just. Thus, unequal treatment can be just. Indeed, unequal treatment is required by just-making reasons in many cases. The impartial demands of justice require that better term papers should receive higher grades. A teacher is showing favoritism, and thus acting unjustly, if he or she gives equal grades to two students who turned in papers of very different quality.

Since justice demands impartiality, it is easy to understand why racial discrimination is unjust and, therefore, morally wrong. But what about preferential admissions for black Americans? Such preferential treatment seems quite the opposite of impartiality and, thus, equally unjust. Perhaps it is. If so, the argument that blacks have no moral right to preferential admissions because this is reverse discrimination is sound. Still, there are two ways one might evade this reasoning. First, one might argue that unequal treatment of blacks is required by some just-making reason. Perhaps one could argue that blacks have a right to a remedy for past injustices or the fact that preferential admissions would be a means to satisfy their right to equal opportunity constitutes such a justicizing reason. Second, one might argue that partiality is morally permissible in admissions because there is nothing unjust in giving places in an entering class to whomever the academic institution prefers. Then, although one would not have shown that preferential admissions is morally required, one would have shown that it is not simply reverse discrimination and thus morally impermissible.

Although justice demands impartiality, justice is not always applicable. In many contexts, there is nothing morally wrong in favoritism or partiality. If I am sending holiday greetings, justice does not demand that I treat all my colleagues in the Philosophy Department equally. I may send cards to my special friends and ignore the others. If I ask who would like to use my tickets to the Saint Louis symphony this evening, justice does not demand that I give the ticket to the most qualified "applicant," the person who would most enjoy or best understand the music from among those who express a desire to use my tickets. Impartiality is not always morally required, although it is when one is grading tests or paying workers. Now is admitting students to an entering class more like giving away tickets or grading exams? More generally, when is partiality unjust? It seems to me that impartial treatment is required when the recipients have a moral claim to receive some sort of treatment. It is because the students have a moral claim to whatever grade each has earned on the test or paper that partiality in grading is unjust. It is because those to whom one sends greeting cards or gives presents have no moral claim to receive any card or present that partiality in such contexts is not unjust. Thus, it may well be that justice is somehow grounded in those rights that ground moral (or legal) claims. This suggests a very different theory of justice.

Justinian, an Eastern Roman emperor, is probably best known for his codification of Roman law, published in 529 A.D. Fundamental to this code was the famous definition of natural justice—to each his own. According to this traditional conception, justice consists in giving each person his or her due, that to which he or she has a right. Thus, justice is essentially a matter of treating individuals in accordance with their respective rights. Since different individuals may have very different rights, equal treatment is not necessarily required by justice. Still, if there are any universal human rights possessed equally by all persons, equal respect for these rights would be an essential part, but only a part, of justice. Justinian's theory explains why it is that justice requires a teacher to give two equally well-researched and written papers the same grade and at the same time requires a teacher to give unequal grades to papers of unequal merit; each student has a right to receive a grade that accurately reflects the quality of his or her performance, and justice demands that each student receive his or her own—the grade to which he or she has a right. Conversely, this theory explains why it is unjust to borrow money from someone and then refuse to repay the debt when it is due; the creditor has a right to repayment and failing to repay the debt is failing to give the creditor what is due.

Justinian's theory is plausible enough so that his formula, "to each his own," has become familiar in the literature of moral philosophy and jurisprudence. The most valuable insight of this theory is that justice and rights are essentially connected. This suggests that we might find this theory of justice useful when we are wondering whether blacks really do have a moral right to preferential admissions. Unfortunately, a little reflection upon the main arguments for and against the view that blacks have such a right reveals that any program of preferential admissions would affect many individuals and that each of these individuals will have moral rights of his or her own. Granted that justice requires that each individual receive the treatment to which he or she has a right, what does justice demand when individual rights conflict? They seem to conflict when preferential admissions for black Americans is at issue. Since black Americans have suffered wrongful injury, American blacks surely have a moral right to a remedy. And preferential admissions would go a long way toward remedying the harm done to blacks in our society. At the same time, preferential treatment for black applicants would necessarily result in the rejection of some white applicants who are better qualified to pursue higher education than some blacks admitted. This certainly seems to violate the moral right of each white applicant to be considered for admission on his or her merits. How can we apply Justinian's theory of justice when the black applicant's right to a remedy thus conflicts with the white applicant's right to fair consideration. Again, the right to equal opportunity of black applicants seems to conflict with the right of academic institutions to use their property as they see fit. Black Americans do not have equal opportunity in our society, and preferential admissions would do much to equalize their opportunity. But to say that this confers upon black applicants any moral claim-right to preferential admissions is to imply that academic institutions are morally bound, whether they wish to or not, to give blacks preferential treatment in their admissions processes. This seems to deny these institutions their property rights, for it denies that they are free to use their academic resources as they wish. One hopes that there is some way to resolve such conflicts between moral rights. But until we can resolve such conflicts, we cannot hope to discover whether blacks have a right to preferential treatment by appealing to Justinian's theory that justice is giving each person his or her own, that to which he or she has a right.

There is an even more fundamental flaw in trying to determine whether black Americans have a moral right to preferential admissions by appealing to this theory of justice. Since justice is supposed to consist in acting in accordance with the rights of those affected, justice is clearly grounded in and derived from rights. To seek to base some moral right upon this theory of justice is, therefore, to use circular reasoning of the most futile sort. One cannot know whether justice demands preferential treatment of blacks in admissions until one knows whether preferential treatment is due to black applicants, that is, whether blacks have a right to preferential treatment. If we are to solve our moral problem in this chapter by an appeal to justice, we obviously need some theory of justice that is prior to and independent of moral rights. We do not want a theory in which rights have no place, of course, but we do need a theory that is not grounded squarely upon presupposed rights.

John Rawls, a contemporary moral philosopher, appeals to our presystematic sense of justice more than to specific moral rights in his very influential book entitled *A Theory of Justice*. In this book, Rawls explains and argues for a theory of *social* justice. It is his view that justice concerns not so much particular actions of individual moral agents, as the basic structure of social institutions, such as the legal system, political structure, and economic system of a society. He proposes two principles by which to assess the social institutions of any society:

1. Each person is to have an equal right to the most extensive total system of equal basic liberties compatible with a similar system of liberty for all; and
2. social and economic inequalities are to be arranged so that they are both (a) to the greatest benefit of the least advantaged, consistent with the just savings principle, and (b) attached to offices and positions open to all under conditions of fair equality of opportunity.

Without going into the details of this theory, let us try to learn something useful from it.

First of all, Rawls suggests that justice is primarily a matter of social institutions. This is highly relevant to the issue we are discussing in this chapter. Preferential admissions is typically proposed and defended as a response to a social problem in our society, as a remedy for past injustices in our predominantly white society and a means for overcoming the social and economic inequality of black Americans. Now the obvious antidote to racial discrimination would seem to be Aristotelian justice, a strict equality or impartiality in the treatment of each individual, black or white. And preferential treatment seems inconsistent with the just treatment of each applicant to a college, university, or professional school. But suppose that Rawls is right and justice is more a matter of institutional structure than individual treatment. Then we must look beyond the admission of this or that black applicant and the rejection of a single white such as Alan Bakke. We must look at the entire pattern of the social institutions in America and the place that institutions of higher education have in our society. We might also notice that the policy of strict neutrality was attempted in educational institutions and seemed to fail. It may be, of course, that it was not tried persistently and imaginatively enough. But others argue that racial discrimination is not merely a matter of prejudicial treatment of individual blacks by individual whites. Many believe that much racial discrimination is based in the very structures of institutions. For example, if blacks generally receive inferior education and have less job opportunity, this is not primarily because teachers or personnel officers in large companies are prejudiced against blacks. It is because most blacks live in areas with a tax base inadequate to pay for high-quality public schools and much hiring, especially for the more advantageous positions, is dominated by a network in which most of the members are whites. If this is true, and obviously one would need evidence to support these claims, then social justice can be achieved in our country only by a restructuring of our social institutions to remove all traces of institutional discrimination against blacks.

What kind of evidence might demonstrate the existence of structural discrimination against black Americans, and how could one tell when our institutions have achieved social justice? There is a vast body of statistical evidence that testifies to the inequality of black Americans. Compared with whites, the life expectancy of blacks is less, the average income is strikingly lower, the percentage of blacks who graduate from colleges and universities is much smaller than their percentage in the total population, etc. It is all too easy to collect large bodies of statistics of these sorts, almost all confirming the inequality of blacks in our society. Interpreting the meaning of such statistics for any assessment of our social institutions is more difficult and should be left to the sociologists. But if, as seems likely, our political and economic system does result in racial inequalities, it is appropriate for a moral philosopher to try to decide what this implies about the justice of our social institutions. Now according to Rawls, social inequality is not always and necessarily unjust. His second principle specifies that such inequalities would be just *if* they were arranged so that they were to the greatest benefit of the least advantaged and were attached to offices and positions open to all under conditions of fair equality of opportunity. Assuming for the sake of argument that blacks, or at least poor blacks, are the least advantaged in our society, are the lower life expectancy, lower wages, poorer education, and inferior housing they receive in our society somehow indirectly to their benefit, perhaps by increasing the total wealth produced in our economic system so that their small share is, nevertheless, larger than the share they would receive in a more egalitarian, but less productive, society? This seems unlikely. Indeed, our society would seem to waste valuable human resources by its failure to develop and use the talents of its black population to the fullest. It seems even more unlikely that the more advantageous positions and offices in America are open to blacks on the basis of fair and equal opportunity with whites. If preferential admissions would overcome or reduce these social injustices, and this remains to be argued, one might base the conclusion that blacks have a right to preferential admissions upon the theory of justice defended by John Rawls.

I shall not attempt this task here, however. For one thing, Rawls' theory of social justice is so complex that it is difficult to draw any very specific conclusions from it. Even were I able to do this, and in a relatively few sentences, there would remain all the arguments on the other side of the issue. It would seem unjust, intellectually if not socially, to ignore them. Therefore, it seems better to return to our original problem and try to speak directly to it, perhaps with some references to matters of justice.

PREFERENTIAL ADMISSIONS DEFENDED

It is useful, even imperative, to distinguish between retrospective and prospective arguments for the moral rights of blacks to preferential admissions. The appeals to remedial justice, unjust enrichment, and reparations owed all look to the past. They attempt to ground a right to preferential admissions upon the wrongful injury that black Americans have suffered, the unjust enrichment that white Americans have received, or reparations owed by whites to blacks for damages inflicted during the history of slavery and racial discrimination in our society. But each of these arguments has serious weaknesses. It is true that any party wrongfully injured by some second party has a right to demand that the wrongdoer remedy the injury. But notice that the remedy is due the injured party, not another, and from the wrongdoer. Can it be shown that the white student rejected because of preferential admissions has wrongfully harmed precisely the individual black applicant accepted in his or her place? Hardly. Similar difficulties arise when one tries to show that the rejected white individual is the one who has been unjustly enriched at the expense of precisely the black accepted in his or her place rather than at the expense of some other black or, more plausibly, blacks in general. This inability to match the individual black who has a right to a remedy or restoration with the individual white against whom his or her right is supposed to hold might be avoided by an appeal to group, rather than individual, rights. Hence, the appeal to the reparations owed by whites as a group to blacks as a group. But then the problem becomes one of determining some fair method of collecting the reparations to be paid and how to distribute those payments to individual blacks. It is not at all clear that it is fair to collect places in entering classes from whites rejected because of preferential admissions programs or that it is fair to distribute all the reparations owed to blacks as a group to those few black applicants accepted by virtue of preferential admissions. Therefore, I suggest that we abandon any attempt to ground a moral right to preferential admissions upon such retrospective arguments. Let us turn instead to prospective arguments, especially the appeals to the basic moral rights to equitable treatment and equal opportunity. I suggest that black Americans do have a moral right to preferential admissions because preferential admissions is an essential means of protecting their rights to nondiscriminatory treatment and equal opportunity in the future.

If racial discrimination in our society were merely the product of individual prejudice and personal animosity, then preferential treatment in admissions processes in American colleges, universities, and professional schools would probably be unnecessary or even immoral. But I believe, on the basis of sociological evidence that is largely but not entirely statistical, that there is also pervasive institutional discrimination in the United States today. Although IQ tests and SAT scores purport to be, and are by their designers surely intended to be, racially neutral, they are very probably biased in favor of whites and against blacks. And given the fact that the majority of those who work in admissions offices are white, and therefore more familiar with and sensitive to standard English than they are to black American English, the reading of essays submitted by applicants tends to favor whites and disfavor blacks. There need be no malice or ill will involved at all. In fact, the individuals participating in our social institutions might well be deeply committed to social justice and the eradication of racial discrimination. Nevertheless, by the very structure of our social institutions and the way they function, black Americans are treated adversely in comparison with whites. To me this suggests that blacks have a right to preferential admissions, among other things, in order to prevent racial discrimination and inequality of opportunity in the future.

In the short run, they have a moral right not to be discriminated against in the admissions processes of our academic institutions. Since the academic institutions that process applications are, at least to some degree, biased against blacks, black Americans have a right to that kind and amount of preferential treatment that would offset this bias and result in equitable admissions treatment. Suppose, to take an artificially simple example, that empirical evidence were to show that SAT scores were on the average biased against blacks by twenty points. Blacks would then have a moral right to ask that admissions offices add twenty points to their scores to balance out this bias and thus prevent their test scores from resulting in racial discrimination against them. Although this is preferential treatment for blacks, white applicants cannot complain of inequitable treatment because there is a just-making reason for their being treated less well than blacks. This argument does not, of course, justify the conclusion that blacks have a moral right to any and all forms of preferential treatment in admissions. Their right is limited to those forms of preferential admissions that will neutralize institutional discrimination against blacks and thereby prevent any new or continuing racial discrimination against them.

In the long run, black Americans have a right to preferential admissions because this is an essential means of restructuring those social institutions that violate their right to equal opportunity in our society. Structural discrimination is pervasive in our society. Blacks are denied equal opportunity because of housing patterns, unequal tax bases for primary schools, broken families that provide less attention and stimulation in the home, policies of hiring and promoting in business organizations, segregation in churches, and many other institutional factors. Given the importance of education in American economic and political life, achieving educational equality is a necessary part, although only a part, of achieving equal opportunity throughout life. But in order to achieve this, educational institutions must be restructured to give blacks an equal chance with whites. There must be more black role models in our educational institutions, more blacks on admissions committees, more black teachers providing guidance and instruction, more blacks in governmental agencies controlling the funding of public and private schools, etc. A means of moving blacks into such positions in our society is through our educational system, and to ensure that they move forward smoothly and quickly we need preferential admissions. This restructuring of social institutions in order to respect the fundamental right of black Americans to equal opportunity will take a long time. Thus, in the long run blacks have a moral right to preferential admissions. But the long run will not, let us hope, be forever. The moral right for which I argue is a temporary one. Blacks have a right to preferential admissions as long as, but only as long as, this is a necessary or most efficient means of achieving equal opportunity for blacks in our society. When institutional discrimination has been eliminated, preferential treatment of any racial group will become morally wrong, a form of racial discrimination.

But why is preferential treatment of blacks today not racial discrimination against whites now? The easy answer will not do. It is sometimes alleged that one can give preferential treatment to blacks without treating whites adversely, for example by adding several places to the entering class and setting these aside for black applicants. In this way, blacks obtain more places while whites are ensured just as many places as they would enjoy without preferential treatment. But this is sophistry. In the enlarged entering class, whites are denied any opportunity to compete for a portion of the places and thus treated less favorably than blacks. No, preferential treatment for blacks is necessarily adverse or unfavorable treatment for whites. Nevertheless, this is not racial discrimination in reverse, and for two very different reasons. First, the rejection of any white applicant by this particular academic institution is only a small part of the picture. The school is considering many applicants for a limited number of places. As an institution, the judgment of whether it discriminates racially must be determined by its treatment of all applicants. When it rejects one or a few whites to avoid discriminating against blacks, it is avoiding as much as participating in racial discrimination. Second, racial discrimination is inequitable treatment because of race. Now inequitable treatment is adverse treatment without any just-making reason. But the institution that rejects a white applicant because of a policy of preferential admissions carefully designed to offset structural discrimination against blacks and/or to equalize their equality of opportunity in our society can be justicized by the appeal to the rights thereby protected, the rights of blacks to equitable treatment and equal opportunity. Therefore, even though it is adverse treatment of whites, it is not inequitable treatment of them.

But do not white applicants have a moral right to be considered on their merits and qualifications alone, just as students have a right to be graded on the merit of their performance in class? I think not. The right of a student to have his or her exam or paper graded on the basis of its merits is a contractual right; it is part of the understanding between the student paying tuition and the academic institution agreeing to provide certain services, including the provision of grades and eventually an official transcript, for monies received. (Even if the student enjoys a full scholarship, he or she has enrolled in the academic institution with this understanding.) The applicant for admission has not yet entered into any comparable contractual relation with the academic institution; he or she is petitioning for admission. Hence, the applicant has no comparable moral right that his or her application be considered purely on its merits. The places in the entering class belong to the institution, and the applicant has no claim to one of them until it is awarded to him or her.

But then I must face the charge that giving blacks a moral right to preferential admission is the unjust confiscation of private property, for it is depriving the academic institution of its right to use its property as it chooses, even if it chooses to reject blacks. My reply would be that no educational institution, at least in our country today, is a purely a private institution. The distinction between public and private colleges and universities is, in a very real sense, a matter of degree. Most public institutions have received donations from former students, friends, or private foundations. Thus, some of their property is genuinely private property. More to the point, every private institution of higher education has derived a considerable portion of its educational resources from the public. At the very least, it has enjoyed a tax-exempt status that has added considerably to the monies available for its educational purposes. Most likely, it has also received government grants for various educational or research programs. It has almost certainly also received, albeit indirectly, tuition payments from students or their families that were in turn derived from government grants or loans. Therefore, the property held by educational institutions is not purely private property. And so to hold that they are morally bound to use some of their resources for social purposes, specifically to ensure equal opportunity in our society, is not an unjust confiscation of private property but rather the just use of property they hold in public trust.

Well, do blacks have a moral right to preferential admissions? I have defended the view that they do. But this is a controversial question on which informed persons of good will can and do differ. It is a question that all citizens and moral agents should think through for themselves. My goal has been to report several of the more important arguments and to explain how I have reached my own conclusion. My hope is that you, my readers, will follow in my steps and improve upon my reasoning. In this, as in so many urgent social issues, clear thinking and moral insight are needed to make our society a better and more just place for all.

STUDY QUESTIONS

1. Some moral philosophers argue that racial discrimination against black Americans can and should be eliminated by nonpreferential affirmative action. What kinds of nonpreferential affirmative action might be used in the admissions procedures of colleges, universities, and professional schools? Would these be sufficient to overcome racial discrimination in our academic institutions? In our society? How do you know?

2. Suppose, for the sake of argument, that nonpreferential affirmative action could eliminate racial discrimination from our academic institutions, but that it would be insufficient to overcome racial discrimination in our society as a whole. Do our educational institutions have any moral obligation to overcome racial discrimination, not merely in themselves, but in society at large? Why or why not? Does it matter whether the university, for example, is a public or a private institution?

3. Even if the arguments for a right to preferential admissions are sound, they surely do not justify any and every form of preferential admissions. Although blacks may have a right to some forms of preferential treatment in admissions, there are other forms, such as admitting totally unqualified black applicants, that would be morally unjustified. How should one define the limits of

any moral right to preferential admissions? Why these limits rather than others?

4. Presumably if Smith injures Jones or damages his automobile by driving recklessly, then Jones has a right to demand that Smith remedy the wrongful injury or damages he has suffered. But suppose that Smith is too poor to pay Jones' hospital bills or auto repairs? Does Jones have any right that someone else remedy the wrong he has suffered? If so, why? If not, does Jones really have a right to a remedy in this situation?

5. Granted that black Americans have a right to a remedy for the injustices they have suffered, against whom does this right hold? That is, who has the corresponding duty to provide the remedy—society at large, educational institutions, white applicants to educational institutions? Why this party rather than some other?

6. Suppose that black Americans do have a moral right to preferential admissions? Against whom does this right hold? That is, who has the moral duty to provide preferential treatment for them in the admissions processes of our educational institutions?

7. Have all or most white Americans been unjustly enriched at the expense of black Americans? If so, do they have any moral obligation to restore such enrichment to blacks? Is preferential admissions the appropriate way to make this restoration? If not, why not?

8. Have colleges, universities, and professional schools in our country been unjustly enriched at the expense of black Americans? If so, how? If so, is preferential admissions the proper way of restoring what they have unjustly received from blacks?

9. Does one nation really owe reparations to an enemy nation for damage done to civilians and their property in time of war? Why or why not? Does it also owe reparations for damage done to military personnel and equipment, such as tanks blown up or ships sunk during the war? Why or why not?

10. Is the analogy between reparations owed by one nation to another after a war and alleged reparations owed by white Americans to black Americans because of slavery and continuing racial discrimination a relevant one? Explain.

11. Reparations owed by one nation to an enemy nation are usually paid in money or in kind, say food or tools to rebuild the property destroyed. Is there any reason why reparations owed by whites to blacks should be paid by preferential admissions rather than in cash? Is there any reason why it should not be paid in this form?

12. Who owes reparations to black Americans—white Americans as a group of individuals, the United States government controlled by whites, academic institutions in our society, or none of the above? Why? Who would be paying reparations under a system of preferential admissions? Is this morally appropriate?

13. Reparations after a war are paid to the nation and then allocated to the individual civilians who have suffered wartime damages. Let us grant that whites owe reparations to black Americans as a group *and* that an appropriate form of payment would be increased educational opportunity. Still, one may wonder whether a system of preferential admissions allocates this educational opportunity to individual blacks fairly? What do you think? Why?

14. Suppose that the social institutions of any society ought to distribute benefits justly. *What* benefits? Should it take private property from individuals and redistribute it more evenly? Should it redistribute livers and kidneys so that

the disparity between the healthy and those disadvantaged by illness or disability would be less? Or should it distribute only *social* benefits, those created by the social institutions themselves? Why?

15. Do individuals have any moral obligation to distribute burdens and benefits justly? If my family is quite well-off but some neighboring family quite poor, do I have any obligation to give my children fewer or less expensive presents in order to give presents to less fortunate children in the neighborhood? Why or why not? Do I have any duty to distribute presents among my own children equally, or may I give what I like to whom I like? Why? If individuals do not have any obligation of distributive justice, why should societies, governments, or educational institutions?

16. One can argue that the right of blacks to equal opportunity implies a right of blacks to preferential admissions. But one can also argue that preferential admissions for blacks violates the moral right of white applicants to an equal opportunity, since it reduces their chances of being admitted to the best educational institutions. Which argument is stronger? Why?

17. To what kind or range of opportunity do blacks have an equal right? That is, do they have a right to equal opportunity to achieve wealth, social standing, and happiness overall *or* a right to equality in each separate opportunity—the opportunity to be admitted to Washington University, the opportunity to run for mayor, the opportunity to be hired as an usher in a local theater, etc.? What difference would this make to the soundness of the arguments for and against preferential admissions based upon the right to equal opportunity?

18. Precisely what is discrimination? Am I discriminating against a student when I give him a C− for an inferior paper and give another student an A for an excellent paper? Suppose I give the former student a C− because he is a male and the other student an A because she is an attractive female? Presumably one ought to be discriminating, but not to engage in racial or sexual discrimination. What is wrong with racial discrimination, anyway?

19. One might try to rebut the charge of reverse discrimination by saying that preferential admissions for blacks is not treating them advantageously merely because they are black, but because they have suffered injustice or would otherwise have less opportunity. Is this attempted rebuttal adequate? Why or why not?

20. Justice requires that one treat similar cases similarly. But similar in which respects? Could preferential treatment for blacks be justified by pointing out that black applicants and white applicants are dissimilar with respect to race? If not, why not? What sorts of dissimilarities might be morally relevant so as to show that preferential admissions is not inequitable treatment? If you think that there are none, how can one know without reflecting upon every conceivable difference?

21. Do white applicants have any moral right to fair consideration? If so, why? Is the right to fair consideration different from the right to equitable treatment? If so, precisely how do they differ? If not, are the arguments from inequitable treatment and from unfair consideration really one and the same argument expressed in different words?

22. Is it really unfair to consider anything other than the qualifications of an applicant when deciding whether or not to admit him or her to an academic institution? Is it unfair for an institution to give preference to children of alumni? Or to veterans returning from wartime service? Or residents of the state in which the academic institution is located? Explain your answers.

23. Qualifications for what? Should a law school consider only the applicant's qualifications to study law, or might it consider also his or her qualifications for the practice of law? Knowing that many lawyers go into politics, may it fairly consider the potential of the applicant to succeed or serve well in politics? Might it consider the applicant's qualifications as a basketball player? Does it matter whether the school has a varsity basketball team as long as its intramural sports program includes basketball?

24. Suppose someone argues that race is a qualification for the practice of law or medicine because black professionals are more likely to serve the unmet needs of the black community than whites. Would this argument, if sound, prove that preferential admissions is not unfair consideration *or* would it prove that admitting black applicants with lower grades or test scores was not preferential treatment at all? Why?

25. The argument that preferential admissions imposes an unfair burden upon those rejected white applicants who would otherwise have been accepted might be countered with the argument from unjust enrichment. After all, these whites are relatively advantaged in our society so that they can doubtless get into some other academic institution of high quality. The burden imposed upon them is, therefore, slight and does little more than balance the unjust enrichment they have received in their families and previous education. Is this attempted refutation sound?

26. Do the colleges, universities, and professional schools own the places to which they admit applicants? Why or why not? Does it matter whether the educational institution is a public or a private one? Why?

27. Does one party ever have a moral right to the property of another? Does the government have a right to take part of my earned income in taxation? Do my children have a right to demand that I leave part of my estate to them and not bequeath it all to Washington University? If so, might black Americans have a right to places owned by an educational institution? If not, why not?

28. Philosophers often try to formulate and defend a general theory of justice, one that applies adequately to the various forms of justice or injustice. Is this a reasonable enterprise, or would they do better to limit themselves to specific theories of justice, theories of distributive justice, remedial justice, or economic justice, for example? Why?

29. Which theory of justice seems to you most nearly adequate? Why? Does this theory help one to understand and assess the various arguments for and against the right of blacks to preferential admissions? If so, how? If not, why not?

30. How, if at all, do you believe that justice and moral rights are connected? Is justice a matter of respecting rights, or are rights grounded in justice, or is neither of these true? Explain.

31. The author tries to evade the difficulties in the retrospective arguments for a right to preferential admissions by appealing to prospective arguments. Do you find this distinction clear? Do you think his strategy helpful? Why or why not?

32. What does the author mean by "institutional discrimination" or "structural discrimination"? Is this racial discrimination in the same sense you defined in response to study question 18? If so, how? If not, is it also morally wrong? Why or why not?

33. Do you believe that there really is institutional discrimination in our educa-

tional institutions and, more broadly, in our society? On what evidence do you base your belief? If there is structural discrimination against blacks, does that imply that they have any moral right to preferential admissions? If so, how? If not, why not?

34. Everything considered, do you believe that black Americans have a moral right to preferential admissions? Defend your conclusion. Do you reach similar conclusions about the alleged right of Hispanic Americans, Asian Americans, or American females to preferential admissions? Why?

BIBLIOGRAPHY

BEDAU, HUGO ADAM, ed. *Justice and Equality.* Englewood Cliffs, N.J.: Prentice-Hall, 1971.

BITTKER, BORIS. *The Case for Black Reparations.* New York: Random House, 1973.

BLACKSTONE, WILLIAM T., AND HESLEP, ROBERT, eds. *Social Justice and Preferential Treatment.* Athens, Ga.: University of Georgia Press, 1977.

BOXHILL, BERNARD R. "The Morality of Reparation." *Social Theory and Practice* 2 (1972): 113–123.

CAPALDI, NICHOLAS. *Out of Order: Affirmative Action and the Crisis of Doctrinaire Liberalism.* Buffalo: Prometheus Books, 1985.

COHEN, MARSHALL; NAGEL, THOMAS; AND SCANLON, THOMAS, eds. *Equity and Preferential Treatment.* Princeton, N.J.: Princeton University Press, 1977.

EAMES, ELIZABETH R. "Quotas, Goals, and the Ideal of Equality." *Journal of Social Philosophy* 13 (1982): 10–15.

FRANKENA, WILLIAM K. "The Concept of Social Justice," in Richard B. Brandt (ed.), *Social Justice.* Englewood Cliffs, N.J.: Prentice-Hall, 1962.

FULLINWIDER, ROBERT K. *The Reverse Discrimination Controversy.* Totowa, N.J.: Rowman and Littlefield, 1980.

GLAZER, NATHAN. *Affirmative Discrimination.* New York: Basic Books, 1976.

GINGER, ANN FAGAN, ed. *DeFunis versus Odegaard and the University of Washington: The University Admissions Case, the Record.* 3 vols. Dobbs Ferry, N.Y.: Oceana Publications, 1974.

GOLDMAN, ALAN H. *Justice and Reverse Discrimination.* Princeton, N.J.: Princeton University Press, 1979.

GROSS, BARRY R., ed. *Reverse Discrimination.* Buffalo: Prometheus Books, 1977.

LECKY, ROBERT S., AND WRIGHT, H. ELLIOTT (eds). *Black Manifesto.* New York: Sheed and Ward, 1969.

O'NEIL, ROBERT M. *Discriminating Against Discrimination: Preferential Admissions and the DeFunis Case.* Bloomington: Indiana University Press, 1975.

RAWLS, JOHN. *A Theory of Justice.* Cambridge, Mass.: Harvard University Press, 1971.

WASSERSTROM, RICHARD. "The University and the Case for Preferential Treatment." *American Philosophical Quarterly* 13 (1976): 165–170.

10
"A RIGHT"

We have been examining philosophically the debate over the moral right to preferential admission. Do black people in our society really have a moral right to preferential admission to colleges, universities, and professional schools? Or is giving blacks preferential treatment in the admissions procedures of our academic institutions reverse racial discrimination, a violation of the right of the white applicants thereby rejected not to be treated adversely because of their race? It is easy enough to assert the existence of one or the other of these rights and thus attempt to settle the issue by emphatic pronouncement, but precisely what does it mean to assert that a right exists? What is a right, anyway?

Probably most of us would be hard put to formulate an illuminating definition of the expression "a right." Dictionaries often tell us that a right is an entitlement. They may well be correct in reporting that "a right" and "an entitlement" are synonymous expressions, but this bit of linguistic information is not very helpful philosophically. Just because the two expressions are synonymous, any obscurity in the first is apt to be reflected in the other as well. The moral philosopher who is unclear about the precise meaning of "a right" is unlikely to be any clearer about the exact meaning of "an entitlement."

The search for an adequate definition of "a right" is not a task of interest to lexicographers only; it is an endeavor with moral and ethical import. This can be seen in several ways. First, ambiguous language often leads to unnecessary and pointless disputes. Although *Roe v. Wade* was widely hailed by feminists as establishing the legal right of a pregnant woman to an abortion on demand, the Supreme Court explicitly denied that it was recognizing any such right. Considerable energy has been wasted, energy that could more profitably have been spent in the discussion of urgent moral causes, in debating whether *Roe* really did recognize a right to abortion on demand. This debate was entirely unnecessary because the disagreement between the feminists and the Court was entirely verbal. They did not really disagree at all; they appeared to disagree only because they were using the expression "a right" in different senses. The feminists were asserting a legal liberty; the Court was denying a legal claim. Since the Court in *Roe v. Wade* did hold that abortion on demand is legally permissible it really did recognize a legal right, in the sense of a liberty, to abortion on demand; since the Court did not hold that a woman's request that her physician perform an abortion imposes any duty to do so, it really did not recognize a right, in the sense of a legal claim, to abortion on demand. There was no real disagreement between feminists and partisans of the Court; there was only a misunderstanding that led to futile wrangling.

Second, the meaning of a statement determines what implications follow logically from it and thus its practical import. If one grants a moral right to disobey a law, provided one does so nonviolently and in order to make a moral protest, does it follow that it is wrong for the government to punish one who engages in civil disobedience? This poses no merely verbal question; it poses an important and controversial issue of public policy, and one with very practical consequences for any civil disobedient. The correct moral conclusion depends upon precisely what it means to assert that the citizen has a moral right to engage in civil disobedience. If this means merely that it is not wrong to do so, then it does not follow that the government wrongs the civil disobedient by punishing him or her. But if this means that the civil disobedient has a moral right in the strong sense, in the sense that it is wrong for others to interfere with his or her doing so, then punishment by the government is correctly condemned as morally wrong.

Third, the meaning of an expression determines when it can be meaningfully used. Presumably it makes perfectly good sense to assert that every normal human being has a right to life, a right that helps to explain why murder is wrong. Presumably it is nonsense to claim that a wart or a mole has a right to life so that a surgeon who removes it is a murderer. But can one meaningfully say that a pig or a chicken has a right to life? There are those who declare that our practice of slaughtering pigs and chickens for food is grossly immoral on the grounds that it violates animal rights. Others believe that such declarations have no moral import because they are literally nonsense; it makes no more sense to say that a pig has a right than to say that a wart has a right. Now if to assert the existence of a right is to assert the existence of a choice that is protected by moral obligations, then it probably is meaningless to apply the expression "a right" to any being incapable of genuine choice. But if "a right" refers to an interest protected by obligations, then it does make sense to ascribe rights to animals, but not to warts, because animals probably do have interests, but warts do not. How seriously one takes the animal rights movement depends upon what it means to talk about moral rights.

Accordingly, it behooves anyone who is deeply concerned about moral issues involving rights to try to become perfectly clear about the meaning of the expression "a right." This endeavor to become clear about the meaning of obscure concepts or to define the meaning of vague and ambiguous language is one of the traditional tasks of philosophy. The history of philosophy has shown that much unnecessary disagreement and paralyzing confusion arises from the attempt to debate questions posed in vague, ambiguous, or obscure language. One of the hallmarks of contemporary philosophy, in ethics as in epistemology and metaphysics, is the persistent effort to use clear and precise language in the discussion of philosophical problems. Let us, therefore, try to find a philosophically helpful definition of "a right" in the hope that clarity on the linguistic level will lead to insight on the moral level.

"A RIGHT": SEVERAL PROPOSED MEANINGS

A Liberty

As usual in philosophy, our problem is not the absence of definitions but the fact that so many different definitions are proposed. The seventeenth-century English political philosopher Thomas Hobbes asserted that a right is a liberty. Accordingly, to say that someone has a right to do something is to say that he or she is at liberty to do so. A liberty is the opposite of an obligation. A person has an obligation to do some act when he or she is bound or constrained to do it. Thus, we have a legal obligation to pay our taxes because we are constrained by the threat of legal sanctions to do so, and we have a moral obligation to seek peace because we are bound by the command of God, who is omnipotent, to do so. A person is at liberty to do something when there is no obligation to refrain from doing it. I am at liberty to stroll upon the common because no law forbids my doing so and there is no threat of sanction to oblige me to keep off this public land. A right is a liberty, and a liberty consists in the absence of any contrary obligation. Thus, "I have a right to free speech" means simply "I am not obliged not to speak freely."

One advantage of this theory is that it explains how rights are associated with freedom. We often appeal to rights in order to defend the freedom of the individual, in order to resist coercion by a government or interference by private persons. The Declaration of Independence and the Bill of Rights both use the rights of the individual as a basis for rejecting governmental policies or actions of an objectionable sort, and an individual usually claims his or her constitutional right to free speech at just that point where someone tries to prevent him or her from saying what he or she wants. It is no accident that attempts to preserve and enlarge human freedom so often appeal to legal or moral rights, if by its very definition a right is a liberty, an area of action in which the right-holder is free to act without constraint. Nor is it any accident that our fundamental constitutional rights are called "civil liberties."

One difficulty with this definition of "right" is that it does not seem to fit the language of passive rights. Sometimes the content of a right is best expressed by a verb in the active voice, for example a citizen's right to demonstrate in protest of some governmental policy or a believer's right to worship at the church or temple of his or her choice. But often the content of a right can be accurately expressed only by a verb in the passive voice, as the creditor's right to be repaid or the individual's right not to be battered by another. Now it is hard to understand how my right not to be battered could possibly consist of any of my liberties, for there is nothing I could do that would constitute exercising this right. Rather I enjoy this right as long as others refrain from beating me up. To be sure, I have a liberty of resisting an attack with all necessary and proportionate force. But this is the exercise of another of my rights, the right to defend myself. Although Hobbes' definition seems to fit our right to act in specific ways well enough, it seems inapplicable to our rights to be treated by others in some specific manner.

A Relative Duty

John Austin, the nineteenth-century English jurist and political philosopher, defined "a right" in terms of a relative duty. His conception of a duty is very much in the spirit of Hobbes: one has a duty to do some act when one is bound or constrained to do it. A legal duty is imposed by some general command of the sovereign. The citizen is bound by the commands of the sovereign, typically expressed in legislation, because these commands are enforced by legal sanctions, penalties imposed by the courts upon those who disobey the law. Presumably, the individual is similarly bound by the moral law because God's commands are enforced with Divine penalties for disobedience. Every law creates a duty, but only relative duties have correlative rights. A duty is relative when it is a duty *to* some assignable or identifiable person or persons; it is then a duty relative to one or more particular persons to whom performance is due. This definition fits passive rights admirably. "The creditor has a right to repayment" simply means that the debtor has a duty *to* the creditor to repay the loan. Not every duty is a relative duty, a duty *to* some right-holder. One also has absolute duties, such as the duties to pay one's taxes or to refrain from suicide. The former is not a relative duty because it is due to the public at large and not to any *assignable* individual or individuals; the latter is not a relative duty because one cannot be obliged or *constrained* by one's own will. According to Austin, "a right" refers to a relative duty; it refers to a relative duty seen from the perspective of the person or persons to whom the performance of that duty is due. Thus, to say that my children have a right to be cared for by me amounts to saying that I have a duty to my children to care for them. What I perceive as my right to be paid for services rendered is, seen from the perspective of Washington University, its duty to pay me for my teaching and research.

A virtue of this theory is that it defines an obscure and problematic expression in terms of a clearer and less problematic one. To be sure, the precise meaning of "a duty" is not entirely clear. But Wesley Hohfeld has shown in his work on legal conceptions that the expression "a legal right" is highly ambiguous, that it is used indiscriminately to refer to legal claims, legal privileges, legal powers, and legal immunities. No one has ever alleged any comparable ambiguity in the expression "a legal duty." Again, paradigm cases of moral duties, such as the duty to keep a promise or the duty not to murder anyone, are fairly easy to find. But it is not easy to find equally uncontroversial examples of moral rights. Indeed, many philosophers go so far as to deny that there are any natural rights, any moral rights independent of social institutions. Thus, it is much easier to know what one is talking about when one talks of duties than when one talks of rights. Since the purpose of any philosophical analysis of an obscure expression is to clarify its meaning, the best definition is the one that uses the clearest language.

Provided, of course, one does not misconstrue the meaning of the expression by reducing it to oversimple concepts. A defect in Austin's definition is that it can plausibly be charged with omitting many essential aspects of a right. Typically rights can be claimed, exercised, waived, renounced, forfeited, or delegated; duties, even relative duties, do not seem to have any of these features. Therefore, to reduce rights to duties seems to be to misrepresent their very nature, for it ignores many of the features that are distinctive of rights and make them important in the law and in morals. No doubt clarity and precision of language, two ideals of contemporary analytic philosophy, are valuable in theory and in practice. But they are purchased at too great a price when a definition of "a right" misinterprets the language of morals.

A Valid Claim

Joel Feinberg, a contemporary American moral philosopher and philosopher of law, defines "a right" as a valid claim. He imagines a community in which there are nonmoral values, virtues, and duties but no rights and asks what would be lacking in it. He suggests that no one would be in the position to *claim* the performance of any duty. No doubt charity is a virtue and those with adequate means have a duty to share their wealth with those in need. But no beggar is in a position to demand as a right that I give him or her a handout because I am free to contribute to other needy individuals or charitable organizations instead. In contrast, my creditor is in a position to demand that I repay him or her, and no other, because a creditor has a right that holds against a debtor. What is distinctive and valuable about rights is the process of claiming, of demanding something as one's due. Claiming is very different from petitioning or begging. The beggar appeals to the mercy of someone in a position to help and depends upon the good will or favor of that person for any gift; the claimant insists upon his or her due and is in a position to demand that the second party perform a duty. One normally claims something by presenting title to it, as one claims one's coat after the play by presenting one's claim check. To have a claim is to be in a position to make a claim. One has a claim when one possesses a title to that thing, evidence sufficient to support one's demand that it be provided to or for one. Every claim is *to* something and *against* someone, for example to a coat and against the coat-room attendant. But not all claims are rights. There can be competing claims to an inheritance or a wallet someone has found, but typically only one of the competing parties can have a genuine right to that thing. A right is a valid claim, a claim that is justified by the applicable set of rules. A legal right is a claim whose recognition and satisfaction is called for by the legal rules of the community; a moral right is a claim justified by the principles of an enlightened conscience.

One strength of this theory of rights is that it can explain the special standing of the right-holder. Only the owner of a coat can claim it as his or her due. Others, of course, can demand to have my coat, just as a gunman can demand that I hand over my wallet. But only I, or my agent acting for me, can claim it as one entitled to it under the rules of the law or morals. Again, only the creditor can waive a right to repayment. If I believe that the heartless banker is immoral in foreclosing on the poor widow's mortgage, I may properly appeal to him to change his mind, or I may protest his cruelty in public. But I cannot, no matter what I do, cancel her debt to him. Only the right-holder can do that. Only I can exercise my right to vote. Another may go to the polls, pretend to be me, and punch holes in a ballot. But this is not exercising my right to vote; it is wrongfully pretending to vote and the vote will, if discovered, be declared legally null and void. The special position of a right-holder is that of a claimant, that of one in a position to claim. This special standing is explained well by the view that a right is a valid claim.

A weakness in this theory is that it seems incapable of interpreting many active rights. Notice that the paradigm cases of claim rights are passive rights, such as the owner's right to be given his or her coat or the creditor's right to be repaid. Now perhaps the claim theory can explain some strong active rights, such as the right to free speech. While Hobbes can say that the citizen's right to free speech consists in a liberty to speak freely on controversial issues, Feinberg can say that the right to free speech is a valid claim that others, both the government and other individuals, not prevent one from speaking out on controversial issues. What Hobbes takes to be a liberty of action Feinberg interprets as a claim against interference. But the latter's strategy will not work for all active rights. I have a right to park in front of the building in which my apartment is located. But since there are many apartment buildings on my street, other drivers often occupy all the spaces in front of my building when I arrive home from work. They have interfered with my parking in front of my apartment, but they have not violated my right to park there. This is because my right to park in front of the building in which I live is a liberty-right and not a claim-right. Such liberty-rights are typical of competitive situations. Each runner has a right to win the race and each team in the American League has a right to win the pennant. But since another runner or team does not violate this right by winning the race or the pennant, this right to win cannot be said to consist in a valid claim against interference with one's winning.

A Protected Choice

H. L. A. Hart, a contemporary jurist and moral philosopher, defines "a right" as a protected choice. I have a right to look over my garden fence at my neighbor, even when she wishes to sunbathe unobserved. This means that I have a liberty of looking or not looking as I choose *and* that others, including my neighbor, have duties not to interfere with my looking by climbing over the fence and beating me up. Not all forms of interference are prohibited; my neighbor may prevent me from observing her sunbathing by building a very high fence around her patio if she wishes. Thus, a right consists in a bilateral liberty, a liberty of acting or not acting in some specific manner, together with a protective perimeter of duties not to interfere with the exercise of this bilateral liberty in certain specified ways. My legal right to park in front of my apartment consists in my bilateral legal liberty to park there or not as I choose together with the legal duties of others not to prevent me from parking or not parking there by disabling me, damaging my car so that it is inoperable, threatening to shoot me if I park there, etc. My moral right to smoke consists of my moral liberty to smoke or not as I like protected by a perimeter of duties of those who object to my smoking not to interfere by destroying my cigarettes, forcefully removing lighted cigarettes from my mouth, or tying me hand and foot.

One advantage of this theory is that it explains the conceptual distinction between a right and a duty. What is the difference between saying that one has "a right" to do something and saying that one has "a duty" to do it? Hart suggests that rights are permissive while duties are mandatory. Although one's rights leave one free choice, one's duties constrain one's choice. To say that I have a right to use the libraries of Washington University is to say that I *may* do so *if* I so choose; to say that I have a duty to grade all written work submitted by my students at Washington University is to say that I *must* do so whether or not I wish to spend my time in this manner. The permissiveness of rights, in contrast to the requiredness of duties, is explained by the view that a right is a protected choice.

But is the distinction between rights and duties that simple? A disadvantage with Hart's definition of "a right" is that there certainly seem to be mandatory rights. We often speak of a child's right to public education and protest that in some communities the right of blacks to serve on juries is violated. But education is compulsory until school-leaving age, and any black called to jury duty is legally (and perhaps morally) required to serve. It is hard to see how Hart's protected choice theory can make sense of these assertions. While the child has a liberty of attending public school and receiving an education, it has no liberty of not doing so; although a black has a liberty of serving on a jury when called to jury duty, he or she is not at liberty to refuse to perform this often arduous duty. Surely it makes sense to say that someone has both a right and a duty to do something, but the theory that places a *bilateral* liberty at the center of every right cannot interpret such language.

A Protected Interest

The twentieth-century jurist John Salmond defined "a right" as meaning an interest protected by a rule. An interest is something in which someone is or should be interested, presumably because it is in his or her interest. A person's interests are the various components of his or her welfare or good—for example, having food, freedom, or wealth. Not all interests are rights, however. I have an interest in becoming famous for my philosophical publications. Not only is this something in which I take a keen interest, something I desire, but it is of value to me because of the personal satisfaction I would derive from it and because fame would probably result in an increased salary. Nevertheless, I have no right to become famous. Only interests protected by rules are rights. Rules protect interests normatively because they are norms of conduct applying to those who might be tempted to invade those interests; primarily they impose upon others duties not to injure some specific interest. My interests in free speech, in voting, and in being paid for services rendered are all protected by legal rules. My interests in remaining alive, having promises to me kept, and not being lied to are similarly protected by moral rules. Hence, all of these constitute rights, some legal and others moral. What we mean by "a right" is simply an interest protected by a rule.

In support of this analysis of the concept of a right it may be said that it explains the value of rights. We ordinarily think of rights as very much worth having, perhaps even valuable enough to fight for. But what is it about rights that makes them so good? If rights are interests, then of course they are good because one's interests are the various components of one's good or one's welfare. According to Salmond's definition, a person's rights consist of those parts of his or her good that are protected by rules. The protection may give social significance and practical force to one's rights, but their value to the individual is explained simply by the fact that they are in his or her interest because they are included in his or her welfare. If a right is by very definition always part of someone's good, then rights are necessarily good, and our ordinary evaluation of rights as valuable is entirely justified.

But can all rights be identified with interests? No doubt most of the rights people possess are in their interest, and they would be less well off were they deprived of them. But is this always and necessarily so? An interest, you will remember, is something in which one is or should be interested because it is in one's interest, something to be desired because one would be better off having it than lacking it. Now many moral philosophers would maintain that the individual has a right to smoke, and even those who deny the existence of any such right presumably understand what is meant by the expression, "a right to smoke." But does this expression refer to any interest of the individual? Presumably an individual can have a right to smoke even when he or she is not in the least interested in exercising it; he or she may dislike the taste of tobacco and abhor the mess associated with smoking. Moreover, smoking may not be in the individual's interest at all, for it probably wastes one's money and impairs one's health. In such a case, smoking is not one of the interests of that individual. Nevertheless, it seems that this individual still has the right to smoke; it is just that he or she would never choose to exercise that right. Apparently, rights cannot be identified with interests, even those protected by a rule.

An Interest-Based Reason

The contemporary moral and legal philosopher Joseph Raz defines "a right" as an interest-based reason. More explicitly, to say that someone has a right to something is to say that, other things being equal, some aspect of someone's well-being (one of his or her interests) is a sufficient reason for holding some other person or persons to be under a duty. He does not so much reject the protected interest theory of rights as to go beyond it. To be sure, in every right there is an interest and one or more duties to protect that interest from invasion or injury. But a right is not merely an interest plus protection; it is no accident that some interests are protected while others are not. Where there is a genuine right, the interest is *a reason for* the protective duty or duties. It is some interest of one party, the right-holder, that justifies imposing one or more duties upon one or more second parties, the duty-bearers. Thus, my moral right to life is a reason for holding others to be under a moral duty not to kill me, and my right to life is itself grounded on my interest in remaining alive. In this way, the expression "a right" means an interest-based reason. Similarly, a statute prohibiting homicide and thereby imposing a duty upon others not to kill me is properly said to confer upon me a legal right to life only if it is thought that my interest in life is a sufficient reason for enacting and enforcing that law.

A considerable virtue of this definition is that it explains the special role of rights in practical reasoning. Suppose that I have borrowed money from a friend and, when the time comes to repay her, I find myself rather short of cash. What reason do I have to repay my creditor? One reason, no doubt, is that if I refuse to pay I may well get into trouble. A friendship I value may be ruined and, if the sum is considerable, my friend may take her case to court. But another, and quite different, reason is that my friend has a right to be paid. While prudential considerations are reasons to hold that I ought to repay my friend, my creditor's right to be repaid is a sufficient reason for holding me under a *duty* to repay. Moreover, this is a duty *to* this individual creditor. I cannot fulfill this duty by using all my available resources to repay my bank, from whom I have also borrowed money, or to contribute to the Red Cross, even though I also have a duty to contribute to charitable organizations. Now, how can we explain how and why rights imply duties to individual right-holders? They impose duties because of the importance of the interests on which rights are based, and they imply duties to individuals because those interests are aspects of the well-being of individuals. Thus, Raz can explain how it is that the essential function of rights in practical reasoning is to ground duties to individuals upon interests.

Many moral philosophers, however, would complain that to define the expression "a right" as an interest-based reason is to beg an important and controversial philosophical question. What are the grounds of moral, especially of human, rights? Although many philosophers agree with Raz that moral rights are grounded on human interests, John Stuart Mill argued that they are grounded on social utility, and contemporary philosopher Ronald Dworkin insists that individual rights are grounded upon a fundamental right to political equality. Theologians typically repudiate all such humanisms and maintain that our fundamental human rights are based upon the will of God. Now to define "a right" as an interest-based reason seems to render the theses of the theologians, of Mill and of Dworkin, meaningless, or at least to prejudice the case against them. Since the grounds of rights are very much in doubt, any definition of the expression "a right" should be neutral between the alternative theories. It is a mistake to try to settle any such substantive issue by definition. If the controversial issue is to be fairly debated and rationally settled, we need a definition of "a right" in which all the plausible philosophical theories can be formulated and that will not prejudice the case against any of them. Therefore, it is a philosophical disadvantage to adopt any definition, like that of Raz, that defines rights in terms of their grounds.

A Side-Constraint

Robert Nozick, another contemporary moral and political philosopher, defines "a right" as a side-constraint. It is a mistake, he argues, to think of rights in terms of interests or aspects of someone's good, even important ones, because then one would be justified in violating someone's rights in order to achieve a greater good, either for oneself or for others. Rights function in a very different manner to rule out using others as a means; they render certain ways of pursuing interests or goals morally or legally impermissible. They specify those ways of treating others that are wrong. This conception of rights is captured in the spatial metaphor of a moral agent pursuing goals located ahead while hemmed in by limits on the side. It is quite natural and entirely proper for an individual to pursue his or her interests, or to further the interests of others. Since I and my family have a legitimate interest in wealth with which to fulfill our basic needs and live a worthwhile life, I may seek an endowed chair in philosophy and the increased salary it carries with it. I may rightfully pursue this goal by publishing books that will enhance my professional reputation or by writing a critical review of a new book by some competitor for the chair. But it is morally impermissible for me to pursue my goal by plagiarizing papers written by my graduate students and publishing them as my own or killing the incumbent so that the chair will be vacant and I can apply for it; such acts violate the property rights of the authors of those papers and the right to life of the person who now holds the chair I seek. Thus, moral and legal rights impose constraints upon any agent pursuing his or her goals by making certain ways of treating others morally or legally impermissible. A right is a side-constraint.

Nozick's conception of a right seems to capture the force of negative rights very well and to explain their moral or legal import. Any right imposes some duty upon second parties. My right to free speech imposes a duty upon the state not to prevent me from speaking out in criticism of the government, and my right to life implies a duty of all others not to kill me. Since these are duties *not* to do certain actions, they are called negative rights. Now, if a right really is a side-constraint, it functions to render certain actions *im*permissible and thereby to impose a duty upon one or more second parties *not* to treat one in that manner. This seems to be precisely what negative rights, such as the right not to be battered or defrauded, do. Accordingly, the definition of "a right" as a side-constraint fits negative rights admirably.

But what of positive rights? This definition seems unable to interpret our talk of positive rights. Creditors frequently assert their "right to be paid" and some political philosophers assert that in our country the unemployed or dependent children have "a moral right to be provided with welfare benefits." If genuine, such rights impose positive duties upon second parties—the duty to pay a certain sum upon the debtor and the duty to provide welfare benefits upon the state. These are positive duties because they are duties to act in certain ways rather than not to act in specific ways. Accordingly, such rights are called positive rights. Now Nozick argues that there are no genuine welfare rights, at least no such moral rights. He might be correct. But we can still understand the assertions of his opponents, those who allege the existence of a positive right to be provided with welfare benefits. But how can Nozick's definition interpret these intelligible, even if controversial, statements, since according to his theory a right is a side-constraint, something that imposes upon others a duty or duties *not* to mistreat the right-holder in certain ways? If the moral and legal import of rights is thus essentially negative, it would appear that any talk of positive rights is nothing but misunderstanding. Surely, this is not so.

An Individual Trump

The contemporary jurist and moral philosopher Ronald Dworkin holds that the expression "a right" should be taken to mean an individual trump over social goals. Like Nozick, Dworkin contrasts rights with goals, but what he emphasizes most is the difference and often the opposition between *individual* rights and *social* goals. This can be seen most clearly in the political arena. If the government decides to publicize the dangers of AIDS, it can justify its action by showing that such publicity promotes the social goal of public health and thereby advances the general welfare. But if the government decides to invade my right to free speech by forbidding me to publish criticisms of its policies, it cannot justify its action merely by showing that it will promote the social goal of reducing divisive controversy. My individual right trumps this social goal and thereby provides me special protection from governmental mistreatment. Dworkin tries to capture the special force of rights, the way in which they protect the individual from wrongful state action, in his metaphor of rights as trumps. The game he has in mind is the justification of action, especially of political actions or governmental actions. The tricks are political decisions. The other suit is social goals or collective goods. These are collective goods in the sense that their value is to be thought of in terms of social utility and ascertained by summing up their good consequences for all members of the community and subtracting all their bad consequences. The point of the metaphor is to suggest that political decisions cannot always be justified by this sort of cost-benefit analysis in which social utility is taken to be merely the sum of the utilities and disutilities for everyone in the society. Thus, to say that individual rights trump social goals is to assert that infringing a right of one individual cannot be justified merely by showing that such action would be socially useful.

The definition of "a right" as an individual trump seems to explain the distributive nature of rights. This is both conceptually and morally important. The very concept of a right ties rights to individual right-holders. It would not make sense to assert the existence of a right that was not someone's right. Every right belongs to someone, and a right of one individual cannot be identified with a right of another individual—even when they each have "the same right." If Jones and Smith have each loaned me ten dollars, then both Jones and Smith have a right to be repaid. But I cannot fulfill Jones' right to be repaid by paying Smith ten dollars, or twenty dollars for that matter. This conceptual tie between a right and the individual who possesses it seems to have important moral implications. It seems to rule out violating a right of one individual in order to benefit, or even to protect the rights of others. Imagine a community in which a white man has raped a black child. The police have only a vague description of the rapist and little hope of detecting and punishing him, but the blacks are angry and demanding justice. If they riot, as seems likely, they will destroy much property and probably injure—possibly kill—several whites. Yet it seems morally wrong to frame and punish an innocent white person, thus violating his moral rights, merely in order to prevent social harm or protect the rights of other individuals. Dworkin's theory seems to explain how it is that the rights *of* individuals give moral or legal protection *to* individuals.

His conception of rights as individual trumps over social goals is most appropriate to the political sphere. It is tailor-made to explain how our fundamental civil rights protect the individual from mistreatment by the government. But it does not seem applicable to the rights of one individual against another individual. Since Jones has loaned me ten dollars, he has a right that I repay him ten dollars when the loan is due. This is a right of one individual, Jones, holding against another individual, me. No doubt his right trumps my personal desire to refuse repayment and spend the money I owe to him upon a bottle of fine wine. But the contrast between individual rights and *social* goals that Dworkin takes to define rights does not seem central to the conception of a right of one individual in relation to that of another individual. Even rights that hold against the state often hold also against other individuals. For example, my right to life imposes a duty upon the state not to execute me without a fair trial and conviction and also a duty upon other individuals not to murder me. Any philosophically adequate definition of "a right" must be general enough to apply outside as well as within the political arena.

Moral philosophers and nonphilosophical moralists often ponder and debate issues concerning rights. In their efforts to think clearly about rights and to assess critically the various arguments advanced for or against the assertion that this or that right exists, philosophers are led to try to clarify the very conception of a right. What do we mean by "a right"? Moral philosophy, ethical theory, and jurisprudence offer a number of plausible definitions. We have examined in cursory fashion the views that "a right" means a liberty, a relative duty, a valid claim, a protected choice, a protected interest, an interest-based reason, a side-constraint, and an individual trump. There is something to be said for each of these definitions, but, as one would expect, none is immune to criticism. The aim of each philosopher must be to carry his or her own critical thinking to the point where it either improves upon one of these theories or culminates in a new and better definition. I shall attempt the latter.

MY OWN PROPOSAL

Earlier in this chapter I mentioned Wesley Hohfeld in passing, but his contribution to the theory of rights is too important to pass over without further discussion. This recent American jurist attempted to identify the fundamental legal conceptions and to display their logical implications or contradictions with one another. Each of these conceptions, he thought, stood for a legal relation between two parties under the law, two parties in a position to confront one another in a suit before a court of law. Through a detailed examination of judicial opinions and other legal texts, he showed that the expression "a legal right" is highly ambiguous because it is used indiscriminately to refer to legal liberties, claims, powers, and immunities. Let me explain and illustrate each of these fundamental legal conceptions.

One party, X, has a legal liberty in face of some second party, Y, to do action A if and only if X has no legal duty to Y not to do A. For example, I have a legal liberty in face of my neighbor to look over my garden fence at her because I do not have any legal duty to her not to do so. X has a legal claim against Y that Y do A if and only if Y has a legal duty to X to do A. Thus, a creditor has a legal claim against the debtor that he or she repay the debt because the debtor has a legal duty to the creditor to repay the loan when due. X has a legal power over Y to bring about legal consequence C for Y if and only if X is able to perform some voluntary action that would be recognized by the courts as having this consequence for Y. For example, I have a legal power to give one of my books to a student because if I were to hand this book to the student and say "Here, this is yours," the courts would recognize my act as transferring legal ownership in the book from myself to the student. X has a legal immunity in face of Y against some legal consequence C if and only if there is no voluntary act that Y could perform that would have this legal consequence for X. Thus, I am legally immune if my wife tries to resign my position at Washington University because there is nothing she can do, not even writing a letter of resignation in my name, that would be recognized by the courts as terminating my appointment at Washington University. Although these four fundamental legal relations are very different, they are all spoken of as legal rights. Hohfeld lamented this ambiguity because, as he demonstrated by his criticism of a number of judicial opinions and juristic pronouncements, it leads to confused thinking and invalid reasoning.

He insisted that, in the strict sense, the expression "a legal right" simply means a single legal claim, a legal claim of one party against one second party. Accordingly, his conception of a right is very similar to Feinberg's. The main difference is that while Feinberg defines a claim in terms of the process of claiming, and takes any implied duties to follow from that, Hohfeld thinks of a claim as the logical correlative of a duty, and takes the power to claim as following from the duty to be claimed. In the end, then, his theory of rights is that of Austin's, for he conceives of a right as the correlative of a relative duty. Indeed, it is this correlation between rights and duties that he used to argue for his theory. It is essential to the very concept of someone's right that it hold against some second party. Since only legal claims imply any correlative legal duties, only legal claims can properly and strictly speaking be called legal rights. Legal liberties, powers, and immunities, important as they are, are not really rights.

Although I firmly believe that Hohfeld's examination of the language of legal rights is immensely important, I cannot agree with his conclusion. What I seek, therefore, is a conception of rights that saves his insights but avoids his basic error. What led him astray, I believe, was trying to identify a legal right with a simple legal relation—a single claim of one party against a second party. He was quite correct in insisting that a right necessarily holds against some second party. But a single legal claim, all by itself, would not hold fast against the second party in any possible confrontation. Let us reexamine the creditor's right to be repaid. Certainly at its center is the creditor's legal claim against the debtor that he or she repay the loan when due. But if this were the entire story, we would not speak of "a right to repayment," because standing alone this claim would not hold against the debtor. Suppose that the creditor did not also have an immunity against having the debtor cancel the debt by pronouncing three times in front of two witnesses the words "I hereby cancel my debt." Then the creditor's claim would not hold fast in any serious confrontation between the right-holder and the duty-bearer. Or suppose that the creditor, in the event that the debtor refuses to repay the loan, had no power to sue for repayment in the courts. Then how would the claim of the creditor be legally binding upon the debtor? Or imagine that although the debtor did have a legal duty to repay the loan, the creditor has no legal liberty of accepting the money tendered in payment of the loan. We would hardly speak of "a right to be repaid" when the creditor is prohibited by law from completing the transaction of repayment. What one should learn from examples such as these, I believe, is that it is a mistake to identify a legal right with a single legal claim. Only a complex of legal claims, liberties, powers, and immunities can constitute a legal right.

Not just any cluster of legal advantages will do, and for the reason Hohfeld stressed. A right of one party necessarily holds against some second party; it is in this sense that the concept of a right is essentially relational. Therefore, a legal right must be a complex of legal positions that confers autonomy upon the right-holder in face of one or more second parties in some possible confrontation. Let me explain. At the core of every legal right is some legal advantage—some legal liberty, claim, power, or immunity. These fundamental legal conceptions identified by Hohfeld are immensely important for our understanding of rights, not because they show that the expression "a right" is ambiguous, but because they enable us to classify rights in a way that makes clear the legally important differences between different sorts or kinds of rights. This core advantage does more than determine the modality of the right; it also unifies the cluster of legal positions into a single complex structure. Around this core element stand a number of associated elements, each of which confers some freedom or control over that core upon the possessor of that core. For example, the creditor has the legal power of waiving his or her core claim against the debtor and thus cancelling the debt; this provides control over the central claim that defines the content of the right to repayment. And the creditor has the bilateral legal liberty to exercise or not exercise this power to waive repayment, a liberty that confers freedom of choice and action regarding the core claim. Each of the other associated elements similarly confers some sort of freedom or control over the core claim upon the creditor. Now freedom and control are essentially connected. The creditor is not free to sue for repayment if he or she has no control over those—either the debtor or anyone siding with the debtor in this confrontation—who would try to prevent him or her from taking the case to court, and the creditor has no real legal control over a recalcitrant debtor unless he or she is free to sue for repayment. Thus, freedom and control are two aspects of what I call autonomy. Accordingly, I conceive of a legal right as a system of legal positions that confers autonomy upon one party in face of one or more second parties in some possible confrontation or conflict of wills.

right to do act A" imply that "P's doing A is not wrong"? Is it ever the case that one has rights it would be wrong to exercise?

2. Among alleged human rights are the rights to life, liberty, property, due process, free association, habeas corpus, free speech, equal opportunity, and education. Which of these can most easily be construed as liberties? Are there any of these that do not seem to be liberties at all? If so, are they rights in the same sense of "a right" that liberties are?

3. The individual sometimes appeals to his or her rights in order to limit or prevent interference or coercion by the state. Does the state or society as a whole also have rights? If so, when would the state be likely to appeal to its rights and for what purpose? If not, why not?

4. Among rights are the rights to free speech, free association, life, liberty, property, privacy, due process, and education. Which of these are active rights and which are passive rights? Are there some rights that are clusters of "subrights," some of which are active and some passive? Are there any rights that cannot be classified as either active or passive?

5. Recently there has been much talk of welfare rights such as the rights to education, medical care, or a decent standard of living. Can such rights be plausibly interpreted as relative duties? If so, whose duties are they? Is there any point in insisting that such things as education or medical care are rights rather than just desirable things for which we should strive?

6. It is sometimes claimed that the rights to education, adequate medical care, and a decent standard of living are human rights. This seems to imply that these rights are possessed by every human being just by virtue of being human. Unfortunately, many human beings live in societies that lack the resources to provide such things to all their members. Does this impossibility mean that human beings can have rights to impossible things like being immune to all disease or being completely happy, *or* that there are no rights to education, or adequate medical care, or a decent standard of living?

7. Consider this argument: Rights are sometimes the grounds of duties; the debtor ought to repay the loan *because* his creditor has a right to be repaid. But the ground or reason for something must be distinct from that for which it is a reason; reiteration is not rational justification. Therefore, a right cannot be identical with the relative duty to which it gives rise. Is this a sound argument? Why or why not?

8. Some moral philosophers hold that although the injured party *ought* to love the person who hates her and forgive the person who harms her, the injuring person has no *right* to be loved or forgiven because he cannot claim it as his due. Again, some maintain that although the owner of a dog or cat has a duty to treat the pet humanely, the animal has no right to humane treatment since only moral agents can possess rights. Do you agree? If so, does this show that there are some relative duties that are not equivalent to rights?

9. The view that a right is a claim and that a claim is to be understood in terms of the process of claiming seems to be faced with a dilemma: If what one is claiming when one claims a right is something independent of the process of making a claim, then a right is something other than the process of claiming and not to be understood in terms of that process. But if there is no right outside the process waiting to be claimed, then there is nothing to be claimed and the process of claiming makes no sense at all. How might Feinberg try to deal with this dilemma? Would any such attempt be adequate?

10. Can one distinguish between having and making a claim? What would it be to

have a claim one never makes? Should a right be defined in terms of having or making a claim? Why?

11. If any claim theory of rights like Feinberg's is to apply to both legal and moral rights, there must be processes of moral claiming analogous to processes of claiming under the law. Are there? If so, describe examples of both legal and moral claiming. If not, should one completely reject Feinberg's theory *or* should one conclude that the expression "a right" means something different in morals from what it means in the law?

12. What is the difference between a valid claim and an invalid claim? What reason, if any, is there to identify a right with a valid claim rather than simply with a claim as such? Do you regard this as a sufficient reason?

13. What is the difference between having a right and having a duty? Does Hart's theory that a right is a protected choice explain what is essential to this distinction? How, for example, could it explain the different legal or moral positions of the creditor, who has a right to be repaid, and the debtor, who has a duty to repay?

14. As a member of the faculty of Washington University, I seem to have a right to use its library facilities and a duty to grade all written work assigned by and submitted to me. Is the former a protected choice and the latter no choice at all? I seem to have both a right and a duty to lecture regularly in the courses I teach. Can one really have both a right and a duty to do the same thing? If so, can Hart explain this? If not, why not?

15. Does the protected interest theory of rights have anything in common with the interest theory of value? Compare and contrast what Salmond means by "an interest" with what Perry (see Chapter 4) means by the same expression.

16. If "a right" means an interest protected by a rule, can there be any natural rights—that is rights independent of human convictions or conventions? Is there any natural law? If so, in what manner might the natural law protect human interests? If not, what might we mean by speaking of moral rights?

17. Suppose that one adopts the view that "a right" means an interest protected by a rule. Then there would seem to be two ways to prove conclusively that blacks do not have a right to preferential admissions. One would be to prove that preferential admissions is not in the interest of black Americans; the other would be to show that this interest is not protected by any rule. Are these really the appropriate sorts of arguments to use to prove that blacks have no right to preferential admissions? If so, are the negative arguments in the previous chapter either disguised forms of these two modes of reasoning or irrelevant arguments? If not, must we reject Salmond's definition of "a right"?

18. Precisely how does the interest-based reason theory of rights differ from the protected interest theory? What are the relative advantages and disadvantages of each sort of theory? Which one do you consider more plausible? Why?

19. Suppose that one denied that "a right" can be defined as an interest-based reason but asserted that rights are grounded in interests. Would such a philosophical position be stronger or weaker than that of Raz? Why?

20. Raz holds that by definition a right is a reason for a duty or duties. Does every right imply some duty? What duty, for example, does my right to park in front of my house imply? Does a right ever imply anything other than or in addition to a duty? Does my right to free speech, for example, imply that I have a liberty to speak freely?

11
CAPITAL PUNISHMENT

*Whoso sheddeth man's blood, by man
shall his blood be shed.*

Genesis 9:6

*No one is hanged who has money in his
pocket.*

Russian Proverb

Many people believe that, as the Declaration of Independence affirms, all
human beings are born with an inalienable right to life. Presumably, the
reason, or at least one of the reasons, that murder is wrong is that it is a
violation of the victim's right to life. But what of the criminal's right to life?
In most societies throughout history, the punishment for murder has been
execution. If the murderer is a human being, and surely he or she is, and if
his or her right to life is inalienable, as human rights are usually taken to
be, then the murderer has a right to life that he has not forfeited by his
criminal act. It would appear that capital punishment is as much a violation
of the fundamental human right to life as murder itself. It seems to follow
that the execution of a condemned criminal is always wrong. This raises the
question of whether there are any circumstances that morally justify capital
punishment.

This question is an issue of lively debate these days. Great Britain
abolished the death penalty in 1969 for all crimes except wartime offenses
such as treason or spying, but with the increase in crimes of violence, there
has been a rising demand for the restoration of capital punishment for
crimes such as the murder of a policeman or a child. In *Furman* v. *Georgia*
(1972), the United States Supreme Court declared unconstitutional any
statute imposing capital punishment at the discretion of the judge or jury,

but it left undecided the constitutionality of the death penalty itself. As a result, many states have since then enacted new statutes making the imposition of the death penalty mandatory in the case of certain crimes such as first-degree murder or kidnapping. The morality and effectiveness of such statutes continues to be debated in Congress and in the state legislatures.

DEFINING THE PROBLEM

Let us try to define this specific moral problem more precisely. The expression "capital punishment" is ambiguous. It often refers to a certain kind of social institution. The institution of capital punishment is one pattern of punishment that forms part of the legal system in many, but not all societies. It involves certain roles like those of the executioner and the criminal and certain rules such as the rule that only a person condemned to death by the courts is to be executed. One may well question the moral justifiability of this social institution, but this is not the question raised here. Instead, let us interpret the expression "capital punishment" as referring to a species of acts, acts of executing someone for conduct judged to be criminal.

The question is whether such acts are right or wrong; this is not to ask whether such acts are virtuous or wicked. Presumably the act of executing an innocent person is wrong, ought not to be done, even when there may be nothing wicked in the act of an executioner who conscientiously performs his painful duty in complete ignorance of any judicial error. Again, even if it is granted that a given act of executing an incurably vicious criminal is right, it would not follow that there is any moral goodness in the act if the executioner performs it in order to enjoy the suffering of the victim rather than from a sense of duty to society. To ask whether an act ought or ought not to be done is not to ask whether it is morally praiseworthy or blameworthy. It is the former, the question of rightness or wrongness, that is at issue here.

Finally, the question is whether capital punishment is *ever* right, whether there are any exceptional circumstances in which the act of executing a condemned criminal may be morally justifiable. No one could seriously maintain that capital punishment is always right, that condemned criminals should always be executed. An act of lynching performed by an enraged mob is a heinous wrong even when the mob has condemned its victim with a mock trial. In a less spectacular way, it is morally wrong to take a criminal's life for any trivial crime like shoplifting or speeding on the highway. The only serious alternatives are that it is always wrong to execute a condemned criminal, no matter how great his or her crime, and that, in a few cases, it is right to take a criminal's life for conduct judged to be very, very wrong. Hence, the question worth discussing is "Is capital punishment ever right?"

individuals is already to begin to exterminate the society. Moreover, certain laws, such as the law prohibiting murder, are necessary if any collection of individuals are to live together in organized society. Hence, to break those laws that alone make the existence of society possible is to threaten that society with death. Capital punishment is sometimes right because it is right for society to exercise its right to self-defense, and in extreme cases capital punishment does defend the society from the attacks of a criminal that threaten its very existence.

Fulfilling a Duty

Executing a condemned criminal is sometimes right because it fulfills the duty of the executioner. Each of us plays many roles in society. I, for example, am a husband, a father, a citizen, and a professor. Each social role brings with it certain duties. As a husband, my duties are at least to support my wife financially, to share certain household responsibilities, and to care for my wife in sickness and in health. To accept the position of professor in a university is to accept the duties of preparing lectures, grading tests and papers, holding regular office hours when students can come for help in their studies, and doing original research as well. Similarly, the social role of public executioner brings with it certain duties, the chief of which is executing those condemned to death by the courts. No doubt it would be morally wrong for you or me to take the life of the criminal, no matter how guilty he or she might be. But it is right for the executioner to perform the act of capital punishment because he or she is acting in fulfillment of his or her duty as public executioner, and it is right to fulfill the duties of one's social role.

These are five arguments for capital punishment. It prevents the criminal from doing additional evil acts. It deters others from committing serious crimes. It is just retribution for the great wrong the criminal has done. It is society's act of killing in self-defense. And it fulfills the chief duty of the executioner. It is worth remembering that none of these arguments pretends to prove that all acts of capital punishment are right; each is intended to show only that it is sometimes right to execute a condemned criminal.

ARGUMENTS AGAINST CAPITAL PUNISHMENT

Any serious moral problem is two-sided. If all or most of the relevant considerations are on one side of the fence, everyone knows where the right course of action lies and there is no real moral problem. In the case of every live moral issue, like that of capital punishment, there is room for sincere and persistent disagreement because plausible arguments on one side can be met with equally plausible arguments on the other side of the issue. Having surveyed the arguments in support of capital punishment, let us look at the arguments of those who insist that capital punishment is always wrong, that it is never right to execute the condemned criminal no matter how evil his crime.

The Moral Law

Capital punishment is always wrong because it is always a violation of the moral law. The moral law consists of those rules that specify which kinds of acts are morally right and which kinds are morally wrong. Historically, it has been thought of in various ways. In the Judeo–Christian tradition, the moral law is usually taken to be the set of commands issued by God, whether limited to the Ten Commandments or including the many mandates inscribed in the books of the Bible. Rationalistic philosophers have tended to ignore or reject revelation and think of moral laws as self-evident truths about right and wrong discoverable by the natural light of human reason. However the moral law may be conceived, it is usually presumed to forbid killing, to prohibit the intentional killing of a human being. Since the moral law declares that killing a human being is always wrong and since the act of capital punishment is obviously an act of killing a human being, capital punishment is always morally wrong.

Monstrous Harm

Capital punishment is always wrong because it is always wrong to do monstrous harm. Although lesser evils may be outweighed by greater goods, there are some acts that do such great harm that under no circumstances could they be morally justified. The Nazi extermination of millions of Jews inflicted such monstrous harm upon these innocent people that no real or imagined benefits to humanity could outweigh its wrongness. On a lesser scale, capital punishment also does almost indescribable harm. By definition, it deprives its victim of his or her very life. The loss of a human life is the greatest of evils because life is the most precious of all human goods. Not only is life the necessary condition of any other good at all, it is intrinsically good to the highest degree. That we prize life above all other things is shown by the way we cling to life and resist death even when everything else seems lost.

In addition to the obvious harm of inflicting death, capital punishment causes cruel and inhuman suffering. It may be that the moment of death is almost painless, although this is not always so. Still, the period of awaiting execution is one of almost unrelieved torture. With few if any interesting activities to distract the condemned prisoner, there is little to think about but impending doom. Under these circumstances, the fear of

society must be fully committed to the sanctity of human life; its members must believe deeply that the life of every human being is inviolable. To suggest that special circumstances justify killing is to open the door to murder; to insinuate that some individuals may be justly killed is to begin to allow the elimination of the physically deformed, the mentally retarded, and the emotionally disturbed whenever caring for these unfortunate souls proves onerous. The security of life and limb and the mutual restraint of anger and aggression so vital to any moral society are undermined by any legal system that practices and sanctions the killing of human beings.

Capital punishment also caters to the baser instincts in the members of society. Although repressed by civilization, deep within human nature are the desires to torture and kill those we hate. These morally evil and socially dangerous desires are excited and strengthened by the spectacle of society taking the lives of those it has condemned. This spectacle, moreover, stimulates a morbid fascination with death, a fascination repugnant to any healthy and sensitive mind.

Finally, although the act of execution is intended to reduce crime by terrifying the potential criminal, in a peculiar way it actually encourages crime by glamorizing the criminal. A person condemned to death becomes famous overnight, and many who learn of his or her terrible fate cannot help but sympathize. That many unfortunate persons are almost fatally attracted to such fame and sympathy is witnessed by the flood of false confessions that follows any capital crime. The same unhappy attraction causes others to perform criminal acts themselves in the pathetic hope of attaining public recognition and even respect. In these various ways, capital punishment corrupts any society that practices it. Since it is always wrong to destroy the moral character of one's society, capital punishment is always wrong.

So they go, five arguments against capital punishment. It violates the moral law that the deliberate killing of human beings is wrong. It is an act of doing monstrous harm. It is an unnecessary evil. It is irremediable. And it corrupts society. Each of these arguments is advanced to establish a very strong conclusion, that the act of executing a condemned criminal is always, not just sometimes or usually, wrong.

CRITICISM OF SOME ARGUMENTS

We have summarized briefly some of the arguments for and against capital punishment. The task of weighing the pro arguments against the con arguments in order to determine which side has the stronger case remains. No argument can be taken at its face value; the reasonable person not only insists that conclusions be supported with reasons, but also subjects all reasoning to critical reexamination. Plausible as an argument may be at first glance, it may fail to establish its conclusion either because it assumes some false premise or because its conclusion does not follow logically from its premises. Let us, therefore, take another and a closer look at two of the arguments concerning capital punishment.

The Moral Law

The first argument to be critically examined is that capital punishment is always wrong because it violates the moral law. Two lines of attack are particularly worthy of note. One questions the content of the moral law; the other questions its very existence.

If there is a moral law, precisely what does it decree? One traditional way of determining the content of the moral law is by consulting revelation—for example, the word of God passed on to us in the Bible. Apparently, the moral law does forbid all acts of killing, for one of the Ten Commandments is "Thou shalt not kill" (Exod. 20:13). Since the act of executing a condemned criminal is obviously an act of killing, it follows that it is against the moral law and, accordingly, morally wrong.

Defenders of capital punishment contend that this commandment cannot be taken literally. Without challenging the authenticity of the passage quoted, they point out that it is not always easy to interpret the real meaning of any isolated quotation from the Holy Scriptures. Each passage must be understood in the light of its entire biblical context. Obviously, God did not mean to forbid every act of killing, including swatting an annoying mosquito or killing cattle for food. At most the Sixth Commandment means "Thou shalt not kill human beings." But if one is to go this far in spelling out the meaning of the passage, why not go farther and read it as "Thou shalt not murder human beings," recognizing that God considers killing in self-defense as morally justified? Since only murder, or the unjustified killing of human beings, is prohibited by the Sixth Commandment, it would be begging the question to use this passage to prove that capital punishment is unjustified.

The obvious reply is that to go so far in watering down the Sixth Commandment is to empty it of all content. God would not have bothered to announce the vacuous truth that unjustified killing is always unjustified; even the fool knows that in his heart. God's purpose in proclaiming the Sixth Commandment was clearly to prohibit the destruction of his creation, the human race. Since all human beings are made in the image of God (Gen. 1:26), God has forbidden the taking of any human life, even that of the sinner or the criminal.

But has He? Another passage from the Mosaic texts is "He that striketh a man with a will to kill him, shall be put to death" (Exod. 21:12). Far from prohibiting capital punishment, this part of the moral law seems to

mands issued by God, then the atheist must deny that any such law exists; for there can be no law, in this sense, without a lawgiver. There are many reasons to deny the existence of God, perhaps the strongest of which is that the existence of evil in our world is incompatible with its having been created by an omniscient, omnipotent, and all-good Being. If there is no divine Creator to issue commands to his creatures, there is no divine command against killing that can be used as the basis for an argument against capital punishment.

The opponent of capital punishment may try to save his or her argument by one or more of the traditional theological moves, explaining the place that evil has in the divine plan or suggesting that the finite human intellect should not presume to fathom the inscrutable purposes of an infinite God. He or she may advance one of the rational proofs for the existence of God or may appeal to revelation to establish His existence. In one way or another, he or she may defend the reality of the moral law by defending the claim that the divine Lawgiver really does exist. The details of any debate between the theist and the atheist belong more properly to theology than to ethics, but anyone interested in ethics should remember that a moral issue can sometimes hinge on a theological one. Another way in which the opponent of capital punishment may try to save this argument is by reinterpreting the moral law in such a way that its existence does not depend upon the existence of God. If the moral law is a set of self-evident truths about right and wrong action, then its reality need not be touched by atheism.

There are, however, other considerations that throw doubt upon the existence of any self-evident moral principles. A statement or proposition is self-evident only if its truth can be seen without proof by any rational person who understands its meaning and pays attention to it. If any moral principles were self-evident, then all rational persons who understood them and reflected carefully upon them should agree that they are true. There are, however, no moral principles universally accepted by all rational individuals. To some it seems self-evident that it is always wrong to deliberately kill a human being; to others reason seems to reveal that it is not wrong to kill under duress of circumstances; to still others it seems more reasonable to condemn killing under duress but to permit it in self-defense. Where rational persons disagree, how can it be contended that there is a truth evident to human reason? No doubt some moral disagreements can be traced to the irrationality, the stupidity, the misunderstanding, or the inattentiveness of one of the disputants; other disagreements cannot be explained away in this fashion. The fact that disagreement concerning basic moral principles resists all reasoning convinces many that there are no self-evident principles of right and wrong. If the moral law is supposed to consist of self-evident principles, then there is no moral law against killing to which one can appeal to condemn capital punishment.

Once more the opponent of capital punishment has two choices. One can try to defend the existence of self-evident moral principles or one can revise his conception of the moral law. If one chooses the former alternative, one can point out that to say that a moral principle is self-evident is not, in spite of popular parlance, to say that it is obvious. When a philosopher says that a principle is self-evident, he or she means that its truth is evident without further evidence to any completely rational person who fully understands its meaning and pays careful attention to it. Only a person whose intellectual powers have fully matured may be able to recognize a complex self-evident principle, and then one may require considerable explanation and great mental effort to see its truth. Hence, persistent moral disagreement need not be incompatible with self-evident moral principles. The possibility always exists that disagreements are due to an incompletely developed reason, or to a partial comprehension of a complex principle, or to an insufficient effort to hold the principle before the mind.

If, on the other hand, the opponent of capital punishment chooses to revise his or her conception of the moral law, he or she can concede that moral principles are not self-evident and then explain that the moral law consists simply of the set of true principles of right or wrong. These principles are not self-evident; they are generalizations from the moral experience of the individual and of society. If it were not possible to generalize about right and wrong in this way, it would be impossible to acquire moral wisdom from past experience or to teach the young how to act morally in recurring types of situations. The moral law that it is wrong to kill human beings is a universal generalization established by reflection on the harmfulness of past acts of murder. Since this moral law prohibits killing, capital punishment is always wrong.

The defender of capital punishment may doubt the existence of any moral law in even this attenuated form. What is now called *situation ethics* is a rejection of moral legalism of every sort. Whether it is thought of as a command of God, a self-evident principle, or a generalization from moral experience, a moral law is a *universal* rule of right or wrong. Situation ethics denies that it is ever possible to truly assert that *all* acts of some specific kind are right or wrong. No doubt the intentional killing of human beings is usually, almost always, wrong. But it is not morally wrong in every case because there are exceptional cases, like killing in self-defense, in which it may be right to kill. Nor is it possible to generalize about such exceptions and to write them into the moral law, for the variety of morally relevant factors is indefinite, and unimagined circumstances can always arise. Each situation must be judged in its own terms because each situation is morally unique. Whether capital punishment is right or wrong depends upon the circumstances and the details of the particular case at hand. There is no universal law to which one can appeal to prove it wrong in every case.

The debate does not stop here, of course, but it is not important for our purposes to follow it to the end. By this time we can clearly see that the argument "Capital punishment is always wrong because it violates the moral law against killing" is subject to criticism. It can be challenged in several ways, two of which involve questioning the content of the moral law and questioning the existence of that law. Such challenges do not show that the argument is to be rejected out of hand, for there are ways of responding to each challenge. What they do show is that one cannot finally judge the strength or weakness of this, or any other, moral argument until one has thought through this process of challenge and response. A deep commitment to the importance of this process of criticism is one of the marks of a genuine philosopher.

Deterrence

Let us now turn our critical attention to a second argument, this time one for capital punishment. The execution of a condemned criminal is sometimes right because it serves as an example to deter other potential criminals. The question usually asked about this argument is whether its factual premise is true. Does capital punishment actually deter the potential criminal? This question takes at least three forms.

(1) *Has reform destroyed the effectiveness of capital punishment as a deterrent?* In the good old days, executions were public and death was brought about in painful and humiliating ways. From the Bible we learn that adulteresses were stoned to death and that thieves were crucified. In England criminals were traditionally hung by the neck until dead and their corpses were displayed on gibbets for all to see. Under such circumstances, it might plausibly be argued that all those who witnessed capital punishment would be terrified enough to desist from any crimes likely to bring a similar fate upon themselves. But the process of reform has transformed capital punishment into something far less terrifying and, therefore, far less effective as a deterrent. For one thing, death is now brought about in the most humane manner possible; the electric chair is swift and the gas chamber an instrument of almost painless sleep. For another, executions now take place in a decent privacy, unseen by the eyes of any potential criminal. It is hardly plausible to claim that an impersonal newspaper account of a quick and painless death at some distant secluded place, should the potential criminal happen to read it, will terrify him or her sufficiently to deter acts of crime.

Those who continue to believe that capital punishment does deter can reply that the reformer overlooks the impact of modern media of publicity and underestimates the power of the fear of death. Capital punishment is big news and popular copy. The criminal awaiting execution, the reactions of his or her relatives, and the execution itself all receive widespread coverage through radio and television, magazines and books, as well as in the newspapers. In modern society, it is impossible for anyone to grow up unaware of and unimpressed by the fact that people are put to death for the most serious crimes. It is not necessary that the actual execution be televised or that it take some inhumane form because the fear of death is so profound and intense in human nature that the mere prospect of death in any form shakes any person to the core. The reform of capital punishment has made it more humane, and therefore more justifiable morally, without undermining its effectiveness as a deterrent.

(2) *What does the empirical evidence show about the effectiveness of capital punishment as a deterrent?* The factual question of whether or not capital punishment really does deter potential criminals is not to be decided by armchair speculation but by scientific investigation. The most obvious sort of evidence is statistical. At one time, when execution still took place by public hanging, it was discovered that of 167 condemned criminals awaiting execution in Bristol prison, 164 had personally witnessed one or more executions. When such a high proportion of those criminals were not deterred by actually seeing others put to death for major crimes, how can any scientific mind continue to believe that execution is an effective deterrent?

The defender of capital punishment can reply that these statistics carry very little scientific weight. The sample is very small and very atypical. A careful scientist will not draw any conclusion until he or she has examined data ranging over a much larger proportion of the total population and in which all segments of that population (noncriminal as well as criminal, rural as well as urban, etc.) are represented. Fragmentary and impressionistic statistics make colorful copy but inadequate evidence.

Social scientists have recently gathered much more massive statistical data, the most significant falling into two classes. The first class of data consists of statistics concerning the frequency of murders per thousand population in adjoining states, one of which does and the other of which does not punish such crimes by execution; adjoining states are selected for comparison in the hope that other variable factors may be held constant. The second class of data consists of statistics concerning the relative frequency of murders in a single state or country before and after capital punishment has been abolished or introduced. Both sets of evidence show that the presence or absence of the death penalty seems to make no statistically significant difference in the frequency of acts of crime. Many regard this statistical evidence as conclusive disproof of the claim that capital punishment is an effective deterrent.

Some of those who justify capital punishment on the grounds that it is a deterrent do not capitulate, however. They contend that such statistical evidence is unreliable because it is always possible to find some set of statistics to confirm one's prejudices; the most favorable data can be selected and analyzed in a way that supports whatever conclusion one began with. If we want to know whether capital punishment really deters the potential criminal, they argue, we should consult the experts, those who have special knowledge of crime and are thoroughly familiar with the criminal mind. Policemen, judges, and prison wardens are overwhelmingly convinced that the death penalty is an effective deterrent. Such authoritative judgments must not be disregarded.

Moreover, self-observation will reveal to any individual the psychological effectiveness of capital punishment. A person can learn most directly and most reliably about human nature by introspection; in looking into oneself one becomes aware of the human nature shared by all people. Upon sincere reflection, each person will discover a personal fear of death in any and all forms. What is true of one human being is true of all. The effectiveness of capital punishment as a deterrent is guaranteed by the powerful and abiding fear of death native to the human mind as revealed to each of us by introspection.

(3) *Who is deterred by capital punishment?* It is poor psychology to generalize about human nature because different people respond very differently to similar stimuli. Self-observation by any normal person, even if it were reliable, would prove at most that the death penalty is an effective deterrent for all *normal* human beings. But for such persons, it is alleged, there is no need for the death penalty. The normal human being is rational enough and sufficiently imbued with a social conscience to be deterred from seriously antisocial acts by inner inhibitions. An investigation of crimes seems to show, however, that at the time of action the mental state of most criminals is such that the fear of death would not deter them at all. The mere existence of the death penalty would not deter the criminal who is oblivious to the punishment legally prescribed for his act. A surprising number of criminals act in the firm belief that they will never be apprehended by the police or that a judge or jury will never impose the death penalty in their case. Why should they be deterred by a penalty they never expect to suffer? Many acts of killing are not premeditated but take place incidentally in the course of committing some other crime; for example, a bank robber may pull the trigger when he intends only to threaten the teller, or a burglar may shoot the householder when resisting capture after being surprised in an attempted theft. Reflection upon capital punishment would hardly deter these criminals from their unpremeditated killings. Many crimes are committed while the criminal is in some abnormal state of mind such that the thought of the death penalty would not come to mind or affect his or her behavior if it did; the jealous husband may kill his wife's lover in the heat of passion, or the paranoid wife may kill her husband in an irrational furor. Since the normal person is inhibited from criminal acts without the threat of the death penalty and since most criminals act under conditions that preclude the psychological effectiveness of the fear of

death, who is left to be deterred by capital punishment? The answer insinuated is that nobody, or almost nobody, is deterred by the act of execution. Hence, deterrence cannot be used as an argument for capital punishment.

The defender of capital punishment may reply that this attack exaggerates the abnormality of the criminal mind. Although a few criminals may be feebleminded or emotionally sick, the vast majority are normal persons who have turned to crime because of environmental factors such as an almost complete lack of economic opportunity, intolerable living conditions, or mistreatment by other persons. Their acts of crime do not prove them to be mentally abnormal or subhuman, for depth psychology has shown that even the best of us have selfish, aggressive, and antisocial impulses. Nor do solid citizens have any monopoly on the milk of human kindness; even thieves usually have enough fellow-feeling and integrity to cooperate within the gang. The average criminal is normal enough to be moved by the fear of death basic to human nature. If not, why is it that almost every criminal condemned to death so strenuously seeks the commutation of his sentence?

Once more we have seen that stating an argument may be only the first step in reasoning about some specific moral problem. Not only must one go on to consider the other arguments that can be given pro and con, one must subject each argument to rational criticism. Criticism may take diverse forms, but let us take note of two fundamental distinctions. One distinction is that between challenging the logical validity of the argument and challenging the acceptability of one of its premises. To challenge the validity of an argument is to charge that its premises, even if true, do not establish the conclusion, that the logical inference from premises to conclusion is mistaken. More often, however, one grants the logic of the argument and charges that one or more of its assumptions is mistaken. Consider the argument that capital punishment does not deter because 164 of 167 criminals awaiting execution in Bristol prison had witnessed executions. To claim that such a small sample proves little or nothing is to challenge the logic of the argument; to suggest that the figures cited are mistaken is to challenge the truth of one of its premises. The other distinction is that between challenging a moral premise and challenging a factual premise. Most of the criticism of the argument that capital punishment violates the moral law centered on the moral assumption that killing is always wrong. Most of the criticism against the argument that capital punishment deters potential criminals challenged the factual assumption that execution is an effective deterrent. Only after this process of criticism can one weigh with any confidence the strength or weakness of any argument.

A CRITICAL CONCLUSION

My own critical conclusion, based on considerable but hardly exhaustive reflection, is that capital punishment is always morally wrong because it is a monstrous and unnecessary evil. We are normally not aware of the horror of capital punishment because we are ignorant of its details and insensitive to the suffering of those who mean little to us, but accounts by those more directly acquainted with executions and more gifted with words than I portray its enormity in a compelling fashion. Death is normally the greatest of evils because it brings the complete and irrevocable end to every human aspiration. The humiliation and suffering of one awaiting death, and of those who know and love the criminal, are grievous and intolerable. That capital punishment is a monstrous evil can hardly be denied.

It might, of course, be contended that this great evil is necessary to save society from the greater evil of additional criminal acts by the criminal himself and others. Fully aware of the radical evil of capital punishment, I wonder whether acts of crime really are worse. In any event, it seems clear to me that capital punishment does not save society from very much crime. No doubt the act of execution does prevent the criminal from continuing his or her life of crime, although the evidence indicates that in many cases persons who commit one capital offense do not repeat such acts even when released from prison. Still, both reliable statistical data and the careful analysis of the psychology of crime seem to me to show conclusively that capital punishment is not an effective deterrent. If it does not accomplish its intended end of saving society from further crime, then it can hardly be a necessary means to that end. Moreover, it is not a necessary means to that end because life imprisonment is an equally effective means. Life imprisonment would, if it were genuinely imprisonment for the rest of the criminal's life, prevent him or her from doing great harm to society in the future. And fear of life imprisonment can serve about as well as fear of death as a deterrent to others, for both are terrifying prospects. Surely life imprisonment is bad enough so that capital punishment is an unnecessary evil.

In fact, life imprisonment may be too evil. While I am most unimpressed by the allegation that capital punishment is necessary as a deterrent to crime, I am gravely bothered by the very real possibility that, of the appropriate penalties for the most serious crimes, it may be the lesser of the two evils. In rejecting capital punishment in favor of life imprisonment, I may have exaggerated the badness of death and underestimated the evils of life imprisonment. To be sure, my death would be a great loss to me and perhaps to a few friends and relatives who love me. But most criminals have little hope of a satisfactory life in society and little of value to look forward to in prison. They tend also to be people who are somewhat isolated and not closely related to others who might care deeply about their loss. Surely, it is not mere life but the good life that is worth prizing; and the life of the criminal convicted of a capital crime offers little that is good and much that is very bad indeed. For that criminal, death may be a release from suffering much more than a loss of value. Moreover, life imprisonment may be an even more monstrous evil than capital punishment. Prison brings with it the physical hardships of cramped and uncomfortable quarters, lack of adequate exercise, and often hard labor. More grievous are the psychological hardships of living continuously without hope or purpose, in utter boredom, and with almost no opportunity to exercise the human faculties of imagination, intelligence, or love. For the dangerous criminal it may mean isolation and the almost complete loss of contact with other human beings. What personal relationships there are are usually abnormal and frustrating in a high degree; interchanges with the guards, prison officials, and other prisoners tend to be characterized by callousness, mistrust, fear, and hate. For younger men or women, the sexual deprivation can be intense; the best one can hope for is masturbation, homosexuality, or sodomy. And while the terror of awaiting execution has a stipulated termination, the horrors of prison life go on through an indefinite future until death brings release. Would not a quick death in the electric chair or gas chamber be more timely and more humane? Perhaps. On this score, I have very real doubts.

In spite of this uncertainty, I continue to believe that capital punishment is always wrong. Probably it is my respect for the right to life that decides this issue for me. I believe, although I do not know how to prove my belief true, that every human being possesses a fundamental right to life. I do not insist that this makes every act of taking human life wrong; I do not think that it is wrong to kill in self-defense. But I do insist that only the most extreme necessity can morally justify the act of killing a human being, and I can see no such necessity in the case of capital punishment. Hence, capital punishment is always wrong.

At least, it is wrong if I am correct in assuming that every human being has a basic right to life. But how can I know whether or not there is a fundamental human right to life? And how can I know whether this right to life, if it does exist, takes precedence over the right of society to punish those condemned for criminal acts? We will turn to the problem of moral knowledge in the next chapter.

STUDY QUESTIONS

1. Well, *is* capital punishment ever right? Try to draw and defend your own reasoned conclusion concerning this specific moral problem.

2. It is often argued that capital punishment is sometimes right because it redeems the criminal's soul through his suffering, or because it vents the wrath of society, or because it molds social values by public condemnation of great wrongs. Can you state each of these arguments fully enough to make explicit its tacit assumptions and to make clear its logical structure?

3. Others argue that capital punishment is always wrong because its vindictive spirit stands in the way of penal reform, or because judge and jury are seldom willing to invoke harsh punishment, or because it usurps God's right to determine the life or death of each human being. Can you formulate each of these arguments in explicit and precise language?

4. On the face of it, life imprisonment and the death penalty should both be completely effective in preventing the condemned criminal from committing further acts of crime. Why does sentencing a criminal to life imprisonment not always succeed in preventing him from performing additional evil acts? Why is the death sentence not always effective either? Which penalty is more effective in preventing crime?

5. Does the fact that a person commits some major crime like murder or rape prove that his personality and character are such as to render him more dangerous to society than those convicted of lesser crimes? Are those who commit capital offenses more or less likely to repeat their crimes than those who commit other sorts of crimes?

6. Imagine that capital punishment could be made an effective deterrent by executing dangerous criminals in the most painful and humiliating manner in full view of close-up television. Would this fact then justify this sort of capital punishment? Why or why not?

7. Would deterrence, if it were in fact effective, morally justify capital punishment? If not, why not? If so, what degree of punishment would it justify? Suppose that rapists are relatively easy to deter while shoplifters, who are hard to detect as long as they steal small items, could be deterred only by great terror. Ought society to punish rape with a modest fine and shoplifting with capital punishment?

8. Does the demand for retribution spring from a vindictive desire to get revenge or from an impartial desire for justice? How do you know? Is the motive relevant to the rightness or wrongness, as opposed to the virtue or vice, of capital punishment?

9. If the principle of retribution requires that the punishment exactly balance the crime, this seems to imply an eye for an eye and a tooth for a tooth. Is it right, therefore, to maim the maimer and to rape the rapist?

10. It is alleged that, however much it may seem required by the theory of justice, in practice capital punishment is unjust because poor and minority groups suffer a disproportionate share of criminal executions. Why might this be so? If so, would this fact prove that criminals ought not to be executed or that our legal system ought to be improved in some other way?

11. Suppose that the principle of retribution, that each person ought to be treated as he deserves, is repudiated. Does it follow that it might be right to punish the innocent or to inflict capital punishment for minor crimes? Suppose that one insists that the punishment ought to fit the crime. What feature of the crime—its moral wrongness, its wickedness, or its social harmfulness—should it fit? What is the measure of its fittingness?

12. Is capital punishment really like killing an attacker in self-defense or is it more like killing a prisoner of war after he has surrendered and is rendered helpless?

13. Does each individual have a right to kill in self-defense? Why or why not? If it is right to kill in self-defense, does this imply that there is nothing wrong in killing human beings? If it is not right to kill in self-defense, does this imply that it is better for the innocent victim to die than for the aggressor to die?

14. Does society, as well as the individual, have a right to kill in self-defense? If so, do social rights have the same ground or justification as human rights? If not, why not?

15. Does the murderer or kidnapper really threaten the life of society? If so, explain precisely and in detail how a single murderer or kidnapper could possibly destroy a whole society. If not, explain how a society can continue to exist without maintaining law and order.

16. Are we obligated to fulfill the duties of our social roles for the most part? If so, what is the ground of this moral obligation? Ought we to fulfill the duties of our social roles in every case? If not, how does one tell when one ought not to do one's duty?

17. Suppose that society ought not to have the practice of capital punishment. Does it follow that the public executioner's acts of fulfilling his duties under that practice are wrong? Is it always wrong for an individual to participate in an imperfect social institution? On the other hand, can the executioner claim that his acts are not wrong because it is society, and not he, that is morally responsible for capital punishment?

18. It is sometimes argued that life imprisonment is a more inhumane punishment than execution because it is a more prolonged suffering and degrades its victims to a mere animal level. Which punishment is really more cruel? Does the criminal really deserve any sympathy from society?

19. Do you believe that it is morally wrong to kill a human being? Can you formulate any universal moral principle that specifies precisely when it is wrong to kill human beings? Can you think of any kinds of cases that might seem to be exceptions to your principle? How does one know whether some seeming exception really is an exception?

20. Suppose that most human beings are unable to state the basic principles of moral law in explicit and exact language. Does it follow that they never know whether a given act is right or wrong? If they can tell right from wrong, how can they recognize a right act without any moral law to serve as a standard of rightness?

21. Is the life of a human being really the most precious of all goods? Why or why not? If its value lies in the fact that it is a necessary condition of the enjoyment of all other goods, is it not also the necessary condition of the suffering of all evils?

22. Is capital punishment a necessary or an unnecessary evil? If it is a necessary evil, what greater evil is it a means of avoiding? If it is an unnecessary evil, what other practicable means is there to save society from further crimes?

23. It is alleged that it is not wrong to do evil when doing evil is a necessary means of avoiding some greater evil. Does this mean that the end justifies the means? If the end does not justify the means, what would justify any means? If the end does morally justify the means, why is this doctrine so often thought to be immoral?

24. It is often alleged that imprisonment is as irremediable as capital punishment because an innocent person pardoned after a few years in prison can never return to anything like his former life. He will have lost his job and find it difficult to find another, will have lost contact with his friends and family, will emerge from a prison a changed person, and will never be fully accepted by society. Are both penalties really irremediable? If so, does it follow that they are both morally unjustified?

25. Is irremediability in itself a reason against some punishment? Would it matter if there were no remedy at all for some slight punishment? If so, exactly why would it matter? If not, is it the seriousness and not the irremediability of capital punishment that is morally objectionable?

26. Some allege that capital punishment corrupts society. Others contend that it teaches moral values by publicly condemning criminal acts. Which view seems more accurate to you? How important a factor is the corrupting or educative impact of capital punishment in determining whether it is right or wrong? If important, does this imply that all the other considerations are irrelevant or trivial? If unimportant, does this imply that the moral character of a society does not matter very much?

27. Since every act can serve as an example to others, it would seem that doing a morally wrong act is always morally corrupting and doing a morally right act is never corrupting. Is this really so? If it is so, does it follow that the argument "Capital punishment is wrong because it corrupts society" is circular because to claim that it corrupts is to presuppose that it is wrong? If it is not so, precisely how could one corrupt society by doing what is morally right?

28. How can we measure or judge the relative evil of capital punishment and life imprisonment? Can we really know the value of either without firsthand experience? Can one person ever experience and compare both?

29. Most of us are largely unaware of the evils of either penalty, and it requires considerable literary skill to convey vividly and in detail the nature of capital punishment and life imprisonment. Does a writer's command of language serve to reveal the objective evil of some penalty to us or only convey his prejudiced condemnation? Is literature ever a valuable source of moral insight? Why or why not?

30. Is there really any fundamental human right to life? If so, does it follow that capital punishment is always wrong? Does it also follow that it is always wrong to kill in self-defense? If not, does it follow that there is nothing wrong in capital punishment?

31. Which of the arguments for and against capital punishment stand up best under critical examination? Which formulation of each is the strongest? Can any of the usual arguments be rejected as worthless? If so, which ones and on what grounds can they be thrown out? If several arguments on both sides of the issue remain, how can one determine where the weight of the evidence lies?

32. The Supreme Court has recently declared that the execution of criminals condemned to death at the discretion of a judge or jury is unconstitutional because it is a cruel and unusual punishment. Such punishment was declared cruel because it is more severe than required by statute, more harsh than necessary to deter potential criminals, offensive to contemporary moral values, and degrading to human dignity. It was held unusual because it is in fact rarely imposed even when permitted by law, and when it is imposed it is inflicted in an arbitrary and discriminatory manner. Could one construct an

analogous argument to prove that capital punishment is not unconstitutional, but morally wrong? If so, how would this argument differ from the argument that capital punishment is wrong because it causes monstrous harm?

BIBLIOGRAPHY

BECCARIA, CESARE BONESANA. *On Crimes and Punishments,* chap. 16. Translated by Henry Paolucci. Indianapolis: The Bobbs-Merrill Co., 1963.

BEDAU, HUGO ADAM, ed. *The Death Penalty in America,* 3rd ed. New York: Oxford University Press, 1982.

BEDAU, HUGO ADAM, AND PIERCE, C. M., eds. *Capital Punishment in the United States.* New York: AMS Press, 1976.

BLOM-COOPER, LOUIS, ed. *The Hanging Question.* Duckworth & Co., 1969.

BOWERS, W. *Executions in America.* Lexington, Mass.: Lexington Books, 1974.

CAMUS, ALBERT. *Reflections on the Guillotine: An Essay on Capital Punishment.* Translated by Richard Howard. Michigan City, Ind.: Fridtjof-Karla Press, 1959.

COOPER, D. *The Lesson of the Scaffold.* Columbus: Ohio State University Press, 1974.

DARROW, CLARENCE SEWARD, AND TALLEY, ALFRED J. *Debate, Resolved: That Capital Punishment Is a Wise Public Policy.* New York: League for Public Discussion, 1924.

INGRAM, T. R., ed. *Essays on the Death Penalty.* Houston, Tex.: Saint Thomas, 1971.

KOESTLER, ARTHUR. *Reflections on Hanging.* London: Gollancz, 1956.

McCAFFERTY, JAMES A., ed. *Capital Punishment.* Chicago: Aldine-Atherton, 1972.

McCLELLAN, G. S., ed. *Capital Punishment.* New York: Wilson, 1979.

MELTSNER, M. *Cruel and Unusual: The Supreme Court and Capital Punishment.* New York: Random House, 1973.

SELLIN, THORSTEN, ed. *Capital Punishment.* New York: Harper & Row, 1967.

VAN DEN HAAG, ERNEST, AND CONRAD, JOHN P. *The Death Penalty: A Debate.* New York: Plenum, 1983.

WILLIAMS, GLANVILLE. *The Sanctity of Life and the Criminal Law.* New York: Alfred A. Knopf, 1957.

12
MORAL KNOWLEDGE

*Each of us should lay aside all other
learning, to study only how he may
discover one who can give him the
knowledge enabling him to distinguish the
good life from the evil.*

Plato in *The Republic*

Ethics becomes practical in the choice situation. It is when an individual must choose between the acts possible in a given situation that he or she can and must put a personal ethical theory into practice. To my mind, the central moral question is "What ought I to do?," asked by the person who must decide how to act. Often it requires a considerable amount of reflection and investigation to discover what the alternatives are, what acts one might do in these particular circumstances. But even after this is discovered, the problem of distinguishing between right and wrong acts remains. Which, among all the acts one might do, is the right act?

Frequently the answer to this very practical question is, or seems to be, obvious. It is clear, when we know something of the situation, that one alternative is right and the others wrong. Sometimes, however, it is far from clear which act is right. The moral agent may have serious doubts about which act is right even after a careful survey of the situation. Again, one may find that one's moral judgment conflicts with that of others. Such disagreement about right and wrong, especially if the parties to the dispute respect one another's character and intellect, can raise or intensify doubt about the right choice in the given situation. Doubt and disagreement about the correct answer to the question "Which act is right?" quite naturally raise another question, "How does one know which act is right?"

Let us imagine, for example, that John Smith, a public executioner, begins to wonder whether it would be morally right for him to carry through the execution scheduled for the next day. His urgent practical problem is "Ought I to pull that electric switch tomorrow?" He is well aware that the criminal has been condemned to death by a duly constituted court and that it is his primary duty as public executioner to carry out such death sentences. Still, reflection upon past executions and what he knows about the penal system may raise many specific moral problems for him. Does society ever have the right to take the life of a human being? Is death the worst of all evils or sometimes a blessing in disguise? Is the individual or society morally responsible for any evil one does in carrying out the duties of one's social role? Is capital punishment ever right? These moral problems may in turn raise many more general theoretical ethical questions. *If* the executioner can establish firmly the ethical principles needed to resolve these specific moral problems, then he can probably make his decision about what he ought to do tomorrow with a clear conscience. But if, as seems more likely, he cannot fully resolve these complex moral and ethical issues, then he is likely to remain in doubt about which of the acts open to him is the right one. What tentative conclusion he can reach may well be put in further doubt by the fact that his wife has come to a very different conclusion. He may have decided that, in the face of personal uncertainty, he ought to carry out his social duty. His wife may be convinced that the act of pulling that electric switch would be morally wrong. She may be less impressed with the stringency of social duties and more sensitive to the horrors of death for the victim and those who care about him. The executioner cannot reject his wife's qualms out of hand as mere sentimentality because he has found her moral judgment sound on past occasions and finds her quite ready on this occasion to support her qualms with reasons. As the executioner struggles with the moral and ethical problems raised by the choice confronting him and finds himself unable to resolve his disagreements with others about what he ought to do in this situation, he may ask, almost in desperation, "How can I know what I ought to do tomorrow?" or even "How can anyone ever know which act is right?"

METAETHICAL PROBLEMS

This question about our moral knowledge is a theoretical ethical question. It does not pose any specific moral problem because it is not limited to any species of act, such as acts of capital punishment or acts of civil disobedience, and because any answer to it is only indirectly applicable to practice. The question concerns our knowledge of the rightness or wrongness of all human actions of every kind, and the answer to it constitutes, if fully developed, an ethical theory. Such an answer would not, however, be a normative ethical theory; it would not affirm or maintain any norm or standard of moral rightness. To explain how one knows which acts are right is not the same as asserting that some act or class of acts actually is right; it is simply to tell one how to go about finding out whether or not some such assertion is true. A theory of moral knowledge need not make any moral judgments. It is a theory about moral judgments, and about the conditions under which they can claim to be genuine knowledge rather than mere conjecture. The question "How does one know which act is right?" poses a metaethical rather than a normative ethical problem.

This is not the first metaethical problem that we have met in our attempt to think through some specific moral issues. We found that in order to evaluate critically the arguments for and against the right of black people to preferential admissions we had to clarify our conception of "a right" because the soundness of these arguments often depended upon the precise meaning of "a right." The question "What do we mean by 'a right'?" is also a metaethical question. The answer to this question proposes a definition of "a right," explains what this word means in the English language. But it does not use the quoted word to make any statement about the existence or nonexistence of any alleged right.

Our concern in this chapter, however, is not so much with the meaning of the language of morals as with the nature of moral knowledge. It is well at the start to make one important qualification in order not to commit the fallacy of complex question, the error of demanding a single answer to what is really more than one question. To ask, "How does one know which act is right?" presupposes that human beings do know right from wrong and that the only interesting problem concerns how we go about gaining this knowledge. It would be better to reformulate our question so that we do not assume dogmatically and without proof that moral knowledge is possible. Let us ask, therefore, "How, if at all, does one know which act is right?" Thus formulated, our question poses two distinct, but related, metaethical problems: Can one know which act is right? And if so, how does one know which act is right?

Both problems concern our moral knowledge, or knowledge of what is morally right or wrong. Precisely what is knowledge? Any satisfactory answer to this important philosophical question belongs more to epistemology than to ethics or moral philosophy. Although it is not our business as moral philosophers to answer this question completely, neither can we completely ignore it. At the very least, we must remind ourselves that quite different conceptions of knowledge are possible and remain on guard lest such differences confuse our discussion of moral knowledge. As far as practicable, we should try to formulate our discussion in terms that will be fair to all the usual theories of knowledge. Moreover, we should try to pose our question in terms of a conception of knowledge that has genuine application to moral issues. Some epistemologists require a great deal of a person before they will grant that he really knows anything; other epistemologists require considerably less of the knower. Sometimes certainty is required for genuine knowledge. One cannot be said to really know something as long as the slightest possibility of error remains. If we insist upon such a strong definition of "knowledge," it is quite likely that the conception of knowledge does not apply to the moral sphere at all. It is very hard, if not impossible, to imagine any method of telling which act is right that rules out every conceivable possibility of error. Other epistemologists maintain that this quest for certainty is inappropriate and conceive of knowledge in terms of a somewhat weaker claim. One can distinguish between genuine knowledge and mere conjecture without claiming certainty for one's beliefs. Knowledge is more reliable than conjecture because the knower is in possession of some reasons to support a belief. The claim that one's belief is reliable and rationally justified seems to be strong enough to be worth insisting upon yet weak enough to be applicable to moral issues. Let us, therefore, conceive of knowledge in this manner throughout this chapter.

The question we are to discuss concerns one species of moral knowledge. It concerns our knowledge of right and wrong, not our knowledge of good and bad, virtue and vice, rights or justice. Moreover, it concerns our knowledge of the rightness or wrongness of individual acts, our knowledge that this act open to the individual moral agent in a given situation is or is not right. There is a considerable advantage in limiting our question to the knowledge of the rightness of individual acts, for this enables us to avoid the confusion that might arise from switching from one sort of moral knowledge to another; at the same time, it indicates as clearly as possible how solutions to this metaethical problem relate to moral decisions. We pay no great price for this gain because most theories about our knowledge of the rightness of individual acts can be extended with only minor modifications to the other sorts of moral knowledge. Enough of preliminaries. On to our question. How, if at all, does one know which act is right?

THEORIES OF MORAL KNOWLEDGE

Ethical Scepticism

The ancient sceptic Sextus Empiricus maintained that there is no way we can know which act is right because no human being can know the truth about right or wrong. This answer is sceptical because it denies the possibility of knowledge; it is ethical scepticism because the sort of knowledge it denies is knowledge of what is morally right or wrong. Notice that ethical scepticism does not deny that there is moral truth. Quite the contrary, it presupposes that in any choice situation there really is a difference between moral right and wrong. Accordingly, it admits that there is in each case a true answer to the question "Which act is right?" What it does deny is that any human being can ever know the answer to this question. In any situation, a person might believe that some one alternative was right and, if he were lucky, his belief might just happen to be true. But such a lucky belief does not constitute knowledge; it is not a reliable belief because the agent has no rational justification for it. The truth is there, and he might stumble upon it. Nevertheless, ethical scepticism insists that there is no way to know, no way to reach a reliable and rationally justified belief, about which act is right. Perhaps God knows, if there is a God, but mere human beings can never achieve moral knowledge.

Ordinarily the ethical sceptic has some fairly definite conception of what moral knowledge, if only we could attain it, would be. In fact, he or she usually holds to moral scepticism just because it seems that the limitations inherent in human nature make it impossible for anyone to achieve this ideal of knowledge he or she conceives so clearly and so tantalizingly. A moral philosopher might believe, for example, that right and wrong are determined by the commands of God and that knowing the commands of someone is hearing that person deliver the command and understanding the words used in the imperative. But he or she might deny our knowledge of right and wrong, believing that no human being can ever be in a position to hear and understand the Word of God. Perhaps when God speaks, He does not make sounds that the human ear is capable of hearing, or perhaps our finite human mind is incapable of interpreting the meaning of the commands of an Infinite Deity. Again, a moral philosopher might believe that rightness and wrongness are nonnatural characteristics of acts and at the same time believe that only the scientific method can give genuine knowledge. If the only way to achieve knowledge is through the empirical method of the natural sciences, then it follows that we cannot know the nonnatural rightness of any act. Once more ethical scepticism results from the conflict between a conception of what knowledge in morals would be— a kind of nonnatural moral science—and the limitations of the empirical methods of attaining knowledge that are available to us.

Is there any reason to accept ethical scepticism that is not grounded in some such limited conception of human knowledge? After all, not every moral philosopher believes that moral knowledge must consist in a revelation of the will of God or in a nonempirical science of nonnatural characteristics. One consideration often adduced in support of ethical scepticism is the persistence of moral disagreement among reasonable and well-informed persons. The mere existence of disagreement about which act is right in this or that situation proves nothing. If factual investigation regularly produced agreement, we would chalk up the initial disagreement to ignorance. If further discussion and reasoning between the disputants normally brought agreement, we would discount initial disagreement in moral judgments as prerational. Nor would the fact that some people are too stupid or too stubborn to be convinced by additional evidence and critical discussion lead us to reject the possibility of knowledge by informed and rational persons. What does seem to support ethical scepticism is the fact that reasonable individuals who have investigated the situation carefully, who seem to agree on all the facts, and who have thought through all the pro and con arguments, so often continue to disagree about which act is right in a given situation. The persistence of this kind of disagreement seems to imply that rational methods are incapable of resolving moral disagreements. If this is so, then it seems pointless and arbitrary to insist nevertheless that one party to the dispute is rationally justified in his moral belief while the other parties lack such justification. With no rational method of achieving reliable belief in moral judgment, moral knowledge is impossible, or so the ethical sceptic argues.

While the ethical sceptic may rest his or her case on the persistence of moral disagreement, an opponent may appeal to situations in which no such disagreement either exists or is easily imaginable. Although there are situations in which the morally right act is in serious doubt, there are also clear cases, situations in which every informed and reasonable person would agree on which act is right. If I am taking a solitary stroll along a mountain canyon and see an amateur climber fall from a cliff ahead of me, of course it would be right for me to come to her assistance and wrong for me to pass her by or rob her as she lies in helpless agony. What possible justification could there be for denying a knowledge of right and wrong in a situation where the difference between right and wrong is as obvious as it is here? To be sure, very few moral choices are as simple or straightforward as this one. There are a great many cases where we do not really know which act is right. It is only natural that we should disagree about complex and ambiguous cases. But the persistence of some moral disagreements should not blind us to the clear cases, the cases in which any rational and informed person can plainly see which act is right. The ethical sceptic denies that anyone can ever know which act is morally right. To refute ethical scepticism it is not necessary to go to the opposite extreme and prove that we can always tell right from wrong. All that is required is to point to a few clear cases, a few cases where moral disagreement is unthinkable. In these cases, few as they may be, we do know right from wrong. If so, it is not the case that no one can ever know which act is right, and ethical scepticism is mistaken.

Ethical Relativism

There is, however, another way to interpret those clear cases, those situations in which doubt or disagreement about which act is right cannot be imagined. Quite possibly, doubt is unthinkable, not because we all know which act is right in these cases, but because there is no moral truth to be either known or doubted. Recall that our central question is "How, *if at all,* does one know which act is right?" Neither the ethical sceptic nor the ethical relativist explains how one knows which act is right, for both repudiate the simpleminded question "How does one know which act is right?" on the grounds that this question falsely presupposes that moral knowledge is possible. They agree that one never does know right from wrong; they disagree, however, on the reason why such knowledge is impossible. The ethical sceptic holds that there is a truth about moral right and wrong, but insists that no human being can achieve any reliable and rationally justified belief about that truth. The ethical relativist goes even further; he or she denies that there is any truth about right or wrong. It is not that there is a moral truth just beyond our cognitive grasp—there is nothing there to be grasped or even groped for. People do, of course, judge this or that act morally right or wrong. However, their judgments are neither true nor false. The distinction between correct and incorrect, rational and irrational, just does not apply to moral judgments. There is no such thing as moral knowledge because knowledge is always a knowledge of some truth; and since moral judgments are neither true nor false, they are not the sorts of things that can be known, or doubted either. Those clear cases in which it is impossible to doubt which act is right do not reveal our moral knowledge; they are cases in which the claim to know is as out of place as is any doubt about the truth. Thus ethical relativism undermines the claim to moral knowledge in a manner even more radical than that of ethical scepticism. While the sceptic denies the claim, the relativist holds that the claim is entirely out of place, not so much mistaken as beside the point.

Ethical relativism is the theory that ethical judgments, including judgments of moral right and wrong, are relative rather than absolute. Relativists may disagree about what ethical and moral judgments are relative to. Some hold that they are relative to the individual judger, that whether an act is to be judged right or wrong depends on what each individual thinks about the act. Other relativists, like the anthropologist Melville Herskovits, maintain that ethical judgments are relative to culture, that whether an act is to be judged right or wrong depends on the culture in which the judger participates. All ethical relativists agree, however, in denying that ethical judgments are absolute. They agree that there is no standard of right and wrong independent of the judger or one's culture to serve as a measure of all moral judgments; there is no universal objective basis for judgments of right and wrong. What this denial really amounts to can be best seen in situations where several judgers make contrary judgments of right and wrong. What the relativist is denying is that, among any set of contrary moral judgments, one judgment is true or rationally justified while all contrary judgments are false or without rational justification. What the relativist is asserting is that moral judgers may disagree without error, that one judgment may be legitimate for one judger while a contrary judgment may be equally legitimate for another.

One strength of ethical relativism is the way in which it comes to terms with cultural relativism. Many moral philosophers believe that ethical relativism is required by the facts established by cultural anthropology. It does seem to be a scientifically proven fact that moral judgments are relative to culture. To say that something is relative to culture is to say two things—that it varies from culture to culture and that it is causally dependent upon culture. Moral judgments clearly vary with the culture. Acts judged wrong in our society, like marrying a second wife or killing a tenth child, are judged right in other cultures, like early Mormon society or some Polynesian societies. Moreover, what causes people to arrive at different judgments of right and wrong is the process of enculturation by which they absorb the mores and values of their respective societies. The moral philosopher's first impulse is to try to overcome this cross-cultural disagreement by appealing to universal moral principles, but the anthropologist is quick to point out that a principle accepted by a moral philosopher in one culture is likely to be rejected by his or her counterpart in another culture. If moral principles are as relative to culture as individual moral judgments are, then it seems to follow that there are no universal standards of right and wrong independent of the judger and his culture. If this is the case, then there is no rational basis for claiming that one moral conclusion is any more justified, objectively correct, or true than another. Thus the scientific fact of cultural relativism seems to require one to adopt the metaethical theory of ethical relativism.

One weakness of ethical relativism is that it seems to be literally incredible. There is no point in advocating it as a philosophical theory simply because no human being, not even the moral philosopher himself, can really believe it. It is easy enough to say that moral judgments are relative rather than absolute; it is impossible to believe it. To see why genuine belief is impossible we must reflect on precisely what it is that ethical relativism requires us to believe. We are required to believe that in every choice situation contrary judgments of right and wrong are equally legitimate because no one judgment is any more true or rationally justified than another. This implies that doubt and debate about which act is right are entirely out of place and inappropriate. We cannot doubt that act A is right, not because we know full well that it is right, but because there is no objective standard in terms of which the judgment that A is right could turn out to be mistaken. Again, it is unreasonable to debate whether act A or act B is the right one because the judgment that A is right is no more and no less rationally justified than the judgment that act B is right. However, when ethical relativists themselves are confronted with complex moral choices, they do not in fact cease to doubt their tentative judgments that this or that alternative is right. And when confronted with moral disagreement, they do not cease and desist from trying to persuade others by reasoning. What this shows is not that ethical relativists are absentminded or illogical, but that no rational person who lives in society and must choose which action is to be done can abstain from doubt and debate about right and wrong. It seems to follow that no person can genuinely and whole-heartedly accept ethical relativism, for this ethical theory would require this humanly impossible suspension of doubt and debate. Any unacceptable theory is unacceptable; that is, any theory that cannot be psychologically accepted by any philosopher ought not to be philosophically accepted by him. Put positively, the only moral theories that are worth serious consider-ation for philosophy are those that could be held by moral philosophers as moral agents. To adopt a theory that one cannot hold to in practice is to engage in self-deception and empty speculation. Therefore, any com-pletely honest and morally concerned philosopher will reject ethical relativism.

Ethical Emotivism

The emotive theory of ethics undercuts the question "How does one know which act is right?" in much the same way that ethical relativism does. We do not know this because there is nothing to be known; judgments of moral right and wrong are not the sort of thing that can be either known or unknown. The emotive theory rejects the possibility of moral knowl-edge, however, on a somewhat different ground than ethical relativism does. Relativism rejects the possibility of moral knowledge on the ground that there is no absolute standard by which any moral truth could be measured. Ethical emotivism rejects the possibility of moral knowledge on the basis of its analysis of the meaning of moral statements. When one understands what it means to say "This act is right" or "That act was morally wrong," one realizes that such sentences could be neither true nor false. Hence, there can be no question of how one knows which moral statements are true; the very question of knowing the moral truth is out of place.

Ethical emotivism in its pure form, maintained by the contemporary British philosopher A. J. Ayer, asserts that normative ethical sentences (sentences saying that something is good or bad, right or wrong) have emotive meaning and denies that such sentences have cognitive meaning. To understand this theory we must understand the distinction it draws between cognitive and emotive meaning. A sentence has cognitive meaning if it asserts or denies some proposition. The sentence is true if the asserted proposition corresponds with the facts and false if what is asserted by it is not the case. A sentence has emotive meaning if it expresses and/or evokes emotions, feelings, or attitudes. To express an emotion is to manifest in overt behavior, linguistic or nonlinguistic, some emotions of the speaker. To evoke an emotion is to cause some hearer or reader to have that emo-tion. Sentences like "Snow is white" or "Smoking causes lung cancer" typi-cally assert propositions; they have cognitive meaning on most occasions. Exclamations like "hurrah" or "shut up" are typically used with emotive meaning. "Hurrah" vents the excitement and joy of the speaker and tends to call forth similar emotions in those who hear his exclamation. The emotive theory of ethics maintains that ethical sentences have emotive rather than cognitive meaning. Thus "Stealing is wrong" should be understood as meaning something like the exclamation "Stealing, ugh!" where emotions of moral disapproval or righteous indignation are expressed and evoked, rather than meaning anything like "Stealing causes suffering" where some fact about stealing is asserted. Since to say that some act or some kind of act is morally right or wrong is not to assert anything at all, obviously there can be no question of knowing whether what is asserted is true or false. Knowledge is out of the question because there is no truth to be known. To our question "How, if at all, does one know which act is right?" the ethical emotivist answers "Not at all." One never does know which act is right because saying or thinking that some act is morally right is not a matter of asserting something that might be known to be true or false, but a matter of expressing and/or evoking moral emotions that make no claim to truth or knowledge.

One advantage of ethical emotivism is that it seems to explain the emotive force of the language of ethics. Talking or thinking about moral issues is obviously not a purely intellectual matter. We normally feel deeply about right and wrong, and our words reflect our feelings. Moreover, to call an act right and wrong usually calls up emotions of moral approval or disapproval in the hearer; the audience responds emotionally to our moral judgments. The emotive theory of ethics can explain this emotional involvement in moral judgment. Of course statements about right and wrong express and evoke emotions, for their meaning is purely emotive. The emotive force of ethical sentences is neither a mystery nor an accident. According to the conventions of our language, words like "right" and "wrong" are properly used to express the moral emotions of the speaker and to evoke similar emotions in the hearer. It is no more surprising that "This act is right" has emotional impact than that "Damn it!" has, for the meaning of ethical sentences, like that of exclamations, is purely emotive.

One difficulty with ethical emotivism is that it is a compound theory; that is, it both asserts that ethical sentences have emotive meaning and denies that they have cognitive meaning. These are distinct and logically independent claims. The difficulty is to provide two sets of evidence for these two theses. Although it is all too easy to slide from "Ethical sentences express and evoke emotions" to "Ethical sentences do not assert or deny propositions," there is no logical connection between these two claims. The emotional force of the language of morals is evidence for the positive thesis that ethical sentences have emotive meaning, but this thesis does not at all imply that they have no cognitive meaning. It is logically possible that sentences like "This act is right" or "That act is morally wrong" *both* express and evoke emotions *and* assert some proposition capable of truth or falsity.

If so, morality may involve truths to be known as well as emotions to be felt. And if moral knowledge is possible, the simpleminded question of how one knows which act is right cannot be rejected out of hand. Let us, therefore, turn from theories like ethical scepticism, relativism, and emotivism that reject the very possibility of moral knowledge to those theories that attempt to explain the nature of our knowledge of right and wrong. How does one know which act is right?

By Consulting an Authority

The first theory of moral knowledge we will consider holds that one knows which act is right by consulting an authority. A child confronted with a difficult moral choice might well ask one of his or her parents which act is right, just as an adult might ask his priest for moral advice. These examples should not, however, mislead us about the nature of the authority possessed by the person one consults. A parent has moral authority over his child; a parent has the right to command the child, at least within certain limits, and the child has a moral obligation to obey the parent's commands. But the kind of authority in question here is of a different sort; it is an epistemological right to be believed rather than a moral right to be obeyed. An authority, as defined by the theory of moral knowledge we are considering, is someone whose opinion is especially reliable, someone whose moral judgments are more likely to be correct than those of the average person. There are many factors that tend to make the judgment of one person more authoritative than that of another, including native intellect, personal experience, factual knowledge, objectivity, and the ability to see logical connections. Suppose that some student is trying to decide whether it would be right or wrong to participate in a few pot parties. In the course of deliberation, he or she may realize the need for the advice of others in order to come to any rationally justified and reliable moral judgment in this case. Unfortunately, the advice of most people would be of relatively little help. Most people either praise the use of marijuana uncritically or condemn it without evidence. There are, however, a few sorts of people who are authorities on the matter. This is not to say that their judgments are infallible, but only that they are more likely than the average person to be correct in their judgments. The doctor will probably know much more than the layman about the physiological and psychological effects of marijuana on the user. Someone who has smoked marijuana regularly is apt to know much more about the experience of drug intoxication than those who have never tried marijuana. A clinical psychologist would be in a particularly good position to assess the danger, if any, of psychological dependence upon this particular drug. A criminal lawyer knows more than the average citizen about the legal penalties for the use of drugs and the likelihood of actually being convicted on the charge of using marijuana. The ideal authority would, I suppose, combine all the sorts of specialized knowledge with a sound insight into morality and a perceptive judgment of particular situations. But short of the ideal, it is still true that the moral judgment of some people is more likely to be correct than the opinion of those lacking in firsthand experience, scientific knowledge, or sound moral judgment. Accordingly, one way to achieve a knowledge of right or wrong is to consult an authority.

One perennially popular and philosophically interesting version of this theory has been recently defended by the Anglican Kenneth Escott Kirk. No doubt the ultimate moral authority is the individual's conscience, for this is the voice of God within each person. But conscience is a still small voice that is often hard to hear and sometimes difficult to interpret with any confidence. Hence, the individual needs to consult the Church, both its official pronouncements and its representative, the priest, in order to arrive at a reliable and rationally justified belief about which act is really right. The Church is the religious community in which the fallible conscience of one individual is subject to correction by the consciences of his fellow Christians, and the Anglican Church carries on through the Apostolic succession an unbroken tradition of the Christian faith. Therefore, the Christian Church is in an authoritative position to interpret the will of God as expressed in individual conscience and in the Bible. The best way for anyone to know which act is right is for him to consult the Church, the authoritative judge of the Divine Lawgiver. The moral judgment of the Church is not infallible, for the Church is a human as well as a Divine institution. But the moral judgment of the Church is authoritative because it is more reliable than that of the average individual.

One argument in support of the theory that one knows which act is right by consulting an authority is that two heads are better than one, especially if the second head is wiser than the first. We often do ask advice on moral problems, and the advice we receive often does help us to reach more reasonable and reliable conclusions about right and wrong. Two heads are often better than one because the two combined are apt to know more of the relevant information than either alone and because the prejudices of the first are often challenged by those of the second. A second head is often better than the first because on any particular moral issue some people are better informed or more thoroughly familiar with the situation than the average person and because on moral issues in general some persons can appeal to sounder moral principles or apply them more perceptively than most. We often do reach rationally justified and reasonably reliable moral judgments based upon the advice of others. Since moral knowledge consists in rationally justified and reliable moral beliefs, one can acquire knowledge of right and wrong by consulting an authority.

This theory cannot, however, be the only answer to our question; it cannot even be the primary and most fundamental answer to it. The appeal to some authority cannot be the only way one comes to know right from wrong; it cannot even be the most important means to moral knowledge. A child might discover which act is right by consulting his or her parent. The parent might in turn reach his or her judgment about the child's act by consulting a priest. But sooner or later this chain of consultation must stop. It cannot be the case that everyone always learns what is right by asking the advice of someone else because the need to ask advice arises precisely from the fact that one does not already know which act is right. If everyone needs to consult an authority, then everyone must lack moral knowledge; and if nobody knows which act is right, then there are no authorities to be consulted. Without authorities to be consulted, the appeal to authority is useless. The same point can be put another way. Someone who is not an authority can, and often does, gain knowledge by consulting someone whose opinion is especially reliable. But the authority, the person whose opinion is rationally justified and therefore especially reliable, must have arrived at an opinion in some other way. Therefore, the method of authority is necessarily a derivative and secondary method. No doubt it is a very practical way for the average person to achieve moral knowledge. But its usefulness presupposes that there is some other and more fundamental way in which the authority, the person whose judgment is more reliable than that of the average person, achieves his or her knowledge of right and wrong. How else, then, does one know which act is right?

By Revelation

A traditional answer, sometimes associated with the appeal to authority, is that one knows by revelation, that God reveals the difference between right and wrong acts to us. Revelation may come firsthand or secondhand to the individual. God may speak directly to the individual human being; a person's conscience is often thought of as the voice of God within. Or the Word of God may be revealed indirectly through the testimony of others to whom God has spoken directly; the Holy Scriptures are often taken to be a written record of the inspiration of saints to whom God has spoken. Either way, by listening to the voice of God within or reading the Word of God in holy books, one can come to know which act is right.

George Finger Thomas, a contemporary Christian moral philosopher, has developed this appeal to revelation in an interesting way. What is revealed to us is the action of God in history, not certain words and sentences spoken by God to human beings. Hence, the literal interpretation of revelation so characteristic of fundamentalist religious thinkers is rejected. Instead, the individual is invited to interpret human history and the Holy Scriptures imaginatively and perceptively to discover their divine meaning. What is revealed in both is the action of God creating the world and the human race, our basic dependence on God, and the record of what happens when we obey or disobey God. From revelation, we may learn the basic truths of the Christian ethics—for example, that all mortal beings owe allegiance to God and that all are created in the divine image. From these principles of the Christian ethics, we may derive universal moral principles—for example, that all human beings ought to be treated with respect or that we have a duty to preserve God's natural creation. We know which individual act is right by applying these moral principles to the situation in which we must choose between alternatives. In this somewhat indirect manner, we know which act is right by revelation.

As a source of moral knowledge, revelation has the tremendous advantage over other means in that it surely must be infallible. There are many ways to guess at right and wrong; human reason can even reach probable conclusions about what one ought to do. But the Word of God is infinitely more reliable because it could not possibly be mistaken. God is, by very definition, divine. To be divine is to be perfect; for the Divine Being is worthy of worship, and only a perfect being would be truly worthy of worship. It follows from God's divinity that He cannot be imperfect in any way. Specifically, He cannot be ignorant of anything and He cannot be at all wicked. Since God is necessarily omniscient, He must have complete and infallible knowledge of right and wrong. Nor would God mislead or deceive us poor human beings, for that would be a cruel and wicked thing to do. Hence, we can trust the Word of God completely. Revelation must be the best of all possible means to moral knowledge because the perfection of its source seems to rule out every possibility of moral error.

The prime difficulty is that revelation may not be available to us. No doubt revelation would be an infallible source of moral knowledge, if only it were easy to obtain and interpret. But it does not follow that we do in fact know which act is right by revelation; for God may not reveal moral truths to human beings, or if He does, He may not reveal moral truths in a manner that can be reliably recognized and readily understood. Most people would sincerely deny that God speaks directly to them; they do not hear His still small voice within. Quite possibly they are correct, and God does not reveal right and wrong to them directly. Even if they are mistaken and God does speak to them, obviously they do not recognize the Word of God in such a way as to give them knowledge of right and wrong.

What, then, of indirect revelation? There can be no doubt that many speakers and writers claim to be inspired by God. The trouble is that they disagree with one another about right and wrong so that we cannot obtain moral knowledge simply by consulting them all. Is there any reliable way of distinguishing between the true prophets of God and those who are misguided or fraudulent? Many of those who sincerely believe that they speak for God may be making public only their personal imaginations or the mores of their society in religious disguise. Less scrupulous speakers may deliberately deceive the public by pretending to have a divine mission in order to gain power, prestige, or wealth. Amid so many doubts and disagreements concerning revelation, it is far from clear that revelation actually exists or, if it does, which proclaimed revelation is genuine. Finally, the identification of genuine revelation would not automatically guarantee the ability to interpret it correctly and understand it fully. The language of God might be too high and mighty for mortals to comprehend. Under such conditions, revelation does not seem to be a very useful or reliable means to the knowledge of right and wrong.

By an Intuition of the Act

While some moral philosophers believe that moral knowledge comes to the individual from outside, from some authority or from a revelation of God, others believe that our native human faculties are the means to moral knowledge. Among the faculties of human nature, the two most plausible sources of moral knowledge are sensation and reason. Through the centuries, the partisans of these two sources have waged an epistemological debate. Empiricists have claimed that knowledge comes primarily from experience, especially sense experience. Rationalists have argued that knowledge is essentially derived from reason, ultimately from intuitive reason. We reason discursively when we draw conclusions step by step through logical inferences from one or more premises. We reason intuitively when we recognize some truth immediately, when we see without further evidence that something is true. Empiricists and rationalists both allow discursive reasoning an important place in moral knowledge. But while the empiricist holds that the premises from which we infer our moral conclusions are known by experience, the rationalist typically insists that the ultimate ethical premises are known by rational intuition.

One version of ethical intuitionism, and one we will consider in this section, is that a person knows which act is right by an intuition of the act. The twentieth-century British moral philosopher E. F. Carritt has maintained that when an individual act is held before the mind, its rightness or wrongness can be seen by a rational intuition. We may need to know certain facts about the act, particularly the various relations in which the agent stands to other persons and the way in which the act will modify the situation, in order to see the act clearly in our mind's eye. But when we do intuit the nature of the act, we will immediately see that it does or does not fit the situation in which it would be done. Thus, we know whether an individual act is right or wrong by intuiting its fittingness or unfittingness to the situation.

In order to understand this theory it is important to be clear on the nature of intuition and of the object intuited. Intuition is a nonsensuous apprehension; it is a direct vision of reason. It is usually thought of as strictly analogous to seeing. I may know which pencil on my desk is red by just looking at the pencils. In seeing the color of the pencil, my eye is directly aware of the pencil; my eye is immediately confronted with the colored object. Similarly, the mind or intellect can be directly confronted with an actual or imagined act. Since it is not any of the sense organs that can do this sort of seeing, it must be human reason that sees the rightness or wrongness of acts. Intuition is this direct vision of reason. It is analogous to sensation in its directness, but it differs in that its content is nonsensuous. One is aware of truth or falsity, rightness or wrongness, not colors or sounds or smells. The object intuited is the individual act—some act that is being observed, or some act that has been done, or some act that is contemplated in the future. Accordingly, one may sense or remember or imagine many characteristics of the act such as its quickness, its power, or its spatial configuration. At the same time, one intuits the rightness or wrongness of the act. For example, any person who saw a large man quickly hit a little old lady very hard and snatch her purse would know by intuition that the act is wrong.

The most straightforward argument for the theory that we know which act is right by an intuition of the act arises from reflection on examples like the one just given. Obviously, we sometimes do know that an act is right or wrong; it is no mere guesswork to judge that the act of striking down a little old lady and taking her purse is wrong. Moreover, we know this immediately, by some sort of direct apprehension. There is no need to sift the evidence, weigh the pros and cons, or proceed through long chains of inference. As soon as we are aware of the act itself we perceive that it is wrong. Hence, there must be some sort of direct awareness of the rightness or wrongness of individual acts. But this direct awareness is not through the external or internal senses. We can see the quickness or feel the force of a blow, but we cannot see or feel the wrongness of the act of striking that blow. Since moral rightness and wrongness are not sensible qualities like colors, tastes, smells, or sounds, they cannot be apprehended by sensation. The only sort of direct awareness a human being has beyond sensation is an intellectual vision or rational intuition. Therefore, we must recognize the rightness or wrongness of an act, at least sometimes, by an intuition of the act.

An argument against this theory is that it seems to imply the absurd conclusion that factual information is unnecessary for moral judgment. If the mind's eye can just look at an act and see its rightness or wrongness, then there would seem to be no need to know any of the other characteristics of the act in order to know whether the act is right or wrong. Unfortunately, it is not normally possible to make reliable judgments of right and wrong in ignorance of the nonmoral features of an act. Whatever one's immediate reaction may be, one does not really know whether it is right or wrong to strike down a little old lady and snatch her purse without first knowing whether she was carrying a bomb into a crowded building, whether the blow injured her or not, and whether the purse was hers or belonged to someone she had just killed. Perhaps this argument against the view that we know which act is right by an intuition of the act can be made clearer by means of an analogy. There are two ways to determine the color of a given pencil. We can know the color indirectly by drawing conclusions from bits of evidence; we can infer that the pencil is red from information about the frequency of the light reflected from its surface or by a chemical analysis of the pigments in its paint. On the other hand, we can know directly that the pencil is red by just looking at it. If we look at the pencil at short range in a clear light, there is no need to gather information about wavelengths or pigments. Such information is unnecessary and beside the point, for the color is there staring us in the eye, as it were. The theory we are considering alleges that we know which act is right much as we know which pencil is red—by direct vision. To be sure, this vision is intellectual rather than sensitive, but it is supposed to be as direct and immediate as sensation. If so, there should be no need to collect information before reaching a conclusion and no danger that a conclusion reached will be shown to be mistaken by further investigation. In the case of judgments of right and wrong, however, factual information is essential to reaching any reliable conclusion, and even informed conclusions are sometimes disproved by later factual investigation. If our knowledge of right and wrong does come from reason, it seems to come from discursive rather than intuitive reason. How can the ethical intuitionist explain this?

By an Intuition of a Moral Principle

The most plausible explanation open to an epistemological rationalist is to say that one deduces a moral judgment of this particular act from a moral principle known by intuition. Richard Price, one of the classical British moralists, has defended this theory of moral knowledge. Although we arrive at the knowledge that an individual act is right or wrong by discursive reasoning, this theory is still a version of ethical intuitionism because the most fundamental part of our moral knowledge is the intuition of the moral principle from which the discursive reasoning starts. Such moral principles are of the form "All acts of kind K are right" or "All acts of kind K are wrong." Examples might be "All benevolent acts are right" or "It is always wrong to kill a human being except in self-defense." Some principles of this form are known by intuition; to understand their meaning is to see their truth. We do not infer their truth from any more basic or fundamental moral principles; we recognize their truth by a sort of direct intellectual vision. Such principles are said to be self-evident. Taken literally, this means that they are their own evidence. What this amounts to is the double claim that we can recognize the truth of the principle simply by reflecting on the full meaning of the principle itself *and* that we do not need any further evidence to know that the principle is true. Having recognized the truth of some moral principle by intuition, we then apply the universal principle to the particular act in question. By subsuming the act under the principle, we are able to deduce the conclusion that this individual act is right (or wrong). Although this moral knowledge is arrived at by deduction, the crucial premise in the inference is the self-evident moral principle known by intuitive reason. Because the rationalist wishes to emphasize this element, he says simply that one knows which act is right by an intuition of a moral principle.

One advantage of this version of ethical intuitionism, at least over the theory that we know which act is right by an intuition of the act itself, is that it seems able to explain the relevance of empirical information. If we know which act is right by an intuition of the act, we should be able to tell the right act by just looking with the mind's eye; it should not be necessary to gather any factual information about the act in question. But if the object of intuition is a moral principle rather than the act itself, we do need to know something about the nature of the individual act because it is such empirical information that enables us to subsume the individual act under the universal principle. Factual information functions as the minor premise in the practical syllogism by which we infer the rightness or wrongness of an act. Suppose, for example, that some person strolling along a beach observes a lifeguard saving the life of an over-ambitious swimmer. How, on this theory, would that person know that the lifeguard's act is right? The starting point of his or her reasoning would be a self-evident principle something like "All acts of saving a human life are right." He or she would then need the factual information, to be established by empirical investigation, that this act is an act of saving a human life. Using the moral principle as the major premise and the factual statement as the minor premise, he or she could readily deduce the moral conclusion that this act is right. In this way, a moral philosopher who wishes to emphasize the role of intuitive reason in moral knowledge can still explain why it is that empirical information is relevant to our knowledge of the rightness or wrongness of particular actions.

One difficulty with this theory is that it requires the existence of self-evident moral principles to serve as the starting points of moral reasoning. Many moral philosophers are highly dubious of the claim that any moral principle is strictly self-evident. When a philosopher labels a moral principle "self-evident," he or she is not using the label in the colloquial sense to mean "obviously true." An ethical intuitionist can, and usually will, agree that it is often very difficult to know whether some moral principle is really true. This is simply because it may be very hard to come to a full and clear understanding of precisely what the principle asserts. Moral agents and moral philosophers can, and frequently do, disagree on matters of principle just because they are unclear on the meaning of the principles involved. What an intuitionist insists, however, is that once a person—perhaps after much explanation and long reflection—really understands a moral principle, he or she will see the truth or falsity of the principle by intuitive reason *and* that he or she will not need or use any other evidence to infer the truth or falsity of the principle. The principle is its own evidence in the sense that reflection on the principle itself, quite apart from one's knowledge or anything else, will make the truth of the principle evident to human reason. One serious difficulty lies in this negative claim that we not appeal to anything other than the principle in seeing its truth. The principle itself is a universal statement, an assertion that all acts of a specified kind are right or wrong. Now, how do we know that *all* acts of a given species are right or wrong? Reflection on what we actually do when we are trying to decide whether to accept or reject some moral principle suggests that what we consider is not just the universal meanings or concepts of the principle itself, but individual cases of the sort specified by the principle. How, for example, might someone come to see that all acts of saving a human life are right? Well, one might remember having observed some acts of lifesaving and, by recalling the nature of these acts, judge them morally right. One might imagine a variety of other acts of lifesaving and recognize that all of these are also right. One might try, without success, to conceive of any act of lifesaving that would be morally wrong. On the basis of reflecting on a wide range of particular instances of saving a human life, one might well conclude that it is always right to save a human life. If, on the other hand, one could imagine any situation in which saving a life would be morally wrong, one would then reject the universal moral principle as false. This suggests that the evidence for a moral principle is not just the meaning of the principle itself but moral judgments of particular acts of the sort specified by the principle in question. If so, the principle is not *self-evident*; it is known by inference from the evidence of particular moral judgments. If moral principles are not self-evident, they cannot be seen to be true by intuition and this theory of moral knowledge is mistaken.

The way in which a moral philosopher answers the question "How, if at all, does one know which act is right?" obviously depends upon a personal general epistemological position, or theory of knowledge. Rationalists hold that knowledge comes primarily from reason. Accordingly, they explain our knowledge of right and wrong in such a way that the central factor is human reason. Since discursive reason must begin with premises known on some other basis, the rationalist usually traces moral knowledge back to intuitive reason. Ethical intuitionists disagree, however, about just what it is that is seen by intuition. Some maintain that it is the rightness or wrongness of an individual act. Others contend that it is some universal principle of right or wrong action. Empiricists, those who believe that knowledge comes essentially from experience, reject all versions of ethical intuitionism. They try to explain how our knowledge of right and wrong results from experience. They do not deny that we reason about moral issues; they grant the importance of discursive reasoning in reaching moral conclusions. They insist, however, that the premises from which we infer the rightness or wrongness of any given act are empirical, known to be true on the basis of experience. Empiricists maintain that the primary or essential element in our knowledge of right and wrong is empirical information about the act. The crucial epistemological problem is precisely how this empirical information is linked to the moral conclusion it supports. We will consider two rather different proposals advanced in recent philosophy.

By Using a Naturalistic Definition

Some empiricists link factual information to moral conclusion by means of a naturalistic definition of an ethical term. Ralph Barton Perry, for example, defined "right" as "conducive to the object of harmonious positive interest." A positive interest is any pro attitude such as desire, love, admiration, or liking. Anything that is the object of a positive interest has some value; to be good is simply to be desired or liked or approved. But most goods can be achieved only at the expense of other goods because interests conflict. My love of silence may conflict with my wife's love of music, and my desire for that last helping of steak may conflict with my son's desire for it. Any object of any positive interest has some value, but only the object of harmonious positive interest has moral value. Something has moral value if and only if it is the object of a set of positive interests, the satisfaction of which does not frustrate some larger set of interests. Now, to say that an act is morally right is to say that it is conducive to that which is morally good. "Right" means conducive to the object of harmonious positive interest.

Perry's definition can be used to determine whether or not some contemplated act is morally right. The first step would be to discover that to which the act is conducive. This would require a scientific investigation of the probable consequences of the act. The next step would be to find out what positive and negative interests various people have toward these various consequences and the degree to which their positive interests are compatible in practice. This part of the investigation would be psychological, for it would be an investigation of the attitudes of human beings. On the basis of all this empirical scientific investigation, one would come to know the relevant factual information about the act, that the act is or is not conducive to the object of harmonious positive interest. If it should turn out that the act is conducive to the object of harmonious positive interest, then it would follow logically that the given act is right. The practical syllogism would go like this: All acts that are conducive to the object of harmonious positive interest are right (by definition). This act is conducive to the object of harmonious positive interest (fact established by empirical investigation). Therefore, this act is right. Thus one knows which act is right by deductive reasoning from empirical information together with a definition of the world "right."

In order for this reasoning from empirical information to moral conclusion to be logically valid, however, the definition must be of a very special sort—it must be a naturalistic definition. A naturalistic definition is one that defines "right"—or any other ethical word—in terms of natural characteristics. A natural characteristic is one that is either given in experience, like yellowness or painfulness, or one that can in turn be reduced to empirical characteristics, as tableness or treeness might be defined in terms of observable features of tables and trees. Only if the word "right" is defined in terms of experience can experienced facts logically imply that some act is right. Empirical characteristics are probably called natural ones because they belong to the world of nature, the world studied by the natural sciences. One knows which act is right, then, by using a naturalistic definition, by deducing the rightness of the act from empirical information about the act together with a definition of the word "right."

Much of the appeal of ethical naturalism lies in the fact that it is not cut down by Ockham's razor. Ockham's razor is the principle that hypothetical entities should not be multiplied beyond necessity. A hypothetical entity is one that is assumed to exist for the purpose of explaining some otherwise anomalous fact, but that is not observed to exist in sensation or introspection. The principle is that we should not assume the existence of any unobserved entities if we can explain all the known facts without any such assumption. Why, for example, is it unreasonable to believe in the existence of Santa Claus? After all, assuming that Santa Claus brings presents to little children would be one way of explaining how the presents get into their stockings on Christmas morning. However, we do not need to assume the existence of any unobserved Santa Claus because we can explain the fact that there are presents in children's stockings on Christmas morning equally well on the assumption that parents bring them. Parents are not, like Santa Claus, purely hypothetical entities. We observe parents every day, and we even observe them doing their Christmas shopping. Since we know on independent grounds that children have parents and that parents play some role in bringing presents, it is simpler to explain the filled-stocking phenomenon on the hypothesis that parents bring the gifts than to assume the existence of an unobserved Santa Claus with very remarkable powers of locomotion and delivery. Similarly, in ethical theory the simpler theory should be preferred to the more complicated explanation.

Ethical naturalism can explain our knowledge of right and wrong in terms of deductive reasoning, experience, and features of our natural world. Since we know on independent grounds that the natural world exists and that human beings have the faculties of reasoning and experiencing, this explanation of moral knowledge need not assume the existence of any purely hypothetical entities. But the theory that one knows which act is right by revelation must assume the existence of an unobserved God and of some faculty of receiving divine messages in the human soul. Ethical intuitionism must assume the existence of nonnatural characteristics of rightness and wrongness in the object and of a very special faculty of intuition in the knower. It is theoretically simpler and more reasonable not to assume the existence of such hypothetical entities if we can help it. It can be argued that ethical naturalism is the best theory of moral knowledge because it explains our knowledge of right and wrong without postulating the existence of any unobserved and unobservable objects or any cognitive faculties not given in introspection.

Is it, however, really unnecessary to assume the existence of something over and beyond the world of nature and the natural faculties of human beings? In part, this depends on whether it is really possible to define ethical words in purely naturalistic terms. G. E. Moore has advanced an argument designed to show that no such purely empirical definition is possible. Consider any definition of the form " 'Right' means N" where "N" stands for a purely natural characteristic. It is always possible to formulate a corresponding question of the form "This act is N, but is it right?" Now *if* the proposed definition were correct, this corresponding question would have to be closed; that is, no one who understood the meaning of the question could be in doubt about or disagree on the answer to the question. In fact, however, this question always remains open. This question remains significant and open to doubt and disagreement no matter what naturalistic definition is proposed. Therefore, no such definition is ever correct. Perhaps the point of this open-question argument can be brought out by an example. Suppose that some moral philosopher suggests that "right" just means "required by the mores of the agent's society." Now consider the corresponding question "This act is required by the mores of the agent's society, but is it right?" If the proposed definition were correct, there could be no doubt or disagreement about the answer to this question; *of course* any act that is required by the mores of the agent's society *must* by very definition be right. In fact, however, there is serious doubt and disagreement about whether some acts required by the mores are morally right. Therefore, this proposed definition must be mistaken. And since the same test counts against every other naturalistic definition one can think of (just think up a few), we can infer by induction that all naturalistic definitions of ethical words are mistaken. If so, then we cannot know which act is right by using a naturalistic definition.

By the Scientific Method

Other empiricists eschew naturalistic definitions and rely instead on the method of the natural sciences. The scientific method is the method of formulating hypotheses and then testing them by experience. Pasteur, for example, formulated the hypothesis that tuberculosis is transmitted from animals to human beings by means of germs in milk. He did not pronounce this as a self-evident truth known by intuition or as a matter of definition; he proposed it tentatively as a statement to be accepted as the basis for further investigation. This hypothesis implies that, if the germs in the milk can be killed by heating, humans who drink the heated milk will probably remain free from tuberculosis. One can test this hypothesis best, if a bit cruelly, by pasteurizing half the milk from infected cows and allowing both halves of the milk to be consumed. The hypothesis implies that most of those who drink the pasteurized milk will not become ill but that most of those who drink the unpasteurized milk will become ill. The method of science is to try the experiment and observe what happens. If the results implied by the hypothesis in fact occur, then the hypothesis is confirmed. If the predicted results are not observed, then the hypothesis is disproved. Although no single test is conclusive, gradually the scientific method can distinguish between true and false hypotheses in this manner.

John Dewey, the American philosopher, has held that the judgment "This act is right" is an empirical hypothesis, a tentative judgment to be tested by experience. We know whether this moral judgment is true or false by using the method of science. Perhaps the label "scientific method" is a bit pretentious, for nothing as technical as laboratory experiments or precise measurement in the field is either possible or necessary. We test the hypothesis that this act is right simply by doing the act and observing the results. The hypothesis is true if it works well in practice, if the act really meets the needs of the problematic situation in which it is done and in fact leads to a more desirable life. Imagine, for example, that my hostess asks me point blank whether I liked the liver and tripe soup she has just served me. Clearly I am confronted with a practical problem, for I want to tell the truth at the same time that I do not want to hurt the cook's feelings by admitting that I could hardly choke the stuff down. Sizing up the situation, I judge that the right act would be to tell a little white lie, to say that the soup was delicious. My moral hypothesis is to be tested by experience; the only way I can know whether the act of lying is really right is to try telling my little white lie and see what happens. If my hostess is made happy and does not become suspicious, if I am invited to more agreeable dinners on future occasions, then experience confirms my hypothesis that the little lie is right. If, on the other hand, my hostess sees through my pretense and becomes deeply wounded at my duplicity or if in the future I must choke down more and more disagreeable culinary creations, then my hypothesis is shown by hard experience to be mistaken. Either way, I know which act is right (or wrong) by the scientific method, by formulating a moral hypothesis and then testing that hypothesis by experience. In morality, as in science, the only way to know is to try and see—to formulate some hypothesis, draw out its implications, and check these implications against experience.

One of the great advantages of this theory of moral knowledge is that it seems to be eminently practical. It sees moral judgments as guides to conduct and accepts or rejects statements about right and wrong by whether they work well when put into practice. In this way, ethics ceases to be idle speculation; morality loses its abstractness and remoteness from life. Moral judgments are no longer external pronouncements from on high; they speak directly to practical problems in a voice that is neither final nor dogmatic. Not only are they relevant to human needs, they can remain relevant when human needs change because moral hypotheses are continuously modified by the process of trial and error. If our knowledge of right and wrong consists of hypotheses confirmed by the test of experience, then obviously moral knowledge must be reliably relevant to human experience and practical choice.

The main problem with this theory lies in explaining precisely how experience can confirm or disconfirm any moral judgment. Many philosophers argue that there is a crucial difference between moral judgments and factual statements, and that only the latter can be established by the scientific method. Suppose I find an unlabeled bottle of liquid. After smelling it cautiously, I formulate the hypothesis that the liquid is an acid. I can test my hypothesis by dipping a piece of blue litmus paper into the bottle. If I observe that the paper turns pink, I have confirmed my hypothesis; if I observe that the paper remains blue, I have disconfirmed my hypothesis. How? What links my experience of the paper turning pink or remaining blue to my hypothesis? The link is a logical one. The factual statement "This liquid is an acid" implies "If I dip a piece of blue litmus paper into it, the paper will turn pink." To be sure, it is only against the background of established scientific laws and a description of the conditions under which the paper is dipped into the liquid that my hypothesis implies that a specified observable result will occur. Still, the experienced result of the experiment confirms or disconfirms the factual hypothesis only because, given these other assumptions, the hypothesis *logically implies* that the specified result will occur. Take away this logical link between hypothesis and predicted results, and whatever results come about would do nothing to verify or falsify the hypothesis because any and every observed result would be equally compatible with the hypothesis. Now many philosophers insist that there is no logical link between a moral judgment and any empirical prediction. What, for example, does "The right act is for me to lie to my hostess" imply about future experience? It does not logically imply that I will be successful in deceiving her so that she will not be hurt by my lie, for she might be even more hurt by hearing the truth. It does not imply simply that my lie will cause my hostess to be happy because telling the truth might have caused such admiration for my moral character that my hostess and I would become lifelong and exceedingly happy friends. There is, it can be argued, a logical gap between moral judgments and empirical predictions such that "This act is right" does not logically imply any factual predictions about the act at all. If this is so, then experience can neither confirm nor disconfirm judgments of right and wrong. The awkward conclusion would seem to be that the scientific method is limited to factual hypotheses; it cannot be used to know which act is right.

BY WEIGHING THE REASONS

How *does* one know which act is right? My own rather tentative answer is that one knows which act is right by weighing the relevant considerations. Judgments of right and wrong do come from human reason, but this reason is neither an intuition of the moral nature of the individual act nor a deduction from some self-evident moral principle. The reasoning required is a weighing of the pros and cons, a weighing of the reasons for doing the act against the reasons for not doing it. Since the reasons are factual statements to be established by empirical investigation, it should not be said that moral knowledge comes from reason rather than experience. Our knowledge of right and wrong comes from reasoning from experience.

Suppose, for example, that a professor is trying to decide whether to cheat on his income tax. Although his regular salary is reported to the Internal Revenue Service, he also has a modest amount of unreported income from giving lectures and acting as a consultant. It would be easy enough to refrain from listing this marginal income and pay a tax on the regular salary only. How does the professor know whether it would be right for him to cheat on his income tax? He must weigh the reasons for cheating against the reasons for not cheating. He really needs the money he would pay in extra taxes in order to keep up his payments on his large mortgage; it is unlikely that he would be detected and punished for his act; and he really does believe that military spending for which much of his tax money would be used is wrong. On the other hand, if he were detected, the result would be disgrace and punishment; he does receive many benefits from his government, benefits made possible by the taxes of the general public; and he strongly approves of many welfare programs that are supported by tax funds. The professor must weigh these and other relevant considerations and make up his mind whether the reasons for cheating on his income tax are more cogent or have more logical force than the reasons against cheating. If he has discovered the more important facts bearing on his decision and if he reflects critically on their relevance and logical force, his final judgment will be knowledge; he will arrive at a fairly reliable and rationally justified judgment of right or wrong.

How do we weigh the relevant considerations in making moral judgments? We cannot put arguments on any scale and read off their weight from the pointer, nor can we literally heft the arguments in our hands to feel their relative weights. What we can and must do is to think through the various arguments and feel their logical force, or lack of it. What we feel is the persuasiveness of the argument, its psychological force. The logical force of an argument is its psychological force after criticism. In weighing an argument, it is not the strength of its first impact upon the mind that counts, but the persuasion it continues to exert after one has reflected on the argument, formulated it as clearly as possible and considered objections to it, discussed its point and its merit with other rational persons, and then reflected some more. The logically valid argument is the one that retains its persuasiveness throughout this critical process of reflection and discussion. We come to know which act is right by subjecting all the pro and con arguments to this sort of criticism and then feeling which seem the more persuasive.

I adopt this theory of moral knowledge primarily, I suppose, because it seems called for by my analysis of the meaning of the expression "morally right." I do not find any of the proposed naturalistic definitions of "right" and "wrong" very convincing. Therefore, I reject the notion that such moral expressions can be defined in terms of empirical characteristics. At the same time, I do not believe that these words stand for nonnatural characteristics to be apprehended by intuitive reason because I do not find any such characteristics before my mind's eye when I reason about right and wrong. What, then, can we mean by the words "right" and wrong"? My thesis is that we use these words to make claims about the rationality of an act. To say that an act is right is to claim that the reasons for doing it outweigh the reasons against doing it. To say that an act is wrong is to claim that the reasons against doing that act are stronger than the reasons for doing it. If this is what we *mean* by "right" and "wrong," then the appropriate way to come to know which act is right would seem to be by weighing all the relevant considerations and judging which set, the pros or the cons, has more logical force.

One difficulty with this theory, and one that causes most philosophers to reject it, is that I must admit that the reasons for a moral judgment do not logically entail it; that is, the logical connection between factual premises and moral conclusion cannot be deductive. Those who hold that all reasoning is deductive, or even either deductive or inductive, must reject my view of moral knowledge because the sort of thinking involved in weighing the pros and cons is neither deductive nor inductive. Personally and philosophically, I prefer to adopt a wider conception of reasoning, for it seems to me that it is a sort of thinking we all use when we decide which act is right and that logical theory must somehow come to terms with it. Surely we could not rationally judge the rightness or wrongness of some act of executing a condemned criminal without weighing the reasons indicated by the arguments for and against capital punishment discussed in the preceding chapter. Accordingly, any adequate metaethical theory must give some sort of plausible account of this sort of reasoning. What seems plausible to me may or may not seem plausible to my reader, whose task is to think critically about the various theories of moral knowledge that have been presented in this chapter, and in the philosophical literature, and to make up his or her own mind on where to take a personal stand.

STUDY QUESTIONS

1. The persistence of moral disagreement is often taken as an argument for ethical scepticism, but on many moral issues there is widespread and persistent moral agreement. Does this latter fact somehow disprove moral scepticism? Why or why not?

2. Sextus Empiricus advanced the argument from balanced arguments. He alleged that, given any rational argument for some moral conclusion, one can always find or invent some contrary argument of equal weight. Is this allegation true? If so, does it establish ethical scepticism? If not, does its falsity prove ethical scepticism false?

3. The refutation of ethical scepticism based upon clear cases assumes that in clear cases we really do know which act is right. How can a person know that he knows something? Does knowing that he knows include or require more than just knowing? If so, what more is required? If not, does a person always know that he is knowing when in fact he is knowing something?

4. There are at least three versions of ethical relativism. The first holds that contrary moral judgments all lack objective validity or truth. The second holds that contrary moral judgments are all equally valid, all are true. The third holds that the moral agent ought always to do that act required by the mores of his society. The first two are metaethical theories about our knowledge of right and wrong. The third is a normative ethical theory about what makes an act right or wrong. Which version, if any, is really implied by the facts of cultural relativity? Explain precisely how the anthropological facts imply the philosophical conclusion. Is the only way a philosopher can deny ethical relativism for him to deny the factual conclusions of cultural anthropology?

5. Is there really any inconsistency in denying that moral judgments are true or false and then going on to give reasons for one's own moral judgments and against contrary judgments? What connection, if any, is there between truth and falsity on the one hand and reasoning on the other? Does it make sense to reason for or against utterances like exclamations or imperatives that are neither true nor false? Why or why not?

6. Pure emotivism holds that ethical sentences have emotive meaning but no cognitive meaning. Mixed emotivism holds that ethical sentences have both emotive and cognitive meaning. Pure emotivism seems to imply that ethical sentences can have no truth-value. Does mixed emotivism also imply this? Why or why not?

7. Does the fact, if it is a fact, that ethical sentences are purely emotive imply that they are not subject to rational criticism? Are there reasons for or against emotions in the same sense that there are reasons for or against beliefs? If so, are emotions true or false? If not, what do we mean when we brand some emotion "irrational"?

8. What is conscience? Is it an emotion or a cluster of emotions? Is it a faculty of rational intuition or the voice of God? Is the theory that one knows which act

is right by consulting one's conscience a theory in addition to those summarized in this chapter? If so, just how does the appeal to conscience differ from these other ways of knowing? If not, with which of the theories presented in this chapter should the appeal to conscience be identified?

9. How can a person rationally choose an authority to consult? If someone does not know the answer to his moral problem himself, how can he recognize a person who does know? If he does know the answer, is not consulting an authority unnecessary?

10. Are there experts in morality as there are experts in medicine or chemistry or carpentry? If so, why are they experts and how did they become experts? If not, does this imply that there are no moral authorities to consult?

11. Precisely how does an authority help us to know which act is right? Do we simply accept the verdict of the authority or do we draw our own conclusion on the basis of what the authority says?

12. Is the appeal to revelation simply a special case of consulting an authority? Is God's relation to the moral law like that of lawyer or of legislator to the law of society?

13. In the case of firsthand revelation, how can a person recognize the still small voice of God? What criteria are there to distinguish between genuine revelation and mere personal conviction?

14. In the case of secondhand revelation, how can anyone recognize a genuine prophet? Are there any tests by which we can distinguish between the speaker or writer who is divinely inspired and one who only claims to be passing on the word of God?

15. Some philosophers claim that they find no nonnatural characteristics of rightness or wrongness before their mind when they reason about moral right and wrong. Assuming that they are sincere, would it be possible for them to intuit rightness or wrongness without realizing that they are doing this? Would it be possible for someone to see colors or hear sounds without realizing that he was doing this? Is this analogy fair? Why or why not?

16. Suppose that the ethical intuitionist claims that factual knowledge is psychologically, but not logically, presupposed by our knowledge of right and wrong. We know which act is right by a direct intellectual vision of the act and not by discursive reasoning from information about the act. Nevertheless, the human mind is not capable of this sort of vision until it has some factual information about the act. Is this a satisfactory explanation of the relevance of factual information to moral knowledge? Why or why not?

17. In order for a moral principle to logically imply that a particular act is right or wrong, the principle must be universal; it must assert that *all* acts of the specified kind are right or wrong. Reflection usually reveals exceptions to any very simple moral principle. To the principle "Killing a human being is always wrong" one seems rationally compelled to add "except in self-defense or under duress of circumstances" and tempted to add "except in a just war or in capital punishment." Is it self-evident whether or not any proposed exception should be written into any moral principle? Can anyone ever know when he has formulated a complete moral principle, one to which no more exceptions are required? If so, how does he know when this stage has been reached? If not, does this rule out the view that one knows which act is right by intuiting a moral principle?

18. People often disagree about the alleged moral truths they claim to see with

their intuitive reason. Does such disagreement show that there is no faculty of intuition or that that faculty is unreliable? Can the intuitionist reply that such disagreements arise only because at least one party to the dispute mistakes his personal opinion for a genuine intuition? Would it be better for him to reply that intuitions are fallible but still sufficiently reliable to give knowledge?

19. Suppose that instead of writing in all the exceptions we were to weaken the moral principle to "Killing a human being is always prima facie wrong." Would this modified moral principle hold without exception? Would it still be possible to deduce any conclusions about the actual rightness or wrongness of any particular act of killing? If not, why not? If so, how would the logical inference look?

20. Suppose that some moral philosopher proposes a definition of "morally right." How might we rationally determine whether his definition is correct? Does the philosopher judge his definitions by the same standards a lexicographer does? Why or why not?

21. The scientist is frequently inventing new expressions or redefining old ones. Cannot the philosopher also define his technical terminology any way he pleases? What would a moral philosopher gain or lose by redefining "morally right" in some convenient way?

22. Suppose that ethical naturalism were correct. What would this imply about the way we do, or should, teach children the meaning of expressions like "right" or "wrong"? Do we in fact teach the vocabulary of morals this way? How do you know?

23. It could be argued that the appeal to the scientific method in ethics presupposes ethical naturalism. The argument would be that experience can serve as a test of a moral judgment only if the moral judgment implies some empirical prediction, and that this logical implication would be possible only if the moral terms used in the judgment were defined empirically. Is this argument sound? Why or why not?

24. Some empiricists look at the fundamental universal principles of right and wrong as definitions of "right" and "wrong." Other empiricists look at them as hypotheses to be tested by experience. Precisely what does this difference in viewpoint amount to? What reason, if any, is there to prefer one view rather than the other?

25. Suppose that "morally right" just means "required by the mores of one's society." Would a moral philosophy built on such a definition turn out to be a version of ethical naturalism or of ethical relativism? Why?

26. Are there any objective criteria that can be used in judging the relevance or weight of some reason advanced on behalf of a moral conclusion? If so, what are these criteria? If not, does this imply that ethical reasoning is entirely subjective and can claim no objective validity?

27. The intuitionist thinks of reasoning as analogous to seeing; it is seeing with the mind's eye. Others think of reasoning as deducing conclusions from assumed premises. Is the reasoning of a scientist establishing his hypothesis by observation or experiment either an intellectual vision or a mere deduction? How does Dewey conceive of reasoning? What conception of human reason best fits the nature of moral deliberation and ethical inference? Why?

28. Kant considers the test of universalizability to be an appeal to pure reason, that is, reason independent of all experience. In what way, if at all, does reason demand universalizability? If universalizability is a necessary condi-

tion of moral rightness, does it follow that we can know which act is right by reasoning? If so, precisely what kind of reasoning?

BIBLIOGRAPHY

AYER, ALFRED J. *Language, Truth and Logic,* 2d ed., chap. 6. London: Gollancz, 1936.
CARRITT, EDGAR F. *Theory of Morals,* chaps. 13 and 14. New York: Oxford University Press, 1928.
DEWEY, JOHN. *Reconstruction in Philosophy,* chap. 7, New York: Holt, Rinehart and Winston, 1920.
EMPIRICUS, SEXTUS. *Scepticism, Man and God,* pp. 31–87. Middletown, Conn.: Wesleyan University Press, 1964.
HERSKOVITS, MELVILLE J. *Man and His Works: The Science of Cultural Anthropology,* chap. 5. New York: Alfred A. Knopf, 1947.
KIRK, KENNETH ESCOTT. *Conscience and Its Problems: An Introduction to Casuistry,* chap. 2. London: Longmans Green, 1927.
MOORE, GEORGE EDWARD. *Principia Ethica.* Cambridge: Cambridge University Press, 1903.
PERRY, RALPH BARTON. *Realms of Value: A Critique of Human Civilization,* chaps. 7 and 8. Cambridge, Mass.: Harvard University Press, 1954.
PRICE, RICHARD. *Review of the Principal Question in Morals.* In *British Moralists,* vol. 2, edited by Lewis Amherst Selby-Bigge, pp. 121–134. Oxford, Eng.: Clarendon Press, 1897.
THOMAS, GEORGE FINGER. *Christian Ethics and Moral Philosophy,* chap. 17. New York: Charles Scribner's Sons, 1955.
WELLMAN, CARL. *The Language of Ethics,* chap. 10. Cambridge, Mass.: Harvard University Press, 1961.

CONCLUSION

Human beings, even philosophers, are essentially active. Human life does not consist so much in a passive awareness of the world as in acting in and interacting with an environment, both natural and social. Throughout his life, a person is doing something, if only chatting or thinking or sleeping. Whatever one may be doing at any given time, one could be doing something else instead. Hence, action and the choice between actions are ubiquitous features of human existence. Most often a person does what he or she does unthinkingly and without deliberation, but many times each day the individual decides what to do. Every decision poses a practical problem, but only the most serious choices pose genuinely moral problems.

Each of us makes innumerable decisions, some of which present insistent moral issues. Ought I to register with the Selective Service as required by law? Would it be right for me to give in to my boyfriend's seductions? Ought I to cheat on my income tax? Is it my moral duty to give up my comfortable life in the university and dedicate my life to helping the victims of urban ghettos? One individual may avoid a moral issue that plagues and perplexes another, but no human being can completely escape the necessity of making moral choices.

THE ASCENT TO THEORY

Any important decision, if only one tries to think it through, raises specific moral problems. Imagine, for example, that a student or a teacher in 1968 received his induction notice and, knowing that if inducted there would be a high probability that he would be required to serve in Vietnam, had to decide whether to report for induction or flee to Canada or remain and refuse induction. As he reflected on the choice confronting him, he would find himself asking questions such as these: Is it always wrong to kill a human being? Is there ever a just war? Is it just for a great power to intervene in the affairs of a small country? Is it ever morally right for a citizen to disobey the country's laws? Is an individual morally guilty for carrying out immoral orders issued by someone in higher authority? Each of these questions, and others like them, poses a specific moral problem. Such problems are general yet specific; each concerns *all* cases of a *specified* kind. Specific moral problems are practical because they arise out of practical decisions and their answers are readily applicable to future practice.

Specific moral problems in turn raise theoretical ethical problems. Someone might, I suppose, answer a specific moral problem by tossing a coin, but the rational person will wish to consider the arguments on both sides of the moral issue. In this text we have summarized some of the arguments bearing on six specific moral issues. We have also learned that the soundness of such arguments depends upon the ethical theories they presuppose. To argue that it is always wrong to kill a human being *because* this violates the law of God presupposes that there is a God, that He promulgates moral laws, and that human beings ought to obey His laws. To argue that it is sometimes right to kill *because* a person sometimes kills in self-defense assumes either that every human being has a right to self-defense or that an attacker forfeits his or her right to life. In this way, the arguments advanced for or against any specific moral conclusion raise theoretical ethical questions. Is there any Divine Lawgiver? Do we have a moral obligation to obey the commands of God? What is the ground of obligation? Are there any universal human rights? Can a human being ever lose his or her natural rights? These questions pose ethical rather than moral problems because each concerns a very wide range of cases not restricted by any specific description. This increased generality is one difference between the ethical question of what makes any act right or wrong and the moral question of whether acts of civil disobedience are ever right. Ethical problems are theoretical because the answer to any such question is an ethical theory, some theory about right or wrong, good or bad.

In the preceding pages we have traced this philosophical ascent from practical choices through moral problems to ethical problems to ethical theories. It is, I believe, important in ethics to begin at the beginning, at the decisions that give birth to ethical theories, for only in this way can the nature of ethics be properly understood. Ethics is not a set of dogmatic pronouncements or simply one intellectual game among others. Its subject matter is defined by moral choice, by the theoretical problems that arise from thinking through practical decisions. And the point of ethics is, ultimately, the solution of the practical problems that arise for any human being trying to live rationally. To really understand ethics, therefore, we must see ethical theories in the context of practice. The goal of the philosopher is to arrive at an ethical theory that will answer satisfactorily the ethical problems that perplex him or her as a persistently thoughtful moral agent.

In the end, the philosopher wants more than to arrive at an ethical theory. For one thing, he or she is not satisfied with an undeveloped theory and wants to formulate a theory in clear and precise language, define or illustrate the meaning of the key terms used in this formulation, draw out some of the theoretical and practical implications of the theory, and present rational arguments to show that the theory is more adequate than rival ethical theories. For another thing, he or she is seeking, not just an isolated ethical theory, but an ethical system. His or her philosophical goal is complete intelligibility and full rational justification. Both understanding and justification require that the philosopher see an ethical theory in its place in a complete and logically interconnected set of ethical theories. Ultimately, he or she will be satisfied with nothing less than an ethical system.

ETHICAL SYSTEMS

First and foremost, an ethical system is a collection of ethical theories, a set of generalizations bearing on moral and practical choice. Each of the even-numbered chapters in this text has collected together a number of different ethical theories, but no chapter has enunciated an ethical system. A system of ethics does not consist of a number of different answers to a single ethical problem, but a number of theories, each of which is an answer to a different ethical problem. Ideally, an ethical system will be *complete*; that is, it will contain, explicitly or implicitly, an answer to every theoretical ethical problem that would arise in fully thinking through the various practical decisions that face human beings. A complete ethical system would have to contain a theory of the end of the law, a theory of rights, a theory of moral knowledge, and many other ethical theories answering to problems that arise in our daily lives. Ethics is driven toward this ideal of completeness by the very nature of philosophical problems. Philosophical problems, including theoretical ethical problems, are inseparable in the sense that they cannot be adequately answered in isolation because the answer to one of them very often hinges on the way in which other problems have been answered. One ethical problem can be fully and finally solved only when all of them have been solved. The philosophical ideal, then, is an ethical system, a complete set of ethical theories.

But it is more. No random collection of unrelated ethical theories, even if it did contain solutions to every conceivable ethical problem, would satisfy a philosopher because it would not make sense of practical choice and human action. The goal of any philosopher is intelligibility, understanding, and theoretical grasp. This can be achieved only if his various theories fit together in some sort of pattern that reveals the connections between things. Hence, the moral philosopher strives for a *coherent* collection of ethical theories. Negatively, coherence rules out logical contradiction. Contradictions are intolerable in any ethical system because it is logically impossible for two inconsistent assertions both to be true. Since any set of ethical theories that contains a logical contradiction must include at least one false or mistaken theory, no such set can be rationally accepted as the truth about ethics. Positively, coherence requires some sort of mutual support. The truth of one ethical theory in the set should somehow render the others more credible. The several theories in an ethical system are not separate answers to isolated ethical problems. They fit together in such a way that any complete justification of one theory tends to justify the other theories as well. As a result, a coherent ethical system must be accepted or rejected as a whole, not bit by bit.

Finally, an ethical system should be *articulate*. The several ethical theories it contains should be explicitly formulated in clear and precise language. As far as possible, the meaning of the language in which these theories are formulated should be defined or explained. Each basic ethical theory needs to be justified; reasons should be given for accepting this answer to the theoretical problem it is intended to solve and for rejecting alternative answers. Moreover, the implications of the basic ethical theories should be drawn out. From a set of basic ethical theories one will be able to infer subordinate ethical theories. For example, from a general theory of the grounds of obligation one might derive an ethical theory about the grounds of political obligation. Specific moral principles may be logically derived from ethical theories; one might derive some principle about the rightness or wrongness of civil disobedience from one's theory of political obligation. Finally, singular moral judgments about individual cases, real or imaginary, may be inferred from the generalizations contained in an ethical system. As the philosopher gives reasons for ethical theories and draws out their implications, the logical structure of the ethical system becomes revealed. It is this that connects the various aspects of practical choice and renders his or her overall view of moral action intelligible.

To sum up, an ethical system is a complete, coherent, articulate set of ethical theories. Ideally, it contains an answer to every theoretical problem that could arise in thinking through any practical decision that any human being might face. These ethical theories must fit together in such a way that each gives some measure of support to the others. The entire set of theories is formulated in clear and precise language, justified with rational arguments, and developed until its logical implications are explicit. It might be said that the skeleton of any ethical system consists of basic ethical theories, derived ethical theories, and moral principles standing in logical relationships to one another. This skeleton is fleshed out by the explanations that are given of its key terms, the reasons that are advanced for adopting it, and the concrete applications that illustrate its practical significance.

Although we have not explicitly discussed ethical systems in this text, we have encountered systematic connections between ethical theories many times. In Chapter 2, we studied the theory that what makes an act right is the law of God. In Chapter 4, we considered the thesis that the good is a vision of God. In Chapters 6 and 12, we discussed the theories that virtue consists in a willing submission to the will of God and that one knows which act is right by a revelation from God. Clearly, these are not isolated and unrelated ethical theories. They are fragments of a system of ethics in which the concept of God is used to tie together the answers given to a wide range of theoretical ethical problems. Moreover, these answers will tend to stand or fall as a set. Whatever justification can be given for the belief in an omniscient, omnipotent, omnibenevolent Creator and Lawgiver will be a rational justification for accepting this ethical system in which such a divinity plays the central role. Any reasons that can be given for adopting the viewpoint of the agnostic or the atheist, however, will count against this entire way of looking at human conduct and moral choice.

Another central and unifying concept we have met frequently is that of utility. It has been held that what makes an act right is either its utility or the utility of the moral rule to which it conforms. The utility of character traits has been used to explain the moral value of an agent. Legal philosophers have debated whether it is the end of the law to promote the utility of the society or the utility of all human beings. And many of the arguments advanced on both sides of the specific moral problems we have considered have asserted the usefulness or harmfulness of some act or practice or law. This frequent use of the concept of utility in moral and ethical debate reveals two things about the nature of an ethical system. The several theories that constitute an ethical system are frequently tied together by the fact that they are formulated in terms of one central and controlling concept; nevertheless, selection of this central concept does not uniquely determine the precise form an ethical theory must take. Utilitarian ethical theories are radically different from theological ethical theories because they are rooted in entirely different concepts. Still, there is room for somewhat different utilitarian systems because the single concept of utility can be used in various ways to formulate theories of obligation or of moral value or of morally justified law.

There are, of course, many other concepts that might be chosen to unify an ethical system. Among the more obvious candidates are the notions of a human interest, the mores of a society, love, nobility, and the intuition of nonnatural characteristics. We need not pursue each of these possibilities now, however, for the two concepts of God and utility are enough to serve as examples of the way in which an ethical system can be built around one central concept. What is important is to remind the reader that our philosophical ascent has been incomplete because we have not attained the systematic ideals of completeness, coherence, and articulateness at which philosophy aims. No one who is deeply concerned about theoretical ethical problems can be fully satisfied until he or she has stated and defended his or her own ethical system.

THE ANATOMY OF ETHICS

The true ethical system is an ideal to be striven for by each philosophical thinker; proposed ethical systems are collections of assertions to be met with in the history of philosophy. By studying the systems of ethics stated and defended in the philosophical literature, we can obtain a fuller understanding of the structure of an ethical system. This structure is doubly revealing, for it reflects the relationships between the many ethical problems that give rise to ethical inquiry and determines the anatomy of the discipline of ethics that seeks to solve these problems.

Any ethical system has both a vertical lineage and a horizontal topography. The vertical lineage consists in the logical derivations by which ethical or moral conclusions are drawn from more fundamental premises. The ancestors of any ethical system, so to speak, are the reasons that are given to justify accepting its most fundamental assumptions, its basic ethical theories. The parents of any ethical system are those highly general and logically primary theories that are used to infer all the conclusions drawn within that ethical system. Succeeding generations are constituted by the conclusions that are successively drawn from those basic premises. They can be roughly divided into derived ethical theories, specific moral principles, and individual practical judgments. In general, this logical descent from first principles through intermediate principles to particular conclusions reverses the philosophical ascent by which practical decisions give rise to moral problems that pose ethical problems. Moreover, this order of logical implication from first premises down to last applications will tend to be expressed in the reasoning used in ethics, both the reasoning by which one may defend a moral principle or ethical theory by deriving it from some more basic theory and the reasoning by which one tests a generalization by seeing whether its implications are acceptable.

The horizontal topography of an ethical system consists in the arrangement of its subject matter, in whatever sense an ethical system can be said to be about values and obligations. The main areas of ethics reflect the basically different kinds of problems that give rise to ethical thinking and determine the main kinds of theories that must be contained in any complete ethical system. Accordingly, the topology of ethics maps the lay of the land to be covered by the discipline of ethics. The heartland of ethics consists of axiology, the theory of value, and deontology, the theory of obligation. Each of these is further subdivided, of course. The theory of value will cover the theory of intrinsic value, theories of various sorts of extrinsic value such as esthetic value or instrumental value, the distinction between moral and nonmoral values, a treatment of the degrees of comparative value, etc. The theory of obligation will include the nature of obligation, the ground of obligation, some consideration of the differences between duties and obligations and mere "oughts," the relation between moral and nonmoral obligation, and many related theories. All the theories of value and obligation located within this heartland belong to normative ethics, for all explicitly or implicitly set up some norm for human conduct. Moral philosophy consists of those specific moral principles that are derived from the general theories of value and obligation. The distinction between ethical theory and moral philosophy is one of degree only; moral principles are more specific than ethical theories and, consequently, more readily applicable to practice. Moral philosophy, like normative ethical theory, takes some stand on what is right or wrong, good or bad. By contrast, metaethics is, or tends to be, morally neutral. It does not use words like "good" or "right" to make normative judgments; it mentions such words in order to clarify their meaning or explain how statements using them can be justified. Metaethics thus contains theories of the meaning of ethical words and theories of the justification of ethical and moral statements. Clustered around normative ethical theory, moral philosophy and metaethics are various and sundry associated theories. Although somewhat removed from the normative core of ethical theory, they all belong to ethics because they all bear upon practical decision. Among these are theories of the psychology of human action, social philosophies concerning the nature of social institutions, and metaphysical theories about the nature of the moral agent, the natural world in which he or she acts, and the existence or nonexistence of God. Any complete ethical system must contain theories to cover this entire territory, and the discipline of ethics must somehow deal with theoretical problems that arise anywhere within this large domain. The task of ethics is almost overwhelming. Is it worth the effort?

THEORY AND PRACTICE

Complicated and demanding as the discipline of ethics may be, philosophical inquiry into ethical problems is doubly rewarding. The inquiry is good for its own sake, and its product, an ethical system, is useful in practice. It is fun to wrestle with theoretical ethical problems. The intellectual activities of formulating theories, finding objections to these theoretical hypotheses, meeting what objections one can and revising a theory when one must—all of these are as enjoyable as any intellectual game like bridge or chess or debating. But constructing and defending an ethical system is more than a game because the ethical theories that compose it can be applied in practice. The fundamental generalizations of any ethical system imply moral principles that can, in turn, guide moral choice and human conduct. Having traced the ascent from practical decision to ethical theory at some length, let us now look briefly at the descent from theory to practice.

What bearing, if any, do ethical theories have on particular decisions of what one should do in a given situation? The simplest answer to this question is that ethical theories tell one what to do, that accepting an ethical system automatically solves all one's moral problems. This is because, given the facts of any situation, the theory is supposed to imply that one act is right and all alternative acts are wrong. On this view, moral deliberation takes the logical form of a practical syllogism. From a major premise supplied by an ethical theory and a minor premise summarizing the facts of the case, we can readily infer a unique moral conclusion. To my mind, however, this answer oversimplifies the connection between theory and practice. We cannot apply theory to practice simply by subsuming the particular case under the theoretical generalization. Two sorts of evidence count against this simple and attractive view. First, if an ethical theory logically entails a unique moral conclusion in any given situation, then it would seem that those who accept different ethical theories would, at least most of the time, arrive at different moral judgments in particular cases. In point of fact, it is remarkably common for two moral philosophers to defend the same moral conclusion by appealing to radically different ethical theories. One can justify the conclusion that war is morally wrong about equally well by appealing to the will of God or to the Kantian theory that all human beings ought to be treated as ends-in-themselves. It can be argued that God has forbidden killing except in self-defense or that it is wrong to use human beings as mere means in power politics. Two very different theoretical premises can lead to the same practical conclusion, that it is immoral for any government to engage in war. Second, and more compelling, is the fact that the same ethical theory can be used to justify contrary moral conclusions. The pacifist and the soldier can each defend his moral stand by appealing to utilitarian considerations. They cannot, of course, agree on all the utilities involved; their estimates of the benefits and harms resulting from fighting must differ. Still, accepting a utilitarian ethical system does not automatically solve the practical problem of deciding what it would be right to do in any complex situation.

The two considerations just advanced might lead us to jump to the opposite extreme and conclude that ethical theories are irrelevant to practice. It does not matter what ethical system an individual accepts, or even whether he has any ethical system at all. The philosophical task of understanding and justifying choice is one thing; the practical task of choosing and acting is an entirely different matter. Ethics, one might imagine, is a fascinating theoretical activity, but it is mere speculation. While I would agree that theoretical ethics is a speculative activity, I would not admit that it is irrelevant to practical decision. Why does practice call for decision? Why are human beings not content to act, simply to do this and that, without deliberating over choices? Human conduct poses practical problems and calls for decisions only because human beings, faced with practical alternatives, want to do the right act, the rationally justified act. But if the point of deliberation is to identify the rationally justified act, then practical problems cannot be solved without considering the reasons for and against any contemplated act. And to accept or reject some practical reason is to take a stand, at least implicitly, on the ethical theory that lies behind that reason. One cannot completely think through any moral decision without raising ethical problems that can be answered only by establishing some ethical theory. Ethical theory is not irrelevant to practice because, as we have seen in this text, ethical problems arise from practical issues.

The truth lies somewhere in between these two extremes. An ethical system does not solve all one's practical problems, but one cannot choose and act rationally without some explicit or implicit ethical system. An ethical theory does not tell a person what to do in any given situation, but neither is it completely silent; it tells one what to consider in making up one's mind what to do. The practical function of an ethical system is primarily to direct our attention to the relevant considerations, the reasons that determine the rightness or wrongness of any act. Ethical egoism tells the agent to consider his or her own welfare and nothing else. Utilitarianism suggests that we consider the welfare of everyone affected by the act in question. A theological ethics might instruct us to listen to the Word of God. Only after accepting some such ethical system do we know what sort of considerations need to be taken into account in making a rational decision. The practical reasoning remains, of course; the ethical system does not weigh the pros and cons and make the decision for us. The factual investigation also remains; it is not the task of ethics to discover the relevant facts of the situation. What ethical theory can do is to guide us toward the relevant facts and away from irrelevant considerations. In this modest way, ethical theory is useful, even essential, to practice.

It follows that what any student of philosophy can hope to learn from a course in ethics is correspondingly modest. One cannot learn the answers to all one's moral problems—or even acquire a moral standard that will enable one to size up every situation and automatically make the right choice. What an ethics course can offer is some direction to and increased skill in thinking about moral issues. Gradually answers to theoretical ethical problems will reveal what considerations are to be taken seriously in making practical decisions. The slow building of an ethical system will ultimately provide a theoretical framework within which to engage in practical thinking. And the more one engages in critical thinking, assessing the various pro and con arguments, the more skillful one becomes in the basic techniques of practical reasoning. These two achievements, learning what to consider and how to consider it, are useful enough to be worth significant effort. These are the real rewards of a course in ethics.

INDEX